Dead Man's Switch

Andrew Parry

Published by Planet Earth Publishing, 2026.

DEAD MAN'S SWITCH

First edition. September 1, 2026.

ISBN: 979-8235244979

Written by Andrew Parry.

Table of Contents

This book is dedicated to all those brave men and women who died to protect the truth.

Introduction — The Truth That Refuses to Die

Imagine possessing information that could expose corruption, reveal a crime, challenge a powerful institution, change a scientific field, or force the public to confront something it would rather not know. Now imagine that the people who would be most threatened by that information know that you possess it. You continue going to work, answering your telephone, meeting friends, traveling, sleeping at night, and attempting to live an ordinary life while carrying something that no longer feels ordinary. You may have documents stored somewhere, recordings that cannot easily be replaced, photographs that establish a sequence of events, correspondence that connects people and decisions, or testimony that exists only because you were present when something happened. Then comes the question that transforms information into a survival problem: what happens to the evidence if you are suddenly unable to protect it?

That question lies at the heart of the dead man's switch.

The phrase itself originated with a very different purpose. In its traditional mechanical form, a dead man's switch is a fail-safe mechanism designed to respond when the person operating a machine releases control, becomes incapacitated, or is otherwise unable to continue performing the required action. The principle is deceptively simple: the continued absence of a signal produces a predetermined consequence. Over time, however, the idea escaped the mechanical world and entered the language of personal security, whistleblowing, journalism, intelligence, activism, digital privacy, and information preservation. Today, the phrase can describe a wide range of systems intended to ensure that information survives when its creator does not.

The modern interpretation is both powerful and potentially dangerous. A person might arrange for sensitive documents to become available if regular communications cease. An archive might be entrusted to several independent custodians. Encrypted material might be preserved in multiple locations. A legal representative might hold instructions concerning what should happen if the creator becomes incapacitated. A journalist might receive evidence with an understanding that further material exists elsewhere. Digital systems might be configured to send notifications when predetermined conditions are met. Technologies such as distributed storage, cryptographic authentication, and blockchain networks have created still more possibilities for preserving information beyond the control of a single individual.

But the existence of technology does not solve the central problem.

It merely changes its shape.

A dead man's switch can preserve information, but it cannot determine whether that information is true. It can release a document, but it cannot automatically establish whether the document is authentic. It can preserve a photograph, but it cannot guarantee that the photograph has been correctly dated or interpreted. It can transmit a recording, but it cannot establish whether the recording has been edited or stripped of important context. It can distribute an archive across multiple locations, but it cannot decide whether publication would expose innocent people to unnecessary harm. The mechanism can preserve the message, but responsibility for interpreting and acting upon the message remains with human beings.

That distinction will guide everything that follows.

This book is not an argument that every mysterious death is an assassination, every disappearance is evidence of a conspiracy, or every person who claims to possess dangerous information is telling the truth. History contains genuine cases of political assassination, institutional corruption, corporate wrongdoing, intelligence abuses, organized crime, retaliation against whistleblowers, and attempts to suppress information. It also contains false accusations, mistaken identities, unreliable testimony, fabricated documents, misunderstood events, exaggerated stories, and conspiracy theories that cannot withstand examination. The existence of one category does not prove the other. A serious examination of dead man's switches must therefore begin with intellectual discipline: documented facts must be separated from allegations, credible evidence from speculation, and established history from stories that remain unresolved.

That approach becomes particularly important because the subject naturally attracts dramatic stories. The idea of someone carrying a secret powerful enough to endanger their life has appeared repeatedly in journalism, espionage narratives, political scandals, organized-crime cases, whistleblower accounts, and popular culture. Sometimes the reality has been just as disturbing as the fiction. At other times, an unexplained event has generated a narrative far more certain than the available evidence allows. The investigator's responsibility is not to make the story more dramatic. It is to determine what can actually be established.

The history of whistleblowing demonstrates why this distinction matters. People who expose wrongdoing can face serious consequences, ranging from professional retaliation and lawsuits to social isolation, surveillance, imprisonment, and, in some circumstances, physical danger. The severity and nature of those consequences vary enormously between countries, institutions, and individual cases. Some whistleblowers receive legal protections. Others discover that formal protections are incomplete or difficult to enforce. Some are believed immediately. Others spend years attempting to persuade authorities, journalists, colleagues, or the public that the information they possess deserves investigation. The dead man's switch emerges within this uncertain territory as a form of contingency planning.

Yet contingency planning is not the same as paranoia.

A person can prepare for an unlikely event without believing that event is inevitable. Insurance works on the same principle. We insure homes against fires without assuming our houses will burn. We maintain emergency supplies without assuming disaster is certain. We create backups because computers fail even when we have done nothing wrong. We make wills because death is unavoidable even though its timing is unknown. A dead man's switch can be understood within the same broader philosophy: important information may deserve protection against circumstances that cannot be predicted. The challenge is determining what level of preparation is proportionate to the actual risk.

That is where psychology enters the story.

Living with sensitive information can alter a person's perception of ordinary life. A missed telephone call may seem significant. An unfamiliar vehicle may attract attention. A change in someone's behavior may become difficult to interpret. Ordinary uncertainty can begin to feel threatening when a person believes that powerful interests may want them silent. Fear can produce hypervigilance, and hypervigilance can produce both useful caution and distorted judgment. The individual may become isolated because trust becomes difficult. Friends may be regarded as potential liabilities. Family members may be excluded for their own protection. The person carrying the information can eventually become trapped between the need for secrecy and the need for help.

This is one reason the human side of a dead man's switch deserves as much attention as its technology. A technically sophisticated system designed by someone under extreme psychological pressure may still contain flawed assumptions. The creator may choose an inappropriate trigger, trust the wrong person, underestimate technical failure, or create a system so complicated that nobody can operate it when the time comes. Fear can encourage preparation, but fear can also undermine preparation. The best contingency planning therefore requires a degree of calm that may be difficult precisely when the system seems most necessary.

Trust becomes the next problem.

Who should receive the information?

The obvious answer might be a family member, but family relationships can introduce emotional pressure, legal complications, and vulnerability. A close friend may be deeply loyal but lack the expertise to evaluate evidence. A lawyer may understand legal risks but operate under professional duties that limit what can be disclosed. A journalist may have the investigative resources to examine a claim but may refuse to publish material that cannot be independently verified. An investigator may know how to establish facts but may be constrained by jurisdiction or institutional authority. A professional custodian may provide technical expertise but may lack personal knowledge of the creator's circumstances.

There is no universal answer because the correct custodian depends upon the information, the risks, the legal environment, and the purpose of the preservation system.

The same complexity applies to the information itself. What deserves protection? A single accusation is different from a collection of original documents. A photograph is different from a financial record. A handwritten note is different from a digitally signed file. A video is different from a transcript. A scientific dataset is different from a personal recollection. A classified document is different from evidence of an ordinary crime. A whistleblower's interpretation of an event is different from the raw evidence upon which that interpretation is based. The strength of a dead man's switch ultimately depends heavily upon the quality of what it preserves.

Evidence also requires context.

Consider a photograph discovered without a date, location, original file, or explanation. It may be genuine, but what does it prove? Consider an email whose surrounding correspondence has disappeared. Its meaning may change depending upon what came before and after it. Consider an audio recording that has been copied repeatedly. Is the copy complete? Has it been edited? Can the original be located? Consider a document that appears authentic but has no reliable chain of custody. How can investigators establish where it came from? These questions are not technical distractions. They are central to whether information can become credible evidence.

This is why preservation and authentication must be considered together.

Modern encryption can protect confidentiality. Cryptographic hashes can help detect changes to digital files. Digital signatures can provide evidence concerning integrity and identity within appropriate systems. Secure storage can reduce unauthorized access. Distributed archives can protect against the destruction of a single copy. Offline storage can reduce certain network-based risks. Cloud systems can make geographically separated backups easier. Each technology can solve particular problems. None of them solves every problem.

The rise of blockchain technology has added another layer to the discussion. Distributed ledgers can create records that are difficult to alter retrospectively within the relevant system, and smart contracts can execute predetermined computational conditions. These capabilities have encouraged claims that blockchain could create nearly unstoppable disclosure mechanisms. Such claims require caution. A blockchain record does not automatically prove that the information entered into it was true. Decentralization does not eliminate legal jurisdiction. Cryptographic permanence does not make a false statement accurate. Technology can make certain forms of information persistence more resilient without transforming information into truth.

Artificial intelligence will make this distinction even more important.

AI can already process enormous quantities of information at speeds impossible for individual investigators. It can search documents, identify patterns, compare language, organize timelines, detect similarities, classify files, and assist researchers in navigating complex archives. Future systems may become increasingly capable of reconstructing relationships among people, documents, transactions, communications, and events. A large dead man's archive could eventually be examined by an AI system that helps investigators understand thousands or millions of interconnected records. Such technology could be extraordinarily valuable.

It could also create extraordinary risks.

An AI system can generate convincing but incorrect conclusions. It can mistake correlation for causation. It can reproduce biases present in its training or data. It can summarize uncertain evidence in language that sounds more confident than the evidence warrants. Generative AI can also create synthetic documents, images, voices, and videos that appear authentic. The future investigator may therefore confront a strange paradox: an enormous archive can be easier to analyze while becoming harder to trust. Provenance and authentication may become more important precisely because artificial intelligence makes information easier to manufacture.

This means the future dead man's switch may not simply preserve files. It may need to preserve the history of those files.

Who created them? When were they created? How were they obtained? Who handled them? Were they modified? Where were they stored? Are there independent copies? What other evidence supports them? What evidence contradicts them? What did the creator personally observe, and what did they learn from someone else? Which conclusions are documented, and which are interpretations? Such questions may eventually become as important as the files themselves.

The legal dimension is equally unavoidable. Sensitive information can intersect with national-security law, privacy law, trade-secret protections, intellectual-property law, confidentiality obligations, evidence rules, defamation law, employment law, and whistleblower protections. The legal status of information can also differ dramatically between jurisdictions. Something that can legally be published in one country may be restricted in another. A document may be evidence of wrongdoing while simultaneously containing information whose unauthorized disclosure creates a separate legal problem. The phrase “the truth must come out” is therefore not a substitute for understanding what can lawfully and responsibly be disclosed.

Ethics adds another layer beyond law.

Suppose an archive contains genuine evidence of serious wrongdoing but also contains private information about people who had no involvement. Should everything be released? Suppose publication could compromise an ongoing investigation. Should disclosure be delayed? Suppose the evidence is incomplete but potentially important. Should it be given privately to investigators rather than released publicly? Suppose a creator wants everything published but the material could place vulnerable people in danger. Does the creator's intention settle the question? These problems have no simple technological solution.

Responsible disclosure requires judgment.

That is why the media can play an important role in the dead man's switch ecosystem. Professional journalists and investigative organizations can evaluate documents, consult specialists, corroborate claims, seek responses from people accused of wrongdoing, and determine whether publication serves a legitimate public interest. They can redact information that unnecessarily exposes private individuals. They can distinguish between what is known and what remains uncertain. They can sometimes protect sources while investigating the information supplied by those sources. The journalist therefore becomes more than a recipient of information. In many circumstances, the journalist becomes another layer of verification.

The same principle applies to lawyers and investigators. A lawyer can help determine the legal implications of particular material. An investigator can evaluate evidence against independent records. A scientific expert can assess technical claims. A financial specialist can examine transactions. A historian can compare documents against established chronology. The strength of a disclosure system can therefore increase when information moves through people with different forms of expertise rather than being released immediately to the entire world.

This book will examine all of these dimensions.

It will begin with the idea itself, tracing the transformation of the dead man's switch from a mechanical fail-safe mechanism into a modern information-preservation concept. It will examine why truth can become dangerous, how people who expose wrongdoing have sometimes experienced retaliation, and why stories of silenced voices must be approached with both seriousness and skepticism. It will then move into the psychological problem of living under perceived threat and the difficult question of whom to trust. From there, the book will examine the conceptual architecture of activation systems, redundancy, physical and digital storage, evidence preservation, encryption, distributed custody, and access management.

The investigation will then turn toward the people who may eventually receive the information. Family members, friends, lawyers, journalists, investigators, professional intermediaries, international organizations, and independent custodians each bring different capabilities and vulnerabilities. The book will examine why no recipient should automatically be regarded as trustworthy simply because of their relationship to the creator. It will also explore why professional independence can sometimes be more valuable than personal loyalty when sensitive information must be evaluated objectively.

Later chapters will consider the technology of delayed disclosure, including automated communication, encrypted systems, distributed networks, blockchain technology, and smart contracts. These technologies will be examined realistically rather than romantically. The purpose will not be to portray any technology as magical or unstoppable, but to understand what it can actually accomplish, what assumptions it depends upon, and how it can fail. A system is only as reliable as its weakest critical dependency.

Failure will therefore receive particular attention.

What happens if the password is lost? What happens if the storage device fails? What happens if the cloud provider closes an account? What happens if the automated system incorrectly interprets a missed check-in? What happens if the intended recipient dies first? What happens if the creator becomes temporarily unreachable? What happens if the information is stolen before the intended trigger occurs? What happens if the archive contains material that should never have been released? The most valuable lesson in contingency planning may be that every system should be designed with its own failure in mind.

Finally, the book will confront the legal and ethical boundaries surrounding disclosure. There is a profound difference between exposing wrongdoing and indiscriminately publishing secrets. There is a difference between evidence of corruption and private information about innocent people. There is a difference between classified information that reveals misconduct and classified information whose disclosure could endanger lives without serving a compelling public interest. There is a difference between a credible whistleblower and an unsupported accusation. The responsibility of truth includes responsibility for the consequences of how truth is revealed.

The central question running through all of these subjects is therefore deceptively simple: **Can the truth survive the person who discovered it?**

The answer depends upon what we mean by truth. If we mean a person's beliefs, those beliefs can survive in writing but may never be proven. If we mean testimony, testimony can survive but remains subject to questions concerning memory and reliability. If we mean evidence, evidence can survive physically or digitally, but its authenticity and context must also survive. If we mean established facts, those facts may become more secure when independent sources converge upon them. The dead man's switch cannot create truth. It can only preserve the possibility that truth will continue to be investigated after its original keeper is gone.

That distinction transforms the entire concept.

The dead man's switch is not ultimately about revenge. It is not about threatening the world with secrets. It is not about assuming that everyone is corrupt or that every unexplained event has a hidden cause. At its most responsible, it is about continuity. It is about ensuring that information does not disappear merely because the person who possessed it disappears. It is about creating a bridge between the present and the future, between a witness and an investigator, between an archive and the people capable of understanding it.

And perhaps that is why the idea remains so compelling.

We live in a world where information can travel across continents in seconds but can also disappear behind a forgotten password. We can preserve millions of files but struggle to determine which ones are authentic. We can duplicate evidence perfectly but also manufacture convincing false evidence. We can communicate instantly but remain vulnerable to surveillance, coercion, technical failure, and human betrayal. Technology has given us unprecedented powers of preservation while simultaneously creating unprecedented problems of verification.

The dead man's switch sits directly inside that contradiction.

It represents humanity's desire to make knowledge survive uncertainty. It acknowledges that people die, disappear, become incapacitated, lose access, change their minds, encounter threats, and sometimes become unable to continue the work they began. It recognizes that institutions can fail and that records can be lost. But it also reminds us that preservation without judgment can become dangerous. The objective is not simply to make information impossible to destroy. The objective is to preserve information in a form that allows responsible people to examine it when the original keeper is no longer present.

That is the journey this book will take.

Along the way, we will encounter documented history, technological realities, psychological research, legal principles, whistleblower experiences, investigative practices, competing interpretations, and difficult ethical questions. Some stories will be disturbing. Some will remain unresolved. Some will demonstrate that fears of retaliation were justified. Others will demonstrate how easily uncertainty can become mythology. The goal is not to force every case into a single explanation. It is to examine the evidence and understand what the evidence can actually support.

Because ultimately, the greatest protection for truth is not secrecy.

It is evidence.

A secret can disappear when its keeper disappears. A rumor can mutate as it travels. A memory can fade. An accusation can be denied. But carefully preserved evidence can remain available for examination long after the original events have passed from living memory. It can be challenged, authenticated, corroborated, interpreted, and reconsidered. It can become part of a historical record that future generations may understand differently from the people who created it.

The dead man's switch, at its deepest level, is therefore an attempt to give evidence a future.

It is a declaration that disappearance does not have to mean erasure. It is an acknowledgment that silence can sometimes be imposed, but that information can be preserved beyond the reach of a single individual. It is a recognition that technology can provide new forms of resilience while introducing new vulnerabilities. And it is a reminder that the survival of information creates a responsibility for those who eventually inherit it.

If the system works, the creator may never know what happens next.

The archive may sit untouched for years. The recipients may debate its significance. Investigators may challenge its claims. Journalists may verify some portions and reject others. Lawyers may determine that certain material cannot legally be published. Historians may eventually discover that the documents illuminate an event nobody living today fully understood. The creator's final message may become part of a larger investigation whose conclusions they could never have predicted.

That uncertainty is not a weakness.

It is the price of allowing the future to judge the past.

A dead man's switch cannot guarantee justice. It cannot guarantee belief. It cannot guarantee publication. It cannot guarantee that the information will even prove to be correct. What it can do, when responsibly conceived, is preserve a pathway through which information can survive long enough to be examined. And sometimes that is the most important protection truth can receive.

Because when the keeper of the information is gone, the real question is not whether the message will automatically be believed.

The question is whether anyone will still be able to find it.

The Dead Man's Switch: An Idea Born from Fear and Necessity

A dead man's switch begins with a deceptively simple idea: something happens when a person can no longer act. In its original mechanical sense, the expression describes a fail-safe mechanism designed to respond when an operator becomes incapacitated, loses control, or stops performing an expected action. The principle can be found in transportation, industrial machinery, military systems, and other environments where the continued presence and attention of a human operator are essential to safety. Instead of assuming that everything will remain normal until someone intervenes, the system is designed around the possibility that the operator may suddenly become unable to intervene at all. That distinction is important because it reveals the deeper logic behind the concept, which is not death itself but the deliberate preparation for an absence of human control. Long before the phrase became associated with whistleblowers and secret files, this underlying principle was already being used to make dangerous systems fail safely when their human guardian could no longer perform the required action.

The expression has therefore always carried a certain darkness, because it forces us to imagine a situation in which a person disappears from the process without warning. A railway engineer might become unconscious, a machine operator might collapse, or a person controlling a dangerous process might simply release the mechanism that they normally hold in place. In each case, the system does not interpret the absence of action as permission to continue indefinitely; instead, it treats the absence as a signal requiring a predetermined response. This is the essence of a fail-safe philosophy, and it is closely related to a broader engineering principle known as "fail-safe" or "dead-man" control. The precise mechanisms differ enormously between applications, but the conceptual structure remains remarkably consistent: continued operation depends upon continued human presence, and when that presence disappears, the system moves into a safer state. In information protection, the same logic can be transferred from machinery to knowledge, creating a system in which information is preserved or communicated if its custodian unexpectedly becomes unavailable. That transformation from physical safety mechanism to information-security concept is what gives the modern dead man's switch its unusual power.

The modern metaphor became especially compelling in an age when information itself could become dangerous. A person might possess documents showing corruption, evidence of financial misconduct, records of institutional abuse, confidential correspondence, photographs, recordings, scientific findings, or testimony concerning activities that powerful people would prefer to remain hidden. The danger in such circumstances is not necessarily that the information will be destroyed immediately, but that the person who knows where it is and understands its significance may disappear before anyone else realizes what has been lost. A dead man's switch attempts to solve that problem by separating the survival of the information from the survival of the individual. Instead of keeping everything inside one person's memory, computer, safe, or private possession, the individual creates some form of contingency in which trusted recipients can eventually obtain information if predetermined conditions are met. The concept therefore represents a shift from protecting a person by keeping information secret to protecting information by ensuring that secrecy cannot depend entirely upon one person's continued existence. That is a profound conceptual change, because it turns information from something passively possessed into something deliberately prepared for survival.

This distinction also explains why the phrase has acquired such a powerful place in popular culture. Fiction has repeatedly imagined journalists, spies, hackers, political dissidents, investigators, and whistleblowers possessing a final package of information that will automatically emerge if they are killed. In films and novels, the mechanism is often portrayed as nearly perfect, with a single button, timed message, hidden file, or automated transmission

capable of bringing down an entire organization after the protagonist disappears. Reality is considerably less dramatic and far more complicated. Real information systems fail, passwords are forgotten, storage devices become corrupted, recipients misunderstand instructions, communication accounts are closed, encryption keys disappear, and automated services change their policies or cease to operate. A genuine dead man's switch is therefore not defined by how dramatic the final disclosure might be but by whether the underlying system has been thoughtfully designed to survive foreseeable failures. The gap between the cinematic version and the real-world version is one of the most important subjects this book will explore.

The history of the concept also tells us something important about the human relationship with technology. Machines are generally designed around predictable assumptions about their operators, yet human beings are inherently unpredictable because they can become distracted, injured, incapacitated, coerced, or killed. Engineers learned that safety cannot depend entirely upon the assumption that a human will always be present and capable of responding correctly. That insight gradually produced mechanisms that detect the absence of expected human action and respond automatically. The dead man's switch is therefore part of a much larger history of designing systems around human fallibility. In engineering terms, this is not pessimism but realism, because reliable systems are designed around known failure modes rather than imagined perfection. When the same principle enters the world of information security, it asks us to confront an equally uncomfortable fact: the person protecting important information is themselves one of the system's vulnerabilities.

Consider what happens when one person becomes the sole custodian of a significant body of evidence. The documents may be perfectly authentic, but if nobody else knows they exist, their evidentiary value may effectively disappear when the custodian does. Even if another person knows that the files exist, they may not know where they are stored, how they are encrypted, which material is genuine, or how the evidence fits together. This is why professional information-security systems emphasize concepts such as redundancy, access control, key management, backup, provenance, and recovery planning. A dead man's switch takes these concerns and places them within a human contingency framework. It asks not merely, "Where is the information?" but, "What happens to the information if the person responsible for it suddenly cannot answer that question?" Once framed this way, the dead man's switch becomes less mysterious and much more recognizable as a specialized form of continuity planning.

The concept becomes especially significant in whistleblowing because whistleblowers frequently occupy an awkward position between information and institutions. They may possess information that cannot easily be transferred through ordinary organizational channels because the very institution responsible for investigating misconduct may also be implicated in it. Sometimes the challenge is not proving that wrongdoing occurred but ensuring that evidence survives long enough to be independently examined. This is where the concept of distributed custody becomes important, because information held by several independent parties is less vulnerable to the disappearance or coercion of any single individual. Yet distribution introduces its own dangers, because every additional person or organization who receives sensitive material can potentially become another point of compromise. The objective is therefore not simply to maximize the number of copies but to construct a rational relationship between availability, confidentiality, authenticity, and safety. A responsible dead man's switch must balance these competing requirements rather than assuming that more copies automatically mean greater protection.

The modern information environment makes this problem simultaneously easier and harder to solve. A person today can create digital copies of enormous quantities of information almost instantly and potentially store those copies in geographically separated locations. Encrypted storage, secure communications, redundant backups, digital signatures, authentication systems, and other technologies provide capabilities that previous generations could scarcely have imagined. At the same time, digital information exists within an ecosystem of service providers, account credentials, software dependencies, changing security standards, surveillance capabilities, data breaches, device failures, and corporate policies. A file stored safely today may become inaccessible years later because the person forgot the password or because the hardware required to read it no longer works. A sophisticated system can therefore fail for remarkably ordinary reasons. The paradox of modern information security is that technological abundance does not eliminate vulnerability; it often creates more layers in which something can go wrong.

There is another dimension to the dead man's switch that is sometimes overlooked: deterrence. A person who believes that damaging them will automatically expose sensitive information may become more difficult to silence. This does not mean that such a system makes anyone invulnerable, nor does it mean that potential aggressors will necessarily believe the threat. In some circumstances, however, uncertainty about what will happen after a person's disappearance can alter the calculations of those who might otherwise attempt intimidation or retaliation. The mechanism becomes a form of informational insurance, because its value lies partly in the consequences that might follow if something happens to its creator. Yet deterrence can become dangerous when the existence of a supposed switch is exaggerated or falsely represented. A person who claims to possess overwhelming evidence when they do not may provoke unnecessary conflict, undermine legitimate investigations, or place innocent people at risk. The credibility of a dead man's switch therefore depends not upon theatrical claims but upon the quality, authenticity, preservation, and responsible handling of the underlying information.

This brings us to one of the central distinctions that will govern the entire subject: protecting information is not the same thing as releasing information. The first is fundamentally a security problem, while the second is a legal, ethical, evidentiary, and social problem. Someone may possess genuine evidence of serious wrongdoing but still need to consider whether immediate publication could expose victims, compromise an investigation, reveal private information, endanger uninvolved individuals, or create false conclusions from incomplete material. A dead man's switch that indiscriminately publishes everything may therefore be less a protection system than an uncontrolled information bomb. Responsible design requires the creator to think beyond personal survival and consider what happens to everyone else when the information leaves their control. The more consequential the material, the more important this distinction becomes.

The concept also raises a difficult question about ownership. Who owns information after its creator dies, and who has the authority to determine what should happen to it? Personal photographs, private correspondence, medical records, financial documents, corporate information, government secrets, scientific research, and evidence of criminal conduct can all have very different legal statuses. A person cannot necessarily transform information into lawful public property simply because they possess it. Nor does the fact that information is important automatically justify revealing every associated detail. In many jurisdictions, legal protections surrounding privacy, trade secrets, classified information, intellectual property, defamation, confidentiality, and evidence can survive beyond the moment when a person decides that disclosure is desirable. A serious dead man's switch must therefore recognize that technological ability does not automatically create legal authority.

The idea becomes even more complicated when the information concerns national security. Governments legitimately classify some information because premature disclosure can reveal intelligence sources, military capabilities, diplomatic strategies, security vulnerabilities, or other sensitive material. At the same time, governments and institutions can also misuse secrecy to conceal misconduct, and history contains well-documented examples of whistleblowers challenging official claims that information should remain hidden. The difficult task is distinguishing legitimate secrecy from secrecy used to prevent accountability. That distinction cannot be resolved merely by declaring that all classified information is dangerous or that all secrecy is suspicious. It requires evidence, context, legal analysis, and often independent investigation. The dead man's switch exists precisely within this tension between the public's interest in truth and the potential harm caused by uncontrolled disclosure.

The same principle applies outside government. Corporations can possess trade secrets, customer information, proprietary research, internal investigations, and legally protected communications. Scientific institutions can hold unpublished findings, research-participant data, experimental records, and intellectual property. Journalists may protect confidential sources whose identities could place them in danger. Lawyers may hold privileged communications, while doctors and other professionals may possess highly sensitive personal information. A person creating an information-release mechanism therefore has to understand that not every secret belongs to them simply because they know it. The ethical question is not only whether something is true but also whether the person releasing it has a legitimate basis for doing so. That is why a mature discussion of dead man's switches must eventually move beyond technology into law, professional responsibility, and moral judgment.

There is also a philosophical dimension hidden inside the mechanism. A dead man's switch is essentially a message sent from one state of existence to another: "If I am no longer able to speak, this information should still have a chance to speak for itself." That idea has appeared in many forms throughout history, from letters entrusted to others to documents hidden for future discovery and testimony preserved against the possibility of retaliation. Modern technology has simply made the mechanism more sophisticated and potentially more reliable. What remains unchanged is the human desire to prevent disappearance from becoming erasure. A person may accept that they cannot control what happens to them, while still trying to control what happens to the evidence they leave behind. In that sense, the dead man's switch is ultimately an attempt to extend human agency beyond the limits of human survival.

Yet there is a danger in romanticizing this idea. Not every person who fears retaliation is actually being targeted, not every unexplained death is an assassination, not every secret document proves a conspiracy, and not every person claiming to possess hidden evidence possesses anything reliable. History provides genuine examples of suppression, corruption, retaliation, and political violence, but it also provides countless examples of misunderstanding, exaggeration, coincidence, fabrication, and confirmation bias. The responsible investigator must therefore resist two equally tempting errors: dismissing every claim of danger as paranoia or accepting every claim of danger as proof. A dead man's switch should be evaluated by the same evidentiary standards applied to the information it protects. The mechanism may preserve a file, but preservation does not transform an unreliable claim into reliable evidence. If anything, the existence of a contingency-release system makes authentication and verification even more important.

This is why evidence preservation will occupy such a central place in the chapters ahead. Information that cannot be authenticated may have little value no matter how securely it is stored. A photograph without provenance may be misunderstood, a recording without context may be misleading, and a document without evidence of authenticity may be dismissed as fabricated. Digital files present additional questions concerning metadata, modification, copying, timestamps, device histories, and chain of custody. The modern dead man's switch must therefore be understood as an information-preservation system rather than simply a disclosure mechanism. Its objective should be to preserve the ability of independent people to evaluate evidence after the original custodian is gone. That distinction may ultimately determine whether the system becomes a vehicle for accountability or merely another source of confusion.

There is an additional practical principle worth emphasizing: simplicity often contributes more to reliability than sophistication. People are naturally attracted to complex systems because complexity appears to offer stronger protection, but every additional component introduces another potential failure. A system requiring several specialized applications, obscure credentials, proprietary hardware, continuous internet access, and complicated instructions may look impressive while being remarkably fragile. Conversely, a carefully documented and redundant arrangement using well-understood technologies may survive for years with relatively little intervention. This is a fundamental lesson of reliability engineering, where unnecessary complexity can increase the number of possible failure modes. The best dead man's switch is therefore not necessarily the most technologically advanced one; it is the one whose essential functions are most likely to remain understandable and recoverable when the person who created it is no longer available.

The concept of redundancy deserves particular attention because it transforms the dead man's switch from a single mechanism into an architecture. If one person has one copy of one document protected by one password and that password is lost, the entire system can fail simultaneously. If evidence is preserved through carefully separated and appropriately protected mechanisms, the failure of one component does not necessarily destroy everything. This resembles the redundancy principles used in aviation, telecommunications, data centers, financial systems, and other environments where catastrophic dependence on a single component is unacceptable. But redundancy must also be balanced against confidentiality, because every additional copy can create another opportunity for unauthorized access. The challenge is therefore to create independence without creating uncontrolled proliferation. That tension between resilience and exposure will appear repeatedly throughout this book.

The dead man's switch also forces us to reconsider the meaning of disappearance. Physical disappearance is only one possibility. A person can become unreachable because of illness, imprisonment, kidnapping, disaster, technological failure, psychological crisis, political displacement, or simple loss of communication. Someone may deliberately stop communicating without wanting anything released, while another person may become temporarily incapacitated and later return. This makes the design of activation conditions far more difficult than popular culture suggests. A system that interprets every unexplained absence as death could cause irreversible consequences based on a temporary circumstance. A responsible system therefore has to account for uncertainty, delay, verification, and the possibility that the creator's intentions may change. The more irreversible the eventual disclosure, the more carefully the triggering conditions need to be considered.

There is, finally, something deeply human about why this concept continues to fascinate us. We live in a world where information can disappear astonishingly quickly despite the enormous capacity of modern technology to preserve it. Servers fail, accounts vanish, institutions change, people forget passwords, witnesses die, archives are destroyed, and memories become unreliable. At the same time, information can travel across the world in seconds once released, making the consequences of a single disclosure potentially enormous. The dead man's switch occupies the narrow space between these two realities: the fragility of human custody and the extraordinary persistence of digital information. It is an attempt to answer an ancient problem with modern tools. What happens to the truth when the person carrying it can no longer speak?

The chapters that follow will examine that question from increasingly practical angles, beginning with the human reasons someone might feel compelled to create such a system and eventually reaching the technologies that can preserve information beyond individual control. We will examine historical cases without assuming that every allegation is true, investigate whistleblowers without turning every whistleblower into a hero, and study security technologies without pretending that technology can eliminate risk. We will also confront the legal and ethical boundaries that become unavoidable when private information crosses into public disclosure. Throughout the book, the crucial distinction will remain between what is documented, what is credible but disputed, what is speculative, and what is demonstrably false. The dead man's switch may promise that a person's information can survive their disappearance, but whether that information deserves to survive into the public record is a separate question. The real challenge, therefore, is not simply learning how to build a switch, but learning how to build one responsibly enough that when the moment comes, the mechanism serves truth rather than merely serving fear.

Resources

1. U.S. Department of Transportation, Federal Railroad Administration, materials concerning railroad operating practices, safety systems, and engineer/operator vigilance devices, which provide useful context for the broader fail-safe principle behind dead-man controls.

2. National Institute of Standards and Technology (NIST), *Security and Privacy Controls for Information Systems and Organizations*, Special Publication 800-53, for foundational concepts concerning contingency planning, access control, system integrity, accountability, and information protection.

3. National Institute of Standards and Technology (NIST), *Contingency Planning Guide for Federal Information Systems*, Special Publication 800-34, for the principles of continuity, redundancy, recovery, and preparation for loss of system availability.

4. National Institute of Standards and Technology (NIST), *Digital Identity Guidelines*, Special Publication 800-63, for authentication and identity-management principles relevant to protecting digital information and access credentials.

5. U.S. Cybersecurity and Infrastructure Security Agency (CISA), guidance concerning data protection, cybersecurity, incident response, backups, and resilience, providing practical context for the vulnerabilities of modern digital information systems.

6. Council of Europe, *Convention on Cybercrime (Budapest Convention)* and associated materials, providing an international legal framework for understanding computer-related offenses, electronic evidence, and cross-border cybercrime.

7. U.S. Securities and Exchange Commission, *Whistleblower Program* materials, for documented information concerning institutional whistleblowing, reporting mechanisms, confidentiality, retaliation concerns, and regulatory disclosure.

8. U.S. Office of Special Counsel, resources concerning federal whistleblower disclosures and prohibited personnel practices, providing primary-source material concerning protected disclosures and retaliation within the federal workforce.

9. Daniel Ellsberg, *Secrets: A Memoir of Vietnam and the Pentagon Papers*, Viking, 2002, providing first-person historical context concerning classified information, whistleblowing, government secrecy, and the personal consequences of unauthorized disclosure.

10. The National Archives, materials relating to the Pentagon Papers and U.S. government records concerning classified information and historical document preservation, useful for understanding the difference between government secrecy, historical evidence, and later public disclosure.

11. International Organization for Standardization, ISO/IEC 27001 and related information-security standards, providing the broader framework of information-security management, risk assessment, access control, continuity, and organizational protection.

12. Bruce Schneier, *Applied Cryptography: Protocols, Algorithms, and Source Code in C*, Wiley, for foundational background on cryptography, secure information handling, and the limitations of technical security.

When the Truth Becomes Dangerous

There is nothing inherently dangerous about truth. A fact can sit quietly in a notebook, a database, a laboratory record, a photograph, a courtroom transcript, or a person's memory without harming anyone, and most facts do exactly that. Information becomes dangerous when it changes what people can know, what institutions can be held accountable for, what money can be lost, what reputations can collapse, or what powerful individuals can no longer conceal. The danger may come from the information itself, from the people who want to suppress it, from the consequences of releasing it, or from some combination of all three. A person who discovers that a corporation is falsifying safety records, that officials are abusing their authority, that organized criminals are influencing public institutions, or that scientific data have been deliberately manipulated may suddenly find that knowledge has changed their relationship with the world around them. The dead man's switch emerges from this uncomfortable territory because it is fundamentally a response to the possibility that possessing important information can make the person who possesses it vulnerable.

The first mistake is to imagine that dangerous information always consists of spectacular secrets. Sometimes the most consequential evidence is remarkably ordinary, consisting of invoices, emails, laboratory notebooks, inspection reports, internal memoranda, photographs, transaction records, meeting minutes, or conversations that appear insignificant when viewed individually. What makes such material powerful is often the relationship between seemingly unrelated pieces of evidence. A single payment may mean little, but a series of payments connected to a decision-maker, a contractor, and an unexplained change in policy can tell a very different story. A laboratory result may appear ambiguous until it is compared with the original experimental records and later publications. A single complaint may be dismissed as an individual's accusation, while hundreds of similar complaints can reveal a pattern that an institution can no longer plausibly characterize as isolated. The danger of information therefore frequently lies not in possessing one extraordinary secret but in possessing enough ordinary facts to reveal a pattern.

This is one reason institutions with legitimate responsibilities for information security distinguish between ordinary information and information whose unauthorized disclosure could cause identifiable harm. The United States classification system, for example, recognizes that certain national-security information may require protection because disclosure could damage defense, intelligence activities, foreign relations, or other defined interests. At the same time, the classification framework explicitly states that information should not be classified merely to conceal violations of law, inefficiency, administrative error, embarrassment, or other matters that do not legitimately require national-security protection. That distinction is fundamental because secrecy and wrongdoing are not synonymous. A secret can be legitimate, and an accusation of wrongdoing can be false, while genuine wrongdoing can sometimes be hidden behind legitimate secrecy. The responsible handling of dangerous information therefore begins with resisting the temptation to treat secrecy itself as proof of guilt.

Corruption provides one of the clearest examples of information acquiring danger through its consequences. Corruption becomes especially threatening when evidence connects public authority with private benefit, because the people who are supposed to investigate misconduct may themselves have relationships with those being investigated. The danger can increase further when corruption intersects with organized crime, where intimidation and violence may become part of the environment surrounding witnesses and investigators. The United Nations Office on Drugs and Crime has documented circumstances in which corruption connected to organized criminal groups creates heightened risks of threats and violence, discourages reporting, and can expose prosecutors, judges, and law-enforcement personnel to serious intimidation. In such environments, information is dangerous not because facts possess some mysterious quality but because people may have powerful incentives to prevent those facts from reaching investigators, courts, journalists, or the public. The person holding the evidence can consequently become part of the risk equation.

Organized crime demonstrates another important feature of dangerous information: the information may be valuable precisely because it connects people who publicly appear unrelated. Criminal organizations rarely operate only through dramatic acts that are immediately recognizable as criminal; they can depend upon financial relationships, intermediaries, compromised officials, corrupt businesses, fraudulent transactions, intimidation, and legitimate-looking commercial structures. Evidence that reveals these connections can therefore be more threatening than evidence documenting an individual crime. A document showing that one person committed an offense may affect one prosecution, whereas evidence demonstrating an institutional network can potentially expose an entire structure. This helps explain why witnesses and investigators can face particular risks when organized criminal groups are involved. The more an investigation threatens the structure rather than merely an individual participant, the greater the incentive may be to disrupt the flow of information.

Political wrongdoing creates a different but equally important problem because political power can influence the institutions responsible for interpreting information. A document showing that a public official lied, misused public funds, interfered with an investigation, abused authority, or violated established rules may have consequences extending far beyond the individual involved. It can affect elections, public confidence, legislation, diplomatic relationships, and the legitimacy of institutions themselves. Yet accusations involving political wrongdoing are also unusually vulnerable to partisan interpretation, selective disclosure, and deliberate manipulation. A genuine document can be presented without context to create a false impression, while a false document can be circulated precisely because it confirms what a particular audience already wants to believe. The danger therefore exists on both sides: suppressing credible evidence can protect wrongdoing, while releasing unverified information can create a different form of injustice.

This is why the person who possesses politically sensitive information has a responsibility that extends beyond simply preserving it. Evidence needs context, chronology, provenance, corroboration, and careful interpretation if it is going to withstand serious scrutiny. A responsible archive should allow an independent investigator to determine where a document came from, whether it has been altered, what events surround it, and whether other evidence supports its claims. Without those elements, information can become more vulnerable rather than more powerful because its opponents can attack its authenticity instead of answering its substance. The objective should therefore be to preserve evidence in a form that permits future verification rather than merely preserving material that supports a preferred narrative. A dead man's switch is strongest when it preserves the possibility of independent examination rather than attempting to dictate the conclusion that examination must produce.

Corporate misconduct creates another category of danger because information can threaten enormous financial interests without involving anything resembling conventional political corruption. Employees may discover fraudulent accounting, manipulation of financial disclosures, unsafe products, environmental violations, regulatory deception, bribery, discrimination, or deliberate concealment of material risks. Modern whistleblower systems exist partly because lawmakers and regulators recognize that employees and insiders can possess information unavailable to outside investigators. The U.S. Securities and Exchange Commission, for example, maintains formal whistleblower protections against retaliation for qualifying reports of securities-law violations and prohibits covered employers from taking certain retaliatory actions against whistleblowers. The existence of such protections is itself evidence of an important institutional reality: reporting wrongdoing can carry risks significant enough that legal systems have created mechanisms specifically intended to protect those who report it. A dead man's switch belongs to a different category of protection, but it addresses the same underlying problem of information being concentrated in people who may fear retaliation.

The legal recognition of retaliation is particularly revealing because retaliation does not always resemble the dramatic violence associated with fictional whistleblower stories. It can take the form of dismissal, demotion, harassment, professional isolation, threats, discrimination, litigation, damage to reputation, or interference with someone's ability to work. The U.S. Department of Labor and OSHA administer numerous whistleblower protection laws covering different forms of protected activity, while federal agencies such as the SEC maintain their own statutory and regulatory frameworks for particular categories of reporting. The existence of these frameworks does not mean every whistleblower is protected from every consequence, because protections vary according to jurisdiction, employment status, subject matter, reporting channel, timing, and other legal requirements. It does demonstrate, however, that the risk surrounding information can be institutional as well as physical. Sometimes the person who needs protection is not someone being hunted in the shadows but an employee whose career becomes increasingly difficult after they challenge a powerful organization.

Intelligence secrets introduce a more complicated category because some information really can be dangerous to disclose even when no wrongdoing is involved. Intelligence operations may depend upon confidential human sources, technical collection methods, diplomatic relationships, military capabilities, or information about vulnerabilities that adversaries could exploit. The U.S. classification framework specifically identifies intelligence activities, intelligence sources and methods, foreign-government information, military operations, and certain scientific or technological matters as categories that can qualify for national-security classification when unauthorized disclosure could reasonably be expected to cause identifiable harm. The existence of legitimate national-security secrets means that a simplistic philosophy of "all hidden information should be exposed" is impossible to defend responsibly. At the same time, secrecy cannot automatically be treated as evidence that the institution holding the information is acting properly. The real question is always what interest is being protected, what evidence supports that protection, and whether the secrecy is lawful and proportionate.

That distinction becomes particularly important for someone considering a dead man's switch involving government information. A person may believe that a document proves misconduct while failing to understand why certain portions are classified, whether the material is authentic, or whether releasing it could expose an innocent source. The information may contain several different categories of material, some legitimately sensitive and some potentially relevant to public accountability. A responsible approach therefore requires separating the question "Is this information important?" from the question "Should all of this information be publicly disclosed?" Those questions can have different answers. The best information-preservation strategy may sometimes involve giving the material to an appropriate lawyer, inspector general, regulator, journalist, or other qualified intermediary capable of evaluating it rather than publishing everything indiscriminately.

Scientific discoveries can become dangerous in an entirely different way. Scientific information can threaten careers, funding arrangements, institutional reputations, commercial interests, intellectual property, or established assumptions within a research community. Research misconduct can involve fabrication, falsification, or plagiarism, and the U.S. National Institutes of Health emphasizes that scientific research depends fundamentally upon trust and integrity. Importantly, scientific controversy should not automatically be confused with scientific misconduct, because disagreement, unexpected results, replication failures, and competing interpretations are normal components of science. The threshold for accusing someone of misconduct is therefore much higher than the threshold for simply disagreeing with their conclusions. That distinction becomes crucial when scientific information is preserved for possible future disclosure because a dead man's switch cannot substitute for replication, peer review, statistical analysis, or independent investigation.

Scientific information can also become dangerous because of what it might enable rather than what it proves. Research involving pathogens, advanced weapons technologies, sensitive biological techniques, powerful computational capabilities, or other dual-use subjects can contain legitimate knowledge whose unrestricted distribution may create security concerns. This is one reason research communities and governments increasingly discuss research security alongside research integrity. The NIH describes research security as including protection of the research enterprise against misappropriation that could harm national or economic security, as well as certain forms of interference. The existence of such concerns does not mean controversial research should automatically be suppressed, but it demonstrates why scientific openness sometimes has to be balanced against other legitimate interests. A person who possesses sensitive scientific information therefore faces a problem much more complicated than simply deciding whether the world has a right to know.

Institutional abuse creates perhaps the most morally difficult category because the information often involves vulnerable people who may already have suffered harm. Evidence concerning abuse in prisons, schools, hospitals, religious organizations, military institutions, police departments, care facilities, corporations, or other powerful organizations can be extraordinarily important for accountability. Yet the evidence may contain names, medical information, personal histories, photographs, communications, or testimony belonging to victims who never consented to becoming public figures. Releasing everything in the name of transparency can therefore reproduce the harm that the disclosure is supposed to expose. The responsible goal is not merely to reveal institutional wrongdoing but to reveal it while minimizing unnecessary exposure of people who did nothing wrong. This is one reason professional investigative processes can be so important when the information concerns vulnerable individuals.

The danger of information is therefore often relational. The same document can be harmless in one context and extremely sensitive in another. A list of names might be meaningless to a stranger but dangerous if it identifies confidential intelligence sources. A laboratory protocol may be ordinary academic material in one field but highly sensitive when connected to a dangerous pathogen. A corporate email may appear trivial until combined with financial records that establish deliberate deception. A photograph can be innocent until its metadata, location, or subjects reveal information that puts someone at risk. Context determines significance, and significance determines risk.

This is also why the idea of "the truth" needs careful handling. People often speak about truth as though it were a single object that can simply be released into the world, but information comes with uncertainty, interpretation, and competing levels of confidence. One fact may be firmly documented, another may be supported by several independent sources, another may be a credible allegation awaiting investigation, and another may be pure speculation. A responsible information-preservation system should maintain those distinctions rather than flattening them into a single narrative. If a dead man's switch releases all material without indicating what is verified and what is uncertain, it can unintentionally make weak claims appear equivalent to strong evidence. The preservation of truth therefore requires preservation of epistemic context.

This problem becomes especially severe in an era of digital manipulation. A photograph can be edited, a recording can be selectively presented, an email can be forged, metadata can be altered, and authentic material can be stripped from its original context. Artificial intelligence has expanded the range of possible manipulations while simultaneously making genuine evidence easier to reproduce and distribute. This does not mean digital evidence is inherently unreliable, but it means that provenance and authentication have become increasingly important. A serious dead man's switch should be imagined as preserving not merely files but the circumstances necessary for those files to be evaluated. The future recipient should be able to ask what the material is, where it came from, how it was obtained, whether it was altered, and what independent evidence supports it.

There is also a subtle danger in believing that possession itself provides protection. Someone might assume that because several people know a secret exists, no one would dare harm them. Another might believe that an encrypted archive is automatically safe because the encryption appears technically strong. Someone else might assume that a journalist will publish anything they receive or that a government agency will automatically investigate every allegation presented to it. None of these assumptions is necessarily correct. Protection depends upon actual relationships, functioning systems, credible evidence, appropriate recipients, and realistic contingency planning. A dead man's switch should therefore never be treated as a magical shield against retaliation.

The strongest reason to study dangerous information is not to cultivate paranoia but to understand incentives. When information threatens money, power, reputation, criminal operations, institutional legitimacy, or personal interests, some people may attempt to suppress it. That does not mean everyone surrounding the information is hostile, nor does it mean suppression will always be violent. Sometimes the resistance is subtle, bureaucratic, legal, professional, or social. Sometimes the institution responds properly and investigates the allegation. Sometimes the allegation collapses under scrutiny. Sometimes the evidence proves more serious than anyone initially imagined. The purpose of a responsible protection system is to preserve the possibility of that investigation regardless of which conclusion ultimately emerges.

This brings us back to the fundamental reason the dead man's switch exists. A person may fear that if they become unavailable, information will disappear with them before anyone has the opportunity to determine what it means. The switch is an attempt to interrupt that possibility by creating continuity between the person who possesses the information today and the people who may need to examine it tomorrow. But continuity alone is not enough. The information must remain secure, authentic, interpretable, and accessible to appropriate recipients without unnecessarily exposing innocent people. The system must also distinguish between genuine incapacity and ordinary silence, because a false activation can produce consequences that cannot easily be reversed. In other words, the real challenge is not merely keeping a secret alive but creating a responsible pathway from secrecy to scrutiny.

The deeper lesson is that dangerous information is rarely dangerous for only one reason. It can threaten someone because it reveals wrongdoing, because it exposes a network, because it contains legitimate security secrets, because it could harm vulnerable people, because it challenges an institution's reputation, or because powerful interests have something to lose. The person holding the information therefore occupies a complicated position between secrecy and accountability. They may have a duty to preserve what they know while simultaneously having a duty not to expose everything indiscriminately. They may need protection while also needing independent scrutiny. And they may have to accept that the most responsible outcome is not immediate public disclosure but controlled preservation until qualified people can determine what the evidence actually establishes.

That is ultimately why the dead man's switch should never be understood simply as a revenge mechanism, a threat against powerful people, or a technological guarantee that secrets will explode into public view after someone's death. At its most responsible, it is a continuity mechanism for information whose disappearance could prevent legitimate investigation or accountability. Its purpose is to keep evidence from being destroyed by the disappearance of its custodian while preserving enough structure around that evidence for someone else to evaluate it properly.

The most important question is therefore not whether information is dangerous, but why it is dangerous, to whom, and under what circumstances. Once those questions are asked seriously, the dead man's switch becomes something far more sophisticated than the popular image of a final secret message. It becomes an attempt to ensure that when the person carrying important knowledge can no longer speak, the evidence does not automatically become silent with them.

Resources

1. U.S. National Archives, Executive Order 13526, *Classified National Security Information*, for the legal framework governing classification, safeguarding, and declassification of U.S. national-security information.

2. U.S. National Archives, *Exemptions from Automatic Declassification*, for the distinction between legitimate continuing secrecy and the public interest in eventual declassification.

3. U.S. Securities and Exchange Commission, *Whistleblower Protections*, for statutory and regulatory protections concerning retaliation against qualifying whistleblowers.

4. U.S. Securities and Exchange Commission, *Whistleblower Frequently Asked Questions*, for additional information concerning retaliation, reporting, and legal protections under federal securities laws.

5. U.S. Department of Justice, Criminal Division, *Whistleblower Frequently Asked Questions*, for current federal guidance concerning corporate whistleblowing, retaliation, obstruction, and cooperation with government investigations.

6. U.S. Occupational Safety and Health Administration, *Whistleblower Protection* resources, for federal whistleblower statutes, anti-retaliation principles, and reporting mechanisms.

7. United Nations Office on Drugs and Crime, *Corruption and Trafficking in Persons*, for evidence concerning intimidation, threats, violence, and reporting barriers when corruption intersects with organized criminal groups.

8. National Institutes of Health, *Research Misconduct*, for definitions and institutional principles concerning fabrication, falsification, plagiarism, research integrity, and reporting suspected misconduct.

9. National Institutes of Health, *Expectations, Policies, and Requirements*, for current research-integrity requirements and responsibilities applicable to federally supported research.

10. National Institutes of Health, *Process for Handling Allegations of Research Misconduct*, for the evidentiary and procedural standards involved in evaluating research-misconduct allegations.

11. National Institutes of Health, *Research Security and Scientific Integrity* materials, for the distinction between research misconduct, research integrity, and research-security concerns.

The Dark History of Silenced Voices

History contains a recurring and unsettling pattern in which people who possess inconvenient information sometimes become targets of pressure, intimidation, retaliation, disappearance, or violence. The pattern is real, but understanding it requires considerably more discipline than simply assembling a catalogue of mysterious deaths and declaring them connected. Some people have unquestionably been murdered because of their political activities, investigative work, testimony, or opposition to powerful interests, while others have died under circumstances that remain disputed despite decades of speculation. Still others became the subjects of conspiracy theories because their deaths occurred at politically sensitive moments even though available evidence does not establish that they were killed for what they knew. The central challenge in studying the history of silenced voices is therefore not finding disturbing cases but determining what the evidence actually permits us to say about each one. That distinction is essential to the philosophy of a dead man's switch because a protection system built around fear must begin with an accurate understanding of the dangers that have genuinely existed.

One of the clearest documented examples is the murder of investigative journalist Daphne Caruana Galizia in Malta in 2017. Caruana Galizia had spent years investigating corruption, political relationships, financial secrecy, and allegations involving powerful figures, and she was killed when a car bomb destroyed her vehicle near her home. The murder produced an extensive criminal investigation and subsequent prosecutions, and Malta's public inquiry concluded that the state had created an environment in which those who exercised journalism could face serious risks and that the state bore responsibility for failing to recognize and address those risks. Her case therefore belongs firmly within the category of documented violence against an investigative journalist rather than merely being an unexplained death surrounded by internet speculation. Yet even here, the historical lesson is more complicated than the simple assertion that "she knew too much." The evidence concerns a network of criminal and political circumstances that must be examined independently rather than reduced to a single theory of motive.

The assassination of Daphne Caruana Galizia also demonstrates why the distinction between journalism and intelligence work matters when studying dangerous information. Investigative journalists routinely work with confidential sources, financial records, leaked documents, corporate filings, public databases, and testimony from insiders, but they do not necessarily know the full significance of every piece of information they receive. Their protection therefore depends not simply on possessing secrets but on maintaining networks of corroboration and ensuring that important evidence does not reside exclusively with one person. Modern investigative organizations have increasingly recognized this problem, developing collaborative reporting models in which sensitive investigations are shared among journalists and institutions across different countries. Such arrangements can reduce the likelihood that eliminating one individual will eliminate an investigation, although they cannot eliminate the physical danger faced by reporters. The lesson for a dead man's switch is straightforward: information becomes more resilient when its existence and significance are not dependent upon a single vulnerable custodian.

Another profoundly documented case is the assassination of Russian opposition politician Boris Nemtsov in Moscow in February 2015. Nemtsov, a prominent critic of President Vladimir Putin, was shot dead on a bridge near the Kremlin, and the murder generated extensive investigations and international concern. The European Court of Human Rights later found serious deficiencies in the investigation, including failures concerning the identification of the person who ordered the killing. This is precisely the kind of case that illustrates why historical analysis must distinguish between the fact of a killing and claims about its ultimate motivation or command structure. It is established that Nemtsov was murdered, but establishing who ordered a killing is a separate evidentiary question. A responsible account must resist the temptation to fill that evidentiary gap with certainty simply because a politically plausible explanation exists.

The history of journalists killed because of their work extends far beyond a handful of famous cases. Organizations such as the Committee to Protect Journalists have documented hundreds of journalists killed in connection with their work over the decades, with particularly severe risks occurring in countries experiencing war, political instability, organized crime, authoritarian repression, and corruption. The United Nations has repeatedly recognized journalist safety as a major international concern, emphasizing that impunity for crimes against journalists can encourage further violence. These cases demonstrate that the danger faced by information holders is not merely an artifact of espionage fiction or conspiracy culture. At the same time, the existence of genuine journalist killings does not mean every murdered journalist was killed because of their reporting. Each case requires its own evidence concerning motive, perpetrators, and circumstances. Statistical patterns establish that the danger exists, but they cannot automatically establish the explanation for an individual death.

The same principle applies to political assassinations. History contains many unquestionably documented political murders, including the assassinations of national leaders, opposition figures, activists, diplomats, and political organizers. The murder of former Lebanese Prime Minister Rafik Hariri in 2005, for example, resulted in an international investigation and later proceedings before the Special Tribunal for Lebanon. The tribunal convicted one individual in absentia for participating in the attack while finding insufficient evidence to establish the responsibility of certain other defendants beyond the required legal standard. The case illustrates an important principle that is easily lost in popular accounts of political violence: complex conspiracies can contain both established facts and unresolved questions. The existence of a coordinated assassination does not automatically mean that every suspected participant or alleged mastermind has been proven responsible. Legal findings can therefore be valuable precisely because they impose evidentiary boundaries on historical narratives.

Some of the darkest examples involve people who were not merely journalists or politicians but witnesses and investigators. Anti-corruption prosecutors, police officers, judges, lawyers, and civil servants can become targets when their work threatens organized criminal interests. The United Nations Office on Drugs and Crime has documented how corruption and organized crime can create conditions involving intimidation, threats, and violence against people involved in law enforcement and justice systems. In such cases, the "silenced voice" may not be someone holding a secret file at all; it may be someone attempting to make an existing body of evidence usable in court. The vulnerability comes from the person's role in converting information into accountability. This distinction matters because it shows that information can become dangerous not only when it is possessed but when someone attempts to make institutions act upon it.

The history of organized crime provides numerous examples of precisely this phenomenon. Investigative journalists who examine criminal organizations can become targets because reporting can expose financial networks, political relationships, trafficking routes, corrupt officials, or hidden ownership structures. Judges and prosecutors can face threats because successful prosecutions can remove criminal organizations' protection and revenue. Witnesses can be intimidated because testimony can transform circumstantial information into admissible evidence. In each situation, the objective of intimidation may not be to destroy information itself but to prevent information from becoming effective. That is a subtle but crucial distinction. The most dangerous moment may occur when evidence moves from private knowledge into a process capable of producing consequences.

One of the most famous historical examples of this broader problem is the murder of Italian anti-Mafia judges Giovanni Falcone and Paolo Borsellino in 1992. Falcone was killed by a massive bomb attack near Capaci, while Borsellino was killed weeks later in another bombing in Palermo. Both men had played central roles in prosecuting Cosa Nostra, and Italian investigations and judicial proceedings established the involvement of organized crime in the attacks. The murders became defining moments in Italy's struggle against the Mafia and demonstrated the extraordinary lengths to which a criminal organization could go to eliminate people involved in judicial enforcement. Their deaths also demonstrate why institutional resilience matters: although the murders killed two individuals, they did not destroy the anti-Mafia investigation or erase the accumulated body of evidence. Instead, the attacks contributed to a profound public reaction and intensified Italy's determination to confront organized crime.

There is a recurring lesson in these cases that deserves careful attention: silencing a person does not necessarily silence information. Sometimes it does the opposite. A violent attempt to suppress information can attract public attention, strengthen investigative determination, motivate additional witnesses, and turn a relatively obscure individual into a symbol of resistance. This is one reason the idea of a dead man's switch possesses both practical and psychological significance. If an investigation is already distributed across multiple people and institutions, eliminating one person may not accomplish the intended objective. Conversely, if all information resides with one individual, the loss of that person can be catastrophic. The historical record therefore suggests that resilience comes less from dramatic final revelations than from ensuring that important evidence has multiple legitimate paths toward preservation and independent scrutiny.

Yet history also contains many deaths that remain genuinely unexplained. These cases present a much greater epistemological challenge because an absence of explanation is not itself evidence of assassination. A person can die unexpectedly from natural causes, accident, suicide, criminal violence unrelated to their professional activities, or causes that investigators simply cannot establish with certainty. The human mind has a powerful tendency to connect unusual events, particularly when they involve famous people, controversial institutions, or emotionally charged political circumstances. Once a theory becomes established within a community, later information may be interpreted through that theory rather than evaluated independently. This is one of the mechanisms through which a legitimate historical mystery can evolve into an unsupported conspiracy narrative. The responsible researcher must therefore preserve uncertainty where the evidence remains uncertain.

The death of British scientist and biological-warfare expert David Kelly provides a useful example of this difficulty. Kelly was found dead in 2003 after becoming a central figure in controversy surrounding claims about Iraqi weapons of mass destruction. His death generated extensive speculation because of his connection to the politically explosive Iraq War and because questions arose about the circumstances surrounding his death. The official inquiry concluded that he died from suicide, while subsequent public debate continued to challenge aspects of that conclusion. Whatever one's interpretation of the controversy, the case demonstrates why "suspicious" and "proven assassination" cannot be treated as interchangeable terms. The existence of unanswered questions may justify further examination, but it does not automatically establish an alternative explanation.

The Kelly case also illustrates how political context can magnify uncertainty. When a person dies while connected to an issue of enormous public controversy, every detail of the death may acquire symbolic meaning. People may reasonably ask whether the person's knowledge created a motive for someone to harm them, but motive alone cannot establish that a crime occurred. Investigators must examine physical evidence, medical findings, communications, timelines, witness statements, financial circumstances, and other relevant information. When alternative explanations survive that examination, the responsible conclusion may remain provisional rather than absolute. Historical research is strongest when it is willing to say, "We do not know." A dead man's switch designed around an unverified assumption can create precisely the kind of catastrophic error that a carefully designed contingency system is supposed to prevent.

The history of intelligence whistleblowers provides another layer of complexity. People who work inside intelligence agencies can possess information that is simultaneously important, classified, technically complex, and difficult for outsiders to interpret. Some disclosures have revealed genuine governmental misconduct or controversial programs, while others have generated serious debates about national security and the appropriate limits of disclosure. The story of Edward Snowden is one of the clearest modern examples, because his disclosures in 2013 revealed extensive information about U.S. and allied electronic-surveillance programs and triggered worldwide debates about privacy, intelligence collection, national security, and government oversight. Snowden's actions remain deeply contested, with supporters describing him as a whistleblower and critics emphasizing the national-security consequences of his disclosures. Whatever one's judgment, the case demonstrates how the same body of information can be interpreted simultaneously as evidence of governmental overreach and as sensitive intelligence whose disclosure creates security risks.

This ambiguity is central to the history of silenced voices because not every person who claims to expose wrongdoing is necessarily correct. Institutions can be corrupt, but institutions can also investigate allegations accurately. Whistleblowers can expose genuine misconduct, but they can also misunderstand events, exaggerate claims, selectively present evidence, or pursue personal grievances. Journalists can uncover suppressed truths, but journalism can also publish inaccurate information. Government officials can conceal wrongdoing, but they can also legitimately protect information whose disclosure would endanger people. The historical record is therefore not a morality play in which the individual always represents truth and the institution always represents deception. The reality is much more difficult, which is precisely why evidence preservation and independent verification matter so much.

Perhaps the most instructive historical pattern is the use of intimidation before violence occurs. People may receive threats, experience surveillance, face harassment, lose employment, encounter lawsuits, become the subject of smear campaigns, or discover that professional relationships have suddenly changed. Such conduct can be difficult to document because each individual incident may have an innocent explanation. A threatening message can be dismissed as a prank, an unexpected dismissal can be described as ordinary business, and an aggressive lawsuit can be defended as legitimate legal action. The pattern becomes significant when independent events begin converging around the same person and the same information. Recognizing patterns without manufacturing them is one of the most difficult skills in investigative research.

Modern whistleblower-protection systems exist partly because lawmakers have recognized that retaliation can suppress important information without requiring physical violence. The U.S. Securities and Exchange Commission, for example, explicitly prohibits certain forms of retaliation against qualifying whistleblowers who report securities-law violations. The U.S. Office of Special Counsel similarly investigates prohibited personnel practices involving certain federal employees and whistleblowers. These systems do not prove that every whistleblower faces retaliation, nor do they eliminate the risks associated with reporting. They demonstrate, however, that the threat of professional or institutional retaliation is sufficiently real to warrant formal legal safeguards. This is an important corrective to the popular assumption that the only meaningful form of silencing is assassination.

The same lesson appears in international journalism. Reporters Without Borders, the Committee to Protect Journalists, UNESCO, and other organizations have documented imprisonment, threats, legal harassment, violence, and killings directed at journalists in different parts of the world. These records reveal that the vulnerability of information holders depends heavily upon political environment, rule of law, organized crime, corruption, armed conflict, and the independence of judicial institutions. In some countries, the principal danger may be physical violence, while in others it may be imprisonment or legal persecution. In still others, intimidation may be economic or professional. The concept of silencing therefore needs to be understood broadly enough to include any deliberate effort to prevent credible information from reaching appropriate scrutiny.

The historical record also warns us against assuming that mysterious deaths are necessarily connected to a person's work. Famous people attract narratives because their lives already carry significance. If an investigator, scientist, politician, journalist, or whistleblower dies unexpectedly, people naturally ask whether the death was related to their work. Sometimes that question leads to legitimate investigation and eventually to evidence of criminal conduct. Other times it produces years of speculation unsupported by reliable evidence. Confirmation bias can cause researchers to remember the unusual cases that fit a theory while ignoring the enormous number of people who possess controversial information and continue living ordinary lives. The absence of an obvious explanation can feel like evidence, but logically it is only an invitation to investigate further.

This is particularly important for the study of assassination claims because assassination is a conclusion about both event and motive. Demonstrating that a person was killed does not automatically demonstrate why they were killed. Demonstrating that someone had enemies does not prove that those enemies ordered a murder. Demonstrating that a death benefited a particular person does not establish that the beneficiary caused it. These distinctions sound obvious when stated abstractly, yet they are frequently abandoned when a case becomes politically or emotionally charged. Serious historical investigation requires maintaining them at every stage. A dead man's switch should be built around evidence rather than around the assumption that the existence of a threat proves the existence of a conspiracy.

There is another reason this discipline matters: false accusations can themselves become dangerous. If sensitive information is released without verification, innocent people may be identified as conspirators, private individuals may become targets, professional reputations may be destroyed, and legitimate investigations may be compromised. The person who creates a disclosure system may believe they are protecting the truth while inadvertently creating a mechanism for amplifying misinformation. This is particularly concerning when digital files can be copied and redistributed indefinitely. Once a damaging accusation enters the public information ecosystem, correcting it may be much harder than releasing it. A responsible dead man's switch must therefore incorporate not only survival mechanisms but also safeguards against premature or indiscriminate disclosure.

The darkest historical cases consequently lead to a surprisingly constructive conclusion. The most effective protection for important information is rarely a single secret held by a single frightened individual. It is a resilient ecosystem in which evidence can be authenticated, preserved, independently corroborated, responsibly transferred, and evaluated by people who are capable of acting upon it. Investigative journalism has increasingly embraced collaborative models for precisely this reason. Major international investigations such as the Panama Papers demonstrated how hundreds of journalists and multiple organizations can work together on enormous collections of sensitive material, making it much harder for pressure against one individual to stop the investigation as a whole. Distributed journalism is not identical to a dead man's switch, but it embodies the same deeper principle: important information becomes harder to suppress when its survival does not depend upon one person's continued ability to speak.

The history of silenced voices therefore gives us neither a simple catalogue of conspiracies nor a reassuring story in which institutions always protect the truth. It gives us something more valuable: evidence of how vulnerable information can become when power, money, crime, reputation, ideology, or national security are involved. Some people have unquestionably been murdered because they challenged powerful interests, while others have died under circumstances that remain disputed. Some whistleblowers have been protected, some retaliated against, some prosecuted, and some celebrated only years after their actions became understood. The historical record demands both vigilance and skepticism because accepting every suspicious death as an assassination is as intellectually irresponsible as dismissing every credible allegation of retaliation. Between those extremes lies the difficult work of evidence-based investigation.

That is where the dead man's switch becomes more than a technological curiosity. Its deepest purpose is to confront the possibility that a person may become unable to protect information before that information has been independently examined. The historical record shows that this possibility is not imaginary, but it also shows that fear can distort judgment and transform uncertainty into certainty without sufficient evidence. A responsible system must therefore protect information without predetermining the conclusion that the information proves. It should preserve evidence so that investigators, journalists, lawyers, regulators, courts, or other qualified recipients can examine it after the original custodian is gone. The goal is not to create an automatic machine for revenge, exposure, or accusation. The goal is to prevent the disappearance of a person from becoming the disappearance of potentially important evidence.

The darkest lesson of history may therefore be that truth rarely survives simply because it is true. It survives because someone preserves it, someone else verifies it, institutions take it seriously, witnesses remain willing to speak, records remain accessible, and evidence can withstand attempts to destroy or discredit it. Sometimes those conditions fail, and the historical record becomes incomplete forever. Sometimes they succeed, allowing information to outlive the people who first discovered it. The dead man's switch is an attempt to deliberately create that second possibility. But as we will see throughout this book, the mechanism is only as responsible as the evidence it protects, the people entrusted with it, and the judgment applied when the time comes to decide what should finally be revealed.

Resources

1. Council of Europe — Daphne Caruana Galizia inquiry materials — documentation concerning the Maltese public inquiry and its findings regarding the circumstances surrounding Caruana Galizia's assassination.

2. Committee to Protect Journalists — Daphne Caruana Galizia[1] — background concerning Caruana Galizia's journalism and assassination.

3. European Court of Human Rights — Nemtsov v. Russia — judicial findings concerning the investigation into Boris Nemtsov's assassination.

4. Committee to Protect Journalists — Journalists Killed[2] — extensive historical database documenting journalists killed in connection with their work.

5. UNESCO — Safety of Journalists[3] — international material concerning violence, impunity, and threats against journalists.

6. Special Tribunal for Lebanon — Hariri assassination case — primary legal materials concerning the investigation and proceedings surrounding the assassination of Rafik Hariri.

1. https://cpj.org/data/people/daphne-caruana-galizia/?utm_source=chatgpt.com

2. https://cpj.org/data/killed/?utm_source=chatgpt.com

3. https://www.unesco.org/en/safety-journalists?utm_source=chatgpt.com

7. Special Tribunal for Lebanon — Judgment in the Ayyash et al. case — legal findings concerning responsibility for the Hariri assassination.

8. United Nations Office on Drugs and Crime — Corruption and Organized Crime[4] — research and international material concerning the relationship between corruption, organized crime, intimidation, and threats to justice systems.

9. Italian Ministry of Culture and institutional memorial resources concerning Giovanni Falcone and Paolo Borsellino and the history of Italy's anti-Mafia struggle.

10. The UK National Archives — The Hutton Inquiry — official archival material concerning the inquiry into the death of David Kelly.

11. UK Parliament — The Hutton Inquiry — parliamentary material concerning the circumstances surrounding the Kelly controversy and inquiry.

12. U.S. Securities and Exchange Commission — Whistleblower Protections[5] — official information concerning retaliation and protections available to qualifying whistleblowers.

13. U.S. Office of Special Counsel — Whistleblower Disclosure — federal whistleblower disclosure procedures and protections.

14. Reporters Without Borders — World Press Freedom Index[6] — comparative international information concerning press freedom, journalist safety, and political environments affecting investigative reporting.

15. Daniel Ellsberg, *Secrets: A Memoir of Vietnam and the Pentagon Papers*, Viking, 2002 — first-person historical account of classified information, government secrecy, whistleblowing, and the personal consequences of disclosure.

16. David E. Sanger, *The Perfect Weapon: War, Sabotage, and Fear in the Cyber Age*, Crown, 2018 — broader context concerning modern information conflict, state power, secrecy, and the vulnerability of information.

17. Bruce Schneier, *Data and Goliath: The Hidden Battles to Collect Your Data and Control Your World*, W. W. Norton, 2015 — useful background concerning surveillance, information power, privacy, and the consequences of centralized information.

18. National Institute of Standards and Technology, *Security and Privacy Controls for Information Systems and Organizations*, SP 800-53 — foundational material concerning access control, accountability, contingency planning, and protection of sensitive information.

---

4. https://www.unodc.org/unodc/en/corruption/?utm_source=chatgpt.com

5. https://www.sec.gov/enforcement-litigation/whistleblower-program/whistleblower-protections?utm_source=chatgpt.com

6. https://rsf.org/en/index?utm_source=chatgpt.com

Whistleblowers, Witnesses, and the Price of Speaking Out

There is a moment in many whistleblower stories when information stops being merely something a person knows and becomes something they feel responsible for acting upon. That transition can be almost imperceptible at first, beginning with an uncomfortable document, an irregular transaction, an unsafe practice, a falsified record, a conversation that does not make sense, or an instruction that conflicts with what the person knows to be true. Most people who encounter troubling information do not immediately become whistleblowers because human beings are strongly influenced by loyalty, career security, social belonging, fear of being wrong, and the desire to believe that an institution will correct its own problems. The decision to speak often emerges only after someone concludes that ordinary channels are ineffective, compromised, or unwilling to address what they have discovered. At that point, the individual is no longer simply observing an institutional problem but entering a conflict between personal security and public responsibility. The history of whistleblowing shows that this decision can produce extraordinary benefits for society while imposing extraordinarily high costs upon the person who makes it.

The word "whistleblower" itself can obscure how different these people and circumstances actually are. A whistleblower might be a government employee exposing misconduct, a corporate accountant reporting financial manipulation, a nurse raising concerns about patient safety, an engineer identifying dangerous defects, a police officer reporting corruption, a scientist challenging research misconduct, or an intelligence employee disclosing information about government activity. Some report internally, some go to regulators, some consult lawyers, some approach journalists, and some eventually make information public. Their legal protections vary dramatically depending upon the country, industry, employment status, subject matter, and reporting channel involved. In the United States, for example, the Occupational Safety and Health Administration administers whistleblower protections under numerous statutes, and those laws can prohibit employers from taking adverse action against employees who engage in legally protected activities. The existence of these protections is important, but it should never be confused with a guarantee that a whistleblower will emerge from the experience professionally or personally unharmed.

The first price of speaking out is often uncertainty. A person may know that something is wrong without knowing exactly what will happen if they report it, whether anyone will believe them, whether the institution will investigate, whether their identity will remain confidential, or whether their interpretation of events will ultimately prove correct. That uncertainty can be more psychologically difficult than a clearly defined threat because the individual is forced to make decisions without knowing which consequences are coming. An employee may continue going to work while wondering whether colleagues know about the complaint, whether management is monitoring them, whether their career has quietly been marked for termination, or whether a seemingly ordinary meeting has another purpose. The person may begin interpreting routine events through the lens of the conflict, sometimes accurately and sometimes incorrectly. This is one reason whistleblowing can become psychologically exhausting even when no physical threat ever materializes.

Retaliation does not have to look like a dramatic act of violence to be effective. U.S. whistleblower-protection authorities recognize adverse actions that can include firing, demotion, reduction in pay or hours, denial of promotion, unfavorable reassignment, disciplinary action, intimidation, harassment, threats, and other conduct capable of discouraging a reasonable employee from raising concerns. Some retaliation is therefore obvious, while other forms can be subtle enough to create plausible deniability. A person may suddenly stop being invited to important meetings, lose responsibilities, discover that colleagues have become distant, or find that opportunities that once seemed routine are no longer available. Because each individual event can have an innocent explanation, proving a pattern can be difficult. The cumulative effect, however, can be substantial, particularly when the individual begins to believe that their professional future has become dependent upon remaining silent.

Career destruction is especially powerful because employment is rarely only about income. A person's occupation can provide identity, professional relationships, status, community, health insurance, retirement benefits, geographic stability, and a sense of competence and purpose. When an employee challenges an institution, the conflict can therefore threaten far more than a monthly salary. A professional who has spent decades building expertise may discover that colleagues no longer want to work with them, prospective employers are reluctant to hire them, or their reputation has become associated with controversy rather than achievement. In extreme cases, the individual may become effectively unemployable within a specialized field because the organizations that could employ them belong to the same professional ecosystem. Research on whistleblowing has documented career, financial, health, reputational, and personal consequences associated with retaliation, illustrating why the decision to report misconduct can become an existential rather than merely occupational calculation.

The psychological consequences deserve particular attention because they are sometimes treated as secondary to the historical drama of the disclosure. A person can survive a legal dispute and still carry the psychological consequences of months or years of uncertainty, conflict, isolation, and distrust. A comparative study of whistleblowers in the Netherlands found substantially elevated levels of reported mental-health problems among its relatively small whistleblower sample, with anxiety, depression, interpersonal sensitivity and distrust, agoraphobia symptoms, and sleeping problems among the conditions examined. The study also reported that large proportions of participants described strongly negative effects on work and income, with substantial effects on family functioning and relationships as well. These findings should not be interpreted as evidence that every whistleblower develops psychological illness, because the study involved a limited sample and cannot establish that whistleblowing alone caused every reported condition. They do demonstrate, however, that the psychological cost of becoming a whistleblower is a serious subject deserving attention alongside the legal and political consequences.

Distrust can become particularly corrosive because whistleblowing often begins with a breakdown of trust. The individual may have once believed that colleagues, supervisors, professional organizations, or government institutions were fundamentally committed to the same standards that they were. Discovering misconduct can fracture that assumption, especially when the first attempts to report the problem produce denial rather than correction. If retaliation follows, the person may begin to question not only the institution but also people who remain inside it. Friends may become uncomfortable discussing the situation, colleagues may avoid contact because they fear association with the whistleblower, and family members may struggle to understand why the individual continues pursuing a conflict that appears to have no obvious end. The result can be profound social isolation even when the whistleblower has technically done nothing wrong.

Witnesses face many of the same pressures, although their position can be different because they may not have initiated the disclosure. A witness might possess direct knowledge of a crime, observe misconduct, hold documents relevant to an investigation, or be able to confirm another person's account. Sometimes the witness is reluctant to become involved because they fear becoming part of a conflict that they did not create. Their hesitation is understandable because testimony can change relationships, employment circumstances, family dynamics, and personal safety. In criminal investigations involving organized crime or corruption, witnesses may face intimidation precisely because their evidence could transform suspicion into a prosecutable case. The United Nations Office on Drugs and Crime has documented how corruption and organized crime can create threats and intimidation affecting people involved in justice systems and reporting mechanisms, demonstrating that the vulnerability of information holders extends well beyond conventional whistleblowers.

Witness intimidation also illustrates why the protection of information cannot be separated from the protection of people. A document can sometimes be copied, but a witness cannot be duplicated in the same way. The person may possess memories, observations, relationships, or contextual knowledge that no file fully captures. If the witness becomes frightened enough to withdraw cooperation, an investigation can lose information that cannot simply be recovered from another source. This is one reason legal systems have developed various witness-protection mechanisms, although their availability and effectiveness vary substantially between jurisdictions. The deeper lesson is that preserving evidence and preserving the conditions under which people can safely testify are complementary objectives. A dead man's switch can potentially preserve documents, but it cannot by itself eliminate the human risks associated with being the person who originally knows what those documents mean.

One of the most instructive whistleblower stories remains Daniel Ellsberg and the Pentagon Papers. Ellsberg had participated in the preparation of a classified Department of Defense study examining U.S. involvement in Vietnam, a massive report that eventually became known as the Pentagon Papers. In 1971, he provided portions of the classified material to newspapers, beginning with *The New York Times*, and the resulting publication created one of the most consequential confrontations between government secrecy and press freedom in modern American history. The National Archives has since released the complete report, consisting of thousands of pages and extensive supporting documentation, allowing researchers to examine the underlying historical record rather than relying solely upon the versions initially published in newspapers. Ellsberg's experience demonstrates that whistleblowing can become a prolonged legal and political struggle rather than a single moment of disclosure.

The government's response to Ellsberg also reveals how retaliation can become more serious when officials perceive information disclosure as a threat to institutional power. Archival records document investigations into the unauthorized disclosure and the government's efforts to investigate Ellsberg and his associates. The Nixon administration also established a secret group that became known as the "Plumbers," initially in response to concerns surrounding leaks and the Pentagon Papers, and members of that group later participated in the break-in at the office of Ellsberg's psychiatrist. National Archives records document the connection between the campaign against Ellsberg and the broader chain of events that eventually became part of the Watergate scandal. The historical significance of this episode lies partly in the fact that the attempt to contain one disclosure ultimately produced evidence of additional abuses of power. It demonstrates the danger created when institutions respond to unwanted information through unlawful or covert retaliation rather than transparent investigation.

Yet Ellsberg's story also demonstrates why the label "whistleblower" should not erase legal complexity. He had obtained and distributed classified government documents without authorization, and prosecutors charged him under federal statutes concerning classified information and government property. The eventual dismissal of the case did not mean that the underlying legal questions surrounding unauthorized disclosure disappeared. Instead, the case became an important part of a continuing national debate about government secrecy, press freedom, national security, and the responsibilities of individuals who possess classified information. The Pentagon Papers themselves were historically significant because they documented internal assessments and policy decisions concerning the Vietnam War, but the process by which they became public also raised serious legal questions. This distinction matters for the dead man's switch because possessing important information does not automatically establish a legal right to publish it.

The Ellsberg case also provides an important lesson about redundancy. The Pentagon Papers were not dependent upon a single copy held by a single person forever. Copies moved among journalists, publications, government offices, libraries, and eventually archival institutions. The National Archives now holds a complete version and related documentation, meaning that the historical record no longer depends upon the survival of the original individuals who handled the material. The resilience of the information emerged through institutional preservation, multiple copies, public scrutiny, and the passage of time. This is conceptually similar to what a dead man's switch attempts to achieve on a much smaller scale: ensuring that information remains recoverable when its original custodian can no longer control it.

Another important example is the modern world of corporate whistleblowing. Employees sometimes discover misconduct through routine professional responsibilities rather than deliberate investigations. An accountant may notice unexplained transactions, an engineer may discover that safety margins have been manipulated, a healthcare worker may observe systematic failures, or a compliance officer may recognize that internal controls are being bypassed. The employee may initially assume that management will want to know, particularly if the organization publicly claims to value integrity and compliance. The crisis begins when internal reporting produces indifference, suppression, retaliation, or instructions to stop asking questions. At that point, the whistleblower must decide whether to escalate the matter externally, and that decision can transform an internal employment problem into a public and potentially legal confrontation.

The existence of formal reporting systems can make this process both safer and more complicated. Many organizations have ethics hotlines, compliance offices, internal audit departments, ombuds services, and legal channels designed to receive allegations of misconduct. Government agencies and regulators may also provide external reporting mechanisms, and some laws protect certain categories of disclosures. The SEC, for example, maintains a whistleblower program designed to receive information concerning possible federal securities-law violations and provides specific protections against retaliation in qualifying circumstances. These channels matter because the responsible response to wrongdoing is not necessarily immediate publication to the entire world. Sometimes the appropriate pathway is confidential reporting followed by independent investigation. The existence of a dead man's switch should therefore not become an excuse to bypass every legitimate reporting mechanism.

At the same time, internal channels cannot be assumed to work perfectly. An organization may have a genuine conflict of interest if the people responsible for receiving complaints report directly to the individuals implicated by those complaints. Employees may also reasonably fear that confidentiality will not be preserved. In some situations, internal reporting can provide an opportunity for the institution to correct a problem before it causes additional harm, while in others it can expose the complainant without producing meaningful action. The correct decision depends upon the facts, the applicable law, the institutional structure, and the nature of the alleged misconduct. A responsible whistleblower must therefore think strategically rather than automatically assuming that internal reporting is either always safe or always useless.

This is where legal advice can become particularly important. Whistleblower laws are not universal shields against retaliation, and their protections often depend upon specific statutory conditions. A person may be protected for reporting one category of misconduct but not another, protected when using one reporting channel but not another, or subject to different rules depending upon whether they are a government employee, private-sector worker, contractor, or professional subject to a separate regulatory framework. Even within the United States, different statutes establish different rights and procedures. OSHA's whistleblower program, for example, covers numerous statutes and provides specific mechanisms for filing retaliation complaints, while other federal agencies administer separate whistleblower programs. The prudent assumption is therefore that whistleblower protection is a legal framework requiring careful interpretation, not a universal promise that anyone who speaks out will be protected.

Lawsuits can become part of the retaliation landscape in ways that are difficult for outsiders to evaluate. A lawsuit may be entirely legitimate, brought by an organization seeking to protect genuine trade secrets or respond to a lawful dispute. It may also be experienced by the whistleblower as a powerful deterrent because litigation consumes time, money, attention, and emotional energy regardless of the ultimate outcome. A person who is already facing professional uncertainty may find the prospect of prolonged litigation overwhelming. The existence of a lawsuit therefore does not itself prove retaliation, just as an employee's accusation of retaliation does not automatically prove unlawful conduct by an employer. Both possibilities have to be investigated independently. This is another reason why the preservation of original documents, correspondence, timelines, and other evidence can become crucial when disputes later move into formal legal proceedings.

Surveillance presents an even more complicated problem because modern technology has made monitoring easier while making it harder for ordinary people to know what is actually happening. Workplace systems can generate extensive records of communications, logins, document access, file transfers, and other activities for entirely legitimate security reasons. Governments possess significant lawful surveillance capabilities under various legal frameworks, while criminal organizations and private actors can also attempt unauthorized monitoring. A person who discovers that their employer has reviewed work communications cannot automatically conclude that they are being targeted because of whistleblowing. Conversely, the existence of ordinary monitoring does not prove that a person has no reason for concern. The correct response is evidence-based assessment rather than assumption, because paranoia and complacency can both lead to dangerous decisions.

The emotional impact of this uncertainty can be profound. A whistleblower may begin checking communications repeatedly, worrying about who has access to information, wondering whether colleagues can be trusted, and replaying conversations to determine whether they revealed too much. The person may begin to feel that ordinary social interactions have hidden meanings. When actual retaliation has occurred, this heightened vigilance may be understandable, but it can still become exhausting. When no retaliation has occurred, the same psychological state can create unnecessary distress and impair judgment. The challenge is therefore to maintain reasonable security practices without allowing fear to become the primary source of decision-making.

Family members can become unintended participants in this process. A whistleblower's spouse, partner, parents, or children may experience financial instability, social pressure, professional consequences, or fear without ever having chosen to become involved. If the whistleblower loses employment, the family may lose income or housing stability. If the person becomes the subject of public controversy, relatives may face unwanted attention. If threats are made, family members may become part of the security calculation even when they have never seen the underlying evidence. This is one of the reasons a responsible information-protection system must distinguish between protecting the whistleblower and exposing the whistleblower's family to unnecessary danger.

The burden can be particularly heavy when the whistleblower begins to feel morally responsible for consequences beyond their control. If an investigation damages a company, employees may lose jobs even when they were not involved in misconduct. If a government disclosure reveals intelligence operations, innocent personnel may become exposed. If a scientific allegation proves false, reputations may be damaged unfairly. If a journalist publishes information involving vulnerable sources, those sources may face consequences they never anticipated. The whistleblower may therefore experience guilt even when they acted in good faith. This moral complexity is rarely captured by the simplistic narrative in which someone discovers a secret, reveals it, and is immediately vindicated.

For this reason, courage should not be confused with recklessness. A courageous person can still seek advice, preserve evidence, evaluate alternatives, protect innocent people, and consider whether a disclosure is proportionate to the wrongdoing alleged. The goal is not to become fearless but to make rational decisions despite fear. A person who possesses potentially important evidence should ideally think about what would happen if they became unavailable, but that does not mean creating an indiscriminate mechanism that publishes every file automatically. The more sensitive the information, the more important it becomes to preserve context and provide trusted recipients with enough information to evaluate what they are receiving. Courage without judgment can produce unnecessary harm, while caution without courage can allow serious misconduct to remain hidden.

This is precisely where the philosophy of the dead man's switch intersects with the psychology of whistleblowing. The switch can be understood as an attempt to reduce the burden placed upon one person's continued survival by creating a contingency for the information itself. Instead of asking the whistleblower to remain permanently available as the sole source of evidence, a carefully designed system can preserve documentation so that other people can examine it if necessary. This may reduce one form of vulnerability, but it does not eliminate the psychological or legal risks associated with the person who created it. It also creates new responsibilities because anyone who receives the material becomes part of the information's chain of custody. The switch therefore cannot replace human judgment; it merely changes when and where that judgment occurs.

There is a deeper lesson here about the relationship between secrecy and courage. People sometimes imagine that the strongest whistleblower is the person who immediately publishes everything, but indiscriminate disclosure can be irresponsible. Other people imagine that the safest approach is to tell nobody, but complete secrecy can ensure that evidence disappears with its owner. Between those extremes lies a more sophisticated approach based upon controlled preservation, independent corroboration, appropriate recipients, and proportional disclosure. The objective is to create enough resilience that the information can survive while avoiding unnecessary exposure of people who do not deserve to be harmed. That is the same balance that responsible investigative journalism, legal practice, archival preservation, and information security attempt to achieve in different ways.

The history of whistleblowing also shows why institutions should not treat every internal critic as an enemy. Organizations that respond constructively to credible concerns can prevent small problems from becoming catastrophic ones. A reporting employee can become an early-warning system, identifying failures before regulators, courts, journalists, or the public discover them independently. Institutions that punish every inconvenient question, however, may unintentionally encourage employees to bypass internal systems altogether. The result can be precisely the loss of control that the organization hoped to avoid. A healthy institution therefore needs mechanisms that allow uncomfortable information to move upward without requiring the person carrying it to become an enemy of the institution.

The opposite lesson is equally important for whistleblowers. Not every institution that challenges an allegation is necessarily engaged in retaliation. Investigations require skepticism, and organizations have legitimate interests in determining whether an accusation is accurate. An employee may misunderstand a policy, interpret incomplete data incorrectly, or mistake an administrative error for intentional misconduct. A professional organization has a responsibility to investigate such claims rather than simply accepting them because the person reporting them appears sincere. Whistleblowers deserve protection from retaliation, but organizations also deserve evidence-based evaluation of allegations. The two principles are not contradictory; they are necessary parts of a functioning accountability system.

The experience of whistleblowers therefore sits at the intersection of morality, psychology, law, technology, and institutional behavior. They are often celebrated after the fact, particularly when history eventually confirms their claims, but the moment in which they make their decision is rarely so clear. They may not know whether they will be believed, whether the evidence will survive scrutiny, whether their career will collapse, whether their family will suffer, or whether the institution will ultimately correct itself. They have to make decisions under uncertainty while carrying information that may have consequences far beyond their own lives. That is an extraordinary burden for any individual. It is also why societies that benefit from whistleblowing have an interest in creating systems that do not require individual courage to substitute for institutional accountability.

The dead man's switch belongs within that larger system rather than outside it. It can provide continuity when a person becomes unavailable, but it cannot determine whether information is true, whether disclosure is lawful, or whether publication serves the public interest. Those questions remain human questions. The technology can preserve a document, but it cannot decide whether the document is authentic. It can deliver a message, but it cannot determine whether the recipient is qualified to interpret it. It can distribute information, but it cannot understand the consequences for victims, witnesses, national security, or innocent third parties. The human beings surrounding the system therefore remain its most important components.

Perhaps the most important lesson is that speaking truth to power is not a single act but a process. It begins with recognizing a problem, continues through evidence collection and verification, proceeds into decisions about reporting and protection, and may eventually lead to investigation, litigation, publication, or institutional reform. At every stage there are opportunities for both courage and error. The whistleblower needs evidence strong enough to survive scrutiny, recipients capable of evaluating it, and protections proportionate to the risks involved. The institution needs mechanisms capable of receiving criticism without automatically treating the critic as an adversary. Society needs journalists, regulators, courts, investigators, and other independent institutions capable of distinguishing genuine revelations from unsupported allegations.

The price of speaking out is therefore not simply the possibility of losing a job or attracting unwanted attention. It can involve uncertainty, isolation, financial instability, damaged relationships, legal pressure, reputational conflict, psychological distress, and sometimes genuine physical danger. Yet the opposite price can also be substantial. Remaining silent when serious wrongdoing is occurring can allow harm to continue, evidence to disappear, victims to remain unprotected, and institutions to learn that misconduct can survive without consequence. The decision to speak is therefore rarely a simple choice between courage and cowardice. It is a difficult calculation involving evidence, responsibility, personal safety, legal rights, and the potential consequences of both action and inaction.

That is why the history of whistleblowers should not be reduced to heroic mythology. The most valuable lesson is not that individuals should become fearless crusaders against every institution they distrust. It is that societies require mechanisms through which credible information can survive the failure of ordinary channels. A dead man's switch represents one possible answer to that problem because it separates the survival of information from the survival of its original custodian. But the switch is only one layer in a much larger architecture of protection, and its existence does not remove the need for evidence, legal advice, secure preservation, trustworthy recipients, and ethical judgment. The ultimate objective is not to make the whistleblower invulnerable, because no technological system can promise that. It is to make the truth less vulnerable to the disappearance, intimidation, isolation, or destruction of the person who first carried it.

In the chapters ahead, we will therefore move from the human cost of speaking into the practical problem of protecting information before a crisis occurs. The question will become increasingly concrete: if a person genuinely possesses evidence that may matter after they are gone, how can that evidence be preserved without creating unnecessary danger? We will examine what should be protected, how evidence can be authenticated, why redundancy matters, how recipients should be chosen, and why the most dramatic disclosure mechanism is often not the safest one. The central principle will remain the same throughout the book: protection should serve evidence, not replace it. A dead man's switch should ensure that important information has a chance to survive, while leaving the final judgment about what that information means to people and institutions capable of examining it responsibly.

Resources

1. U.S. Occupational Safety and Health Administration — Whistleblower Protection Program[1] — primary-source material concerning federal whistleblower rights, retaliation, complaint procedures, and protections.

2. OSHA — Retaliation and Adverse Actions[2] — useful for defining retaliation, including dismissal, demotion, reduced hours, intimidation, harassment, threats, and other adverse employment actions.

3. OSHA — Whistleblower Protection FAQs[3] — provides information on protected activity, reasonable good-faith reporting, retaliation, causation, and different forms of adverse action.

4. U.S. Securities and Exchange Commission — Whistleblower Protections[4] — official material concerning retaliation protections applicable to qualifying SEC whistleblowers.

5. R. K. A. van der Velden et al., "Mental Health Problems Among Whistleblowers: A Comparative Study," *Journal of Occupational and Environmental Medicine*, available through PubMed Central. The study examines anxiety, depression, interpersonal distrust, sleep problems, and other psychological consequences reported by whistleblowers.

6. "Whistleblowing as an anti-corruption strategy in health and pharmaceutical organizations in low- and middle-income countries: a scoping review," available through PubMed Central, examining career, financial, health, reputational, and personal consequences associated with whistleblowing and retaliation.

7. National Archives — The Pentagon Papers[5] — primary archival material concerning the Vietnam Task Force report, its classification, disclosure, publication, and subsequent declassification.

8. National Archives — National Archives and Presidential Libraries Release Pentagon Papers[6] — detailed archival account of the 1971 disclosures, the copies made, the publications involved, and the eventual release of the complete report.

9. National Archives — Pentagon Papers Project[7] — useful for understanding document provenance, archival preservation, incomplete early public versions, and the eventual effort to reconstruct the historical record.

1. https://www.whistleblowers.gov/?utm_source=chatgpt.com
2. https://www.whistleblowers.gov/know_your_rights?utm_source=chatgpt.com
3. https://www.whistleblowers.gov/faq?utm_source=chatgpt.com
4. https://www.sec.gov/enforcement-litigation/whistleblower-program/whistleblower-protections?utm_source=chatgpt.com
5. https://www.archives.gov/research/pentagon-papers?utm_source=chatgpt.com
6. https://www.archives.gov/press/press-releases/2011/nr11-138.html?utm_source=chatgpt.com

10. National Archives — Investigation of Unauthorized Disclosure of Classified Information to The New York Times by Daniel Ellsberg[8] — archival primary-source material concerning the government's investigation of Ellsberg and the legal consequences of the Pentagon Papers disclosure.

11. National Archives — Watergate Records and Ellsberg Investigation — primary-source documentation concerning the White House response to the Pentagon Papers and the activities surrounding the investigation of Ellsberg.

12. Daniel Ellsberg, *Secrets: A Memoir of Vietnam and the Pentagon Papers*, Viking, 2002, for a first-person account of the Pentagon Papers, government secrecy, disclosure, prosecution, and the personal consequences of whistleblowing.

13. U.S. Department of Labor, OSHA, *Whistleblower Investigations Manual*, for additional background concerning the investigation of retaliation complaints and the evidentiary issues involved in establishing protected activity and adverse action.

14. United Nations Office on Drugs and Crime, materials concerning corruption, organized crime, witnesses, justice-sector personnel, intimidation, and threats, for the broader international context surrounding witnesses and information holders in criminal investigations.

---

7. https://declassification.blogs.archives.gov/2011/02/14/pentagon-papers-project/?utm_source=chatgpt.com

8. https://www.archives.gov/files/research/jfk/releases/docid-32989638.pdf?utm_source=chatgpt.com

From Physical Mechanism to Digital Lifeline

The phrase "dead man's switch" began with something much more tangible than secret documents, encrypted archives, or automated messages waiting for a person to disappear. In its original engineering sense, a dead man's switch is a fail-safe mechanism designed to respond when a person stops actively maintaining control, usually because of incapacitation, unconsciousness, or death. Railways, industrial machinery, elevators, locomotives, and other systems have employed related forms of vigilance control because machines can become dangerous when an operator is suddenly unable to act. The underlying principle is deceptively simple: continued operation requires evidence that the responsible human being is still present and capable of exercising control. If that evidence disappears, the system moves into a safer state. Modern information-based dead man's switches borrow this logic and turn it upside down, because instead of stopping a machine when its operator becomes unavailable, they can cause information to become available when its custodian can no longer intervene.

The mechanical dead man's switch therefore provides the conceptual foundation for everything that follows in this book. Its genius is not in detecting death directly, because most mechanical systems have no ability to determine whether someone has actually died. Instead, they detect the absence of an expected human action. A train operator may have to maintain pressure on a control, periodically acknowledge a warning, or perform some other continuous activity demonstrating attentiveness. If that activity stops, the system assumes that something may be wrong and initiates a predetermined response. The mechanism is therefore based upon a proxy for human availability rather than biological certainty. This distinction becomes extremely important when the same concept is transferred into digital systems, because an email server, cloud platform, or cryptographic protocol also cannot inherently know that a person has died; it can only detect that certain expected conditions have or have not been satisfied.

Historically, the idea emerged from the practical problem of human failure within increasingly complex technological systems. As transportation and industrial machinery became faster, heavier, and more powerful, the consequences of an incapacitated operator became more severe. Engineers consequently developed systems designed to make dangerous equipment fail safely when human control was interrupted. Railway vigilance devices are particularly illustrative because they combine monitoring, warning, and automatic intervention. The exact mechanisms vary across technologies and jurisdictions, but the engineering philosophy is consistent: a system should not depend entirely upon the assumption that its operator will always remain conscious, attentive, and physically capable. The dead man's switch was therefore never primarily about death. It was about designing systems that anticipate human absence and respond predictably when that absence occurs.

This distinction explains why the expression eventually became attractive as a metaphor for information protection. Imagine someone possessing evidence that could become important if they suddenly disappeared. Their problem is fundamentally different from that of a train operator, but the structural question is similar. What happens if the person who controls a critical system is suddenly unable to act? If the answer is "nothing," then the information may disappear with them. If the answer is "the information automatically becomes available," then the system has created continuity beyond the individual. The modern dead man's switch is therefore an information-continuity mechanism. Its purpose is not necessarily to reveal secrets immediately, but to create a condition under which the disappearance or prolonged inactivity of the information holder does not automatically destroy access to the material.

The earliest information-based versions did not require sophisticated technology. A person could leave documents with a lawyer, trusted friend, journalist, bank, or other custodian and provide instructions about what should happen if they failed to make contact. A sealed envelope could contain evidence, instructions, passwords, or the location of additional records. A periodic telephone call could serve as the human check-in, with the recipient instructed to take action if the calls stopped. Even a simple calendar reminder combined with a trusted intermediary could create a rudimentary form of dead man's switch. These arrangements lacked the automation and redundancy of modern systems, but they introduced an important idea: information can be given a contingency plan independent of the original owner's continued availability.

The next major transformation came with electronic communication. Email changed the economics of information preservation because a message could be created once and transmitted across geographical boundaries almost instantaneously. Instead of leaving a physical envelope in one person's possession, someone could maintain digital copies in several accounts or arrange for a message to be sent automatically under specified conditions. Automated email systems made it possible to transform a human reminder into a machine-mediated process. Scheduled messages, recurring notifications, and server-side automation could provide increasingly sophisticated ways to establish proof of continued activity. The dead man's switch was beginning to move from an object into a process.

But automation introduces an important problem that mechanical engineers understood from the beginning: false activation can be dangerous. A railway vigilance system that stops a train unnecessarily is inconvenient; a system that releases sensitive information prematurely can create legal, personal, professional, or physical consequences. An automated email may be triggered because someone lost access to an account, forgot a password, became hospitalized, travelled somewhere without connectivity, or simply failed to complete a scheduled check-in. None of those circumstances necessarily means that the information should be released. A digital dead man's switch therefore needs to distinguish between absence and genuine incapacity as carefully as possible. Since digital systems cannot reliably detect death by themselves, the design problem becomes one of reducing false positives and false negatives rather than attempting to achieve impossible certainty.

The rise of personal computers transformed the storage side of the problem as well. Documents that once required filing cabinets could now exist as digital files that were inexpensive to duplicate and easy to transport. This dramatically increased the possibility of redundancy. A sensitive document could theoretically exist on several encrypted drives, removable media, servers, and other storage systems simultaneously. Duplication protects against one of the oldest enemies of information: physical destruction. Fire can destroy paper, water can ruin photographs, a burglar can steal a filing cabinet, and an investigator can seize a physical archive. Digital information introduces different vulnerabilities, but it also creates the possibility of geographically distributed copies that can survive the destruction of any one location.

The crucial distinction is between copying information and protecting information. Making ten copies of an unencrypted document does not necessarily make it secure; it may simply create ten opportunities for unauthorized access. Likewise, storing a password on ten devices does not make the password resilient if every device is compromised through the same account or security weakness. Effective redundancy requires independence. If all copies depend upon one cloud account, one password, one encryption key, or one administrator, the apparent redundancy may be largely illusory. A resilient system therefore needs to consider not only how many copies exist but also how independently those copies can survive failure. This principle will become increasingly important when we examine distributed storage later in the book.

Encryption changed the nature of the problem again. Before widespread encryption, physical possession of a document often meant possession of its contents. Digital encryption made it possible to separate possession of the storage medium from possession of readable information. An encrypted drive could contain thousands of documents while revealing almost nothing to someone who lacked the necessary key. This created a powerful tool for information custodians, particularly those handling material that could expose sources, violate privacy, or create security risks. At the same time, encryption introduced a new single point of failure: the key. If the information survives but the decryption key disappears, the archive may become permanently inaccessible.

This creates one of the fundamental paradoxes of secure information storage. The stronger the protection, the more carefully access credentials must be preserved. A completely open archive is easy to recover but easy to compromise. A heavily encrypted archive may be almost impossible for an unauthorized person to read but equally impossible for legitimate recipients to access if the owner disappears without leaving an appropriate recovery mechanism. The dead man's switch therefore becomes a problem of controlled succession. Someone has to determine who should eventually possess the ability to decrypt the information, under what conditions, and with what safeguards against premature access. Security is not simply about keeping everyone out; it is about keeping the wrong people out while ensuring that the right people can eventually get in.

Cloud computing dramatically expanded the possibilities for information continuity. Instead of storing important files on a single computer in a home or office, individuals could place them on remote servers operated by specialized providers. This meant that physical disasters affecting the user's location no longer necessarily destroyed the information. A flood, fire, theft, or hardware failure could occur without eliminating the remote copy. Cloud platforms also made synchronization possible, allowing information to exist across multiple devices while remaining connected to a central service. For the person designing a dead man's switch, this created an attractive possibility: the archive could exist somewhere beyond their immediate physical environment and potentially remain available even if they could no longer reach it personally.

Cloud storage, however, does not eliminate trust; it relocates it. The user must trust the provider's security practices, authentication systems, infrastructure, legal policies, account-recovery procedures, and continued operation. A cloud provider may be extremely secure against ordinary attackers while still being subject to lawful demands for information under applicable law. An account may be suspended, credentials may be lost, a payment may fail, or the provider may change its policies. A cloud archive is therefore not an independent universe outside institutional control. It is another layer in the chain of custody. The correct question is not whether cloud storage is "safe" or "unsafe," but what threats it protects against and which new dependencies it creates.

The emergence of encrypted cloud storage attempted to address some of these concerns by allowing users to encrypt information before or during storage. End-to-end encryption and client-side encryption can reduce the amount of plaintext information available to a service provider, depending upon the architecture. Yet even the strongest cryptography cannot solve every problem. Metadata can reveal information about activity, account access can still be compromised, authentication credentials can be stolen, and users can accidentally expose decrypted files. A technically sophisticated encryption system can therefore be undermined by weak passwords, compromised devices, poor operational security, or careless sharing. The dead man's switch is ultimately a socio-technical system, meaning that its security depends upon both technology and human behavior.

The development of automated scripting and cloud computing introduced another possibility: conditional execution. A computer program can monitor events, dates, authentication records, network activity, or other predetermined conditions and then perform an action automatically. This is conceptually much closer to the original mechanical dead man's switch because the machine no longer requires a person to manually initiate the final action. The challenge is defining the condition correctly. A timer is simple, but human life is not. A system based solely upon a date can trigger even when the person is alive and well, while a system based upon a missed check-in can fail because of technical problems rather than actual incapacity. The more sophisticated the trigger becomes, the more important it is to understand precisely what event the system is measuring.

This is why a dead man's switch should never be described as literally knowing when its owner dies. In most practical implementations, it does nothing of the sort. It knows that a deadline passed, that a confirmation was not received, that a credential was not refreshed, or that another predefined condition occurred. Human beings then interpret that condition as evidence that the person may no longer be available. This distinction is not merely technical semantics. It determines how much confidence should be placed in the trigger and how much additional verification should occur before sensitive information is released. A system that treats a missed check-in as absolute proof of death is inherently vulnerable to false activation.

Distributed networks extended the concept further by reducing dependence upon centralized infrastructure. Instead of maintaining a single copy under one person's control, information could be divided or replicated across multiple independent participants. Peer-to-peer systems, distributed databases, decentralized storage networks, and other architectures explored different ways of making information resilient even when individual nodes fail. The underlying principle resembles redundancy in physical engineering: if one component disappears, the system should continue functioning. But distribution introduces its own complexities, including authentication, coordination, availability, governance, and the question of who ultimately controls the information.

Blockchain technology added another layer of possibility because blockchains are designed around distributed ledgers maintained across networks of participating computers. Smart contracts can encode conditional logic that executes according to predefined rules when supported conditions are satisfied. This has led to experimentation with decentralized escrow, automated payments, document notarization, and other applications that can be conceptually related to dead man's switches. Yet blockchain should not be treated as a magical solution to information survival. A blockchain can provide durable records and automated execution within its technical environment, but it does not inherently determine whether a person is dead, whether a document is authentic, whether a recipient is trustworthy, or whether releasing information is lawful.

The distinction between preserving proof and preserving content becomes especially important here. A blockchain can be useful for establishing that a particular digital fingerprint, such as a cryptographic hash, existed at a particular point in time. That can contribute to evidence integrity because later investigators can compare the hash of a document with the recorded value. But the blockchain does not necessarily contain the document itself, and storing sensitive material directly on a public blockchain can create serious privacy and permanence problems. Once information is published to an immutable public ledger, removing it may be impossible or extremely difficult. A technology designed for permanence can therefore be a poor place for information that may later need to be withdrawn, corrected, or legally restricted.

The evolution from mechanical devices to blockchain systems reveals a remarkable continuity beneath the technological differences. The hardware has changed almost beyond recognition, but the fundamental question remains the same: what should happen when the person responsible for something can no longer perform the action expected of them? In a railway, the answer may be to stop the machine. In an information system, the answer might be to notify a trusted recipient, unlock an archive, release a document, or initiate a verification process. The mechanism changes, but the philosophy remains one of preplanned response to human unavailability. That continuity is what makes the term "dead man's switch" so useful despite its very different modern applications.

The modern digital environment also allows several mechanisms to be combined. A person might maintain encrypted records offline while keeping encrypted copies elsewhere. A trusted recipient might hold one part of an access arrangement while another recipient holds another part. An automated system might send notifications if check-ins stop without immediately releasing the underlying material. A legal representative might hold instructions concerning what should happen to the archive. A cryptographic timestamp could help establish when particular documents existed. None of these measures needs to be sufficient by itself. Their combined purpose is to create layers so that the failure of one component does not automatically destroy the entire system.

Layering is one of the most important concepts borrowed from engineering and information security. A building designed to withstand one type of failure may still collapse under another, so engineers use multiple independent safety measures. Cybersecurity follows a similar principle through defense in depth. Authentication, encryption, backups, access controls, monitoring, physical security, and recovery procedures can each address different classes of risk. A dead man's switch can adopt the same philosophy. Instead of asking whether one automated trigger is foolproof, the designer should ask how many independent safeguards would need to fail before the system produces the wrong result.

The evolution of digital communication also changed the geography of secrecy. Physical archives once had obvious boundaries: a safe, a house, an office, a bank vault, or a government facility. Digital information can cross borders without the owner's physical movement. A file stored on a server may be replicated across data centers in multiple jurisdictions. An email can pass through infrastructure belonging to several countries. A cloud account may be governed by contractual terms and laws that differ from those of the person who created it. This creates enormous possibilities for resilience but also introduces complicated questions concerning jurisdiction, privacy, lawful access, and evidence handling. The international nature of digital storage means that information protection can no longer be understood purely as a physical security problem.

The development of secure messaging systems further transformed the information environment. Encrypted messaging can allow sensitive communications to move between people without relying upon traditional email infrastructure. Some systems emphasize end-to-end encryption, minimizing the ability of intermediaries to read message contents. Others incorporate disappearing messages or device-specific protections. These technologies can be valuable for legitimate privacy and security purposes, including protecting journalists and sources, but they also introduce new risks when users misunderstand how the systems actually work. A disappearing message is not necessarily unrecoverable, and an encrypted communication is not necessarily anonymous. Screenshots, backups, compromised devices, metadata, and human error can all undermine assumptions about confidentiality.

This is a recurring theme in the evolution of the dead man's switch: every technological improvement creates both new capabilities and new failure modes. Mechanical systems could break, electrical systems could lose power, email accounts could become inaccessible, cloud providers could suspend accounts, encryption keys could be lost, automated scripts could malfunction, and distributed networks could experience governance or availability problems. No technology abolishes uncertainty. It merely changes the structure of the uncertainty. The responsible designer therefore thinks in terms of failure analysis rather than technological faith. The question is always, "What happens when this component fails?" rather than, "Can this technology guarantee success?"

Artificial intelligence is now beginning to extend this evolution into another territory. Modern AI systems can analyze large volumes of information, classify documents, identify relationships, summarize evidence, monitor specified conditions, and assist with workflows that would previously have required substantial human labor. In principle, AI could help maintain an archive, detect changes, verify whether certain routine conditions have occurred, or assist authorized recipients in navigating a large body of evidence. But AI introduces a critical new problem because an automated system capable of interpreting information is not necessarily capable of understanding its moral, legal, or factual significance. An AI model can misclassify a document, misunderstand context, or confidently produce an incorrect interpretation. For highly sensitive information, automation should therefore assist human judgment rather than silently replace it.

The same caution applies to biometric systems. Fingerprints, facial recognition, voice recognition, and other biometric technologies can help authenticate identity, but they are not magical proof of a person's condition. A biometric system can determine whether presented characteristics correspond sufficiently to stored patterns, but it does not inherently know whether a person is acting freely, whether their account should remain active, or whether information should be released after a medical emergency. Biometrics are particularly difficult as long-term secrets because biological characteristics cannot simply be changed in the same way that passwords can. Once compromised, the underlying identifier may remain compromised indefinitely. Consequently, biometric activation can be one component of an authentication architecture but should not automatically be treated as a complete dead man's switch.

Another emerging concept is the use of geographically distributed release conditions. A system might theoretically respond differently depending upon where authorized devices, people, or infrastructure are located. Such mechanisms could be useful for resilience because a system that depends upon one geographic location is vulnerable to local disasters or interference. But location data also raises significant privacy and security issues. A location-based system may produce false signals when devices lose GPS accuracy, network connectivity changes, or people travel unexpectedly. As with every other trigger, the technology can measure a condition but cannot automatically understand its meaning.

Perhaps the most profound transformation has been psychological rather than technological. The traditional dead man's switch was associated with machinery and danger, while the digital version is increasingly associated with personal autonomy over information. Individuals can now possess archives containing documents, photographs, financial records, research data, correspondence, testimony, and other material that may outlive them. The problem of digital inheritance has therefore become much larger than the question of whistleblowing. People need systems for ensuring that legitimate information reaches heirs, lawyers, researchers, journalists, organizations, or other intended recipients after death or incapacity. The dead man's switch is one specialized expression of this broader problem of digital succession.

Yet sensitive information requires a distinction between inheritance and disclosure. A family archive may appropriately pass to heirs, while evidence concerning alleged wrongdoing may require review by lawyers or journalists. Medical records may need strict confidentiality, while historical documents may eventually belong in an archive. Corporate information may be governed by contractual duties, while personal correspondence may involve the privacy of people who are still alive. A universal "release everything" switch therefore makes little sense. The modern information environment demands differentiated handling according to the nature of the material, the rights of other people, and the legal framework governing it.

This is why the most sophisticated dead man's switch is often not a single trigger at all. It is an architecture of conditional access. Some information may be released immediately to one trusted recipient. Other material may require verification. Some documents may remain encrypted until a legal representative authorizes access. Other evidence may be preserved indefinitely without public release. A system can therefore distinguish between notification, preservation, authentication, review, and publication rather than treating them as one event. This approach is far more consistent with the lessons learned from both engineering safety systems and modern information security.

The history of the dead man's switch consequently tells a larger story about humanity's relationship with technology. We began with machines that needed protection from the failure of their operators. We then developed digital systems capable of preserving information beyond the physical lives of their owners. Eventually, networks became capable of distributing that information across institutions and geographical boundaries. Cryptography allowed us to control access, cloud computing allowed us to separate storage from physical location, and distributed systems allowed us to reduce dependence upon centralized infrastructure. Each generation solved certain problems while creating new ones, forcing the next generation of designers to think more carefully about trust, authentication, redundancy, and failure.

The essential principle has remained remarkably stable throughout this evolution. A system should anticipate the possibility that the human being at its center will become unavailable. It should have a predefined response to that condition. It should fail in a controlled rather than chaotic manner. It should avoid unnecessary dependence upon any single component. It should preserve the ability of legitimate people to recover what matters. And above all, it should distinguish between the technical detection of inactivity and the human interpretation of what that inactivity means. These principles are more durable than any individual technology because they describe the architecture of the problem rather than the tools of a particular era.

The modern dead man's switch is therefore best understood not as a gadget but as a philosophy of continuity. An email, encrypted drive, cloud account, blockchain contract, physical vault, or distributed archive is merely a component. The real system consists of triggers, evidence, authentication, redundancy, recipients, legal constraints, and carefully defined consequences. A person designing such a system is effectively asking what parts of their knowledge should survive them, who should have access, how that access should occur, and what safeguards should prevent a premature or malicious release. Those questions cannot be answered by technology alone. They require judgment about evidence, responsibility, privacy, law, and human vulnerability.

The journey from the physical dead man's switch to the digital lifeline therefore marks a profound shift in what it means to survive through information. A machine can stop when its operator disappears, but information can continue moving long after its creator is gone. That possibility is both empowering and dangerous. The same technology that allows evidence to survive assassination, disappearance, accident, or incapacitation can also release false accusations, private information, stolen secrets, or misunderstood material into the world. The objective is consequently not maximum automation or maximum exposure. It is controlled continuity: creating a system in which important information has a greater chance of surviving while preserving enough safeguards to ensure that survival does not automatically become indiscriminate publication.

The chapters that follow will build upon this technological history by examining what an information-based dead man's switch must actually contain. We will look at triggers, check-ins, physical and digital storage, encryption, redundancy, distributed custody, recipient selection, legal considerations, and the increasingly sophisticated technologies that can participate in a contingency system. The central engineering lesson will remain with us throughout: every system should be designed around the assumption that something will eventually fail. The central human lesson is equally important: when the information matters, the cost of failure may be measured not in broken machinery but in lost evidence, damaged lives, or truths that disappear permanently. A well-designed dead man's switch is an attempt to ensure that when one human link in the chain is broken, the information does not necessarily break with it.

Resources

1. U.S. Federal Railroad Administration, materials concerning railroad safety systems and locomotive engineer vigilance, for historical and regulatory context surrounding human-failure protection in railway operations.

2. U.S. Department of Transportation, Federal Railroad Administration, *49 CFR Part 229 — Railroad Locomotive Safety Standards*, particularly provisions concerning alerters and locomotive control systems, for the regulatory background to modern railroad vigilance mechanisms.

3. International Electrotechnical Commission, IEC 61508, *Functional Safety of Electrical/Electronic/Programmable Electronic Safety-Related Systems*, for the broader engineering principles of fail-safe design, functional safety, fault tolerance, and risk reduction.

4. National Institute of Standards and Technology, *Cryptographic Standards and Guidelines*, for authoritative background on encryption, cryptographic keys, authentication, hashes, and secure information systems.

5. National Institute of Standards and Technology, *Digital Identity Guidelines*, Special Publication 800-63, for authentication, identity proofing, authenticators, and the limitations of digital identity systems.

6. National Institute of Standards and Technology, *Security and Privacy Controls for Information Systems and Organizations*, Special Publication 800-53, for access control, contingency planning, system integrity, auditability, and information-security architecture.

7. National Institute of Standards and Technology, *Guide to Enterprise Patch Management Planning*, for broader context concerning lifecycle management and the importance of maintaining security systems over time.

8. Bruce Schneier, *Applied Cryptography*, Wiley, for foundational treatment of cryptographic systems, authentication, keys, digital signatures, and the distinction between cryptographic strength and operational security.

9. Bruce Schneier, *Secrets and Lies: Digital Security in a Networked World*, Wiley, for the broader principle that information security is a socio-technical problem involving people, procedures, incentives, and technology rather than cryptography alone.

10. NIST Cybersecurity Framework 2.0[1] — contemporary framework for identifying, protecting, detecting, responding to, and recovering from cybersecurity risks.

11. CISA — Secure Cloud Business Applications — government guidance concerning cloud security, identity, access management, configuration, and risks associated with cloud environments.

12. NIST — Blockchain Technology Overview[2] — technical background on distributed ledgers, blockchain architecture, consensus, cryptographic hashes, and related concepts.

13. NIST — Blockchain and Related Technologies[3] — additional technical resources concerning blockchain systems and their applications.

1. https://www.nist.gov/cyberframework?utm_source=chatgpt.com

2. https://www.nist.gov/publications/blockchain-technology-overview?utm_source=chatgpt.com

3. https://www.nist.gov/blockchain?utm_source=chatgpt.com

14. Satoshi Nakamoto, "Bitcoin: A Peer-to-Peer Electronic Cash System," 2008, for the foundational description of a decentralized blockchain-based network and cryptographic proof structure.

15. Electronic Frontier Foundation — Surveillance Self-Defense[4] — practical educational resources concerning encryption, secure communication, account security, metadata, device security, and threat modeling.

16. Signal — Signal Protocol documentation[5] — technical documentation concerning the cryptographic architecture underlying modern end-to-end encrypted messaging.

17. Internet Engineering Task Force — OpenPGP specification and standards[6] — technical background concerning public-key encryption, digital signatures, and secure email.

18. National Archives — Digital Preservation — useful institutional background concerning long-term preservation, authenticity, accessibility, and the challenges of maintaining digital records over time.

19. Library of Congress, *Digital Preservation at the Library of Congress*, for the long-term preservation problems associated with changing formats, storage media, metadata, authenticity, and technological obsolescence.

20. National Institute of Standards and Technology, *NIST Special Publication 800-57: Recommendation for Key Management*, for the practical problem of creating, protecting, distributing, rotating, recovering, and eventually destroying cryptographic keys.

21. Ross Anderson, *Security Engineering: A Guide to Building Dependable Distributed Systems*, Wiley, for a comprehensive treatment of security architecture, distributed systems, human factors, failure modes, and dependable system design.

22. NIST — Artificial Intelligence Risk Management Framework[7] — framework for understanding and managing risks associated with AI systems, particularly relevant when AI is incorporated into automated information-management or decision processes.

23. CISA — Zero Trust Maturity Model[8] — useful for understanding why modern security architectures avoid assuming that any single user, device, network, or location is automatically trustworthy.

24. ISO/IEC 27001, *Information Security Management Systems*, for the broader governance principle that information security requires organizational processes, risk assessment, controls, and continual improvement rather than technology alone.

25. Internet Archive — Wayback Machine[9] — an important practical example of large-scale distributed digital preservation and the challenge of maintaining access to information as websites and technologies change.

---

4. https://ssd.eff.org/?utm_source=chatgpt.com

5. https://signal.org/docs/?utm_source=chatgpt.com

6. https://www.openpgp.org/?utm_source=chatgpt.com

7. https://www.nist.gov/itl/ai-risk-management-framework?utm_source=chatgpt.com

8. https://www.cisa.gov/resources-tools/resources/zero-trust-maturity-model?utm_source=chatgpt.com

9. https://web.archive.org/?utm_source=chatgpt.com

Living Under Threat: Fear, Courage, and Psychological Survival

Living with information that may be dangerous is psychologically different from simply possessing information that is important. An important document can sit quietly in a drawer while its owner goes about an ordinary life, but information perceived as dangerous can change the way a person interprets almost everything around them. A telephone call that would once have seemed routine may suddenly appear significant, an unfamiliar vehicle may attract attention, and an unexpected conversation with a colleague may become something to analyze afterward. Sometimes those perceptions are justified because genuine threats do occur, particularly when information concerns organized crime, corruption, political violence, corporate wrongdoing, or sensitive government activity. Sometimes they are not justified, and ordinary events become frightening because prolonged uncertainty has altered the person's sense of safety. Understanding this distinction is one of the most important psychological challenges in designing any responsible dead man's switch, because fear can encourage sensible preparation while uncontrolled fear can produce decisions that make an already difficult situation considerably worse.

Threat perception begins with uncertainty. When a person knows exactly what is happening, they can often formulate a response, but when they suspect that something may be happening without possessing enough information to confirm it, the mind begins filling the gaps. Human beings are naturally pattern-seeking organisms, and the ability to detect possible danger has evolutionary value because failing to notice a genuine threat can have serious consequences. The problem is that the same cognitive machinery can generate false alarms when evidence is incomplete. A person who possesses sensitive information may therefore become increasingly attentive to ambiguous events, searching for connections between circumstances that may or may not be related. The more consequential the information appears, the stronger the temptation can become to interpret uncertainty as evidence. Psychological survival begins with recognizing that danger assessment itself is a process requiring evidence, calibration, and periodic reassessment.

Fear is not necessarily a sign of weakness. In a genuine threat environment, fear can be an adaptive response that increases attention, encourages preparation, and motivates a person to avoid unnecessary exposure. The body's stress response can produce increased alertness, faster heart rate, changes in attention, and heightened readiness for action. These responses are useful when a person needs to respond quickly to immediate danger, but they can become exhausting when activated repeatedly over long periods. A person who believes that danger is always present may remain physiologically and psychologically prepared even when no immediate threat exists. The resulting state can make rest difficult and can gradually interfere with concentration, relationships, work, and ordinary decision-making.

Psychology has long studied the consequences of prolonged stress because the human nervous system is not designed to remain indefinitely in a state of emergency. Chronic stress is associated with changes in sleep, mood, attention, memory, and physical functioning, although individual responses vary substantially. The National Institute of Mental Health recognizes that stress can affect both mental and physical well-being and distinguishes ordinary stress responses from more serious conditions requiring professional attention. The important point for someone protecting sensitive information is that psychological strain can affect the very cognitive abilities required to manage that information responsibly. A person who is exhausted, frightened, isolated, and constantly alert may have greater difficulty evaluating evidence objectively. Security planning must therefore include the psychological condition of the person operating the system rather than treating the human being as an infinitely reliable component.

Hypervigilance is particularly relevant because it can emerge when a person believes that danger may be present but cannot determine exactly when or where it will appear. Hypervigilance involves excessive attention to potential threats and can cause an individual to monitor surroundings, communications, people, and unexpected events with unusual intensity. In some circumstances, heightened vigilance is an appropriate response to credible danger. The problem occurs when the level of vigilance becomes disproportionate to the available evidence or remains elevated long after the immediate threat has passed. A person can begin to treat every ambiguity as potentially meaningful, creating a feedback loop in which increased monitoring produces more ambiguous information, which then produces even more monitoring. Without external reality checks, this process can become increasingly difficult to interrupt.

The difference between vigilance and hypervigilance is therefore not simply the amount of attention being paid. It concerns whether attention remains proportionate, flexible, and evidence-based. A careful person might notice an unusual event, record it, investigate whether there is an independent explanation, and then adjust their assessment. A hypervigilant person may notice the same event and continue searching for additional evidence that confirms an existing fear. The first approach allows information to change the conclusion, while the second can become increasingly resistant to disconfirmation. This distinction is crucial for anyone constructing a threat assessment because a security system that responds to every perceived anomaly can eventually become unusable. Good security does not mean believing every danger is real; it means creating procedures capable of distinguishing credible indicators from ordinary uncertainty.

Isolation can intensify the problem. People who possess sensitive information may deliberately avoid discussing it because they fear compromising confidentiality. That instinct can be rational, especially when the information concerns identifiable individuals, protected sources, classified material, criminal investigations, or other sensitive subjects. But secrecy can gradually reduce access to ordinary emotional support because the person cannot easily explain why they are anxious, why they are changing routines, or why they need to take unusual precautions. Friends may interpret withdrawal as indifference, while family members may perceive unexplained behavior as irrational or secretive. The individual may then retreat further because explaining the situation feels impossible. A security measure intended to protect information can therefore unintentionally create a psychological environment in which the person becomes increasingly alone with their fears.

This is one reason confidentiality should not be confused with complete isolation. Sensitive information can sometimes be compartmentalized so that trusted people know enough to provide support without receiving the underlying material. A lawyer may need to know the legal circumstances without possessing every document. A therapist may need to understand that someone is under significant stress without being told confidential details. A family member may need to know how to respond to an emergency without knowing the contents of a protected archive. The objective is to preserve necessary confidentiality while preventing the individual from becoming psychologically isolated. This distinction between information access and human support will become increasingly important when we examine the selection of recipients later in the book.

Trust becomes particularly difficult when a person begins to believe that information may put them at risk. Under ordinary circumstances, trust is built through repeated interactions and shared experience. Under perceived threat, however, the person may begin evaluating relationships according to security rather than affection. A colleague who once seemed reliable may suddenly appear vulnerable to pressure. A friend may be considered too curious. A relative may be excluded because of professional connections. The person may begin creating mental categories of people who are safe, unsafe, uncertain, or compromised. Some of these judgments may be accurate, but others may be based on fear rather than evidence. Maintaining the ability to distinguish uncertainty from demonstrated unreliability is therefore essential.

Trust should also be understood as multidimensional. A person can be trustworthy in one context and inappropriate in another. Someone may be completely loyal but have poor digital security. Another person may possess excellent technical expertise but lack the discretion required for sensitive personal information. A lawyer may understand legal confidentiality but not have the technical ability to manage encrypted archives. A journalist may know how to protect sources but may have a different standard for publication than the information holder expects. The right question is therefore not simply, "Do I trust this person?" but rather, "Do I trust this person with this particular responsibility under these particular circumstances?" That shift from personal trust to role-based trust is one of the foundations of sound security architecture.

Fear can also alter decision-making through what psychologists describe as attentional narrowing. When people perceive serious danger, attention may become concentrated on the perceived threat at the expense of broader considerations. This can be beneficial during an immediate emergency because it allows rapid action. It becomes problematic when complex decisions require consideration of multiple competing consequences. A frightened person may focus intensely on preventing an imagined disclosure while overlooking the possibility that an automatic release could expose an innocent family member, identify a confidential source, violate a legal obligation, or publish material that has not been verified. The more important the information, the more damaging such omissions can become. A responsible contingency system should therefore be designed during periods of relative calm whenever possible, rather than improvised in the middle of a crisis.

This is one of the strongest arguments for preparing a dead man's switch before it becomes urgently necessary. Planning made during calm periods can be deliberate, documented, and reviewed. Planning made during a perceived emergency may be dominated by fear and urgency. The difference is similar to the difference between writing an evacuation plan before a fire and deciding where to run after the building is already burning. A person who believes they may possess dangerous information should ideally establish procedures while they can still think clearly about verification, access, recipients, legal constraints, and possible unintended consequences. The objective is not to assume that disaster will occur. It is to reduce the number of critical decisions that would otherwise have to be made under extreme pressure.

Courage is often misunderstood in precisely this context. Popular culture tends to portray courage as the absence of fear, but psychologically and historically, courage is better understood as action undertaken despite fear. A person who feels no fear in a genuinely dangerous situation may simply be unaware of the danger. A person who recognizes the risks and nevertheless acts according to carefully considered principles may be demonstrating something closer to genuine courage. This does not mean that every decision to disclose information is courageous, because reckless action can sometimes create unnecessary harm. Courage becomes constructive when it is combined with judgment, proportionality, and responsibility. The objective is not to eliminate fear but to prevent fear from becoming the sole author of one's decisions.

The moral dimension of whistleblowing can make this especially difficult. A person may believe that remaining silent allows wrongdoing to continue while speaking creates serious personal danger. The individual may feel responsible for people who could be harmed if the information remains hidden. At the same time, disclosure may expose people who were not involved in the wrongdoing or may reveal information whose consequences are difficult to predict. The person is therefore caught between competing responsibilities rather than simply choosing between good and evil. Moral courage in these circumstances involves recognizing that several legitimate interests may exist simultaneously. Protecting the truth, protecting innocent people, respecting lawful confidentiality, and preventing further harm may all matter at once.

The psychological burden becomes heavier when the individual begins to believe that nobody else can understand the situation. This belief can emerge naturally when information is highly confidential. A person may think that explaining the problem would itself create unacceptable risk, so they carry the entire burden internally. Over time, this can produce a dangerous asymmetry: the individual knows everything while everyone else knows almost nothing. If the person becomes incapacitated, the people around them may have no idea what information exists or how to access it. From a dead man's switch perspective, this is precisely the problem that contingency planning is intended to solve. The system should allow enough information to survive without requiring the person to tell everyone everything while they are alive.

One solution is compartmentalization. Instead of giving one person complete knowledge of the entire archive, different people can have different responsibilities. One may know where an encrypted archive exists. Another may possess an authentication credential. A lawyer may hold instructions concerning legal review. A journalist may know that evidence exists without receiving the entire archive immediately. This approach reduces the consequences if one person becomes compromised, unavailable, or simply makes a mistake. It also reduces the psychological pressure on the original information holder because the entire future of the information no longer rests on their memory and continuous availability. Compartmentalization, however, must be designed carefully because excessive fragmentation can make legitimate recovery impossible.

Memory itself becomes an important issue under prolonged stress. Sleep deprivation, anxiety, and cognitive overload can affect attention and recall, particularly when a person is trying to remember complex procedures while simultaneously managing fear. This means that a dead man's switch should not depend upon the owner remembering every detail of its operation. Instructions should be written clearly, access arrangements should be documented securely, and recovery procedures should be tested periodically. The system should assume that human memory is fallible. A person who says, "I will remember exactly what to do if something happens," has not created a reliable contingency plan; they have created a dependency on a biological system operating under potentially extreme stress.

The same principle applies to passwords and encryption keys. People frequently create security systems that are technically strong but practically fragile because they rely upon one person remembering a complicated credential indefinitely. A forgotten password can make a perfectly preserved archive inaccessible. Conversely, writing a password on an easily discoverable piece of paper can undermine the entire security model. The solution is not necessarily maximum complexity but controlled recoverability. Key-management systems exist precisely because secure information requires mechanisms for authorized recovery, rotation, backup, and revocation. The human problem and the technical problem are therefore inseparable.

Fear can also create a desire for certainty that technology cannot provide. Someone who feels threatened may want a system that guarantees that their information will be released if anything happens to them. But no technological architecture can simultaneously guarantee perfect detection of death, perfect authentication, perfect preservation, perfect secrecy, perfect delivery, and perfect interpretation. Every system contains assumptions. The responsible approach is therefore to identify those assumptions explicitly and design safeguards around them. A missed check-in might mean death, hospitalization, travel, imprisonment, loss of connectivity, or simple forgetfulness. The system must account for these possibilities rather than pretending they do not exist.

This is why a verification window can be psychologically and technically valuable. Instead of releasing information immediately when a check-in is missed, a system can initiate a warning period during which the individual has opportunities to confirm that they are safe. Trusted intermediaries may also attempt contact through predetermined channels. Only after the defined period and verification process have failed would the system proceed to the next stage. Such a structure does not eliminate false activation, but it can substantially reduce the probability that a temporary interruption becomes an irreversible event. The psychological benefit is equally important because the individual can know that the system contains safeguards rather than functioning like a hair trigger.

The concept of a "hair trigger" is particularly dangerous when dealing with sensitive information. A person who is frightened may initially believe that maximum sensitivity provides maximum protection. In reality, excessive sensitivity can make the system less reliable because it increases the frequency of false alarms. If a system repeatedly triggers when nothing serious has happened, recipients may begin ignoring its warnings. This is the information equivalent of the boy who cried wolf. Reliability requires a balance between responsiveness and discrimination. A good system should be sensitive enough to respond to genuine danger without being so sensitive that ordinary life becomes indistinguishable from catastrophe.

There is also a social dimension to maintaining secrecy. People often underestimate how much behavioral information can reveal even when they carefully protect documents. Sudden changes in routines, unusual meetings, unexplained anxiety, altered communication habits, or visible security measures can attract attention. The problem is not that such behavior proves anything, but that humans infer information from patterns. Someone who becomes dramatically secretive may inadvertently signal that they possess something worth discovering. This does not mean that a person should behave recklessly or ignore security. It means that operational security includes ordinary behavior as well as passwords and encryption. The safest system is often one that does not create unnecessary signals about its own existence.

This principle also applies to digital behavior. A person may carefully encrypt documents while repeatedly accessing them from insecure devices, using the same password across multiple accounts, or storing recovery information in predictable locations. The strongest encryption cannot compensate for compromised endpoints. Likewise, an elaborate automated switch is of limited value if the attacker can simply access the account controlling it. Security therefore depends upon the entire chain from device to credential to storage to recipient. Psychological stress can make these mistakes more likely because anxious people may rush, improvise, or repeatedly check systems in ways that create additional vulnerabilities. Calm procedures are therefore a security control in their own right.

The psychological experience of secrecy can also produce a strange relationship with time. When a person believes that something terrible may happen eventually, the future becomes psychologically present. They may continually rehearse hypothetical scenarios: What if I disappear? What if someone takes my computer? What if I am followed? What if my family becomes involved? What if the documents are destroyed? Some scenario planning is useful because it identifies vulnerabilities before they become emergencies. Excessive rehearsal, however, can become a form of mental captivity in which the person spends more time imagining catastrophe than living their actual life. The purpose of contingency planning should be to reduce uncertainty, not to create an endless cycle of fear.

One of the healthiest distinctions a person can make is between preparation and prediction. Preparing for a possible threat does not require believing that the threat will definitely occur. A homeowner can install a smoke detector without expecting the house to burn down. A traveler can carry emergency identification without expecting an accident. An organization can maintain backups without expecting every primary server to fail. In the same way, an information holder can create a contingency archive without concluding that they are destined to be killed or disappear. This distinction allows preparedness to exist without allowing fear to dominate everyday life.

Professional psychological support can sometimes play an important role in maintaining this balance. Speaking with a qualified mental-health professional does not require revealing confidential documents or compromising sensitive information. A person can discuss stress, sleep problems, fear, isolation, decision-making difficulties, and the emotional burden of secrecy without disclosing information that should remain protected. Professional support can provide an external perspective that is neither emotionally entangled with the information nor dependent upon the person's immediate social circle. This can be particularly valuable when the individual is struggling to distinguish credible danger from anxiety-driven interpretation. Seeking help should therefore not be regarded as evidence that the threat is imaginary; it can simply be part of maintaining the psychological capacity to respond rationally.

Trusted professional relationships can serve a similar function in other domains. A lawyer can help distinguish legally protected information from information that can be disclosed. A security professional can help evaluate technical vulnerabilities. An investigative journalist can assess whether evidence meets publication standards. A financial professional may understand risks involving corporate or financial records. These roles provide something that a frightened individual often lacks: specialized external judgment. The objective is not to surrender control to other people but to avoid making every decision inside a single mind operating under stress. A well-designed protection strategy distributes not only information but also expertise.

The concept of psychological resilience is therefore closely related to information resilience. Resilience does not mean that a person never becomes frightened, angry, exhausted, or uncertain. It means that they retain enough flexibility to adapt, reassess, recover, and continue making decisions when circumstances change. A resilient information holder can revise a threat assessment when new evidence appears. They can recognize that a suspected threat may have an ordinary explanation. They can also escalate their precautions when independent evidence demonstrates that the risk has increased. The ability to change one's mind in response to evidence is not weakness; it is one of the strongest forms of psychological security.

The danger of becoming psychologically trapped by one's own information is particularly important in cases involving secrecy. The person may begin to think of themselves as the sole guardian of a truth that nobody else can understand. That identity can become emotionally powerful, particularly when the individual believes that exposing the information would make them a target. The role can gradually become part of how they understand themselves. But information does not become more reliable because its custodian feels personally responsible for it. In fact, the more personally attached someone becomes to a conclusion, the more important independent verification becomes. A dead man's switch should therefore protect evidence, not reinforce an individual's identity as the heroic or persecuted keeper of a secret.

This distinction is vital because history contains both genuine whistleblowers and people whose interpretations of events were later found to be mistaken. A person can sincerely believe something without possessing sufficient evidence to establish it. Sincerity and accuracy are different qualities. A responsible information system should preserve the original evidence in a way that allows others to evaluate it independently rather than automatically converting the owner's interpretation into an unquestionable public claim. This is one of the most important ethical principles in the entire subject. The dead man's switch should preserve the possibility of truth rather than manufacture certainty.

The human problem therefore cannot be solved by technology alone. Encryption can protect a file, but it cannot calm a frightened mind. Automation can send a message, but it cannot determine whether the underlying fear is justified. Distributed storage can preserve evidence, but it cannot determine whether that evidence has been interpreted correctly. A biometric system can authenticate a person, but it cannot decide whether their information should be released. The technology provides mechanisms, while human beings provide judgment. The quality of the final outcome depends upon how intelligently those two elements are combined.

The most mature approach to living under threat is therefore neither denial nor obsession. Denial assumes that nothing dangerous can happen, while obsession assumes that every ambiguous event confirms danger. A disciplined approach occupies the difficult middle ground. It acknowledges credible risks, documents evidence, establishes proportionate safeguards, seeks independent perspectives, protects necessary confidentiality, and periodically reassesses assumptions. It also recognizes the psychological cost of remaining permanently prepared for catastrophe. The goal is not to live as though death is approaching every day. The goal is to construct enough resilience that if something genuinely goes wrong, the consequences do not automatically include the disappearance of everything the person was trying to protect.

This is ultimately why the dead man's switch should be understood as an extension of human resilience rather than a replacement for it. The switch exists because human beings are vulnerable, but the person designing it remains the most important component of the system. Their judgment determines what information matters, their discipline determines whether the evidence is preserved properly, their choices determine who receives access, and their emotional state influences whether the system is designed rationally or reactively. A technically impressive mechanism created in panic may be less reliable than a simple mechanism created calmly and tested repeatedly. The strongest protection is therefore not the most dramatic technology but the architecture that remains dependable when the person at its center is frightened, exhausted, distracted, or unavailable.

The history of whistleblowing teaches us that speaking can carry a price, but psychology teaches us something equally important: anticipating that price can itself become a burden. People who believe they possess dangerous information may begin living in the shadow of hypothetical consequences long before anything actually happens. Their challenge is to preserve enough caution to remain safe without allowing fear to consume their capacity for ordinary life. That balance requires evidence, external perspective, careful planning, and systems that reduce the number of decisions that must be made under pressure. It also requires accepting that uncertainty cannot always be eliminated. Sometimes the most rational position is simply to acknowledge what is known, what is suspected, and what remains unknown.

The dead man's switch emerges from that recognition of uncertainty. It says, in effect, that a person does not have to know exactly what the future will bring in order to prepare responsibly for the possibility that they will no longer be able to act. The system can preserve information, establish contingencies, and provide instructions without requiring its creator to predict the future. But it must be designed around reality rather than fear. The distinction is fundamental because the purpose of a contingency system is to make the future less dangerous, not to make the present unbearable. Preparation should create psychological breathing room rather than eliminate it.

The next stage of this book will therefore examine how secrecy itself should be managed. If information is sensitive enough to require protection, the central question becomes how much should remain secret, how much should be exposed, and who should know what. Complete secrecy can protect information while making recovery impossible. Complete exposure can guarantee survival while creating unnecessary danger. Between those extremes lies the principle of controlled disclosure, in which information is compartmentalized according to its sensitivity, purpose, and recipient. Understanding that balance is essential because a dead man's switch is ultimately not just a mechanism for releasing information. It is a mechanism for deciding what should survive, who should eventually see it, and under what circumstances the truth should finally be allowed to leave the hands of the person who first carried it.

Resources

1. National Institute of Mental Health — 5 Things You Should Know About Stress[1] — authoritative background on stress, its effects, and when stress can become a significant health concern.

2. American Psychological Association — Stress Effects on the Body[2] — accessible scientific background concerning physiological and psychological responses to prolonged stress.

3. American Psychological Association — Understanding Chronic Stress[3] — background on prolonged stress and its potential effects on cognition, mood, sleep, and physical health.

4. National Center for PTSD — Hyperarousal and Hypervigilance — clinical background concerning heightened alertness, exaggerated threat perception, sleep disruption, and related symptoms.

5. National Institute of Mental Health — Coping With Traumatic Events — guidance concerning psychological responses to threatening or traumatic experiences and approaches to maintaining functioning.

6. Shelley E. Taylor, *The Tending Instinct: How Nurturing Is Essential to Who We Are and How We Live*, Times Books, 2002 — useful psychological context concerning social support, stress, and human responses to threat.

7. George A. Bonanno, *The End of Trauma: How the New Science of Resilience Is Changing How We Think About PTSD*, Basic Books, 2021 — research-based discussion of resilience, adaptation, and the variability of human responses to traumatic stress.

8. Bruce Schneier, *Beyond Fear: Thinking Sensibly About Security in an Uncertain World*, Copernicus Books, 2003 — particularly relevant to the distinction between genuine security assessment and fear-driven security decisions.

9. Bruce Schneier, *Click Here to Kill Everybody: Security and Survival in a Hyper-connected World*, W. W. Norton, 2018 — useful for understanding the interaction between technological systems, human vulnerability, interconnectedness, and security failures.

10. Daniel Kahneman, *Thinking, Fast and Slow*, Farrar, Straus and Giroux, 2011 — foundational discussion of cognitive biases, judgment under uncertainty, attentional processes, and the ways human decision-making can deviate from purely rational models.

11. National Institute of Standards and Technology — Risk Management Framework — useful methodological foundation for identifying threats, assessing risk, selecting controls, and continuously reassessing security assumptions.

12. National Institute of Standards and Technology — Cybersecurity Framework 2.0[4] — broader framework for risk identification, protection, detection, response, and recovery.

---

1. https://www.nimh.nih.gov/health/publications/so-stressed-out-fact-sheet?utm_source=chatgpt.com

2. https://www.apa.org/topics/stress/body?utm_source=chatgpt.com

3. https://www.apa.org/topics/stress/chronic?utm_source=chatgpt.com

4. https://www.nist.gov/cyberframework?utm_source=chatgpt.com

13. CISA — Secure Our World[5] — practical guidance concerning account security, passwords, multifactor authentication, phishing, and everyday cybersecurity behavior.

14. Electronic Frontier Foundation — Surveillance Self-Defense[6] — practical resources for people facing elevated digital-security concerns, including threat modeling, device security, encryption, metadata, and secure communications.

15. U.S. Department of Justice — Witness Security Program — historical and legal background illustrating the institutional recognition that witnesses can face serious retaliation and security risks.

16. United Nations Office on Drugs and Crime — Witness Protection[7] — international background concerning witness protection, intimidation, organized crime, and the need to safeguard people whose testimony is important to investigations.

17. U.S. Department of Labor — Whistleblower Protection Program[8] — authoritative background concerning retaliation protections and the institutional mechanisms available to qualifying whistleblowers.

18. U.S. Securities and Exchange Commission — Whistleblower Program[9] — official information concerning confidential reporting, whistleblower protections, and the handling of securities-law allegations.

19. National Institute of Standards and Technology — Key Management Guidelines[10] — useful technical background for understanding why secure information systems must account for key storage, recovery, protection, and loss.

20. Ross Anderson, *Security Engineering: A Guide to Building Dependable Distributed Systems*, 3rd ed., Wiley, 2020 — comprehensive treatment of security architecture, human factors, threat modeling, resilience, failure modes, and the interaction between people and technology.

21. National Archives — Digital Preservation — institutional guidance relevant to long-term information survival, authenticity, accessibility, and preservation planning.

22. International Organization for Standardization, ISO 22301, *Security and Resilience — Business Continuity Management Systems*, for the broader principle of planning for disruption, maintaining critical functions, and designing recovery mechanisms before emergencies occur.

5. https://www.cisa.gov/secure-our-world?utm_source=chatgpt.com

6. https://ssd.eff.org/?utm_source=chatgpt.com

7. https://www.unodc.org/unodc/en/organized-crime/witness-protection.html?utm_source=chatgpt.com

8. https://www.whistleblowers.gov/?utm_source=chatgpt.com

9. https://www.sec.gov/enforcement-litigation/whistleblower-program?utm_source=chatgpt.com

10. https://csrc.nist.gov/projects/key-management?utm_source=chatgpt.com

Trust Is the Weakest Link

Every dead man's switch eventually arrives at the same uncomfortable question, regardless of how sophisticated the technology may be: who, exactly, should be trusted when the original custodian can no longer make the decision? Encryption can protect a file, redundancy can preserve it, and automation can initiate a release, but eventually some person or institution must interpret instructions, authenticate circumstances, safeguard material, or decide whether disclosure is appropriate. That human decision point creates a vulnerability that technology alone cannot eliminate. A perfectly encrypted archive is useless if its intended recipient cannot recover it, while a technically secure system can become catastrophically insecure if access is handed to someone who is careless, compromised, coercible, or simply unable to understand the responsibility they have been given. The problem of trust is therefore not an accessory to a dead man's switch; it is one of its central engineering problems.

Trust is often discussed as though it were a personal quality that someone either possesses or lacks. In reality, security professionals generally approach trust more cautiously because people behave differently under different circumstances and because even honest individuals can make serious mistakes. A person can be loyal but technologically careless, intelligent but impulsive, courageous but easily pressured, or highly competent but legally unable to act on certain information. Someone who would never intentionally betray a friend might nevertheless lose an unencrypted laptop, click a malicious link, reuse a compromised password, or casually discuss sensitive matters in an inappropriate setting. The relevant question is therefore not simply whether a person is "good." It is whether that person is capable of performing a specific security responsibility reliably under the circumstances in which the information may eventually become important.

This distinction between trustworthiness and suitability is fundamental. Imagine someone who has spent twenty years proving that they are personally loyal but has no experience handling confidential records. They may be an excellent friend and a poor custodian. Conversely, a professional archivist may possess extraordinary skills for preserving information but have no personal relationship with the person who created it. The first individual may provide emotional trust, while the second provides procedural competence. A strong system may require both. The mistake is assuming that because someone is trusted in one dimension, they are automatically trustworthy in every other dimension.

The family is usually the first place people look when thinking about succession. Family members often have deep emotional bonds with the information holder and may have an obvious interest in protecting their legacy. They may also be easier to contact than professional intermediaries and may remain connected to the person's affairs long after death. Yet family relationships can become complicated when sensitive information creates legal, financial, reputational, or physical risks. A spouse may be emotionally overwhelmed, a child may be too young or inexperienced, another relative may have conflicting interests, or a family member may become a target simply because they are associated with the information. Family trust can therefore be genuine while still being inadequate for the role of information custodian.

There is another difficulty with family custody: emotional proximity can affect judgment. Someone grieving a death may be more inclined to believe everything the deceased believed and less inclined to question the interpretation of ambiguous evidence. They may also feel a powerful obligation to fulfill the person's final wishes even when circumstances have changed. That emotional loyalty can be admirable, but it can also create pressure to publish material that should instead be independently verified. A family member may interpret release as an act of love or loyalty rather than as a decision carrying consequences for other people. For this reason, sensitive evidence may require an intermediary capable of applying professional distance.

Friends occupy a similar but somewhat different position. A close friend may know the person's character, understand their concerns, and recognize which information mattered most to them. Friendship can provide a level of loyalty that formal institutions cannot easily reproduce. But friendship is also vulnerable to changing circumstances. People move, relationships deteriorate, financial pressures arise, health changes, and personal loyalties shift. A person who appears ideal at the time an archive is created may be living an entirely different life five or ten years later. Trust must therefore be treated as something that requires periodic review rather than something permanently established by a single conversation.

Journalists introduce a particularly important category because their professional role is built around handling information, evaluating evidence, cultivating sources, and determining whether matters of public interest warrant publication. Investigative journalists can possess considerable experience protecting confidential sources and working with sensitive material. They may also have institutional support from an established newsroom, editors, legal counsel, digital-security specialists, and established publication procedures. Yet journalists are not neutral storage devices. Their professional responsibility includes editorial judgment, meaning that they may decide not to publish material that cannot be verified or that creates disproportionate harm. Someone handing information to a journalist must therefore understand that "I want this published" does not necessarily mean "this journalist is obligated to publish it."

The relationship between whistleblowers and journalists is consequently based on a particular form of negotiated trust. The source must trust the journalist to protect confidential information, while the journalist must trust the source sufficiently to invest time and resources in investigating the claims. Both sides have incentives to question the other. A source may fear that the journalist will expose them, while a journalist may worry that the source has exaggerated, misunderstood, or selectively presented evidence. This tension is not necessarily a weakness. In serious investigative reporting, skepticism can be one of the mechanisms that protects the public from false conclusions. A trustworthy journalist should not merely preserve a secret; they should subject the underlying claims to verification.

Lawyers represent another category of professional trust. Legal counsel may be particularly valuable because attorneys operate within professional and ethical frameworks concerning confidentiality, conflicts of interest, and representation. In appropriate circumstances, legal advice can help an information holder understand what may lawfully be disclosed, what obligations may restrict disclosure, and what mechanisms exist for protecting evidence. But lawyers are not interchangeable. Different lawyers specialize in different areas of law, and an attorney experienced in one field may be poorly positioned to advise on another. Furthermore, attorney-client confidentiality is governed by specific legal doctrines and circumstances rather than functioning as an unlimited guarantee that every communication with every lawyer is protected.

This is why a person should not assume that simply handing a document to a lawyer automatically makes the document legally protected. The nature of the relationship, the purpose of the communication, applicable law, and the lawyer's professional role all matter. There may also be conflicts of interest, jurisdictional issues, or other limitations. The appropriate legal structure depends heavily upon the circumstances. For a dead man's switch involving genuinely sensitive information, professional legal advice should therefore be obtained before assuming that an informal relationship provides the desired protection.

Investigators present another possibility. Depending upon the circumstances, this could include private investigators, corporate investigators, law-enforcement personnel, regulatory investigators, or specialist organizations. Their advantage may be expertise in evaluating evidence, interviewing witnesses, documenting events, and establishing chains of custody. Their limitation is that every investigator operates within a particular mandate. A private investigator works for a client, a regulator works under statutory authority, and law enforcement operates within legal procedures and jurisdictional boundaries. Giving information to an investigator therefore does not mean that the information will necessarily be handled according to the creator's preferred outcome.

Organizations can sometimes provide stronger continuity than individuals. A newsroom, law firm, university, nonprofit organization, professional association, archive, or other established institution may have policies that survive the departure or death of any one employee. This institutional continuity is one of the most powerful forms of redundancy available. A person can disappear while the organization continues operating. The institution may also possess secure infrastructure, legal resources, professional staff, and established procedures for handling confidential material. Yet institutions have their own vulnerabilities, including leadership changes, policy changes, funding pressures, internal conflicts, mergers, acquisitions, cyberattacks, and legal obligations.

Institutional trust is therefore not automatically superior to personal trust. An organization may be more resilient but less aligned with the original custodian's intentions. A journalist might personally promise confidentiality while the newsroom later changes ownership. A company might have excellent security procedures while its legal department decides that certain material cannot be retained. A nonprofit might appear permanent until funding disappears. The key issue is institutional succession. If the system is designed to survive the death of one individual, it should also consider what happens if the institution itself changes.

Professional intermediaries can bridge some of these problems. An intermediary may be responsible for holding instructions, coordinating access, maintaining records, or verifying conditions without necessarily possessing the complete archive. This arrangement can reduce the risk that any one person has complete control. It can also create a procedural buffer between the information holder and the eventual recipient. The intermediary's role should be clearly defined, however, because ambiguity creates opportunities for disagreement and failure. If nobody knows whether the intermediary is supposed to preserve, investigate, release, or destroy information, the system has not actually solved the succession problem.

Anonymous custodians introduce a more unusual form of trust. A person may theoretically distribute information through systems in which the eventual custodian's identity is not known to the original creator. This can reduce certain risks because the custodian cannot easily be targeted through personal relationships. But anonymity creates a corresponding problem: the information holder has less ability to assess the custodian's reliability. There may be no reputation to evaluate, no professional obligations to enforce, and no obvious mechanism for correcting mistakes. Anonymous systems can reduce dependence upon personal trust while increasing dependence upon technical and procedural trust. The risk has not disappeared; it has merely moved.

This principle is sometimes described as the difference between trusting people and trusting systems. A system can reduce the amount of trust placed in any individual by distributing responsibilities across multiple parties and using cryptographic controls. For example, access to an archive might require more than one independent authorization. One person may possess part of an authentication mechanism while another controls another component. Neither can act alone. This kind of architecture is related to threshold cryptography and secret-sharing techniques, in which a secret can be divided into multiple pieces so that a predetermined number of participants must cooperate before reconstruction is possible.

The advantage is obvious. If one person becomes compromised, the entire system does not necessarily collapse. The disadvantage is equally important. Every additional participant introduces another possibility of loss, misunderstanding, collusion, or unavailability. A five-person system is not automatically more secure than a two-person system simply because it has more participants. Complexity can become its own vulnerability. If the system requires three of five people to cooperate but two have moved away, one has died, and another has forgotten their credentials, the theoretically resilient architecture may become practically unrecoverable. Redundancy must therefore be balanced against operational simplicity.

The same principle applies to passwords and encryption keys. A person may decide that several trusted individuals should each know a password, believing that this creates backup access. In reality, it creates multiple copies of the same secret and therefore multiple points of compromise. A more sophisticated design separates authentication factors or uses threshold mechanisms rather than simply duplicating credentials. The goal is to make unauthorized access difficult while legitimate recovery remains possible. Security architecture is fundamentally about controlling combinations of conditions. A single password held by one trusted person creates one type of risk; multiple independent factors held by different custodians create another.

Trust also has a temporal dimension. Someone may be trustworthy today and unsuitable tomorrow. People experience financial difficulties, relationship breakdowns, addictions, ideological changes, career changes, legal problems, and ordinary changes in priorities. None of these possibilities means that a person should be treated with suspicion simply because humans are imperfect. It means that contingency systems should not be designed as though relationships are frozen in time. Long-lived information requires long-lived governance. A system created at age thirty may still contain sensitive material at age sixty, while the people originally chosen as custodians may no longer occupy the same roles in the creator's life.

Periodic review is therefore essential. A responsible custodian should know who has access, what each person is responsible for, whether credentials remain valid, whether storage systems still function, and whether the original instructions still reflect the creator's intentions. This does not mean constantly rebuilding the system. It means recognizing that security arrangements decay. Passwords become obsolete, software changes, cloud services disappear, encryption standards evolve, relationships change, and legal circumstances develop. A dead man's switch that is never tested may eventually become nothing more than a comforting idea.

Testing also reveals a subtle psychological problem. People often confuse the existence of a security mechanism with proof that the mechanism works. A backup that has never been restored is an assumption, not a demonstrated recovery capability. An emergency contact who has never been briefed may not know what to do. An encrypted archive whose decryption process has never been tested may contain corrupted or incomplete data. A recipient who has never received a simulated notification may not recognize the message as legitimate. Testing transforms assumptions into evidence. In a system whose purpose is to function during an extraordinary event, that distinction can be decisive.

Another challenge is coercion. Trust is often evaluated under normal circumstances, but a person who willingly accepts responsibility may behave differently if threatened, bribed, blackmailed, legally compelled, or otherwise pressured. This is particularly important when information could have serious consequences for powerful individuals or institutions. A trusted custodian may be completely honest and still be unable to resist an overwhelming external pressure. Security design therefore seeks to reduce the amount of power concentrated in any one person. Compartmentalization, access controls, and multi-party authorization can make coercion less effective because no single individual possesses everything necessary to compromise the entire system.

The concept of least privilege is useful here. In information security, users should generally receive only the access necessary to perform their legitimate responsibilities. Someone responsible for verifying that a check-in has occurred may not need to read the underlying documents. Someone responsible for preserving an encrypted archive may not need the decryption key. A lawyer may need access to specific records but not to unrelated personal material. A journalist may need evidence relevant to a story but not the passwords controlling the entire archive. Separating responsibilities reduces the damage that can occur when one account or individual is compromised.

This approach also protects recipients from unnecessary responsibility. Imagine giving a friend access to a massive archive containing confidential medical records, financial information, allegations against third parties, and other unrelated material merely because the friend is trusted. The friend has now inherited a legal and ethical burden they may never have wanted. A more carefully designed system would give them only what they need to perform their assigned role. Good security protects not only the information holder but also the people asked to help protect it. The less unnecessary information a custodian possesses, the less they can accidentally expose.

The same principle applies to family members. Someone may be willing to help preserve a parent's records but unwilling to become responsible for publishing accusations against powerful people. Someone may agree to contact a lawyer but not to contact the media. Someone may be comfortable storing a sealed package but not opening it. These distinctions should be established before an emergency rather than discovered afterward. Clear boundaries reduce emotional conflict because recipients understand that they are carrying out a defined responsibility rather than improvising a response to a crisis.

There is also a danger in selecting custodians solely because they share the information holder's beliefs. Agreement can feel like trust because people are naturally more comfortable with those who see the world as they do. But a custodian who never challenges assumptions may actually be less valuable than one who is willing to ask difficult questions. Evidence requires scrutiny, particularly when accusations are serious. A trustworthy recipient should be capable of saying, "I believe you may be right, but I need to verify this before acting." Intellectual independence can therefore be a stronger form of loyalty than unquestioning agreement.

This becomes especially important when the information concerns alleged wrongdoing. The creator may possess genuine evidence, but they may also have incomplete context, outdated information, or interpretations that later prove incorrect. A recipient who immediately accepts every conclusion may amplify an error. A recipient who carefully preserves the original material while seeking independent corroboration can protect both the truth and innocent people. The distinction between preserving evidence and endorsing allegations should remain explicit. A dead man's switch should ideally ensure that evidence survives, not that every interpretation attached to it becomes automatically authoritative.

Trust also intersects with authentication. Even a legitimate recipient can become vulnerable if an attacker impersonates them. An email that appears to come from a trusted lawyer may not actually have been sent by that lawyer. A message requesting access credentials may be fraudulent. A phone call may be spoofed. Digital systems therefore require methods for verifying identity independently rather than relying solely upon familiar names or contact details. The more valuable the information, the more important independent authentication becomes. A dead man's switch should never assume that the person who claims to be the recipient is necessarily the person the creator intended.

This is one reason predetermined communication channels can be valuable. If a recipient's identity can be verified through an independently established method, the chance of social engineering is reduced. The details of such arrangements should themselves be protected because revealing the verification process may make it easier for an attacker to impersonate the recipient. The principle is broader than any specific technology: never allow the same compromised channel to prove both identity and authorization. If an attacker controls the communication path, they should not automatically gain the ability to redefine who is trusted.

Trust can also fail through simple misunderstanding. Instructions written years earlier may use ambiguous language. A phrase such as "release the files if something happens to me" sounds straightforward until someone asks what "something" means. Does hospitalization count? Temporary disappearance? Arrest? Loss of communication? Mental incapacity? Death? A serious but recoverable emergency? The recipient may interpret the instruction differently from the creator's intention. The more consequential the information, the more carefully the conditions should be defined. Precision is not bureaucratic fussiness; it is a way of reducing conflict among people who may later have to make difficult decisions under pressure.

Legal and ethical constraints can further complicate trust. A recipient may receive information with instructions that conflict with applicable law or professional obligations. A lawyer may be unable to follow an instruction that would violate legal requirements. A journalist may have ethical reasons not to publish identifying details. A family member may discover that the material contains private information belonging to other people. An organization may have statutory obligations that override the creator's preferred outcome. A mature dead man's switch therefore recognizes that instructions exist within a larger legal and ethical environment. Personal wishes matter, but they are not always the only relevant authority.

The strongest systems consequently tend to distribute trust rather than maximize it. Instead of searching for one perfect person, the designer asks which responsibilities can be separated. One person can maintain the archive. Another can hold part of the authentication structure. A lawyer can advise on legal questions. A journalist can evaluate public-interest publication. A family member can provide emergency context. An independent professional can verify whether predetermined conditions have occurred. The architecture becomes a network of limited trusts rather than a single enormous trust. This can be much more resilient because the failure of one relationship does not necessarily destroy the entire system.

Yet there is a point at which distribution becomes counterproductive. If every decision requires six people to coordinate, the system may fail because coordination itself becomes impossible. People may be asleep, travelling, unreachable, unwilling, or uncertain about their responsibilities. Excessive complexity can also increase the chance that confidential information spreads beyond those who genuinely need it. The goal is therefore not maximum fragmentation. It is sufficient separation of responsibilities to prevent catastrophic dependence upon any one person while retaining practical recoverability.

The idea that trust is the weakest link should therefore be understood carefully. Human beings are not inherently the weakest part of every security system. Sometimes humans are the strongest component because they can recognize context, adapt to unexpected circumstances, and exercise judgment where automated systems cannot. The vulnerability arises when human judgment is assumed to be perfect, permanent, and incorruptible. People make mistakes, change, forget, misunderstand, and respond differently under pressure. Good architecture acknowledges these realities rather than pretending they can be engineered away. The objective is to design a system that remains reasonably safe even when people behave imperfectly.

Ultimately, trust should be treated as a measurable responsibility rather than an emotional declaration. Ask what the person must do, what could prevent them from doing it, what information they actually need, what happens if they become unavailable, and how their actions can be independently verified. Ask whether their role depends upon a relationship that may change or an institution likely to survive. Ask whether another person can perform the same function if necessary. Ask what happens if the recipient is honest but mistaken, competent but unavailable, loyal but compromised, or trustworthy but legally constrained. These questions transform the vague concept of trust into something that can actually be designed around.

The dead man's switch ultimately exists because its creator cannot guarantee that they will always be present to protect what they know. But once that realization is accepted, another follows immediately: nobody else can guarantee it either. The answer is not to search endlessly for a mythical person who can be trusted with everything. It is to create an architecture in which responsibility is appropriately divided, evidence can be independently evaluated, access can be controlled, and no single failure automatically destroys the whole system. Trust remains necessary, but it no longer has to be absolute. The most resilient system is one in which people are trusted carefully, for defined purposes, with defined powers, and within a structure designed to survive their inevitable imperfections.

That principle will shape everything that follows. The next stage is to examine the tension between secrecy and exposure, because deciding whom to trust is only half the problem. A person can choose the most trustworthy custodian in the world and still make a disastrous decision about how much information that custodian should receive. The central question becomes not simply who should know, but what they should know, when they should know it, and what safeguards should stand between private possession and public disclosure. That is where the dead man's switch becomes something more complicated than a contingency mechanism: it becomes an architecture for controlled revelation.

Resources

1. Bruce Schneier, *Secrets and Lies: Digital Security in a Networked World*, Wiley, 2000 — foundational discussion of security as a combination of technology, people, processes, incentives, and institutional behavior.

2. Ross Anderson, *Security Engineering: A Guide to Building Dependable Distributed Systems*, 3rd ed., Wiley, 2020 — extensive treatment of trust models, human behavior, authentication, compartmentalization, failure modes, and dependable security architecture.

3. National Institute of Standards and Technology — Zero Trust Architecture, SP 800-207[1] — authoritative treatment of the principle that trust should not be granted automatically based solely on network location or previous assumptions.

4. NIST Cybersecurity Framework 2.0[2] — framework for identifying, protecting, detecting, responding to, and recovering from cybersecurity risks.

5. NIST Digital Identity Guidelines, SP 800-63-4[3] — authoritative material concerning identity proofing, authentication, authenticators, and assurance levels.

6. NIST Special Publication 800-57 — Recommendation for Key Management — important for understanding the protection, distribution, recovery, and lifecycle management of cryptographic keys.

1. https://csrc.nist.gov/publications/detail/sp/800-207/final?utm_source=chatgpt.com

2. https://www.nist.gov/cyberframework?utm_source=chatgpt.com

3. https://pages.nist.gov/800-63-4/?utm_source=chatgpt.com

7. NIST Special Publication 800-53 — Security and Privacy Controls[4] — provides extensive controls relevant to least privilege, access management, separation of duties, contingency planning, and accountability.

8. Cybersecurity and Infrastructure Security Agency — Zero Trust Maturity Model[5] — useful practical framework for reducing implicit trust and strengthening identity, device, application, and data controls.

9. Electronic Frontier Foundation — Surveillance Self-Defense[6] — practical resources on threat modeling, secure communication, device security, encryption, and protecting sensitive information.

10. U.S. Department of Labor — Whistleblower Protection Program[7] — authoritative information concerning whistleblowers, retaliation protections, and reporting mechanisms.

11. U.S. Securities and Exchange Commission — Whistleblower Program[8] — official information on confidential reporting and protections associated with qualifying securities-law whistleblowers.

12. Society of Professional Journalists — Code of Ethics[9] — useful for understanding journalistic responsibilities concerning verification, minimizing harm, independence, and accountability.

13. Committee to Protect Journalists — Safety Kit[10] — resources concerning journalist safety, source protection, digital security, and risk assessment.

14. Reporters Without Borders — Handbook for Journalists — international resources concerning journalist safety, source protection, and reporting in hostile environments.

15. American Bar Association — Model Rules of Professional Conduct[11] — professional standards concerning confidentiality, conflicts of interest, duties to clients, and legal representation.

16. American Bar Association, Model Rule 1.6, *Confidentiality of Information*, for the professional framework surrounding lawyers' duties concerning information relating to clients.

17. National Institute of Standards and Technology — Cryptographic Standards and Guidelines[12] — background on cryptographic mechanisms used to reduce dependence upon personal trust.

18. Adi Shamir, "How to Share a Secret," *Communications of the ACM*, Vol. 22, No. 11, 1979 — foundational paper introducing Shamir's Secret Sharing, an important mathematical approach to dividing a secret among multiple participants.

19. NIST — Privacy Framework[13] — useful for understanding why information protection must consider not only security but also privacy risks affecting people whose information is contained in an archive.

---

4. https://csrc.nist.gov/publications/detail/sp/800-53/rev-5/final?utm_source=chatgpt.com

5. https://www.cisa.gov/resources-tools/resources/zero-trust-maturity-model?utm_source=chatgpt.com

6. https://ssd.eff.org/?utm_source=chatgpt.com

7. https://www.whistleblowers.gov/?utm_source=chatgpt.com

8. https://www.sec.gov/enforcement-litigation/whistleblower-program?utm_source=chatgpt.com

9. https://www.spj.org/ethicscode.asp?utm_source=chatgpt.com

10. https://cpj.org/safety-kit/?utm_source=chatgpt.com

11. https://www.americanbar.org/groups/professional_responsibility/publications/model_rules_of_professional_conduct/?utm_source=chatgpt.com

12. https://csrc.nist.gov/projects/cryptographic-standards-and-guidelines?utm_source=chatgpt.com

20. National Archives — Digital Preservation — institutional perspective on preserving information across technological and organizational change.

21. United Nations Office on Drugs and Crime — Witness Protection[14] — international context concerning witness vulnerability, retaliation, confidentiality, and protective structures.

22. U.S. Department of Justice — Justice Manual, Confidentiality and Witness-Related Materials — useful institutional context for understanding how sensitive information can be handled within formal legal systems.

23. Daniel Kahneman, *Thinking, Fast and Slow*, Farrar, Straus and Giroux, 2011 — relevant to the psychological limitations of human judgment, particularly under uncertainty and pressure.

24. Paul C. van Oorschot, *Computer Security and the Internet: Tools and Jewels*, Springer, 2020 — technical background on authentication, authorization, security architecture, and the practical limitations of security mechanisms.

25. Internet Engineering Task Force — Security Area and RFC Repository[15] — primary technical standards environment for many of the protocols underlying modern Internet security and authentication.

13. https://www.nist.gov/privacy-framework?utm_source=chatgpt.com

14. https://www.unodc.org/unodc/en/organized-crime/witness-protection.html?utm_source=chatgpt.com

15. https://www.ietf.org/standards/?utm_source=chatgpt.com

Secrecy, Exposure, and the Psychology of Insurance

A dead man's switch is unusual because its power may exist even when nothing ever happens. The files may never be released, the emergency messages may never be sent, the recipients may never be contacted, and the mechanism may remain dormant for decades. Yet the person who creates such a system may feel safer simply because they know that their information has a path to survival beyond their own continued existence. That psychological effect resembles insurance in an important respect: insurance provides value even when the insured event never occurs because the existence of a contingency changes the person's exposure to uncertainty. A dead man's switch can operate in much the same psychological space, transforming the fear of losing information into the knowledge that some form of continuity has been deliberately established. The paradox is that a mechanism designed for catastrophic circumstances may produce its most immediate benefit during ordinary life.

The concept of insurance is fundamentally about transferring or managing uncertainty. People insure homes they hope never burn down, vehicles they hope never to crash, and lives they expect to continue for many years. The purchase does not mean that catastrophe is expected; it means that catastrophe has been recognized as possible and that consequences have been planned for in advance. Information protection can involve a similar logic, although the mechanisms and legal implications are very different. A person who creates a contingency archive is effectively saying that their ability to protect certain information should not depend entirely upon their continued physical presence. The archive becomes a form of informational continuity planning. It is not necessarily an expression of paranoia or an expectation of death, but a recognition that human beings can become unavailable for many reasons.

That distinction matters because the popular image of a dead man's switch is often dominated by dramatic scenarios. Films and novels portray a threatened individual secretly holding explosive information and arranging for its automatic publication if anything happens to them. Real-world information protection is usually less theatrical. People lose access to accounts, suffer accidents, become seriously ill, disappear during disasters, lose devices, forget passwords, die unexpectedly, or become unable to communicate for ordinary reasons. Organizations themselves can disappear, change ownership, or lose archives. The underlying problem is therefore broader than assassination. It is the problem of informational dependency. If one person's continued availability is the only thing preventing important evidence from being lost, the system contains a single point of failure.

The psychology of insurance begins with this reduction in perceived vulnerability. When people believe they have no contingency plan, uncertainty can become mentally consuming. Every possible failure remains open because there is no established response. Once a credible contingency exists, the mind can sometimes shift from constant anticipation toward ordinary functioning. This does not require the contingency to be perfect. A person may simply feel more secure knowing that their family has emergency instructions, their important documents are backed up, and a trusted professional knows how to respond if they become unavailable. The psychological value comes partly from converting an undefined threat into a defined procedure. Planning gives uncertainty boundaries.

This is closely related to the psychological concept of perceived control. Human beings generally cope better with uncertainty when they believe they have meaningful influence over what happens next. A person cannot control whether an accident occurs, whether a political situation changes, or whether another individual behaves maliciously. They can, however, control whether important information has been duplicated, whether trusted recipients have been designated, and whether recovery procedures exist. This distinction between controlling an event and controlling one's preparedness for an event is crucial. A contingency plan does not guarantee safety. It can nevertheless reduce the consequences of circumstances that cannot be controlled.

The sense of protection created by preparation can also change behavior. Someone who previously believed that one lost device could destroy years of evidence may become less anxious after creating secure backups. Someone who feared that nobody would understand their records after their death may become more comfortable because clear instructions exist. Someone who worried that a trusted source might disappear may create a preservation mechanism before continuing an investigation. In each case, the system changes the person's perceived risk environment. That psychological change can influence how they work, communicate, and make decisions. The effect may be beneficial if it produces greater confidence and disciplined preparation.

But perceived protection can also create overconfidence. This is one of the most important dangers in the psychology of security. A person who believes they have created an impenetrable dead man's switch may become less cautious because they feel protected by it. They may store information carelessly, disclose more than necessary, or assume that the mechanism will function automatically regardless of circumstances. Security researchers have repeatedly emphasized that perceived security and actual security are not the same thing. A system can feel reassuring while containing vulnerabilities its owner does not understand. The psychological benefit of a contingency mechanism therefore has to be balanced against the risk that confidence exceeds capability.

This phenomenon is sometimes discussed in security research through the idea of risk compensation. When people perceive themselves as safer, they may sometimes alter their behavior in ways that increase exposure to risk. The exact strength of this effect varies by context, and it should not be treated as a universal psychological law. Nevertheless, the possibility is highly relevant to information security. If someone believes that every document will automatically be released if they disappear, they may stop maintaining secure backups or verifying access. If they believe an encrypted cloud archive is sufficient, they may ignore the security of the device used to access it. If they believe trusted recipients will solve everything, they may never establish clear instructions. A dead man's switch should therefore increase preparedness, not become an excuse for reducing it.

The psychological concept of deterrence introduces another layer. Deterrence occurs when the anticipated consequences of an action influence someone to refrain from taking that action. The classic examples come from criminal justice, military strategy, and security policy, where an actor is discouraged from committing an act because the expected cost is perceived as too high. A dead man's switch can potentially create a similar dynamic if a threatening actor knows that harming or silencing the information holder could cause sensitive information to become public. The crucial word is "potentially," because deterrence depends upon the other party believing both that the mechanism exists and that it will actually function.

This makes credibility central. An alleged dead man's switch that nobody believes exists is unlikely to deter anyone. A mechanism that appears credible but has never been tested may also provide less deterrent value than its creator assumes. Conversely, publicly announcing every detail of a contingency system can create unnecessary risks and may undermine the security of the information it is intended to protect. Deterrence therefore exists in a difficult space between secrecy and signaling. The potential adversary needs enough reason to believe that retaliation could produce unwanted consequences, but does not necessarily need to know precisely how the mechanism works. The design problem becomes one of credible uncertainty.

This is where the psychology of insurance and the psychology of deterrence intersect. Insurance protects against the consequences of an event after it occurs, while deterrence attempts to reduce the probability that the event occurs in the first place. A dead man's switch can potentially perform both functions. If something happens to its creator, the information may survive. If a potential aggressor believes that the information will survive and become public, the aggressor may decide that eliminating the creator is counterproductive. The first mechanism is resilience. The second is deterrence. Neither should be assumed automatically, but both are legitimate concepts for understanding why contingency systems can matter even when they are never activated.

History provides examples of deterrence operating through uncertainty, although establishing a direct causal relationship in individual cases can be difficult. States maintain strategic capabilities partly because potential adversaries must account for possible retaliation. Businesses maintain continuity systems because competitors, customers, and regulators expect them to survive disruptions. Individuals install alarms because potential intruders may be discouraged by the possibility of detection. In each case, the protective mechanism can influence behavior without being physically activated. The same logic can apply to information protection. If a person is known to have distributed copies of sensitive evidence, the uncertainty surrounding those copies may become part of the risk calculation of anyone considering retaliation.

However, deterrence can fail spectacularly when the threatening actor is irrational, desperate, misinformed, or unaware of the contingency. It can also fail when the actor believes they can neutralize every copy. This is why a responsible dead man's switch should never be treated as a guarantee against violence. It may reduce certain incentives for retaliation, but it cannot eliminate them. A person should not assume that possessing damaging information makes them safer simply because others know it exists. In some circumstances, the opposite may be true. The existence of a contingency system can increase perceived stakes and therefore requires careful consideration of whether signaling its existence is itself safe.

Secrecy consequently becomes a strategic variable. The creator must decide what should remain completely private, what should be known to selected custodians, and what, if anything, should be publicly acknowledged. This is not a simple spectrum from secret to public. Information can exist in layers. Someone may know that an archive exists without knowing where it is stored. Another person may know where it is stored but not possess the key. A lawyer may know that legal instructions exist without knowing the underlying contents. A journalist may know that evidence has been preserved without receiving access until verification occurs. This layered structure allows the creator to create confidence in continuity without necessarily exposing the entire substance of the information.

The psychological effect of secrecy can be complicated by this layering. Complete secrecy can make the creator feel isolated because nobody else knows what exists. Complete exposure can create vulnerability because too many people know too much. Controlled disclosure provides an intermediate condition in which enough people know enough to ensure continuity while the underlying material remains protected. This resembles compartmentalization used in other security environments. The psychological advantage is that the creator no longer has to carry the entire burden alone. The operational advantage is that no single person necessarily possesses enough information to compromise the entire system.

There is also a psychological distinction between having a secret and having evidence. People sometimes speak about "my secret" when what they actually possess is a mixture of documents, memories, interpretations, rumors, and conclusions. A contingency mechanism can preserve all of these things, but preservation does not make them equally reliable. A video statement may accurately record what someone believed without proving that the underlying allegation was true. A photograph may establish that an event occurred without proving why it occurred. An internal document may reveal a decision without revealing every motive behind it. The psychological desire to protect a secret can therefore become confused with the evidentiary obligation to preserve verifiable facts.

This is why a responsible information insurance system should preserve provenance. Provenance means maintaining information about where evidence came from, when it was obtained, how it was handled, and whether it has been altered. A file without provenance can be difficult to authenticate later. A photograph without context may be misunderstood. A recording without metadata may raise questions about when or how it was created. The psychological comfort of knowing that "I have the files" is therefore insufficient. The stronger form of security is knowing that the files can still be evaluated as evidence if they ever need to be used.

The same principle applies to personal testimony. A person's written or recorded account may be extremely important because it preserves information that might otherwise disappear. But testimony remains testimony. The creator may remember events accurately, partially, or incorrectly. They may also have interpreted events according to information available at the time. A dead man's switch can preserve the account, but it should not automatically convert personal testimony into objective fact. This distinction protects the integrity of the eventual disclosure. The recipient should be able to say what is documented, what is claimed, what is corroborated, and what remains uncertain.

The psychological appeal of automatic disclosure can sometimes obscure this problem. Automatic systems feel powerful because they appear to remove human hesitation. If the creator dies, the system releases everything. If the creator fails to check in, the archive goes public. Such simplicity can feel reassuring. But sensitive information rarely exists in circumstances simple enough for absolute automation to be ideal. A missed check-in may have a harmless explanation. A recipient may discover that some documents implicate innocent people. New evidence may emerge that changes the interpretation. A legal order may affect what can be disclosed. An automatic mechanism cannot understand these developments unless they have been incorporated into its design.

This is why the strongest concept of information insurance is not necessarily "release everything if I disappear." It is continuity with judgment. The system should preserve the ability of appropriately authorized people to examine the circumstances and determine the correct response. In some cases, the correct response may be immediate disclosure. In others, it may be legal review, investigative verification, limited disclosure, or continued preservation. The objective is to ensure that disappearance or incapacity does not automatically destroy the information while avoiding the opposite mistake of publishing everything without context. A dead man's switch should preserve options rather than eliminate them.

The psychological benefit of this approach can be substantial. Knowing that trusted people have a defined role reduces the feeling that everything depends upon one person's constant vigilance. The creator can continue working without repeatedly imagining every possible failure. The recipients know that they are part of a defined structure rather than being suddenly handed an unexplained archive. The system itself becomes a form of psychological scaffolding. It supports human decision-making without pretending to replace it. That distinction becomes particularly important when the stakes involve allegations against powerful people, classified material, confidential sources, or information capable of causing serious harm.

There is another form of deterrence that does not involve threatening anyone directly: the deterrent effect of accountability. Institutions may behave differently when individuals know that wrongdoing could eventually be documented and preserved. Employees may be less willing to destroy records if they believe independent copies exist. Organizations may take allegations more seriously if they know evidence has been preserved outside their control. A person considering retaliation may hesitate if they believe retaliation itself will be documented. Again, these effects cannot be assumed in every situation. But the possibility that evidence can survive attempts to suppress it can alter the strategic environment surrounding misconduct.

This is one reason distributed archives can have significance beyond individual safety. If evidence exists in multiple independent locations, destroying one copy does not necessarily eliminate the evidence. That creates a different relationship between power and information. An institution may control its own servers, offices, employees, and internal records, but it may not control independent copies maintained elsewhere. The psychological effect on both sides can be significant. The information holder may feel less vulnerable because no single seizure can erase everything, while the institution may recognize that suppression is less likely to succeed. Distribution therefore creates both technical redundancy and potential psychological leverage.

But distribution should not be confused with indiscriminate duplication. Every additional copy can create another opportunity for unauthorized disclosure. The objective is controlled redundancy, not uncontrolled proliferation. Information should be duplicated according to a threat model that considers confidentiality, availability, integrity, and recoverability. A highly sensitive archive may require fewer carefully protected copies rather than dozens of ordinary ones. A public-interest dataset may eventually benefit from widespread distribution because its survival is more important than secrecy. Different information requires different architectures. The psychology of insurance begins with the same principle as technical security: protection should correspond to the consequences of failure.

The creator's perception of those consequences also matters. People tend to value losses differently depending on how personally connected they are to the information. A person may be more concerned about a private family record than a public document, even if the public document has greater historical significance. Another may regard evidence of institutional wrongdoing as worth enormous personal risk. These values influence how much effort someone is willing to invest in protection. A rational system should therefore begin by identifying what is actually being insured against. Is the primary concern loss, destruction, unauthorized access, manipulation, retaliation, legal exposure, or failure to reach the appropriate audience? Without answering that question, it is difficult to design a useful contingency.

The phrase "dead man's switch" can itself influence psychology because it sounds final. It suggests that the creator expects death and has decided what should happen afterward. For some people, that framing may create a sense of seriousness and resolve. For others, it may increase anxiety and encourage catastrophic thinking. The terminology can therefore shape the emotional relationship with the system. In many practical contexts, "continuity plan," "emergency disclosure protocol," or "information succession plan" may be psychologically more accurate. The underlying mechanism is not necessarily about death. It is about ensuring that a critical process continues when its primary operator becomes unavailable.

This broader framing also makes the concept relevant to ordinary people. A researcher might maintain an archive so years of work are not lost if their computer fails. A journalist might protect source material against confiscation or accidental destruction. A scientist might preserve experimental records independently of a laboratory's institutional systems. A business owner might ensure that critical records remain accessible after an unexpected death. A family might preserve legal documents and instructions so that survivors are not forced to reconstruct everything during grief. None of these situations requires a dramatic conspiracy. They all involve the same underlying principle: important information should not depend upon a single point of human failure.

The psychological value of preparation becomes clearest when something actually goes wrong. People who have established emergency procedures often have fewer decisions to make during the crisis itself. They know where information is stored, who has responsibility, and what sequence of actions should occur. This reduces improvisation. Improvisation is not always bad, but under stress it can produce inconsistent decisions and accidental disclosure. A prepared system converts some of the crisis response into routine procedure. The paradox is that the system may feel most useful when it is least visible. Its greatest achievement may be preventing a crisis from becoming an information catastrophe.

Yet there is an ethical limit to the insurance analogy. Insurance normally compensates for loss within a defined contractual framework. A dead man's switch can affect people who never agreed to its consequences. The release of information can expose private individuals, reveal confidential sources, affect legal proceedings, damage reputations, or create security risks. The creator therefore cannot assume that because the information belongs to them; every consequence of disclosure is theirs alone to decide. Other people's rights and interests may be embedded within the archive. The psychological comfort of having an escape mechanism must never replace ethical consideration of those who may be affected.

This is especially important when the information contains personal data. An archive may contain names, addresses, correspondence, medical information, financial records, photographs, or testimony belonging to people other than its creator. Automatic publication could transform a system designed to protect one person into a mechanism that harms many others. The responsible approach is therefore to separate the creator's legitimate interest in preserving evidence from the unnecessary exposure of unrelated private information. Redaction, controlled access, staged disclosure, and professional review can all help preserve this distinction. Information insurance should protect the truth without treating human privacy as collateral damage.

There is also an important difference between deterrence and retaliation. A legitimate contingency system is designed to preserve information or ensure continuity. A retaliatory system is designed primarily to punish someone by releasing information if they take a particular action. The two can overlap psychologically, but their ethical and practical implications differ. Retaliatory thinking can encourage escalation because each side begins trying to increase the consequences imposed on the other. A continuity-oriented system instead asks what should happen to the information regardless of who is responsible for the crisis. This shift from revenge to preservation can make the architecture both safer and more defensible.

The strongest psychological position is therefore one of preparedness without obsession. The creator acknowledges that important information could be lost and establishes reasonable safeguards. They do not need to monitor the system every minute or interpret every unexpected event as evidence of impending danger. They can periodically test the mechanism, update recipients, review legal considerations, and then return their attention to ordinary life. The system becomes background infrastructure rather than a permanent psychological presence. That is arguably the healthiest expression of information insurance. Preparation should create freedom from constant fear rather than a new reason to remain afraid.

The paradox becomes even more interesting when we consider that the dead man's switch may never need to function. If the information holder lives a long life, nothing happens, and the archive is eventually closed or incorporated into an ordinary estate, the mechanism could still have been valuable. It may have encouraged better documentation, stronger backups, clearer relationships, and more disciplined thinking about evidence. It may have provided psychological confidence during difficult periods. It may even have discouraged someone from attempting retaliation. None of these outcomes requires a dramatic activation event. The value can exist entirely in the reduction of vulnerability.

That is the deeper meaning of informational insurance. It is not primarily about expecting disaster. It is about refusing to allow disaster to determine whether important information survives. The mechanism acknowledges that people are mortal, institutions are imperfect, technology fails, relationships change, and circumstances can become unpredictable. It responds by creating continuity beyond the individual. But because information can harm as well as help, continuity must be accompanied by judgment. The most mature dead man's switch is therefore not a weapon waiting to fire. It is a carefully designed bridge between one person's knowledge and the future's ability to evaluate it.

Once this psychological foundation is understood, the next problem becomes practical. If information is going to survive beyond its creator, what exactly should be preserved? Not everything a person owns deserves the same level of protection, and not every secret should automatically be released. Some materials may be irreplaceable evidence, some may be personal records, some may be allegations requiring corroboration, and some may be irrelevant or dangerous if exposed. The architecture of protection must therefore begin with classification. Before deciding how information will be released, we must determine what information is actually worth protecting in the first place.

Resources

1. Daniel Kahneman, *Thinking, Fast and Slow*, Farrar, Straus and Giroux, 2011 — foundational work on judgment under uncertainty, cognitive biases, risk perception, and decision-making.

2. Gerd Gigerenzer, *Risk Savvy: How to Make Good Decisions*, Viking, 2014 — useful examination of how people understand uncertainty and make decisions when probabilities and consequences are difficult to evaluate.

3. Paul Slovic, "Perception of Risk," *Science*, Vol. 236, No. 4799, 1987 — foundational research on the psychology of risk perception and why perceived risk does not always correspond directly to statistical risk.

4. Paul Slovic, Ellen Peters, "Risk Perception and Affect," *Current Directions in Psychological Science*, Vol. 15, No. 6, 2006 — important research concerning the influence of emotional reactions on risk judgments.

5. Robert J. Shiller, *The New Financial Order: Risk in the 21st Century*, Princeton University Press, 2003 — broader conceptual discussion of risk management, uncertainty, and mechanisms designed to reduce vulnerability to unpredictable events.

6. Bruce Schneier, *Beyond Fear: Thinking Sensibly About Security in an Uncertain World*, Copernicus Books, 2003 — particularly relevant to distinguishing genuine security improvements from security theater and fear-driven behavior.

7. Bruce Schneier, *Secrets and Lies: Digital Security in a Networked World*, Wiley, 2000 — useful for understanding security as an interaction between technology, human behavior, incentives, and institutional processes.

8. Ross Anderson, *Security Engineering: A Guide to Building Dependable Distributed Systems*, 3rd ed., Wiley, 2020 — extensive treatment of security architecture, trust, redundancy, failure modes, human factors, and dependable systems.

9. NIST Cybersecurity Framework 2.0[1] — authoritative framework for identifying, protecting, detecting, responding to, and recovering from cybersecurity risks.

10. NIST Risk Management Framework — useful framework for identifying risks, evaluating controls, and continuously reassessing security assumptions.

1. https://www.nist.gov/cyberframework?utm_source=chatgpt.com

11. NIST Contingency Planning Guide for Federal Information Systems, SP 800-34[2] — practical foundation for continuity planning, recovery strategies, alternate processing, and information availability.

12. NIST Digital Identity Guidelines[3] — relevant to authentication and the problem of ensuring that authorized recipients are actually the people or entities intended to receive information.

13. NIST Recommendation for Key Management, SP 800-57 — technical foundation for protecting cryptographic keys and designing recoverable security systems.

14. CISA — Secure Our World[4] — practical guidance concerning account protection, authentication, phishing, and everyday cybersecurity behavior.

15. Electronic Frontier Foundation — Surveillance Self-Defense[5] — practical guidance concerning threat modeling, secure communication, encryption, device security, and protection of sensitive information.

16. National Archives — Digital Preservation — authoritative perspective on maintaining information integrity and accessibility over time.

17. NIST Privacy Framework[6] — relevant to the distinction between protecting information and protecting the privacy of people whose information is contained within an archive.

18. Adi Shamir, "How to Share a Secret," *Communications of the ACM*, Vol. 22, No. 11, 1979 — foundational work on secret sharing and distributing sensitive information among multiple participants.

19. Committee to Protect Journalists — Safety Kit[7] — practical resources concerning journalist safety, source protection, threat assessment, and digital security.

20. Society of Professional Journalists — Code of Ethics[8] — relevant to verification, minimizing harm, independence, accountability, and responsible publication.

21. U.S. Department of Labor — Whistleblower Protection Program[9] — official context concerning whistleblower reporting and protections against retaliation.

22. U.S. Securities and Exchange Commission — Whistleblower Program[10] — official information concerning confidential whistleblower reporting and associated protections.

23. American Bar Association — Model Rules of Professional Conduct[11] — relevant to professional confidentiality, conflicts of interest, and the responsibilities of lawyers handling sensitive information.

---

2. https://csrc.nist.gov/publications/detail/sp/800-34/rev-1/final?utm_source=chatgpt.com

3. https://pages.nist.gov/800-63-4/?utm_source=chatgpt.com

4. https://www.cisa.gov/secure-our-world?utm_source=chatgpt.com

5. https://ssd.eff.org/?utm_source=chatgpt.com

6. https://www.nist.gov/privacy-framework?utm_source=chatgpt.com

7. https://cpj.org/safety-kit/?utm_source=chatgpt.com

8. https://www.spj.org/ethicscode.asp?utm_source=chatgpt.com

9. https://www.whistleblowers.gov/?utm_source=chatgpt.com

10. https://www.sec.gov/enforcement-litigation/whistleblower-program?utm_source=chatgpt.com

11. https://www.americanbar.org/groups/professional_responsibility/publications/model_rules_of_professional_conduct/?utm_source=chatgpt.com

24. Karl Weick, Kathleen Sutcliffe, *Managing the Unexpected: Sustained Performance in a Complex World*, 3rd ed., Wiley, 2015 — useful organizational perspective on resilience, uncertainty, failure, and maintaining reliable operations in complex environments.

25. Nassim Nicholas Taleb, *Antifragile: Things That Gain from Disorder*, Random House, 2012 — broader conceptual treatment of resilience, redundancy, uncertainty, and systems designed to withstand unpredictable events.

Planning for the Unthinkable

The hardest contingency plans are the ones people create for events they hope will never happen. Death is difficult to contemplate, disappearance is frightening, imprisonment is disruptive, incapacitation can arrive without warning, and the sudden loss of communication can occur for reasons having nothing to do with deliberate interference. Yet the very fact that these events are difficult to imagine is precisely why they deserve deliberate consideration before a crisis occurs. Planning for the unthinkable does not mean predicting catastrophe or assuming that the worst interpretation of every event is correct. It means recognizing that a person's ability to protect important information can disappear suddenly and that a system designed around uninterrupted human availability contains an obvious weakness. The purpose of contingency planning is therefore not to make frightening events inevitable, but to ensure that important information and legitimate responsibilities do not become casualties when circumstances change.

A useful contingency plan begins by defining the problem without immediately choosing the technology. People often make the mistake of starting with a tool, asking whether they should use automated email, cloud storage, encryption, blockchain systems, or some other mechanism. The better question is what failure the system is intended to prevent. If the concern is death, the problem may be succession and preservation. If the concern is temporary incapacitation, the problem may be continuity of access. If the concern is imprisonment, the problem may be the inability to communicate or authorize decisions. If the concern is coercion, the problem may involve both personal safety and the protection of information. Different threats produce different requirements, and a system designed around the wrong failure can appear sophisticated while solving very little.

The first conceptual distinction is between an event and a condition. Death is an event with a relatively definitive outcome, while disappearance or loss of communication may be ambiguous. A person can be unreachable because they are travelling, hospitalized, asleep, disconnected from the Internet, or experiencing an ordinary technical problem. Someone can also be unreachable because they have been detained, abducted, injured, or deliberately prevented from communicating. The system cannot automatically know which explanation is correct unless it has access to reliable evidence. This means that a missed communication should normally be treated as a signal requiring evaluation rather than immediate proof of catastrophe. Good contingency planning begins by respecting uncertainty.

Death presents the clearest example because it ultimately creates a permanent change in the information holder's ability to act. Yet even here, the planning problem is more complicated than it first appears. A system may need to distinguish confirmed death from a prolonged absence of communication. It may need to preserve records for heirs, lawyers, investigators, or journalists. It may need to separate personal information from evidence intended for public disclosure. It may need to account for legal requirements concerning estates, privacy, intellectual property, and confidential records. A responsible posthumous information plan therefore cannot simply be a timer that publishes everything. It must consider what should happen to different categories of information after the creator is no longer available.

Disappearance is considerably more difficult because the word itself contains uncertainty. A missing person may be voluntarily absent, involuntarily detained, injured, lost, or deliberately hiding. A dead man's switch designed around disappearance must therefore include a verification process rather than treating silence as conclusive evidence. This is where graduated responses become useful. An initial missed check-in might generate a private reminder. A longer period might notify a trusted intermediary. A still longer period might initiate an investigation or activate a predetermined review process. Only after appropriate conditions have been satisfied might a higher level of disclosure become possible. The principle is simple: uncertainty should produce investigation before irreversible action whenever circumstances permit.

Imprisonment introduces another complication because the individual may still be alive and capable of making decisions but unable to communicate freely. Depending on the jurisdiction and circumstances, a detained person may have restricted access to devices, accounts, legal counsel, or outside contacts. They may also be subject to legal processes that change what can safely or lawfully be communicated. A contingency plan should therefore distinguish between physical absence and loss of autonomy. Someone can be alive but temporarily incapable of managing their information. The system should preserve continuity without assuming that the person's silence necessarily means consent to disclosure.

Incapacitation creates a similar problem. An accident, illness, injury, neurological event, or other medical emergency can leave a person unable to communicate while their information remains important. The individual may recover days or weeks later and discover that an automated system released sensitive material because they were temporarily unable to check in. This is one of the strongest arguments against simplistic triggers. The system needs to distinguish between temporary incapacity and permanent unavailability whenever possible. It should also define what authority, if any, another person has to act during incapacity. These questions move the dead man's switch from the realm of dramatic storytelling into the much more complex territory of continuity and delegated authority.

Coercion is perhaps the most difficult condition because the person may appear to be functioning normally while their decisions are no longer entirely voluntary. A person under threat may send a message, cancel a contingency, hand over credentials, or make statements that appear authentic but were produced under pressure. Traditional authentication systems are often designed to answer the question, "Is this really the person?" Coercion raises a different question: "Is the person acting freely?" No simple technical mechanism can completely solve that problem. The most practical response is to avoid designing the entire system around a single voluntary action that can be compelled.

This distinction has important consequences for emergency instructions. A person might be tempted to create a secret phrase indicating that they are in danger, but any such mechanism must be considered carefully because a coercive actor might discover or demand it. The broader principle is that the system should not rely upon one easily compelled signal. Multiple independent indicators may provide greater confidence than a single message. Even then, no mechanism can guarantee that coercion will be detected. The objective is to make the system more resilient to uncertainty and pressure rather than pretending that technology can eliminate human vulnerability.

Sudden loss of communication is the most ordinary of these extraordinary conditions. Internet outages, damaged devices, travel, power failures, natural disasters, account lockouts, and network disruptions can all make someone temporarily unreachable. A contingency system that interprets every outage as an emergency will generate false activations. False activations can themselves become dangerous because they expose sensitive information, erode trust in the system, and train recipients to disregard future warnings. Reliability therefore requires tolerance for ordinary failure. A system that cannot distinguish inconvenience from catastrophe is not robust; it is merely reactive.

This is why time becomes a central variable. The longer a person remains unavailable, the more significant the absence may become, but time alone does not prove what happened. A missed daily check-in is relatively weak evidence because ordinary interruptions are common. A prolonged absence combined with failed contact attempts, unusual circumstances, and independent indicators may provide stronger evidence. The exact timing must therefore reflect the consequences of false activation as well as the consequences of delayed response. If premature disclosure could seriously harm innocent people, a longer verification window may be justified. If delayed access could result in the permanent loss of critical evidence, a shorter response may be appropriate.

The architecture should consequently be based on thresholds rather than assumptions. A threshold is a defined condition that must be satisfied before a particular action occurs. It might involve elapsed time, independent confirmation, multiple failed contact methods, authentication by designated people, or some combination of these factors. Thresholds make the system predictable. They also allow the creator to separate different levels of response. A low-level threshold might preserve information without releasing it. A higher threshold might notify a professional intermediary. The highest threshold might authorize carefully defined disclosure. This graduated structure is more flexible than treating the switch as an all-or-nothing mechanism.

Redundancy is equally important. If the entire contingency system depends upon one server, one email account, one device, one password, or one human custodian, the system contains a single point of failure. A person can lose a phone, an account can be suspended, a storage service can experience an outage, and a custodian can become unavailable. Redundancy means ensuring that the failure of one component does not destroy the entire chain. But redundancy must be deliberate because every additional copy or access point creates another potential security vulnerability. The goal is not to create infinite copies. It is to create enough independent paths that predictable failures do not become catastrophic.

Independence is particularly important when evaluating redundancy. Five copies stored on five devices in the same building do not provide the same protection as copies maintained through genuinely independent systems. If a fire destroys the building, all five copies disappear together. If one administrator controls every account, compromise of that administrator may expose everything. If every recipient communicates through the same platform, a platform-wide outage can affect them simultaneously. True resilience comes from reducing correlated failures. The system should therefore consider not merely how many backups exist but whether they are vulnerable to the same event.

The same principle applies to human custodians. Three people who all work for the same organization may not provide genuine independence if the organization can restrict all three simultaneously. Three relatives living in the same household may be affected by the same emergency. Three digital administrators using the same compromised authentication infrastructure may represent one practical point of failure. Independence is therefore a structural property rather than a numerical count. A resilient plan asks what could affect all participants at once. It then attempts to create separation around those common vulnerabilities.

Information itself should also be divided according to consequence. Not every document deserves the same level of protection. Some material may be ordinary personal records. Some may contain confidential correspondence. Some may document alleged wrongdoing. Some may identify vulnerable sources. Some may contain information whose public release would create serious harm. A useful contingency plan classifies information according to sensitivity, evidentiary value, and consequences of disclosure. This allows different material to follow different pathways. The system becomes more precise because it no longer treats every file as equally urgent or equally dangerous.

Classification also helps prevent the psychological temptation to treat everything as equally important. When a person is frightened, every piece of information can begin to feel connected to the central threat. This can lead to enormous archives containing irrelevant material that increases complexity without improving protection.

Complexity creates more opportunities for errors. The better approach is to identify the information that genuinely matters and document why it matters. A smaller, well-organized archive can be more useful than a massive collection whose contents nobody can interpret. Contingency planning is therefore partly an exercise in disciplined selection.

The question of authenticity must be addressed at the same time. If a person disappears, recipients may eventually receive files claiming to have come from them. How will anyone know that the material is genuine? Digital signatures, cryptographic hashes, trusted timestamps, metadata, independent copies, and documented provenance can all contribute to authentication. None is magic. A digital signature can demonstrate that a particular key signed a file, but the security of the key itself still matters. A hash can demonstrate that a file has not changed since the hash was created, but it does not establish that the original file was truthful. Authentication and truth are therefore separate questions.

The distinction between evidence and interpretation becomes particularly important after an unexpected event. A personal statement may explain what the creator believed had happened. Supporting documents may establish certain facts. Other materials may contradict some of the conclusions. A responsible contingency system should preserve these layers separately. Recipients should be able to identify original records, later commentary, and personal interpretations. This protects the integrity of the archive and gives independent investigators the ability to reach their own conclusions. The objective is to preserve evidence in a form that remains useful even when the creator is no longer available to explain it.

Documentation should also explain the architecture itself. A sophisticated system that nobody understands is not a reliable system. The creator should document what each component does, who has responsibility, what happens if a component fails, and what conditions activate different stages. These instructions should be understandable to someone who did not design the system. Technical jargon can be included where necessary, but critical procedures should not depend upon the creator's memory. If a lawyer, family member, investigator, or journalist must eventually operate the system, they should be able to understand the basic logic without reconstructing it from fragments.

The architecture should also distinguish between preservation and publication. These are not the same action. Preservation means ensuring that information remains available and intact. Publication means making information available to an audience. A person can preserve evidence without deciding that it should immediately become public. This distinction provides an important safety valve. If an unexpected event occurs, the first response can be to secure the archive rather than release it. Professional review can then determine what should happen next. In many circumstances, this is safer and more ethically defensible than automatic publication.

This separation creates the possibility of staged disclosure. The first stage might simply notify designated custodians that a contingency condition has occurred. The second might provide access to a limited set of instructions. The third might allow professional review of selected evidence. The final stage might involve publication or transfer to appropriate authorities. Each stage creates an opportunity to detect mistakes. If the initial assumption proves wrong, the process can stop before irreversible disclosure occurs. The architecture therefore behaves less like a detonator and more like a sequence of gates.

Legal considerations must be incorporated into this planning from the beginning. Different jurisdictions treat privacy, confidential information, intellectual property, evidence, communications, estate administration, and national-security material differently. A person cannot assume that an instruction written in one country will have the same legal effect in another. Nor can they assume that a recipient has unlimited authority to publish material simply because the creator requested it. Legal review is particularly important when the archive contains third-party personal information, classified material, trade secrets, or information connected to ongoing litigation. The safest conceptual framework is to treat legal constraints as part of the architecture rather than as an obstacle encountered after the switch activates.

This is also where the distinction between lawful whistleblowing and indiscriminate leaking becomes important. There are circumstances in which disclosure of wrongdoing may serve a powerful public interest. There are also circumstances in which disclosure can violate legitimate confidentiality, endanger innocent people, interfere with investigations, or expose information unrelated to the alleged misconduct. A contingency system should not assume that "important" automatically means "public." The purpose of planning is to preserve the information long enough for appropriate judgment to be exercised. This is particularly important when the creator may no longer be present to explain context.

Another essential principle is revocability. Circumstances change, and a person may legitimately decide that an earlier contingency arrangement is no longer appropriate. A system created during one investigation may become unnecessary after the investigation ends. A trusted recipient may become unsuitable. A legal situation may change. New evidence may invalidate an earlier conclusion. If the system cannot be safely updated or revoked, it can become a liability. The creator should therefore consider how instructions are amended, how old copies are retired, and how recipients know which version is authoritative.

Version control is especially important for long-lived archives. Imagine that a person creates an emergency instruction in 2026 and updates it in 2028. If both versions remain accessible, which one should a recipient follow? Without a clear method of identifying the current version, the system can produce contradictory instructions. This is a mundane technical issue with potentially extraordinary consequences. Dates, version identifiers, authentication methods, and explicit supersession rules can reduce confusion. The more complex the system becomes, the more important administrative discipline becomes.

A contingency plan should also account for the possibility that its creator becomes unavailable before the system is complete. People often imagine that they will finish everything later. They intend to organize documents, test backups, choose recipients, consult a lawyer, and document procedures when they have more time. Yet unexpected events do not respect schedules. A partially completed system may therefore be worse than a simple system that is functional today. This creates a practical principle: establish a reliable minimum architecture first, then improve it progressively. A basic functioning contingency system provides more protection than a theoretically perfect system that remains unfinished.

Testing should follow the same logic. A test should ideally simulate failure without actually causing irreversible disclosure. The purpose is to discover whether people understand their roles, whether credentials work, whether archives can be recovered, whether instructions are comprehensible, and whether false activations can be cancelled. Testing can also reveal assumptions that were invisible during design. A recipient may discover that a supposedly simple procedure requires specialized software. An encrypted archive may depend upon an obsolete application. A backup may exist but contain an incomplete version of the evidence. Testing converts theoretical resilience into demonstrated resilience.

The human response should also be considered. If a contingency system activates, recipients may be frightened, confused, or uncertain about what they have received. They may wonder whether the creator is dead, missing, detained, or simply unreachable. They may also worry about legal consequences. Instructions should therefore tell them what not to do as well as what to do. They should know whether they are expected to preserve the material, contact counsel, verify circumstances, or take some other authorized step. Clear instructions reduce the possibility that panic will cause accidental disclosure.

The system should also anticipate compromise. Suppose an attacker discovers that a dead man's switch exists. They may attempt to access the archive, disable the trigger, impersonate recipients, or create false evidence suggesting that the creator is safe. A responsible threat model therefore considers both passive failure and active interference. The goal is not to construct an invulnerable system, because no system is invulnerable. It is to identify which failures would be catastrophic and then prioritize protection around them. Security architecture becomes more effective when it concentrates effort on consequences rather than on the pursuit of an abstract idea of perfect security.

This is where threat modeling becomes particularly useful. A threat model asks what is being protected, from whom, under what circumstances, and what the consequences would be if the protection failed. The answers should be specific. "Hackers" is not a sufficient threat model because different attackers possess different capabilities and incentives. An ordinary thief, a hostile employer, a sophisticated criminal organization, a government agency, an abusive partner, and a curious acquaintance represent very different threat environments. The architecture should reflect the actual circumstances rather than an imagined universal adversary. Overestimating threats can make a system unnecessarily complicated, while underestimating them can create dangerous vulnerabilities.

The consequences of false activation should receive equal attention. Security discussions often focus on preventing unauthorized access but neglect the possibility that the system itself may authorize disclosure incorrectly. A false trigger can be just as damaging as a successful attack if it exposes confidential evidence to the wrong people. This means that reliability and security are interconnected. The system must not merely resist attackers. It must also resist its own tendency to misinterpret ambiguous events. Verification, delay periods, multiple conditions, and human review can all help reduce this class of failure.

The concept of graceful degradation is valuable here. A resilient system should not move directly from "everything works" to "everything is exposed" when one component fails. Instead, it should have intermediate states. If an email account becomes inaccessible, perhaps another communication channel remains available. If one custodian disappears, another can perform the same role. If a storage provider fails, an independent archive remains intact. If automated triggering becomes unreliable, manual review can continue. Graceful degradation means that failure in one component reduces capability without destroying the entire architecture.

The same principle applies to the creator's own changing circumstances. A person may initially be the sole operator, but over time they may gain employees, collaborators, lawyers, family responsibilities, or institutional affiliations. Their information may also become more sensitive or less sensitive. The contingency plan should evolve with those changes. A static plan gradually becomes inaccurate. Periodic review should therefore ask whether the original assumptions remain valid. The most important assumption of all is that the system still reflects the creator's actual intentions.

There is also a philosophical dimension to planning for the unthinkable. Every contingency plan represents a decision about what should survive the planner. A person cannot preserve everything indefinitely. Storage has limits, attention has limits, and recipients have limits. Choosing what survives is therefore an act of judgment. It reflects what the creator considers historically, legally, personally, or socially significant. This can make contingency planning unexpectedly clarifying. By asking what would matter if they were suddenly gone, people are forced to distinguish between what is merely accumulated and what is genuinely important.

That exercise can also reduce fear. When everything feels important, everything feels vulnerable. Once the essential information has been identified, the problem becomes more manageable. The person can separate ordinary material from critical evidence, personal records from public-interest information, and irreplaceable material from information that can easily be reconstructed. The archive becomes smaller, clearer, and easier to protect. Psychological uncertainty decreases because the individual has converted a vague fear into a defined set of responsibilities. Planning therefore becomes both an information-management exercise and a way of regaining perspective.

Ultimately, planning for the unthinkable is an exercise in accepting uncertainty without surrendering to it. Death cannot be prevented by an information system. Disappearance cannot always be explained immediately. Imprisonment can remove a person's freedom to act. Incapacitation can interrupt communication without warning. Coercion can compromise voluntary decision-making, and technical failures can imitate emergencies. The purpose of the dead man's switch is not to defeat all of these conditions. It is to ensure that the failure of one human being's availability does not automatically become the failure of everything they were responsible for protecting.

The strongest contingency plan therefore has several characteristics that may initially seem contradictory. It is cautious without being paranoid, redundant without becoming chaotic, secure without becoming impossible to recover, automated without surrendering all judgment, and protective without assuming that disclosure is always the correct outcome. It recognizes that people make mistakes and that systems fail. It builds opportunities for verification before irreversible action. It preserves evidence separately from interpretation and preservation separately from publication. Most importantly, it is designed while the creator still has the time and psychological distance to make rational decisions.

The next question is where these principles become operational. Once the threats have been identified and the architecture has been conceptualized, the system needs a trigger: some condition that tells the mechanism that normal human control may no longer be available. That sounds straightforward until we examine the possibilities. Should the trigger be a missed daily check-in, a weekly confirmation, a specific condition, an independent report, a combination of signals, or a deliberate human decision? Each choice creates different advantages and different failure modes. The next chapter therefore begins the technical heart of the book by asking the deceptively simple question on which the entire mechanism depends: what, exactly, should trigger the switch?

Resources

1. National Institute of Standards and Technology — Risk Management Framework — authoritative framework for identifying threats, assessing risk, selecting controls, and continuously monitoring security assumptions.

2. NIST Cybersecurity Framework 2.0[1] — useful framework for understanding cybersecurity through identification, protection, detection, response, and recovery.

3. NIST Special Publication 800-34 — Contingency Planning Guide for Federal Information Systems[2] — foundational guidance on contingency planning, recovery strategies, alternate processing, and information-system continuity.

4. NIST Special Publication 800-53 — Security and Privacy Controls[3] — extensive controls concerning contingency planning, access control, separation of duties, incident response, authentication, and system integrity.

1. https://www.nist.gov/cyberframework?utm_source=chatgpt.com

2. https://csrc.nist.gov/publications/detail/sp/800-34/rev-1/final?utm_source=chatgpt.com

5. NIST Zero Trust Architecture, SP 800-207[4] — relevant to the principle that authorization should not rest solely upon implicit trust.

6. NIST Digital Identity Guidelines[5] — technical guidance concerning authentication, identity assurance, authenticators, and identity-related risks.

7. NIST Recommendation for Key Management, SP 800-57 — important for key protection, lifecycle management, backup, recovery, and cryptographic access control.

8. NIST Guide to General Server Security, SP 800-123 — useful background for protecting server-based infrastructure supporting information-continuity systems.

9. CISA — Secure Our World[6] — practical guidance concerning authentication, account protection, phishing, device security, and everyday cyber resilience.

10. CISA — Cybersecurity Performance Goals[7] — practical security baseline emphasizing resilience, backups, identity management, and protection against common failure modes.

11. Electronic Frontier Foundation — Surveillance Self-Defense[8] — practical material on threat modeling, secure communications, encryption, device security, and protecting sensitive information.

12. Ross Anderson, *Security Engineering: A Guide to Building Dependable Distributed Systems*, 3rd ed., Wiley, 2020 — comprehensive treatment of dependable systems, threat modeling, human factors, failure modes, authentication, and security architecture.

13. Bruce Schneier, *Beyond Fear: Thinking Sensibly About Security in an Uncertain World*, Copernicus Books, 2003 — important conceptual treatment of security, threat assessment, tradeoffs, and the difference between actual and perceived protection.

14. Bruce Schneier, *Secrets and Lies: Digital Security in a Networked World*, Wiley, 2000 — foundational discussion of the interaction between cryptography, systems, people, procedures, and institutional vulnerabilities.

15. Adi Shamir, "How to Share a Secret," *Communications of the ACM*, Vol. 22, No. 11, 1979 — foundational work on threshold-based secret sharing and distributing critical information among multiple participants.

16. National Archives — Digital Preservation — authoritative material concerning preservation, integrity, accessibility, and long-term survival of digital information.

17. NIST Digital Preservation Resources — useful background for the technical and organizational challenges of maintaining digital records over time.

3. https://csrc.nist.gov/publications/detail/sp/800-53/rev-5/final?utm_source=chatgpt.com

4. https://csrc.nist.gov/publications/detail/sp/800-207/final?utm_source=chatgpt.com

5. https://pages.nist.gov/800-63-4/?utm_source=chatgpt.com

6. https://www.cisa.gov/secure-our-world?utm_source=chatgpt.com

7. https://www.cisa.gov/cross-sector-cybersecurity-performance-goals?utm_source=chatgpt.com

8. https://ssd.eff.org/?utm_source=chatgpt.com

18. International Organization for Standardization — ISO 22301 Business Continuity Management[9] — international standard concerning organizational continuity and the preparation required to maintain critical functions during disruption.

19. International Organization for Standardization — ISO/IEC 27001 Information Security Management Systems[10] — international framework for systematic information-security risk management and organizational controls.

20. National Institute of Mental Health — Coping With Traumatic Events — relevant psychological background concerning responses to threatening events and the importance of maintaining adaptive coping mechanisms.

21. Daniel Kahneman, *Thinking, Fast and Slow*, Farrar, Straus and Giroux, 2011 — useful for understanding judgment under uncertainty and why contingency systems should not rely entirely upon intuition or emotionally driven decisions.

22. Gerd Gigerenzer, *Risk Savvy: How to Make Good Decisions*, Viking, 2014 — relevant to reasoning under uncertainty and evaluating risks without demanding impossible certainty.

23. U.S. Department of Labor — Whistleblower Protection Program[11] — institutional context for protected disclosures and the risks associated with retaliation against whistleblowers.

24. U.S. Securities and Exchange Commission — Whistleblower Program[12] — official information concerning confidential reporting and whistleblower protections within the securities regulatory framework.

25. Committee to Protect Journalists — Safety Kit[13] — practical guidance relevant to risk assessment, source protection, digital security, and contingency planning for journalists and sensitive sources.

---

9. https://www.iso.org/standard/75106.html?utm_source=chatgpt.com

10. https://www.iso.org/isoiec-27001-information-security.html?utm_source=chatgpt.com

11. https://www.whistleblowers.gov/?utm_source=chatgpt.com

12. https://www.sec.gov/enforcement-litigation/whistleblower-program?utm_source=chatgpt.com

13. https://cpj.org/safety-kit/?utm_source=chatgpt.com

What Should Trigger the Switch?

Every dead man's switch ultimately depends upon a single decision, whether that decision is made by a machine, a trusted person, or a combination of both: something has happened, and the system must now determine whether its normal state has ended. This sounds simple until we examine what "something has happened" actually means. A person can stop responding because they have died, disappeared, been imprisoned, become incapacitated, lost access to communication, travelled somewhere without connectivity, forgotten to check in, or deliberately chosen to remain silent. A technical system cannot automatically understand the difference between these circumstances merely because a message was not received. The central design problem is therefore not creating a trigger that reacts to silence, but creating a trigger that interprets silence responsibly.

The word "trigger" can itself be misleading because it suggests a single event that produces an immediate consequence. In a sophisticated contingency system, the trigger should instead be understood as a decision condition. It represents the point at which available evidence has become sufficient to justify moving from one state of the system to another. That movement might be from normal operation to warning, from warning to verification, from verification to restricted access, or eventually from restricted access to disclosure. The trigger is therefore better understood as part of a decision architecture than as a simple switch. This distinction is important because irreversible actions require stronger evidence than reversible ones.

The first question should always be what the system is actually trying to detect. If the objective is to protect information after death, then the system needs evidence of death or a sufficiently reliable posthumous process. If the objective is to protect information after prolonged disappearance, the system needs to detect sustained unavailability rather than death specifically. If the objective is continuity during incapacitation, the system needs a mechanism that permits another authorized person to act without prematurely treating the situation as permanent. If the objective is protection against coercion, the system needs to account for the possibility that apparent communication may not represent free consent. Different objectives produce different trigger conditions. A single universal trigger is therefore unlikely to be appropriate for every situation.

The most basic trigger is time. A person establishes an interval during which they are expected to confirm that everything remains normal. If confirmation does not occur, the system begins a response. This is attractive because time is objective and easy for software to measure. A clock does not become confused by emotion, uncertainty, or changing interpretations. Yet time alone says nothing about why the person failed to respond. The longer the silence continues, the stronger the reason for concern may become, but duration is still only an indirect indicator of the underlying event.

This creates the problem of false positives. Imagine a person who normally confirms their status every evening. One night they forget. A system that immediately releases sensitive information would convert an ordinary human mistake into an irreversible event. The same thing could happen because of a lost phone, an Internet outage, a dead battery, travel, hospitalization, or a change in schedule. False positives are particularly dangerous in information systems because disclosure cannot always be undone. Once sensitive information has been distributed, deleting the original file does not retrieve every copy. A responsible trigger must therefore be designed around the consequences of being wrong.

False negatives create the opposite problem. A system may fail to activate even though the person is genuinely unavailable. Perhaps the person remembers to send one final confirmation while under circumstances that prevent them from acting freely. Perhaps an attacker gains access to their account. Perhaps the system itself fails silently. Perhaps the person becomes incapacitated immediately after completing a check-in. In such circumstances, an apparently functioning system may provide false reassurance. Reliability therefore requires attention to both types of error. A trigger that activates too easily is dangerous, but a trigger that almost never activates can be equally useless.

This is a classic decision problem under uncertainty. In statistical terms, the system is attempting to infer an unobserved condition from observable signals. The actual condition might be "the creator remains safely available," "the creator is temporarily unavailable," or "the creator can no longer exercise control." The observable signals might include missed check-ins, failed communications, account activity, independent confirmations, or reports from designated people. None of these signals necessarily proves the underlying condition. They provide evidence from which a decision can be made. The quality of the system therefore depends upon the quality, independence, and reliability of those signals.

The distinction between signal and proof should remain central throughout the design process. A missed email is a signal. A failed phone call is another signal. A report from a trusted person is a stronger signal in some circumstances. A legally recognized death record may provide substantially stronger evidence of death. The system should not treat all signals as equivalent. Instead, it should assign different levels of confidence to different forms of evidence. This creates the possibility of a graduated response in which weak signals initiate investigation while strong signals authorize more consequential actions.

One of the most useful concepts here is a state machine. In computing, a state machine describes a system that moves between defined conditions according to specified events or inputs. A dead man's switch can be conceptualized in the same way. The normal state might mean that the creator is actively confirming availability. A warning state could begin after a missed confirmation. A verification state could follow repeated failures. A restricted state might preserve the archive while authorized people investigate. A final disclosure state could occur only after predetermined conditions are satisfied. This structure allows the system to behave differently at different levels of uncertainty.

Such a model also makes cancellation possible. Suppose a person misses a check-in because their phone was destroyed while travelling. The system enters a warning state and perhaps notifies a designated contact. The person later re-establishes communication and confirms that everything is normal. The warning can then be cancelled without any sensitive information having been released. This is fundamentally different from a binary system in which silence immediately produces publication. Reversibility is one of the strongest protections against accidental activation. The closer the system moves toward irreversible disclosure, the stronger the evidence should become.

A second important principle is separation of detection from authorization. The mechanism that detects an unusual condition does not necessarily need to be the mechanism that authorizes disclosure. A timer might detect prolonged silence. A trusted intermediary might verify circumstances. A lawyer might determine legal consequences. A journalist might evaluate evidentiary significance. A separate custodian might control the archive. Separating these functions reduces the danger that one compromised component can make the entire decision. It also introduces human judgment where automated interpretation would be inadequate.

This is similar to the principle of separation of duties used in information security and organizational governance. Critical actions can require more than one person or process. One person may initiate a transaction while another approves it. One system may identify an anomaly while another determines the response. The same principle can be adapted to information continuity. A system could recognize that a creator has become unavailable without giving the detection mechanism unilateral authority to publish everything. The architecture becomes more resilient because no single error necessarily produces the final consequence.

The problem becomes particularly serious when the trigger concerns death. Death is a legal and biological event, but a software system generally does not possess direct access to the underlying fact. It might receive information from another person or service, but then the reliability of that source becomes relevant. An automated system that relies on an unverified message could be manipulated. A system that requires official documentation may introduce delays. There is therefore a tradeoff between speed and certainty. The appropriate balance depends on the nature of the information being protected and the consequences of premature disclosure.

Disappearance is even harder to detect because disappearance is not a binary technical condition. Someone can be missing from their normal digital environment while remaining perfectly safe. They may deliberately disconnect from technology. They may travel to an isolated location. They may decide that their previous check-in routine is no longer appropriate. A trigger that interprets digital silence as physical disappearance therefore risks confusing privacy with danger. This is why a robust system needs explicit expectations. The creator should define what constitutes an unusual absence rather than allowing software to invent its own definition.

Incapacitation requires another conceptual distinction: inability versus unwillingness. A person may choose not to communicate, or they may be physically incapable of communicating. The system cannot reliably infer the difference from silence alone. External evidence may sometimes help, but even external evidence can be incomplete. A hospital admission, for example, might explain why someone cannot respond, but the system may not have legitimate access to such information. A trusted contact may know that the person is safe but unable to manage their affairs. A contingency architecture should therefore avoid treating every failure to communicate as evidence that disclosure is appropriate.

Voluntary silence is particularly important because privacy is not itself a failure condition. People have legitimate reasons to withdraw from communication. They may want time away from work, family, media, or technology. They may change their communication habits. They may decide that an earlier contingency plan is no longer necessary. A system that punishes silence with automatic disclosure undermines personal autonomy. The creator should therefore have clearly defined ways to suspend or modify the mechanism. A dead man's switch should protect the creator's intentions, not override them merely because they became temporarily unreachable.

This leads directly to the concept of an emergency override. An override allows an authorized person or the creator to stop an impending activation when circumstances demonstrate that the trigger was inappropriate. But the override itself creates security questions. Who is authorized to use it? How is that person's identity established? What prevents an attacker from forcing the override? What happens if the person who controls the override becomes unavailable? Every new control creates another potential vulnerability. The objective is not to eliminate all complexity but to balance competing failure modes.

The architecture can therefore use multiple independent signals. Instead of relying on a single missed check-in, the system might consider the passage of time together with failed communications and another independently obtained indicator. The principle resembles multi-factor authentication, although the signals here concern circumstances rather than identity. Each independent factor reduces the probability that one ordinary failure will produce an incorrect conclusion. Independence is essential. If all signals originate from the same compromised account or device, apparent redundancy may be illusory. Three confirmations generated by one broken system are still effectively one signal.

Geographic information presents another possible signal, but it should be treated carefully. Location data can be incomplete, inaccurate, unavailable, or deliberately disabled. A device may appear to remain in one location while the person is somewhere else. A person may intentionally switch off location services for legitimate privacy reasons. Geographic triggers can therefore contribute evidence but should rarely be treated as definitive proof of a person's condition. Location can be particularly useful for continuity systems that depend on known travel or operational zones, but its limitations must be recognized. Privacy concerns also make indiscriminate location monitoring inappropriate in many circumstances.

Digital activity can create another source of evidence. Account access, device activity, message responses, or other authenticated actions may demonstrate that a system remains under someone's control. Yet digital activity is not equivalent to human presence. Credentials can be stolen. Devices can be shared. Automated processes can generate activity without the owner being involved. An account may continue sending scheduled messages after its owner has become incapacitated. Digital traces should therefore be treated as evidence rather than proof of wellbeing. Their value depends upon how difficult they are to fake and how closely they correspond to the condition the system is attempting to detect.

Biometric systems create similar questions. A biometric signal can sometimes provide stronger evidence that a particular person is physically present, but it cannot establish that the person is acting freely. Fingerprints, faces, voices, and other biometric characteristics can also present security and privacy challenges. A biometric trigger might therefore answer the question of identity while failing to answer the question of consent. This distinction becomes critical in coercion scenarios. A system that confirms the correct person but ignores the possibility of coercion can produce a technically authenticated but substantively false decision.

Coercion is one of the strongest arguments for designing triggers around patterns rather than single events. If a person suddenly changes their normal communication behavior, cancels every contingency, transfers access, or sends unusual instructions, these changes might warrant attention. But unusual behavior is not proof of coercion either. People change jobs, relationships, routines, devices, and priorities all the time. The system should therefore avoid converting behavioral anomalies directly into accusations or automatic disclosure. Instead, anomalies can initiate a verification process. This preserves the distinction between detecting something unusual and deciding what it means.

A useful trigger architecture can consequently be described as a ladder of confidence. At the lowest level, something unusual occurs. The system records it and perhaps sends a private notification. At the next level, repeated anomalies produce a request for verification. At a higher level, independent evidence supports the conclusion that normal control has been disrupted. Only at the highest level does the system authorize a predefined response. This approach has an important psychological advantage because it reduces the pressure placed on any single event. The system does not have to be certain immediately because it has been designed to gather confidence progressively.

The timing between these levels is also important. Short intervals reduce the risk of prolonged inaction but increase the possibility of false activation. Longer intervals reduce false positives but may delay access to information that could be time-sensitive. There is no universally correct interval. The correct timing depends upon the nature of the information, the threat environment, the reliability of communication channels, and the consequences of delay. A

system protecting ordinary personal records can tolerate much longer uncertainty than one preserving evidence that may disappear or be destroyed. Timing must therefore be connected to consequence rather than selected arbitrarily.

The creator should also consider what happens during the verification period. A warning that nobody receives is functionally useless. Notifications should therefore have redundancy. But again, redundancy must be balanced against confidentiality. Sending sensitive information to multiple channels merely to guarantee delivery can create unnecessary exposure. The notification can instead contain minimal information necessary to prompt an authorized response. The principle is to separate notification from disclosure. A person may need to know that a contingency event has occurred without immediately receiving the underlying evidence.

This distinction becomes especially important when considering public release. Public publication should generally represent a much higher threshold than private preservation. Once information reaches the public domain, control is effectively lost. Copies can be downloaded, mirrored, archived, quoted, altered, and redistributed. Even if an original publication is removed, secondary copies may remain indefinitely. The trigger for preservation can therefore be relatively sensitive while the trigger for public disclosure should generally be considerably more demanding. This creates a useful hierarchy of consequences. The more irreversible the action, the stronger the trigger should be.

There should also be a distinction between disclosure to a professional intermediary and disclosure to the general public. A lawyer, journalist, investigator, regulator, or other qualified recipient may be capable of reviewing information responsibly before publication. This provides an additional layer of judgment. The system can preserve evidence and make it available to an appropriate professional without automatically publishing accusations worldwide. That approach is especially valuable when the information is complicated, potentially defamatory, classified, or likely to affect innocent people. Professional review cannot eliminate all risks, but it can provide context that an automated mechanism cannot.

The creator should be particularly careful about triggers based on subjective conditions. Phrases such as "if I am in danger," "if they try to silence me," or "if something suspicious happens" may express genuine intentions but are difficult for a machine to interpret consistently. Such language needs to be translated into observable conditions if automation is involved. Otherwise, the system depends upon someone later deciding what the original instruction meant. Ambiguity may be acceptable in a personal note, but it becomes dangerous when connected to irreversible technical action. Good design converts broad intentions into clear decision criteria.

At the same time, excessive precision can create its own problems. If the trigger requires an extraordinarily specific chain of events, the system may fail to activate under circumstances that were not anticipated. Real life is rarely as orderly as a flowchart. A person might experience an emergency that falls just outside the defined conditions. The architecture therefore needs both specificity and flexibility. Specificity reduces ambiguity, while flexibility allows authorized people to respond to unforeseen circumstances. This is another reason why staged systems are generally stronger than single-condition mechanisms.

The possibility of technical failure must remain in the model. Servers fail. Software contains bugs. APIs change. Accounts are locked. Encryption keys become inaccessible. Storage providers shut down services. Domain names expire. Operating systems change. Automated scripts stop running. A trigger that depends upon a fragile technological chain may fail precisely when it is needed. This means that the trigger itself should have redundancy and monitoring. A system cannot assume that because it was functioning last month, it will still be functioning when a crisis occurs years later.

The creator should therefore establish a means of detecting whether the trigger mechanism itself remains operational. This creates an important distinction between "nothing has happened" and "the system has not detected anything." Silence from a monitoring system is not necessarily evidence that everything is normal. The system might simply have stopped working. Health checks, independent monitoring, periodic testing, and documented recovery procedures can help address this problem. In technical terms, observability is part of reliability. A system that cannot tell whether its own critical components are functioning is difficult to trust.

There is a deeper philosophical problem hidden within all of this. The creator is attempting to encode a future decision while knowing that they cannot predict the future circumstances in which the decision will be applied. They are effectively writing instructions for a future version of themselves who may not be present. That requires humility. The creator should avoid assuming that their current understanding of a situation will remain correct forever. They should also avoid writing instructions that depend upon emotional conditions likely to change. A durable contingency system should capture enduring principles rather than temporary anger or fear.

This is particularly important when the information concerns allegations against other people. A person may genuinely believe that someone has committed wrongdoing, but the belief may later prove incomplete or mistaken. An automatic trigger that publishes accusations without review can cause permanent reputational damage. The archive should therefore preserve the underlying evidence and the creator's account while allowing independent evaluation. The system's purpose should be to prevent information from disappearing, not to guarantee the creator's interpretation. Preservation of evidence and judgment about evidence should remain separate functions.

The same caution applies to classified or restricted information. The existence of a contingency plan does not automatically override legal restrictions. A person may believe that public disclosure is morally justified, but the legal consequences can still be significant. Furthermore, indiscriminate publication can expose operational details, identities, or capabilities that have nothing to do with the underlying wrongdoing. A responsible architecture therefore needs a legal and ethical pathway between possession and publication. The trigger should not be designed as a mechanism for bypassing every institution or legal constraint. It should be designed to preserve the possibility of lawful and responsible action when ordinary channels fail.

Another important consideration is the creator's changing intentions. A person might establish a system at a time when they fear retaliation and later decide that disclosure is no longer appropriate. Perhaps the underlying issue has been resolved. Perhaps the information has been independently published. Perhaps new facts have changed the situation. Perhaps the person has decided that the consequences of disclosure would now outweigh the benefits. The system must therefore permit legitimate updates. Otherwise, yesterday's emergency instruction could become tomorrow's unintended catastrophe.

Periodic review is consequently not optional in a serious long-term system. The creator should revisit the trigger conditions, recipients, storage locations, authentication mechanisms, legal assumptions, and underlying evidence. The review should ask a deceptively simple question: if the system activated today, would I still want it to behave exactly as currently configured? If the answer is no, the architecture needs revision. A contingency plan is not a document written once and forgotten. It is a living system whose validity depends upon continued alignment with reality.

The ultimate objective is not to create a trigger that is infallible. No trigger can achieve that. The objective is to create a trigger that behaves rationally when information is incomplete. It should be conservative when consequences are irreversible, responsive when delay creates serious risk, and capable of escalating gradually as evidence accumulates.

It should distinguish signals from proof and preservation from publication. It should allow human judgment where machines cannot reliably interpret circumstances. Above all, it should fail in a controlled manner rather than turning uncertainty into catastrophe.

The dead man's switch therefore becomes something more sophisticated than a mechanism waiting for silence. It becomes an information decision system built around uncertainty, verification, redundancy, and consequence. Its strength does not come from making an aggressive assumption about what silence means. Its strength comes from refusing to make that assumption too quickly. The creator's real task is to design a pathway from uncertainty toward justified action. Once that pathway exists, the next question is how much of it should be automated and how much should remain under deliberate human control.

That question leads directly into the next stage of the architecture. Automation can make a system faster, more consistent, and less dependent upon human memory, but automation can also magnify errors at machine speed. Manual control provides judgment and flexibility, but humans forget, hesitate, become unavailable, and make mistakes. The central challenge is therefore not choosing between automatic and manual activation as if one must always replace the other. It is determining where automation should begin, where human judgment should intervene, and where irreversible decisions should require more than one layer of confirmation.

Resources

1. NIST Risk Management Framework — provides a structured approach to identifying, assessing, managing, and continuously monitoring security risks.

2. NIST Cybersecurity Framework 2.0[1] — useful for understanding identification, protection, detection, response, and recovery as interconnected elements of resilient system design.

3. NIST Special Publication 800-53, Security and Privacy Controls for Information Systems and Organizations[2] — relevant to contingency planning, access control, authentication, separation of duties, system integrity, auditability, and incident response.

4. NIST Special Publication 800-34, Contingency Planning Guide for Federal Information Systems[3] — foundational guidance on contingency planning, recovery, alternate processing, and information-system resilience.

5. NIST Special Publication 800-61, Computer Security Incident Handling Guide[4] — useful for understanding detection, analysis, response, escalation, and recovery following security incidents.

6. NIST Special Publication 800-207, Zero Trust Architecture[5] — relevant to continuous verification and the principle that trust should not be assumed merely because an entity previously authenticated.

7. NIST Digital Identity Guidelines[6] — authoritative guidance on identity proofing, authentication, authenticators, and digital identity assurance.

---

1. https://www.nist.gov/cyberframework?utm_source=chatgpt.com

2. https://csrc.nist.gov/publications/detail/sp/800-53/rev-5/final?utm_source=chatgpt.com

3. https://csrc.nist.gov/publications/detail/sp/800-34/rev-1/final?utm_source=chatgpt.com

4. https://csrc.nist.gov/publications/detail/sp/800-61/rev-2/final?utm_source=chatgpt.com

5. https://csrc.nist.gov/publications/detail/sp/800-207/final?utm_source=chatgpt.com

6. https://pages.nist.gov/800-63-4/?utm_source=chatgpt.com

8. NIST Recommendation for Key Management, SP 800-57 — relevant to cryptographic keys, authentication infrastructure, key protection, recovery, and lifecycle management.

9. Ross Anderson, *Security Engineering: A Guide to Building Dependable Distributed Systems*, 3rd ed., Wiley, 2020 — comprehensive treatment of dependable systems, threat modeling, failure modes, authentication, human factors, and security architecture.

10. Bruce Schneier, *Beyond Fear: Thinking Sensibly About Security in an Uncertain World*, Copernicus Books, 2003 — useful conceptual framework for evaluating security decisions according to threats, consequences, tradeoffs, and actual effectiveness.

11. Bruce Schneier, *Secrets and Lies: Digital Security in a Networked World*, Wiley, 2000 — important discussion of the interaction between technical systems, human behavior, authentication, and operational security.

12. Adi Shamir, "How to Share a Secret," *Communications of the ACM*, Vol. 22, No. 11, 1979 — foundational work on threshold-based information sharing and distributing critical secrets across multiple participants.

13. Barbara Liskov, "From Viewstamped Replication to Byzantine Fault Tolerance," in *Replication*, Springer, 2010 — relevant to thinking about distributed systems, failures, agreement, and the difficulty of maintaining reliable decisions when components cannot always be trusted.

14. Leslie Lamport, Robert Shostak, Marshall Pease, "The Byzantine Generals Problem," *ACM Transactions on Programming Languages and Systems*, Vol. 4, No. 3, 1982 — foundational work concerning distributed agreement in the presence of faulty or deceptive participants.

15. CISA — Cross-Sector Cybersecurity Performance Goals[7] — practical security guidance concerning resilient architecture, authentication, backups, logging, and recovery.

16. Electronic Frontier Foundation — Surveillance Self-Defense[8] — practical guidance on threat modeling, secure communications, authentication, device security, and protection of sensitive information.

17. National Archives — Digital Preservation — authoritative material concerning long-term preservation, integrity, accessibility, and management of digital records.

18. Daniel Kahneman, *Thinking, Fast and Slow*, Farrar, Straus and Giroux, 2011 — useful background concerning decision-making under uncertainty, cognitive bias, and the limits of intuitive judgment.

19. Paul Slovic, "Perception of Risk," *Science*, Vol. 236, No. 4799, 1987 — foundational research on perceived risk, uncertainty, and the psychological factors influencing decisions about danger.

20. Gerd Gigerenzer, *Risk Savvy: How to Make Good Decisions*, Viking, 2014 — relevant to practical decision-making under uncertainty and the difficulty of translating incomplete information into rational action.

21. Karl E. Weick, Kathleen M. Sutcliffe, *Managing the Unexpected: Sustained Performance in a Complex World*, 3rd ed., Wiley, 2015 — important organizational perspective on resilience, anomaly detection, uncertainty, and high-reliability systems.

---

7. https://www.cisa.gov/cross-sector-cybersecurity-performance-goals?utm_source=chatgpt.com

8. https://ssd.eff.org/?utm_source=chatgpt.com

22. ISO 22301 — Security and Resilience, Business Continuity Management Systems[9] — international framework for maintaining critical functions and preparing for disruptive events.

23. ISO/IEC 27001 — Information Security Management Systems[10] — international standard for systematic information-security risk management and organizational controls.

24. Committee to Protect Journalists — Safety Kit[11] — practical resources for threat assessment, journalist security, source protection, and contingency planning.

25. U.S. Department of Labor — Whistleblower Protection Program[12] — official resource illustrating the legal and practical context in which individuals may need to preserve information while facing retaliation or loss of ordinary institutional protection.

---

9. https://www.iso.org/standard/75106.html?utm_source=chatgpt.com

10. https://www.iso.org/isoiec-27001-information-security.html?utm_source=chatgpt.com

11. https://cpj.org/safety-kit/?utm_source=chatgpt.com

12. https://www.whistleblowers.gov/?utm_source=chatgpt.com

Automatic, Manual, and Conditional Activation

Once we have decided what circumstances might justify a dead man's switch, we encounter the next problem, which is deceptively simple but technically and ethically profound: who or what should decide when the switch activates? A human being can understand context, recognize unusual circumstances, and exercise judgment that no automated system can fully reproduce. A machine, however, does not forget, become frightened, hesitate, or change its mind under pressure, and it can monitor conditions continuously without fatigue. Neither approach is inherently superior because each fails in different ways. The real question is how much authority should be given to automation, how much should remain with people, and where conditional logic can provide a bridge between the two. The strongest systems are therefore not necessarily the most automated ones, but those that place each kind of decision in the environment where it is most reliable.

The simplest model is manual activation. In this arrangement, the person possessing the information decides that circumstances have become sufficiently serious and deliberately initiates the release process. This approach has an obvious advantage because the person knows the context better than any machine. They can evaluate whether a threat is genuine, whether the information is accurate, whether disclosure remains justified, and whether innocent people could be harmed. Human judgment also provides flexibility when circumstances do not fit the assumptions built into a technical system. Yet manual activation has a fundamental weakness: it assumes the person will remain alive, conscious, free, informed, and capable of acting at precisely the moment the mechanism is needed.

That assumption can fail in numerous ways without requiring anything sinister. An accident can leave someone unconscious. A medical emergency can prevent communication. A natural disaster can destroy communications infrastructure. A person can lose access to their devices or accounts. They can become trapped somewhere without connectivity or simply be unable to remember the procedure they established months or years earlier. If the entire contingency system depends upon a conscious decision at the critical moment, then the system may disappear with the person's ability to make that decision. Manual control therefore offers excellent contextual judgment but poor protection against sudden loss of agency.

There is another weakness that is more psychological than technical: hesitation. Someone who believes they are in danger may repeatedly postpone activation because disclosure has serious consequences. They may worry about family members, colleagues, reputations, legal exposure, or the possibility that they have misunderstood what is happening. This hesitation is entirely human and sometimes beneficial because it prevents reckless decisions. But it can also defeat the purpose of a contingency mechanism. A person can spend years preparing information and then fail to release it because the moment of decision becomes emotionally overwhelming. Manual systems therefore place considerable weight on human courage at exactly the point when fear may be greatest.

Automatic activation attempts to solve this problem by transferring the decision from the individual to a predefined mechanism. The creator establishes conditions in advance, and the system responds when those conditions are met. The classic example is a scheduled confirmation. The person must periodically demonstrate that they remain available. If the expected confirmation does not occur, the system begins its predefined process. Automation removes the need for a final decision during a crisis. The system can continue operating even when the creator cannot. This is the defining attraction of the automated model.

Automation also provides consistency. A machine does not decide that Tuesday's missed check-in is serious while Wednesday's is not because it feels differently. If the same conditions are present, the same rules can be applied.

Automation can monitor clocks, schedules, account states, and other measurable conditions continuously. It can also initiate notifications without waiting for a person to remember. In situations where delay could result in permanent loss of information, this persistence can be extremely valuable. The machine effectively becomes a custodian of an instruction made while the creator was still capable of thinking clearly.

Yet automation introduces a different class of danger: it can execute a wrong decision perfectly. A machine may faithfully follow instructions while having no understanding of whether those instructions remain appropriate. If a person misses a check-in because they are travelling, the system does not know that they are travelling unless the architecture provides some way to establish it. If a server fails, the system may interpret the absence of a confirmation as evidence that the person is unavailable. If an account is compromised, an attacker may manipulate the signals upon which the automated decision depends. Automation therefore eliminates certain human errors while introducing machine-mediated errors.

This is why the phrase "set and forget" should be treated with suspicion. A dead man's switch that was reliable when created may become unreliable as technology changes. Email services modify authentication requirements. Cloud providers change APIs. Software dependencies become obsolete. Devices fail. Passwords expire. Cryptographic systems evolve. The creator's circumstances also change. A recipient who was trusted five years ago may no longer be appropriate. Information that once seemed safe to disclose may become legally or ethically problematic. An automated system that is never reviewed can eventually execute yesterday's instructions in tomorrow's circumstances.

Scheduled confirmation is a particularly interesting middle ground because it does not require the system to determine whether an emergency has occurred. It merely asks whether the creator has demonstrated continued availability. This reduces the amount of interpretation required from the machine. The system does not need to know whether someone has died, disappeared, or been imprisoned. It only needs to know that an expected confirmation did not arrive. The missing confirmation then becomes a signal that something may have changed. The architecture can subsequently move into a verification phase rather than immediately releasing information.

The frequency of confirmation changes the character of the system. Very frequent confirmations can provide strong evidence of current availability but increase inconvenience and the likelihood of accidental failure. Less frequent confirmations reduce the burden on the creator but increase the period during which an emergency can go undetected. There is no universally optimal schedule. The appropriate interval depends upon the consequences of delayed activation, the likelihood of ordinary communication failures, and the nature of the information being protected. A system protecting long-term historical documents might tolerate a much longer interval than one protecting evidence that could disappear within days.

The system can also use grace periods. A missed confirmation does not necessarily produce an immediate escalation. Instead, the system can provide an opportunity for the creator to correct the missed event. This might involve additional reminders or a secondary confirmation method. The important principle is that the first failure should usually be treated as evidence of uncertainty rather than proof of catastrophe. Grace periods reduce false positives. They also make the system more compatible with ordinary human life, where missed appointments and interrupted communications are inevitable.

Conditional activation goes further by allowing multiple conditions to interact. Rather than saying, "If there is no response for seven days, release the archive," the architecture can establish several states and requirements. A missed confirmation might initiate a warning. Repeated missed confirmations could initiate verification. Independent evidence of an emergency could increase the system's confidence. A designated custodian might then be authorized to review the situation. Only after additional conditions are satisfied would the system move toward disclosure. Conditional logic transforms the switch from a timer into a decision process.

This approach resembles fault-tolerant engineering because it recognizes that individual signals can fail. In a resilient system, one component failing should not automatically produce the most severe outcome. Several indicators can instead be evaluated together. If a scheduled confirmation fails but the creator's other authenticated activity remains normal, the system might remain in a warning state. If the confirmation fails and several independent channels also become unavailable, concern may increase. If a trusted intermediary independently confirms a serious event, the system may move to a higher state. The exact implementation can vary, but the underlying principle is that confidence should accumulate rather than being determined by one ambiguous signal.

Conditional systems also make it possible to distinguish between different kinds of action. Not every trigger needs to release the same information. A low-confidence event might preserve the archive and alert a custodian. A medium-confidence event might permit restricted access to selected documents. A high-confidence event might authorize broader disclosure subject to legal and professional review. This is more sophisticated than the traditional image of a switch that simply "goes off." The system becomes a controlled progression. Each stage corresponds to a different level of confidence and consequence.

The idea of consequence is crucial because not all errors are equally damaging. If a system sends a harmless reminder to the creator because of a missed check-in, the cost of a false positive may be negligible. If it sends a notification to a trusted intermediary, the cost may be somewhat greater. If it publishes allegations, confidential identities, or sensitive evidence worldwide, the cost can be enormous and potentially irreversible. The stronger the consequence, the stronger the activation requirements should generally be. This principle provides a rational basis for layered activation. It connects the strength of the evidence to the seriousness of the action.

Manual systems can also benefit from conditional logic. Human activation does not have to mean pressing a single button labelled "release everything." A creator can establish a set of predefined decisions that reduce the burden of improvisation. They might decide that certain information should be preserved regardless of circumstances while other information should be disclosed only after independent review. They might establish different recipients for different categories of evidence. They might define conditions under which the system should remain dormant. By making these decisions in advance, the creator preserves human judgment while reducing the amount of judgment required during a crisis.

This produces a useful distinction between decision-making and decision execution. The human can decide in advance what should happen under specified circumstances. The machine can then execute that decision when the conditions are met. This is one of the most powerful roles for automation. Instead of asking a machine to interpret a complex human situation, the creator asks the machine to reliably execute a clearly defined instruction. The machine handles repetition and timing. The human establishes purpose, boundaries, and exceptions. This division of responsibility can be much more robust than asking either humans or machines to do everything.

There is also a fourth possibility: human-in-the-loop activation. Under this model, automation detects a condition but does not complete the final action without human confirmation. The system might recognize that a creator has missed several confirmations and automatically notify designated custodians. Those custodians then investigate and decide whether the next stage should occur. This approach sacrifices some speed in exchange for judgment. It is particularly attractive when false disclosure would be more damaging than delayed disclosure. The challenge is ensuring that the human reviewers themselves remain available and trustworthy.

Human-in-the-loop systems also introduce their own failure modes. A custodian may ignore the notification. They may misunderstand the instructions. They may be unavailable at the critical moment. They may disagree with other custodians. They may be compromised or coerced. They may have a conflict of interest. The architecture must therefore consider what happens if the human layer fails. One answer is multiple custodians. Another is a secondary automated escalation. Another is a professional intermediary who assumes responsibility after a defined period. Again, the goal is not to eliminate every possible failure but to prevent one failure from ending the entire process.

Multiple custodians raise the question of consensus. Must everyone agree before an action occurs, or is one authorized person sufficient? Requiring unanimous agreement provides strong resistance to unilateral error but can make the system fragile because one unavailable person can block the process. Requiring only one person's approval increases responsiveness but creates greater dependence on that individual. Threshold arrangements provide a middle ground. A predefined number of authorized participants can be required to approve a significant action without requiring everyone to participate. This general principle has deep roots in distributed systems and cryptographic secret-sharing research.

Threshold approaches are particularly useful when the consequences of activation are substantial. Instead of giving one person complete authority over an archive, the creator can distribute responsibility among several independent custodians. The system can require a predetermined subset of those custodians to agree before sensitive material becomes accessible. This does not guarantee safety, because the custodians can still collude or make mistakes. But it reduces the probability that one compromised individual can unilaterally activate the final stage. It also provides resilience if one participant becomes unavailable.

The distinction between independence and redundancy remains important here. If all custodians are close associates who share the same interests, employer, physical location, and communication infrastructure, multiple approvals may provide less protection than expected. A resilient design considers correlated failure. If one event can compromise every custodian simultaneously, the system remains vulnerable despite the apparent number of participants. Independence can involve different institutions, locations, communication channels, or professional roles. The objective is to make it difficult for one event to control every decision path.

A conditional system can also include negative conditions, which are sometimes overlooked. Most trigger designs ask what must happen for activation to occur. A stronger architecture also asks what conditions should prevent activation. For example, the existence of a valid cancellation signal might halt an escalation. A confirmed voluntary absence might suspend the timer. A legal injunction or professional review might temporarily prevent publication. A newly discovered problem with the evidence might require additional evaluation. Negative conditions create brakes within the system. They are essential because a safe mechanism needs not only an accelerator but also a means of stopping before an irreversible action.

This is particularly important when dealing with technical failure. Suppose a scheduled confirmation system depends upon a particular online service. If that service stops operating, the absence of confirmation might look exactly like the absence of the creator. Without an independent system-health signal, the architecture cannot distinguish "the person did not check in" from "the mechanism could not receive the check-in." A robust design therefore monitors itself. It should have some way of determining whether its own critical components remain operational. Otherwise, silence from the system may be mistaken for silence from the human.

Testing is another essential part of activation design. A mechanism that has never been tested is a hypothesis, not a dependable system. Testing should examine ordinary scenarios, missed confirmations, communication outages, account failures, changes in schedules, replacement of devices, and recovery from partial failures. It should also test whether the people involved understand what their notifications mean. A technically functioning trigger can still fail operationally if the recipient does not know what to do. Testing therefore needs to include both technical and human components. The objective is to discover failures while they are still reversible.

Testing also provides an opportunity to measure false activation. A system can appear impressive on paper while producing frequent warnings in practice. Every false warning consumes attention and may eventually create complacency. If recipients receive repeated alerts that turn out to be harmless, they may begin ignoring future alerts. This is a classic problem in alarm systems. The value of an alarm depends partly upon whether people trust that it represents something meaningful. A dead man's switch should therefore be designed to minimize unnecessary alerts without sacrificing appropriate sensitivity.

The architecture should also distinguish between detection and disclosure channels. An automated system may use one channel to determine whether the creator is active and another to deliver notifications. The archive itself may be stored separately from both. This separation can reduce the consequences of compromise. If an attacker gains access to the notification mechanism, they should not automatically gain access to the underlying evidence. If a storage system fails, the detection mechanism should not necessarily fail with it. Independent components create opportunities for cross-checking. They also make the overall architecture more complicated, which means documentation becomes increasingly important.

One of the most tempting approaches is to make the system extremely sophisticated. Designers can imagine combining biometric authentication, geographic data, artificial intelligence, blockchain records, encrypted messaging, multiple cloud providers, physical storage, and automated decision engines. Such complexity can appear to provide extraordinary protection. But every additional component introduces dependencies and potential failure modes. A system with twenty moving parts has twenty opportunities for incompatibility, misconfiguration, or failure. Complexity is therefore not synonymous with resilience. Sometimes the strongest architecture is the one that uses the fewest components necessary to achieve the required protection.

This leads to an important engineering principle: simplicity should be measured by behavior, not by the number of technologies involved. A system may use several technologies while still presenting a simple operational process. Conversely, a single application may conceal extraordinary complexity beneath its interface. The creator should understand what happens from beginning to end. What generates the signal? How is the signal authenticated? What happens if it is missing? Who receives the notification? What can they access? What prevents accidental release? What happens if the service fails? What happens if the creator returns? If these questions cannot be answered clearly, the system is not yet mature.

The possibility of malicious manipulation must also be considered. Someone who knows a dead man's switch exists may attempt to force activation or prevent activation. They might interfere with communication channels, compromise credentials, impersonate the creator, or attempt to persuade a custodian that an emergency has occurred. The architecture therefore needs to protect both the trigger and the information about the trigger. Secrecy surrounding the existence of a system may sometimes provide an additional layer of protection, but secrecy should not be treated as a substitute for security. A mechanism that fails completely when discovered is inherently fragile.

There is also a subtle danger in making activation too dependent upon artificial intelligence. AI systems can analyze patterns and identify anomalies at a scale that humans cannot easily match. They can potentially evaluate communication patterns, system states, and other signals. But anomaly detection is not the same as understanding. An AI system may identify behavior that statistically differs from a person's normal routine without knowing whether the difference represents danger, travel, personal choice, or ordinary life. False confidence can be especially dangerous when AI output is treated as an authoritative decision rather than one source of evidence. AI can assist with detection and prioritization, but consequential decisions should remain subject to appropriate controls.

The same caution applies to predictive systems. A system that attempts to predict whether someone is in danger based upon behavioral patterns may appear more advanced than a simple timer. Yet prediction introduces assumptions about normal behavior. It can also create opaque decisions that are difficult for recipients to understand or challenge. If the system activates because an algorithm has assigned a high probability to danger, someone should still be able to determine what evidence produced that assessment. Explainability becomes especially important when the consequence is irreversible disclosure. The more powerful the automated decision, the more important it becomes to understand its limitations.

Manual, automatic, and conditional activation can therefore be viewed as three points on a continuum rather than mutually exclusive alternatives. Manual activation maximizes human context but depends upon human availability. Automatic activation maximizes persistence and consistency but risks acting on incomplete information. Conditional activation combines signals and stages to manage uncertainty, while human-in-the-loop designs add judgment where automated interpretation becomes unreliable. A mature architecture may use all three. Automation can monitor, conditional logic can escalate, and humans can authorize consequential actions. The system becomes a partnership between machine reliability and human judgment rather than a contest between them.

The final design should also reflect the information's sensitivity. For relatively harmless material, automation can reasonably be more aggressive. For highly sensitive evidence, the activation threshold should be much higher. If the information could identify vulnerable people, reveal confidential sources, expose private records, or create serious legal consequences, additional verification is warranted. If the material is already public or poses little risk, a simpler trigger may be sufficient. The architecture should therefore be proportional to consequence. There is little value in building a highly elaborate system for information that does not require extraordinary protection.

Ultimately, the question is not whether the switch should be automatic or manual. The more useful question is which decisions should be automatic and which should remain human. Machines are well suited to repetitive monitoring, time measurement, notification, integrity checks, and other deterministic tasks. Humans are better suited to interpreting context, weighing competing interests, evaluating ambiguous evidence, and considering ethical consequences. Conditional logic can connect the two by determining when a situation has become sufficiently unusual to require escalation. This division of labor recognizes the strengths of each without pretending that either is infallible.

A well-designed dead man's switch should therefore behave less like a trapdoor and more like a carefully engineered emergency procedure. It should notice when something changes, allow time for correction, seek additional evidence, escalate when appropriate, and preserve opportunities for human review. It should be capable of continuing when the creator cannot act but should not interpret every interruption as proof of catastrophe. It should protect information before deciding to publish it. Most importantly, it should be designed around the consequences of being wrong, because the true measure of a trigger is not how dramatically it activates but how responsibly it behaves when the available information is incomplete.

The next challenge is time itself. Every activation philosophy requires some temporal framework, whether it is a daily confirmation, a weekly check-in, a fixed period of silence, a conditional deadline, or a series of escalating intervals. Too little time can produce false activation, while too much time can render the system ineffective. The timing mechanism must also account for travel, technical outages, changing routines, and the possibility that an emergency unfolds gradually rather than at a precise moment. The following chapter therefore examines one of the most deceptively important design decisions in the entire architecture: how often should a person have to say, in one form or another, "I am still here"?

Resources

1. NIST Risk Management Framework — foundational framework for identifying threats, evaluating risk, selecting controls, and continuously monitoring whether those controls remain effective.

2. NIST Cybersecurity Framework 2.0[1] — useful framework for understanding cybersecurity through governance, identification, protection, detection, response, and recovery.

3. NIST Special Publication 800-53 — Security and Privacy Controls[2] — particularly relevant to contingency planning, access control, authentication, separation of duties, system integrity, auditability, and incident response.

4. NIST Special Publication 800-34 — Contingency Planning Guide for Federal Information Systems[3] — provides foundational guidance for contingency planning, recovery, alternate procedures, and information-system resilience.

5. NIST Special Publication 800-61 — Computer Security Incident Handling Guide[4] — relevant to detection, analysis, escalation, response, and recovery when abnormal conditions occur.

6. NIST Special Publication 800-207 — Zero Trust Architecture[5] — relevant to continuous verification and avoiding assumptions based solely upon previous authentication or trusted status.

7. NIST Digital Identity Guidelines[6] — provides authoritative guidance concerning authentication, identity assurance, authenticators, and digital identity risks.

8. NIST Recommendation for Key Management, SP 800-57 — relevant to authentication keys, cryptographic credentials, lifecycle management, protection, backup, and recovery.

9. Adi Shamir, "How to Share a Secret," *Communications of the ACM*, Vol. 22, No. 11, 1979 — foundational research underlying threshold secret-sharing approaches in which multiple participants can collectively control access without any single participant possessing the complete secret.

10. Leslie Lamport, Robert Shostak, Marshall Pease, "The Byzantine Generals Problem," *ACM Transactions on Programming Languages and Systems*, Vol. 4, No. 3, 1982 — foundational work concerning agreement and reliability when components in a distributed system may fail or behave dishonestly.

---

1. https://www.nist.gov/cyberframework?utm_source=chatgpt.com

2. https://csrc.nist.gov/publications/detail/sp/800-53/rev-5/final?utm_source=chatgpt.com

3. https://csrc.nist.gov/publications/detail/sp/800-34/rev-1/final?utm_source=chatgpt.com

4. https://csrc.nist.gov/publications/detail/sp/800-61/rev-2/final?utm_source=chatgpt.com

5. https://csrc.nist.gov/publications/detail/sp/800-207/final?utm_source=chatgpt.com

6. https://pages.nist.gov/800-63-4/?utm_source=chatgpt.com

11. Barbara Liskov, "From Viewstamped Replication to Byzantine Fault Tolerance," in *Replication*, Springer, 2010 — useful background for distributed agreement, fault tolerance, and resilient system architecture.

12. Ross Anderson, *Security Engineering: A Guide to Building Dependable Distributed Systems*, 3rd ed., Wiley, 2020 — comprehensive treatment of dependable systems, threat modeling, authentication, human factors, security architecture, and failure modes.

13. Bruce Schneier, *Beyond Fear: Thinking Sensibly About Security in an Uncertain World*, Copernicus Books, 2003 — useful for understanding security tradeoffs, threat assessment, incentives, and the distinction between perceived and actual security.

14. Bruce Schneier, *Secrets and Lies: Digital Security in a Networked World*, Wiley, 2000 — important discussion of security as a system involving technology, people, procedures, authentication, and operational assumptions.

15. CISA — Cross-Sector Cybersecurity Performance Goals[7] — practical guidance on resilient security architecture, authentication, backups, monitoring, and recovery.

16. Electronic Frontier Foundation — Surveillance Self-Defense[8] — practical resources on threat modeling, secure communications, authentication, device security, and protection of sensitive information.

17. Karl E. Weick and Kathleen M. Sutcliffe, *Managing the Unexpected: Sustained Performance in a Complex World*, 3rd ed., Wiley, 2015 — relevant to high-reliability organizations, anomaly detection, resilience, and managing unexpected events.

18. Daniel Kahneman, *Thinking, Fast and Slow*, Farrar, Straus and Giroux, 2011 — useful background on human judgment, cognitive bias, uncertainty, and decision-making under pressure.

19. Paul Slovic, "Perception of Risk," *Science*, Vol. 236, No. 4799, 1987 — influential research concerning how people perceive, evaluate, and respond to risk and uncertainty.

20. Gerd Gigerenzer, *Risk Savvy: How to Make Good Decisions*, Viking, 2014 — useful for understanding practical decision-making when information is incomplete and probabilities are uncertain.

21. National Archives — Digital Preservation — relevant to maintaining reliable, accessible, and authentic digital information over time.

22. ISO 22301 — Business Continuity Management Systems[9] — international framework for preparing organizations and systems to continue functioning during disruptive events.

23. ISO/IEC 27001 — Information Security Management Systems[10] — international standard for systematic information-security risk management and security controls.

24. Committee to Protect Journalists — Safety Kit[11] — practical resources relevant to threat assessment, source protection, secure communications, and contingency planning.

---

7. https://www.cisa.gov/cross-sector-cybersecurity-performance-goals?utm_source=chatgpt.com

8. https://ssd.eff.org/?utm_source=chatgpt.com

9. https://www.iso.org/standard/75106.html?utm_source=chatgpt.com

10. https://www.iso.org/isoiec-27001-information-security.html?utm_source=chatgpt.com

11. https://cpj.org/safety-kit/?utm_source=chatgpt.com

25. U.S. Department of Labor — Whistleblower Protection Program[12] — official context concerning protected disclosures and retaliation risks faced by individuals reporting wrongdoing.

12. https://www.whistleblowers.gov/?utm_source=chatgpt.com

Time, Redundancy, and the Architecture of Failure

The most dangerous assumption anyone can make about a dead man's switch is that the system will work exactly as designed when the moment of crisis finally arrives. That assumption is understandable because every contingency plan begins with an imagined sequence of events in which one thing follows another predictably. The person fails to check in, the system notices, a warning is issued, a verification period begins, and eventually the information is released according to instructions established in advance. Real life rarely behaves so neatly. Communications disappear, devices break, people become unavailable, passwords are forgotten, organizations change, services shut down, and circumstances develop in ways nobody anticipated when the original plan was created. A serious dead man's switch therefore has to be designed not only for the emergency it is intended to address, but also for the possibility that the mechanism itself will fail at exactly the wrong time.

This is the central idea behind resilience engineering. A resilient system does not assume that its components will remain perfect; it assumes that some components will eventually fail and asks what happens next. That distinction changes the entire philosophy of contingency planning. Instead of asking whether a particular mechanism is reliable, we ask how the overall system behaves when that mechanism becomes unreliable. Instead of assuming that a person will always be available, we establish alternatives. Instead of assuming that a server will remain online, we consider independent storage. Instead of assuming that a scheduled check-in will always arrive, we create grace periods and secondary signals. The objective is not perfection but controlled degradation, meaning that the system should lose capability gradually rather than collapsing completely after its first failure.

Time is the first component of this architecture because nearly every dead man's switch contains some temporal assumption. Someone must check in every day, every week, every month, or according to some other predetermined schedule. The system must decide how long to wait after a missed confirmation. It may then need to wait again before escalating. Eventually, it may reach a point at which the absence of communication is considered sufficiently significant to justify further action. Time therefore acts as both a detector and a filter. It allows the system to distinguish an isolated interruption from a sustained absence. But time can also become a source of failure when its intervals are chosen without considering the realities of human behavior.

A daily check-in illustrates the problem clearly. A daily confirmation creates frequent evidence that the person remains available, which can be valuable when circumstances are changing rapidly. Yet it also creates 365 opportunities every year for an ordinary mistake to occur. The person may forget once, become distracted, travel somewhere without connectivity, or simply decide to sleep through the reminder. If every missed confirmation immediately produces escalation, the system will generate unnecessary alarms. If the system responds too aggressively to ordinary interruptions, people may eventually stop trusting it. A useful system therefore has to balance sensitivity against tolerance for normal human error.

A weekly schedule produces a different balance. There are fewer opportunities for accidental failure, but a genuine emergency may remain undetected for longer. A monthly schedule reduces administrative burden still further but creates an even larger period of uncertainty. None of these intervals is universally correct. The appropriate interval depends upon what the system is protecting, how quickly the information could become unavailable, how serious the consequences of premature disclosure would be, and how reliable the communication environment is. Time must therefore be treated as a risk-management variable rather than a convenient number selected at random.

The idea of a grace period provides one of the simplest ways to reduce false activation. A missed check-in does not immediately cause the final action. Instead, it begins a temporary state in which the creator has an opportunity to re-establish contact. The system might issue reminders or initiate an alternative verification process. If the person returns during this period, the event can be closed without further consequences. This creates an important buffer between detection and irreversible action. The buffer acknowledges that silence is ambiguous and gives ordinary life a chance to explain it.

Grace periods can also be graduated. The first missed confirmation might produce a private reminder. A second could produce a stronger warning. A prolonged absence might notify a designated custodian. Only after additional conditions are satisfied would the system move toward release. This resembles the escalation procedures used in many safety-critical environments, where an initial anomaly does not immediately produce the most serious response. The system gathers information as the situation develops. Each escalation corresponds to increasing confidence that something significant has happened.

The length of a grace period should also reflect the consequences of delay. If the information is historical and unlikely to disappear, there may be little reason to respond quickly. If the information concerns an unfolding event, delay might matter considerably more. Yet urgency should not automatically eliminate safeguards. Rapid disclosure of incorrect or incomplete information can create damage that cannot later be repaired. The designer must therefore consider two competing forms of risk: the risk that waiting will allow something valuable to be lost and the risk that acting too quickly will cause unnecessary harm. The correct timing lies somewhere between those two dangers.

This is where the concept of a risk window becomes useful. Every contingency system operates within a period during which action remains meaningful. Before that window, activation may be unnecessary. After it, activation may be too late. The purpose of timing is to maximize the probability that the system responds during the meaningful portion of that window. This requires understanding the information itself. Evidence that exists only temporarily may require faster preservation. Information that can remain securely stored for decades may justify slower verification. Timing should therefore be designed around the lifespan and consequence of the information, not merely around the convenience of the person operating the system.

Redundancy addresses a different but related problem. Time protects against uncertainty about human availability, while redundancy protects against uncertainty about system components. If one storage device fails, another may preserve the information. If one communication channel disappears, another can carry the notification. If one custodian becomes unavailable, another may remain capable of acting. If one service provider shuts down, an independent copy may survive elsewhere. Redundancy therefore creates alternatives. But redundancy is valuable only when those alternatives are genuinely independent.

This distinction is frequently misunderstood. Copying the same file five times onto five devices located in the same room may look redundant, but a fire, flood, theft, or other physical event can destroy all five simultaneously. Likewise, storing five backups with the same cloud provider may not provide meaningful independence if one account is compromised or the provider experiences a systemic failure. True redundancy requires consideration of correlated failure. The question is not simply how many copies exist, but whether one event could destroy them all. A smaller number of genuinely independent copies can be more resilient than a large number of superficially different copies.

Geographic separation is one obvious form of independence. Information stored in different physical locations is less vulnerable to a single local disaster. Organizational separation can provide another layer. Two independent service providers may fail differently. Human separation can matter as well. If all custodians belong to the same household, organization, or social circle, they may share the same vulnerabilities. Independent custodians can reduce the likelihood that one event eliminates every decision-maker simultaneously. Redundancy is therefore as much about independence as it is about duplication.

The same principle applies to communication. A dead man's switch that depends entirely upon one email account contains a single point of failure. If the account is locked, compromised, discontinued, or inaccessible, the system may become silent. Adding another communication channel can reduce that risk. But the additional channel should not simply replicate the same dependency. If both channels depend upon the same device, password, or network, they may fail together. Communication redundancy should therefore be evaluated across the entire chain from sender to recipient.

There is also a danger in excessive redundancy. Every additional component creates another credential to manage, another system to maintain, and another potential point of misconfiguration. More backups can create more confusion about which version is authoritative. More custodians can create disagreements. More communication channels can produce inconsistent instructions. More software can create more dependencies. Redundancy therefore has diminishing returns when it becomes uncontrolled complexity. The objective is not to create as many alternatives as possible but to create enough independent alternatives to survive credible failure scenarios.

Independent custodians deserve particular attention because people can be both the strongest and weakest components of a contingency system. A trusted person can interpret circumstances, recognize nuance, communicate with professionals, and intervene when technology behaves unexpectedly. Yet people also become unavailable, make mistakes, change relationships, face conflicts of interest, or become subject to pressure. A system relying on one human custodian therefore contains a significant single point of failure. Multiple custodians can provide resilience, especially when they have clearly defined responsibilities. But the more people who are involved, the more important governance and communication become.

One solution is to give different custodians different roles. One person might hold knowledge about the existence of the archive. Another might control access credentials. Another might have authority to contact a professional intermediary. Another might possess instructions concerning the creator's wishes. This separation can prevent any single person from controlling everything. It can also reduce the consequences if one custodian becomes compromised. The principle is similar to separation of duties in information security. Critical authority is divided so that one compromised component does not automatically control the entire system.

Another approach is threshold authorization. Instead of requiring one particular individual to act, the system can require a predefined number of authorized participants. This creates resilience against individual absence. If one person cannot respond, others can still proceed. At the same time, no single custodian necessarily has unilateral authority. Threshold arrangements can be especially useful for highly consequential actions. Their effectiveness depends on careful selection of participants and secure management of whatever credentials or information they require. The underlying principle is straightforward: critical decisions should not depend upon one fragile human link when multiple independent links are available.

The architecture of failure should also consider the failure of the creator's own assumptions. When people construct contingency plans, they naturally imagine the threats they already understand. They may think about death because that is the traditional meaning of a dead man's switch. They may think about disappearance because it is easier to imagine than prolonged incapacitation. They may think about hacking because digital security is familiar. But the system may actually fail because of something mundane. A forgotten password, an expired credit card, a discontinued phone number, an unmaintained domain, or an obsolete application can destroy a sophisticated plan. The boring failures deserve as much attention as the dramatic ones.

This is why lifecycle management is essential. A contingency system created today may be expected to operate for years. During that period, almost every component surrounding it can change. Software is updated. Security standards evolve. Cloud services merge or disappear. People change jobs and addresses. Legal circumstances develop. Relationships change. Encryption algorithms become obsolete. Devices are replaced. A system that does not have a maintenance process will eventually become less reliable even if nothing actively attacks it. Long-term protection requires periodic review as well as initial construction.

Testing should therefore be treated as part of the system rather than as an optional exercise. A backup that has never been restored is not equivalent to a verified backup. A contact who has never been asked to perform their role may not understand what is expected. A notification system that has never been tested may fail silently. A recovery procedure that exists only in the creator's memory is vulnerable to the very event the system was designed to survive. Testing turns assumptions into evidence. It reveals weaknesses while they can still be corrected.

Testing should also include failure injection. In engineering and information security, systems can be evaluated by deliberately simulating failures and observing how they respond. The purpose is not to cause permanent damage but to discover hidden dependencies. What happens if the primary communication account becomes inaccessible? What happens if the creator misses a scheduled confirmation? What happens if a custodian does not respond? What happens if one storage location disappears? What happens if the person returns after an escalation has begun? Each scenario can reveal a different weakness. The system becomes stronger when its designers learn how it behaves outside normal conditions.

A particularly important test concerns recovery after a false alarm. Suppose the system enters an escalation state and then the creator becomes available again. Can the process be stopped cleanly? Can temporary notifications be withdrawn where possible? Can access permissions be restored? Can the system return to normal operation without leaving confusing residual states? Recovery matters because a contingency system must handle not only the emergency but also the possibility that the emergency was misunderstood. A system without recovery logic is effectively assuming that every activation will be correct. That is an unreasonable assumption.

Another important failure mode is credential loss. Digital systems often depend upon passwords, encryption keys, authentication devices, recovery codes, or other credentials. If the creator becomes unavailable and nobody else can access the relevant information, the archive may be perfectly preserved yet practically useless. This creates a paradox in information security: protecting information too effectively can make it inaccessible to the people who are supposed to receive it. The solution is not necessarily weaker security. It is deliberate planning for authorized recovery. Access continuity must be considered alongside confidentiality.

There is an equivalent human problem. A person may carefully distribute information among trusted custodians but fail to explain what each person is supposed to do. One custodian may believe their role is simply to preserve the material. Another may believe they are authorized to publish it. A third may assume someone else is responsible. The result can be paralysis at the moment action is required. Clear role definitions are therefore as important as technical controls. A resilient system depends upon both information architecture and organizational architecture.

The system should also distinguish between preservation redundancy and activation redundancy. These are not the same thing. Having multiple copies of an archive does not guarantee that anyone will know when to access them. Conversely, having multiple people aware of an activation condition does not guarantee that the underlying evidence remains available. The archive and the trigger represent different dependencies. Each requires its own redundancy. Ideally, the failure of one should not automatically destroy the other.

This distinction becomes particularly important when considering cloud storage. Cloud systems can provide geographic distribution, automated replication, versioning, and convenient access. They can also create dependencies on providers, authentication systems, Internet connectivity, and account recovery mechanisms. A cloud archive should therefore not automatically be regarded as a permanent vault. Long-term preservation requires consideration of provider continuity, data export, account access, encryption, integrity verification, and independent copies. The cloud can be one component of a resilient system, but it should rarely be treated as the entire system.

Offline storage presents the opposite tradeoff. Physical media can remain disconnected from online attacks and may provide an important independent copy. Yet physical media can degrade, become obsolete, be lost, or become unreadable because the necessary hardware disappears. A storage device sitting untouched for ten years is not necessarily a healthy archive. The information must remain retrievable. This means preservation includes both the data and the ability to interpret and access it. Long-term storage is therefore a process rather than simply a location.

The same principle applies to encryption. Encryption can protect sensitive information from unauthorized access, but the system must preserve the ability to decrypt it when the appropriate conditions arise. If the encryption key disappears with the creator, the contingency plan may become an elaborate mechanism protecting an inaccessible archive. Key management therefore belongs inside the failure architecture. The system must consider not only who should not be able to access the information, but also how authorized access will remain possible after the creator is unavailable.

A resilient system should also assume that some failures will happen simultaneously. A natural disaster could eliminate a person's physical access to devices while disrupting local communications. A targeted attack could compromise both an account and the device associated with it. A corporate failure could affect storage, authentication, and billing simultaneously. A legal event could affect the creator and the person who was supposed to act on their behalf. Thinking only about isolated failures can therefore produce a false sense of security. The strongest architectures examine combinations of failures and ask whether the system still has at least one viable path forward.

This is the logic behind defense in depth. No single security control should be expected to stop every threat. Instead, several layers should provide overlapping protection. If one layer fails, another remains. In a dead man's switch, those layers might involve time-based monitoring, multiple communication channels, independent custodians, separate storage locations, authentication controls, professional review, and recovery procedures. Each layer addresses a different failure mode. The architecture becomes resilient not because any one component is perfect, but because the components do not all fail in the same way at the same time.

Yet defense in depth should not become an excuse for unnecessary complication. Every layer needs a purpose. A sophisticated system that nobody understands may be less reliable than a simpler system that has been thoroughly tested. The creator should be able to explain the entire chain of custody from the original information to the final authorized recipient. They should know what happens when everything works and what happens when individual components fail. They should also know which components are essential and which are merely supplementary. Clarity is itself a form of resilience.

There is another dimension to redundancy that concerns evidence integrity. Multiple copies are useful only if they remain identical or their differences can be explained. If one archive contains an altered document and another contains the original, recipients need a way to determine which version is authentic. Cryptographic hashes, digital signatures, timestamps, and documented chain-of-custody procedures can help establish whether files have changed. The technical mechanism is less important than the principle. Preservation means maintaining not merely availability but confidence that the preserved material has not been silently altered.

This is especially important when the information may eventually be examined by journalists, investigators, lawyers, regulators, courts, or historians. A collection of files without provenance can be difficult to evaluate. Who created the document? When was it created? Has it been modified? How was it obtained? Who had access to it? Were copies made? Were the original files preserved? These questions can determine whether evidence is taken seriously. A dead man's switch should therefore protect context as well as content. Information without provenance can lose much of its evidentiary value.

The architecture should also anticipate the possibility that the information itself becomes obsolete. Perhaps the issue that motivated the contingency plan is resolved. Perhaps the alleged wrongdoing is independently documented. Perhaps new evidence contradicts an earlier conclusion. Perhaps the identities of people involved change. A system that automatically releases everything after a fixed period can become disconnected from reality. Periodic review can prevent this. The creator may need to update the archive, revise recipients, or cancel particular disclosures while retaining other preservation instructions.

Cancellation is consequently part of resilience. A system designed only to activate but not to deactivate is incomplete. The creator should have a clear method for withdrawing or modifying instructions while they remain capable of doing so. This method should itself be protected against unauthorized interference. The challenge is to make cancellation easy enough for legitimate changes but difficult enough that an attacker cannot simply disable the entire system. This is another example of competing requirements that cannot be solved by technology alone. Good architecture emerges from understanding the tradeoff.

There is also a human tendency to underestimate maintenance because maintenance feels less dramatic than creation. Building an encrypted archive can feel like a significant accomplishment. Reviewing it every six months can feel tedious. Yet long-term systems usually fail through neglect rather than dramatic attack. A person creates a plan, becomes busy, changes devices, forgets the credentials, and assumes everything remains intact. Years later, the system exists only in theory. Maintenance is therefore not an administrative afterthought. It is part of the mechanism itself.

The deepest lesson of redundancy is that survival depends upon pathways rather than objects. A backup drive is not the goal. The goal is continued access to information. A trusted person is not the goal. The goal is continued human capacity to make an appropriate decision. An automated trigger is not the goal. The goal is ensuring that an important intention survives the creator's inability to act. Once the objective is understood in this way, the architecture becomes easier to evaluate. Every component can be judged by the question of whether it preserves a viable path when another component fails.

This perspective also changes how we think about the phrase "foolproof." There is no truly foolproof dead man's switch. Every system operates within assumptions about technology, people, law, communication, time, and circumstance. Claiming otherwise encourages complacency. A more realistic objective is graceful failure. When something goes wrong, the system should preserve as much functionality and protection as possible. A missed check-in should not automatically become public disclosure. A failed server should not destroy the only copy. An unavailable custodian should not leave the archive permanently inaccessible. A compromised account should not necessarily expose everything.

The architecture of failure is therefore not a pessimistic addition to the dead man's switch. It is the heart of the concept. The entire reason to create such a system is that ordinary assumptions about continuity may no longer hold. If the system itself depends upon uninterrupted normality, it contradicts its own purpose. It must assume that people disappear, communications fail, technology changes, and unexpected events occur. It must continue functioning under conditions substantially different from those in which it was created. That is what transforms a contingency idea into a resilient information-preservation system.

Ultimately, time provides the rhythm, redundancy provides the alternatives, and failure analysis provides the discipline that holds the architecture together. Check-in intervals determine how quickly uncertainty becomes significant. Grace periods prevent ordinary interruptions from becoming emergencies. Multiple triggers reduce dependence upon ambiguous signals. Independent custodians and storage locations protect against correlated failure. Testing, maintenance, and recovery procedures ensure that the system remains more than a theoretical arrangement of instructions.

A dead man's switch becomes genuinely meaningful only when it has been designed with the expectation that something will eventually go wrong. The creator should not ask whether the system can survive a perfect execution of the original plan. The better question is what happens when the first assumption fails, followed by the second, and perhaps the third. If the system still contains a viable path toward preservation, verification, and appropriate action, it has achieved something much more valuable than technological sophistication. It has achieved resilience. The next question is where the information itself should live, because even the most carefully engineered trigger is useless if the evidence it is supposed to protect is stored in one fragile place.

Resources

1. NIST Special Publication 800-34 — Contingency Planning Guide for Federal Information Systems[1] — foundational guidance on contingency planning, recovery strategies, alternate procedures, and maintaining information-system operations after disruption.

2. NIST Cybersecurity Framework 2.0[2] — provides a broad framework for governance, identification, protection, detection, response, and recovery, all directly relevant to resilient contingency architecture.

3. NIST Special Publication 800-53 — Security and Privacy Controls[3] — includes controls concerning contingency planning, system recovery, alternate storage, backup, incident response, access control, authentication, and separation of duties.

1. https://csrc.nist.gov/publications/detail/sp/800-34/rev-1/final?utm_source=chatgpt.com

2. https://www.nist.gov/cyberframework?utm_source=chatgpt.com

3. https://csrc.nist.gov/publications/detail/sp/800-53/rev-5/final?utm_source=chatgpt.com

4. NIST Special Publication 800-61 — Computer Security Incident Handling Guide[4] — relevant to incident detection, escalation, response, recovery, and post-incident evaluation.

5. NIST Special Publication 800-57 — Recommendation for Key Management — authoritative guidance on cryptographic key lifecycle, protection, backup, recovery, and key-management risks.

6. NIST Digital Identity Guidelines[5] — relevant to authentication, identity assurance, authenticators, recovery, and maintaining authorized access.

7. NIST Special Publication 800-207 — Zero Trust Architecture[6] — useful for understanding continuous verification and reducing dependence on implicit trust.

8. CISA — Cross-Sector Cybersecurity Performance Goals[7] — practical guidance concerning backups, authentication, incident response, recovery, and resilient cybersecurity architecture.

9. National Archives — Digital Preservation — relevant to the long-term preservation, integrity, accessibility, and management of digital records.

10. Library of Congress — Digital Preservation at the Library of Congress[8] — provides authoritative background on sustaining digital information and addressing long-term preservation challenges.

11. ISO 22301 — Security and Resilience, Business Continuity Management Systems[9] — international framework concerning organizational resilience and continuity during disruptive events.

12. ISO/IEC 27001 — Information Security Management Systems[10] — international standard for systematic information-security risk management and organizational controls.

13. Ross Anderson, *Security Engineering: A Guide to Building Dependable Distributed Systems*, 3rd ed., Wiley, 2020 — extensive treatment of dependable systems, security architecture, failure modes, human factors, and distributed-system resilience.

14. Bruce Schneier, *Beyond Fear: Thinking Sensibly About Security in an Uncertain World*, Copernicus Books, 2003 — useful framework for evaluating security measures according to threats, consequences, tradeoffs, and actual effectiveness.

15. Bruce Schneier, *Secrets and Lies: Digital Security in a Networked World*, Wiley, 2000 — explores the interaction between technology, people, procedures, authentication, and security assumptions.

16. Adi Shamir, "How to Share a Secret," *Communications of the ACM*, Vol. 22, No. 11, 1979 — foundational research behind threshold secret-sharing and distributing control among multiple participants.

---

4. https://csrc.nist.gov/publications/detail/sp/800-61/rev-2/final?utm_source=chatgpt.com

5. https://pages.nist.gov/800-63-4/?utm_source=chatgpt.com

6. https://csrc.nist.gov/publications/detail/sp/800-207/final?utm_source=chatgpt.com

7. https://www.cisa.gov/cross-sector-cybersecurity-performance-goals?utm_source=chatgpt.com

8. https://www.loc.gov/preservation/digital/?utm_source=chatgpt.com

9. https://www.iso.org/standard/75106.html?utm_source=chatgpt.com

10. https://www.iso.org/isoiec-27001-information-security.html?utm_source=chatgpt.com

17. Leslie Lamport, Robert Shostak, Marshall Pease, "The Byzantine Generals Problem," *ACM Transactions on Programming Languages and Systems*, Vol. 4, No. 3, 1982 — foundational work on agreement and reliability in distributed systems when components can fail or behave maliciously.

18. Karl E. Weick and Kathleen M. Sutcliffe, *Managing the Unexpected: Sustained Performance in a Complex World*, 3rd ed., Wiley, 2015 — important work on high-reliability organizations, resilience, anomaly detection, and responding to unexpected events.

19. Charles B. Perrow, *Normal Accidents: Living with High-Risk Technologies*, Princeton University Press, 1999 — influential examination of complex systems, interacting failures, and the difficulty of predicting how multiple failures can combine.

20. Nancy G. Leveson, *Engineering a Safer World: Systems Thinking Applied to Safety*, MIT Press, 2011 — systems-engineering approach to understanding accidents, unsafe interactions, constraints, and complex-system failure.

21. Electronic Frontier Foundation — Surveillance Self-Defense[11] — practical guidance on threat modeling, authentication, secure communications, device security, and protecting sensitive information.

22. Committee to Protect Journalists — Safety Kit[12] — practical resources concerning risk assessment, source protection, digital security, physical safety, and contingency planning for journalists.

23. U.S. Cybersecurity and Infrastructure Security Agency — Incident Response and Recovery — practical government resources for preparing for, responding to, and recovering from cyber incidents.

24. Internet Engineering Task Force — RFC 4949, Internet Security Glossary[13] — useful technical reference for terminology concerning security, reliability, authentication, failure, and related concepts.

25. SRE Book — Site Reliability Engineering, Google[14] — valuable technical resource for understanding reliability engineering, monitoring, failure budgets, redundancy, incident response, and designing systems that continue operating under failure.

---

11. https://ssd.eff.org/?utm_source=chatgpt.com

12. https://cpj.org/safety-kit/?utm_source=chatgpt.com

13. https://www.rfc-editor.org/rfc/rfc4949?utm_source=chatgpt.com

14. https://sre.google/sre-book/table-of-contents/?utm_source=chatgpt.com

Physical, Digital, and Hybrid Dead Man's Switches

The dead man's switch began as a physical idea long before anyone imagined encrypted cloud storage, automated messaging, or distributed digital archives. Its original logic was mechanical: a person remained in control while they were actively applying pressure or maintaining a position, and the mechanism responded when that control disappeared. Modern information-preservation systems have inherited the underlying principle while moving it into an entirely different technological environment. Today, a dead man's switch can involve paper documents inside a secure repository, encrypted digital files distributed across several locations, automated communications, or combinations of physical and digital systems. Each approach solves certain problems while creating others. The central question is therefore not which technology is most advanced, but which architecture remains dependable when the assumptions surrounding it begin to fail.

A physical dead man's switch is the most intuitive model because information can exist independently of computers and networks. Documents can be printed, photographs can be stored on physical media, notebooks can contain instructions, and physical objects can be deposited with trusted custodians or secure repositories. Such materials do not require an Internet connection merely to exist. They can survive changes in software, operating systems, online platforms, and cloud providers. Physical records can also provide an important sense of permanence because their existence is tangible and directly observable. Yet physical storage is vulnerable to fire, flood, theft, deterioration, accidental destruction, and simple loss.

The greatest strength of physical storage is independence from digital infrastructure. A paper document does not require a server to remain online, and a printed photograph does not become inaccessible because a software company changed its terms of service. This independence can be extremely valuable when the intended preservation period is long. Historical archives demonstrate that physical records can survive for generations under appropriate conditions. But physical independence should not be confused with physical invulnerability. Paper can decay, magnetic media can deteriorate, optical media can become unreadable, and storage facilities can disappear. Every physical medium has its own preservation requirements.

Physical repositories also introduce the question of custody. If a person places sensitive information in a safe, vault, safety-deposit arrangement, or other physical location, someone must eventually be able to retrieve it. That person may be the creator, a designated custodian, an attorney, an executor, or another authorized recipient. Access arrangements can become complicated after death or incapacitation. Legal ownership may not automatically translate into immediate access. A repository can therefore protect information while simultaneously making it difficult to retrieve. Security and accessibility must be designed together.

There is also a fundamental distinction between secrecy and preservation. A document hidden so effectively that nobody can find it may remain perfectly confidential but fail as a dead man's switch. The purpose of the system is not simply to prevent unauthorized access. It is to preserve the possibility of authorized access when the creator can no longer provide it personally. That requires some form of continuity of custody. The intended recipients must know that the repository exists, know how their authority is established, and understand what conditions permit access. A secret that disappears with its creator is not a successful contingency system.

Digital systems approach the problem from the opposite direction. Instead of depending upon physical custody, they can use electronic storage, automated communication, cryptographic protection, and networked distribution. Digital information can be copied rapidly and accurately. It can be stored in multiple geographic locations. It can be transmitted across borders almost instantly. It can also be searched, indexed, authenticated, and organized more efficiently than large physical collections. These properties make digital systems extremely powerful for information continuity. At the same time, they create dependence upon infrastructure that can change or disappear.

The first digital dependency is electricity. Almost every modern digital archive ultimately depends upon powered equipment somewhere in the chain. Even cloud storage, which appears remote and abstract to the user, ultimately exists on physical computers operating in physical facilities. Those facilities require electricity, cooling, networking, maintenance, security, and personnel. The cloud therefore does not eliminate physical infrastructure. It merely moves that infrastructure elsewhere. Understanding this distinction is important because digital systems are sometimes treated as if they exist outside the physical world. They do not.

The second dependency is software. A file can survive physically while becoming difficult or impossible to interpret. Proprietary formats may become obsolete. Applications may disappear. Encryption systems may change. Authentication standards may evolve. Operating systems may stop supporting old software. Digital preservation therefore involves more than copying bits. It requires maintaining the ability to interpret those bits. This is one reason archival organizations emphasize formats, metadata, integrity, documentation, and migration. A digital archive that cannot be understood is technically present but functionally lost.

The third dependency is identity and access control. A digital archive can be extraordinarily secure while remaining useless if nobody knows how to authenticate as an authorized recipient. Modern security systems increasingly rely on multiple factors, recovery mechanisms, cryptographic keys, and identity verification. These controls are designed to prevent unauthorized access, but they create a continuity problem when the original account holder disappears. The question becomes how legitimate authority can survive the loss of the person who originally controlled the account. A dead man's switch must therefore consider succession as carefully as security.

Digital systems offer one particularly powerful capability that physical systems struggle to provide: automation. A computer can monitor time, send reminders, record confirmations, initiate notifications, and perform predefined actions without human intervention. This allows a contingency system to continue operating even when its creator cannot. Automation can also provide precise logging. The system can record when a check-in occurred, when a warning was generated, and when a particular state changed. Such records may become valuable later because they establish a history of how the mechanism behaved. Yet automation remains dependent upon the reliability of the software and infrastructure executing it.

An automated system can fail silently. A scheduled task may stop running. An account may become inaccessible. A service may change its interface. A payment method may expire. An application may be discontinued. A security update may break compatibility. The creator may never know that the system has ceased functioning. This is why digital continuity requires monitoring. The system should ideally have some mechanism for determining whether its own critical components remain operational. Otherwise, the creator may possess the illusion of protection without the reality of it.

Offline digital archives occupy an interesting middle ground. A hard drive, solid-state device, optical disc, or other removable medium can hold substantial amounts of information without remaining connected to the Internet. Offline storage reduces exposure to many forms of remote compromise. It can also provide independence from online service providers. But offline does not mean permanent. Physical media can fail, become damaged, be misplaced, or become unreadable. The devices required to access them may eventually disappear. Offline storage therefore solves some problems while creating others.

The correct question is not whether a storage medium is "secure" but secure against what. A disconnected drive may be highly resistant to remote hacking but vulnerable to physical theft. A cloud archive may be geographically distributed but vulnerable to account compromise. Paper may be immune to software obsolescence but vulnerable to fire. A safe may protect against casual access but provide little protection against environmental disaster. Security is always relative to a threat model. The architecture must therefore begin with the threats that matter rather than with a particular technology.

This is why hybrid systems are often attractive. A hybrid architecture combines physical and digital mechanisms so that each can compensate for weaknesses in the other. A creator might preserve original documents physically while maintaining encrypted digital copies in geographically separated locations. Digital systems might handle monitoring and notification while physical repositories preserve authoritative originals. A trusted custodian might hold one component while another remains under independent professional control. The purpose is not technological complexity for its own sake. The purpose is to create independent pathways to preservation and authorized access.

Hybrid systems can also separate different functions. The trigger mechanism does not necessarily need to contain the information itself. A digital service can determine that an unusual condition has occurred while a separate physical repository holds the underlying evidence. Conversely, a physical instruction can explain how to access a digital archive. This separation can prevent compromise of one component from exposing everything. It can also make the system more resilient because the trigger and archive do not share exactly the same failure dependencies. A failure in one layer does not automatically destroy the other.

One of the most useful distinctions in hybrid architecture is between the authoritative copy and the working copies. The authoritative copy is the version designated as the reference record. Working copies may be created for review, analysis, transmission, or professional evaluation. Maintaining this distinction can help prevent confusion when files are modified or updated. It also allows the creator to preserve an original record while permitting authorized recipients to work with duplicates. The concept becomes particularly important when information may eventually have evidentiary significance.

Digital integrity mechanisms can strengthen this architecture. Cryptographic hashes can provide a mathematical fingerprint of a file, allowing later users to determine whether the file has changed. Digital signatures can provide evidence concerning authenticity and authorship when implemented appropriately. Timestamps and metadata can help establish chronology. None of these mechanisms proves that the underlying information is truthful. They instead help answer a narrower question: has the digital object changed since a particular point in time? This distinction is critical because authenticity and truth are different properties.

Physical documents have analogous evidentiary considerations. Original papers may contain signatures, handwriting, annotations, physical characteristics, or other information that can be difficult to reproduce perfectly. Photographs can contain contextual information not captured in a digital summary. Physical evidence may therefore have value beyond the information represented in a scanned copy. A hybrid archive can preserve both. Digital copies provide accessibility and redundancy, while physical originals preserve material characteristics. Together they can create a stronger evidentiary record than either medium alone.

The problem of duplication nevertheless requires discipline. A creator may assume that making many copies automatically creates resilience. But if every copy is generated from a corrupted source, duplication merely reproduces the corruption. If every copy uses the same encryption key and that key is lost, the entire collection may become inaccessible. If every copy is stored under the same account, one credential compromise may expose them all. Redundancy must therefore consider not only the number of copies but also the independence of their creation, custody, authentication, and recovery mechanisms. Multiple copies are valuable when they fail differently.

Geographic diversity is one important form of independence. A local disaster should not be able to destroy every copy. Organizational diversity can also matter. If all copies depend upon the same provider, they may share common vulnerabilities. Technological diversity can provide another layer. A physical archive, an offline digital copy, and an independently maintained online archive may fail under different circumstances. Diversity should not become chaotic complexity, but deliberate variation can protect against common-mode failure. The system should be constructed so that one category of failure does not remove every pathway.

There is also a question of frequency. Digital systems make duplication cheap, which can encourage constant copying. But every additional copy requires some form of inventory and management. The creator needs to know which version is current, which copies are encrypted, who can access them, and whether they remain intact. Physical archives generally make duplication more cumbersome, but this can encourage greater discipline. Neither environment is automatically better. What matters is whether the archive remains understandable, current, and recoverable.

Long-term preservation introduces the issue of technological migration. Digital information sometimes needs to be moved from one format, storage medium, or system to another before the original becomes obsolete. This can involve converting files, replacing storage devices, updating documentation, or changing authentication arrangements. Migration itself creates risk because every transfer can introduce errors. The solution is verification. After migration, the creator or custodian should be able to confirm that the new copy corresponds to the original. Long-term preservation is therefore an active process rather than a single act of storage.

The same principle applies to physical media. A document stored in a climate-controlled environment may require periodic inspection. A hard drive may eventually need to be copied to newer media. An optical disc may require migration before compatible readers disappear. A physical vault may need new access arrangements if ownership changes. The archive must therefore have a maintenance lifecycle. The system should specify not only where information is stored but how its continued usability will be confirmed. Preservation without maintenance is merely delayed deterioration.

Digital systems also create the possibility of rapid global distribution, which can be both their greatest advantage and their greatest danger. A document can potentially reach thousands of recipients within seconds. That can make censorship or localized destruction more difficult. But once information has been distributed, control becomes extraordinarily difficult. Copies may persist indefinitely. Recipients may alter the material or remove its context. Innocent people can become exposed. Sensitive information can spread far beyond its intended audience. Automation should therefore be used cautiously when the final action is irreversible.

A physical repository offers greater control over distribution. A custodian can inspect documents before handing them to another party. A lawyer can review materials before deciding what may be disclosed. A journalist can evaluate evidence before publication. But physical control also creates bottlenecks. One person can refuse access, disappear, lose the key, or become unavailable. A purely physical system may therefore preserve information without guaranteeing that it reaches anyone. Again, the issue is not choosing the perfect medium. It is designing a pathway that survives plausible failures.

Accessibility and confidentiality are naturally in tension. The more accessible information becomes, the greater the risk of unauthorized access. The more tightly it is protected, the greater the risk that legitimate recipients cannot obtain it. This is one of the fundamental dilemmas of information security. A dead man's switch intensifies the problem because the person who originally balanced these competing requirements may no longer be present. The architecture must therefore encode both the security requirement and the succession requirement. Neither can safely be treated as an afterthought.

The physical world also provides an important advantage that digital systems sometimes obscure: people understand physical custody intuitively. If a sealed envelope is delivered to a lawyer and placed in a secure file, there is a clear chain of custody. If a digital file moves through several cloud systems, automated services, encryption layers, and accounts, the chain can become harder for nontechnical people to understand. This does not make digital systems less trustworthy. It means that their trustworthiness depends more heavily upon documentation. The creator should be able to explain where the information exists and what happens to it as it moves through the system.

A useful hybrid architecture can therefore assign each medium the task it performs best. Physical storage can preserve original records and provide independence from digital infrastructure. Digital storage can provide redundancy, searchability, rapid duplication, and remote access. Automated systems can provide monitoring and scheduled communication. Human custodians can provide contextual judgment. Professional intermediaries can provide legal or editorial evaluation. The architecture becomes a network of complementary capabilities rather than a single mechanism expected to solve every problem. Resilience emerges from the relationships between the components.

There is another reason to favor deliberate hybridity: technological uncertainty. A person establishing a dead man's switch today cannot know which services will still exist ten or twenty years from now. Some current platforms will disappear. Others will merge, change ownership, or radically alter their security models. New standards will emerge. Old systems will become unsupported. Physical archives face fewer changes in some respects, but they too are affected by environmental conditions, ownership changes, and technological obsolescence. A hybrid architecture spreads this uncertainty across different environments. The failure of one technological ecosystem does not necessarily eliminate the entire plan.

The legal environment adds another layer of complexity. Physical documents may be subject to property, inheritance, privacy, or evidentiary rules. Digital accounts can involve contractual terms, access restrictions, jurisdictional questions, and platform policies. Information crossing national borders may encounter different legal regimes. A technically elegant system may therefore encounter practical obstacles when someone attempts to activate it. Legal continuity should be considered when determining who can access physical and digital repositories. The most secure archive in the world is not useful if legitimate recipients cannot lawfully obtain it.

Privacy deserves equal attention. A dead man's switch can contain not only information about wrongdoing but also private communications, personal records, identities of sources, family information, and material concerning people who never consented to disclosure. A system designed around maximum exposure can therefore cause harm beyond its intended purpose. The architecture should separate information according to sensitivity where possible. Some material may require preservation but not public disclosure. Other material may be appropriate for professional review but not immediate publication. Physical and digital systems can both support such distinctions if they are designed deliberately.

One of the strongest arguments for a hybrid system is therefore not simply redundancy but controlled access. Different layers can be given different permissions. A digital index might reveal that an archive exists without revealing its contents. A physical custodian might hold original documents while an encrypted digital copy provides emergency continuity. A lawyer might receive access to one category of material while a journalist receives another. A designated family member might possess instructions without possessing the sensitive evidence itself. Separation reduces the likelihood that one person's mistake or compromise exposes everything.

The architecture should also preserve instructions separately from evidence. The evidence may be enormous, complicated, and constantly changing, while the instructions may be relatively simple. Keeping them separate makes maintenance easier. If the recipient changes, the instruction layer can be updated without reconstructing the archive. If evidence changes, the instruction framework can remain intact. The instructions can explain what the creator intended, who should review the material, what conditions should trigger escalation, and what limitations should apply. This separation is useful in both physical and digital environments.

There is also value in maintaining an inventory. A creator may know that "the files are in the archive" without remembering precisely which files exist, which versions are authoritative, or where the backups are located. A basic inventory can provide continuity without exposing the underlying contents. It can identify categories of records, storage locations, responsible custodians, and preservation dates. Such documentation becomes especially valuable if someone else must assume responsibility. The inventory is effectively a map of the system. Without a map, redundancy can become indistinguishable from confusion.

A dead man's switch should also be judged by recoverability rather than simply by survival. Imagine an archive that survives for fifty years but requires a password that nobody possesses. Technically, the information has survived. Practically, it has been lost. Conversely, an archive that remains accessible but has been silently modified may also have failed. Resilience therefore requires at least three qualities: continued existence, continued accessibility to authorized people, and confidence in integrity. A strong architecture considers all three. Storage is only the first stage of preservation.

The broader lesson is that there is no universally safest medium. Physical systems fail physically. Digital systems fail digitally. Human systems fail socially. Hybrid systems can fail through complexity or poor coordination. Every architecture has a different risk profile. The correct choice depends upon the information, the threat environment, the required preservation period, the people involved, the legal context, and the consequences of accidental disclosure. A system designed for one person may be inappropriate for another. The architecture should therefore begin with requirements rather than technology.

The strongest principle may be the simplest: never allow one dependency to become synonymous with survival. If the archive exists only on one computer, the computer becomes the archive. If it exists only in one cloud account, the account becomes the archive. If only one person knows how to retrieve it, that person becomes the archive. If only one password unlocks everything, that password becomes the archive. A resilient system distributes these dependencies so that the loss of one does not necessarily mean the loss of the whole.

This brings us back to the original purpose of the dead man's switch. The mechanism exists because the creator anticipates a future in which they cannot personally guarantee the survival of information. Physical, digital, and hybrid systems are simply different ways of solving that continuity problem. None eliminates uncertainty. None guarantees that every future event can be predicted. But each can be evaluated according to how well it preserves information, maintains authorized access, resists common failures, and prevents premature disclosure. The choice of architecture should therefore be deliberate rather than fashionable.

Ultimately, the most reliable dead man's switch may not look like a switch at all. It may be a carefully connected ecosystem in which physical evidence, digital archives, automated monitoring, independent custodians, authentication systems, and documented instructions support one another. The physical layer provides independence from network failure. The digital layer provides distribution and automation. The human layer provides judgment. The hybrid layer provides resilience when any one environment becomes unreliable. The result is not invulnerability but continuity—the ability of important information to remain available and meaningful even when the person who originally possessed it is no longer able to protect it.

Once the architecture has been selected, however, another question becomes unavoidable: what exactly should be placed inside it? Not every document, photograph, recording, message, or personal file deserves the same level of protection. Some material may establish facts, some may provide context, some may identify sources, and some may simply reflect the creator's interpretation. The next chapter therefore turns away from the machinery of preservation and toward the information itself, asking what kinds of data actually deserve protection and how they should be distinguished from material that could create unnecessary risk if released.

Resources

1. NIST Cybersecurity Framework 2.0[1] — provides a broad framework for identifying, protecting, detecting, responding to, and recovering from cybersecurity risks.

2. NIST Special Publication 800-53 — Security and Privacy Controls[2] — relevant to access control, contingency planning, system integrity, authentication, auditability, backup, and separation of duties.

3. NIST Special Publication 800-34 — Contingency Planning Guide for Federal Information Systems[3] — foundational guidance concerning contingency planning, backup, recovery, alternate storage, and system resilience.

4. NIST Special Publication 800-57 — Recommendation for Key Management — relevant to cryptographic keys, key protection, recovery, backup, and lifecycle management.

5. NIST Digital Identity Guidelines[4] — authoritative guidance on authentication, identity assurance, authenticators, and account recovery.

6. NIST Special Publication 800-88 — Guidelines for Media Sanitization[5] — useful for understanding the security implications of digital storage media throughout their lifecycle, including disposal and reuse.

7. National Archives — Digital Preservation — authoritative material concerning long-term preservation, authenticity, accessibility, metadata, and management of digital records.

8. Library of Congress — Digital Preservation[6] — extensive resources concerning preservation of digital materials, sustainability, formats, storage, and long-term access.

---

1. https://www.nist.gov/cyberframework?utm_source=chatgpt.com

2. https://csrc.nist.gov/publications/detail/sp/800-53/rev-5/final?utm_source=chatgpt.com

3. https://csrc.nist.gov/publications/detail/sp/800-34/rev-1/final?utm_source=chatgpt.com

4. https://pages.nist.gov/800-63-4/?utm_source=chatgpt.com

5. https://csrc.nist.gov/publications/detail/sp/800-88/rev-1/final?utm_source=chatgpt.com

9. Library of Congress — Sustainability of Digital Formats[7] — useful for understanding file-format sustainability and the risks of technological obsolescence.

10. ISO/IEC 27001 — Information Security Management Systems[8] — international framework for information-security risk management and organizational controls.

11. ISO 22301 — Security and Resilience, Business Continuity Management Systems[9] — relevant to continuity planning, resilience, and maintaining critical functions during disruption.

12. CISA — Cross-Sector Cybersecurity Performance Goals[10] — practical recommendations concerning backups, authentication, recovery, and resilience against common cyber threats.

13. CISA — Cybersecurity Resources Roadmap[11] — government resources covering cybersecurity, resilience, incident response, and infrastructure protection.

14. Electronic Frontier Foundation — Surveillance Self-Defense[12] — practical resources concerning threat modeling, secure communications, authentication, device security, and protecting sensitive information.

15. Internet Engineering Task Force — RFC 4949, Internet Security Glossary[13] — technical reference for terminology involving authentication, integrity, confidentiality, availability, and security architecture.

16. Ross Anderson, *Security Engineering: A Guide to Building Dependable Distributed Systems*, 3rd ed., Wiley, 2020 — comprehensive treatment of dependable systems, security architecture, human factors, distributed systems, and failure modes.

17. Bruce Schneier, *Secrets and Lies: Digital Security in a Networked World*, Wiley, 2000 — important discussion of digital security as an interaction between technology, people, procedures, authentication, and operational assumptions.

18. Bruce Schneier, *Beyond Fear: Thinking Sensibly About Security in an Uncertain World*, Copernicus Books, 2003 — useful framework for evaluating security mechanisms according to threats, consequences, tradeoffs, and actual effectiveness.

19. Adi Shamir, "How to Share a Secret," *Communications of the ACM*, Vol. 22, No. 11, 1979 — foundational research underlying threshold approaches for distributing control over sensitive information among multiple participants.

20. Leslie Lamport, Robert Shostak, Marshall Pease, "The Byzantine Generals Problem," *ACM Transactions on Programming Languages and Systems*, Vol. 4, No. 3, 1982 — foundational work concerning distributed agreement and resilience when components can fail or behave dishonestly.

---

6. https://www.loc.gov/preservation/digital/?utm_source=chatgpt.com

7. https://www.loc.gov/preservation/digital/formats/?utm_source=chatgpt.com

8. https://www.iso.org/isoiec-27001-information-security.html?utm_source=chatgpt.com

9. https://www.iso.org/standard/75106.html?utm_source=chatgpt.com

10. https://www.cisa.gov/cross-sector-cybersecurity-performance-goals?utm_source=chatgpt.com

11. https://www.cisa.gov/resources-tools/resources?utm_source=chatgpt.com

12. https://ssd.eff.org/?utm_source=chatgpt.com

13. https://www.rfc-editor.org/rfc/rfc4949?utm_source=chatgpt.com

21. Charles B. Perrow, *Normal Accidents: Living with High-Risk Technologies*, Princeton University Press, 1999 — influential analysis of interacting failures and the difficulties of maintaining complex systems under unexpected conditions.

22. Nancy G. Leveson, *Engineering a Safer World: Systems Thinking Applied to Safety*, MIT Press, 2011 — systems-engineering treatment of safety, failure, interactions, and complex-system design.

23. SAA Digital Preservation Technical Guidelines[14] — supplementary archival context for managing digital information over long periods.

24. Committee to Protect Journalists — Safety Kit[15] — practical material concerning threat assessment, source protection, digital security, physical safety, and contingency planning.

25. International Council on Archives — Digital Records and Archives Resources[16] — international archival perspective on the preservation, authenticity, management, and accessibility of records.

14. https://wwws.loc.gov/preservation/digital/?utm_source=chatgpt.com

15. https://cpj.org/safety-kit/?utm_source=chatgpt.com

16. https://www.ica.org/?utm_source=chatgpt.com

Designing for Survival: Multiple Layers of Protection

The moment a dead man's switch becomes important is precisely the moment when ordinary assumptions about continuity can no longer be trusted. The creator may be dead, missing, imprisoned, incapacitated, isolated, or otherwise unable to intervene, while the information itself may be exposed to technological failure, human error, legal complications, physical destruction, or deliberate interference. A system built around one device, one account, one storage location, or one trusted individual therefore contains a contradiction at its center. It claims to protect information when its creator is no longer available, yet it remains dependent upon a single point of continuity. Designing for survival means breaking that dependency into multiple layers so that the loss of one component does not automatically become the loss of everything.

The concept is closely related to defense in depth, a principle developed across information security, engineering, military planning, aviation, and other fields in which catastrophic failure must be prevented despite uncertainty. Defense in depth does not assume that one protective measure will always succeed. Instead, it places different safeguards around the same critical objective so that one failure encounters another layer. In information preservation, those layers might involve separate storage locations, independent custodians, different communication channels, authentication safeguards, physical archives, digital copies, and documented recovery procedures. The purpose is not to make the system unnecessarily complicated. The purpose is to ensure that the system has more than one path toward survival.

The first step is identifying what must actually survive. This sounds obvious, but it is often where contingency plans become vague. A person may believe they are protecting "the evidence," when in reality they possess a mixture of original documents, photographs, recordings, correspondence, personal notes, interpretations, source identities, and background material. Each category can have a different preservation requirement. Some information may need to remain confidential, some may need professional review, and some may eventually be suitable for public disclosure. Designing multiple layers becomes easier when the information has first been classified according to its importance, sensitivity, authenticity, and intended use.

Once the information has been classified, the next question is what would constitute a catastrophic loss. Catastrophic loss does not necessarily mean physical destruction. Information can be effectively lost because nobody can authenticate access, because the only person who understands the archive becomes unavailable, because encryption keys disappear, because a storage service closes an account, or because recipients cannot determine which version is genuine. It can also be lost through premature disclosure if sensitive material is released before it can be properly evaluated. Survival therefore has two dimensions: keeping the information available and keeping it under appropriate control. A resilient system must protect both.

Redundancy is the most familiar layer of protection. If one copy exists, its destruction ends the archive. If several independent copies exist, one failure does not necessarily end it. But redundancy must be meaningful. Five copies stored in the same room are effectively one copy when the room burns. Five accounts controlled by the same compromised password may be five doors opened by one key. Several backups maintained by one provider may share the same infrastructure. Genuine redundancy requires independence between the things being duplicated. The objective is not simply more copies, but more opportunities for the information to survive.

This principle is sometimes described as avoiding a single point of failure. A single point of failure is any component whose loss can bring down the entire system. It may be obvious, such as a single hard drive, or subtle, such as one person who possesses every password. It can even be an assumption rather than an object. For example, a system may depend upon the assumption that the creator will remain capable of periodically updating it. Once that assumption fails, the system fails with it. A proper resilience review therefore asks not only "What components do we have?" but also "What must remain true for the system to continue working?"

Independence is consequently more important than quantity. Two independent repositories may provide greater resilience than ten repositories that share the same vulnerability. A physical archive and an independently maintained digital archive may fail differently. Two custodians living in different locations may be less vulnerable to the same local emergency than two people living together. Two unrelated communication channels may be more useful than several accounts dependent upon the same service. The architecture should therefore seek diversity in failure modes. When possible, different components should not share the same infrastructure, credentials, physical location, or human dependency.

Geographic separation is one of the clearest examples. A local disaster can destroy an entire collection if all copies remain nearby. Fire, flooding, earthquakes, storms, theft, or building failure can affect everything within a relatively small area. Geographic separation reduces this risk by placing important components in different locations. The exact distance required depends upon the threat environment and the value of the information. The underlying principle is simple: an event that can destroy one location should not automatically be capable of destroying every location.

Geographic distribution, however, introduces its own complications. Different jurisdictions may have different legal requirements concerning privacy, data access, evidence, inheritance, and disclosure. A physical repository in one country may be governed by different rules from a digital service located elsewhere. A custodian may be legally unable to access material held in another jurisdiction without following specific procedures. Geographic diversity therefore needs legal and administrative consideration. Separation increases resilience against physical disasters but can increase complexity in governance.

Distributed custody addresses another category of failure: the disappearance or compromise of one person. If one individual holds all the information and all the access credentials, that individual becomes an enormous vulnerability. They might die, become unavailable, lose the credentials, change their mind, become compromised, or simply misunderstand their responsibilities. Distributed custody spreads responsibility among several people or institutions. One person might preserve the physical archive, another might hold a digital copy, and another might know how authorized access is established. The arrangement can be designed so that no single person has to carry the entire burden.

Distributed custody does not mean indiscriminate sharing. The principle is controlled distribution. Each participant should receive only what is necessary for their role. A custodian may need to know that an archive exists without knowing every detail contained within it. A professional intermediary may need access to a particular category of material without possessing the entire collection. A family member may hold instructions concerning the creator's wishes without being entrusted with highly sensitive evidence. Separation of knowledge can reduce the consequences of a compromised participant. It can also prevent unnecessary exposure of people who never agreed to become part of the system.

There is a delicate balance here because excessive fragmentation can create a different form of failure. If nobody has enough information to understand their role, the system can become inert. Imagine an archive divided among six people, each possessing one small piece of the puzzle, while nobody knows who is responsible for coordinating the pieces. Every component survives, but the system does not function. Distributed custody therefore requires clear governance. Participants need to know what their responsibilities are, what conditions justify action, whom they should contact, and what limits apply to their authority.

This is where separate access mechanisms become valuable. Information and authorization do not always need to travel together. A physical repository might contain the original documents while a separate system maintains instructions about access. A digital archive might hold encrypted information while authorized recovery depends upon independently maintained credentials. A professional intermediary might possess authority to evaluate material without controlling the underlying storage. Separating these functions can prevent one compromise from exposing the entire system. It also allows different layers to be replaced without reconstructing everything from scratch.

Authentication deserves particular attention because it represents the boundary between security and accessibility. A dead man's switch needs to prevent unauthorized access while ensuring that legitimate recipients can eventually gain access when appropriate. If authentication is too weak, an attacker may obtain the material. If it is too strong without a recovery mechanism, the intended recipients may be locked out permanently. This is especially important when the original account holder is no longer available. The architecture must therefore anticipate succession. Authorized access should not depend entirely upon knowledge that disappears with the creator.

Cryptographic protection can strengthen the digital layers, but encryption does not eliminate the need for sound architecture. An encrypted archive is only as resilient as its key-management process. If the key is stored alongside the encrypted material in an easily accessible location, confidentiality may be compromised. If the key exists nowhere except in the creator's memory, continuity may be compromised. If several people hold fragments without clear recovery procedures, authorized access may become impossible. Cryptography protects information from unauthorized readers, but key management determines whether authorized readers can ever reach it.

This is one reason threshold approaches can be useful conceptually. Instead of allowing one individual to possess complete authority, access can require cooperation among a predefined group. Secret-sharing research has demonstrated mathematically defined ways to distribute information so that a specified number of participants are required for reconstruction. Such approaches can reduce dependence on one custodian. They also introduce operational complexity. The participants must remain available, understand their responsibilities, and preserve whatever material is required for recovery. The mechanism should therefore be chosen because it solves a real dependency, not simply because it is technically impressive.

Another layer concerns the distinction between storage and notification. A system can preserve the evidence without being able to tell anyone that it exists. Conversely, a notification can reach the intended recipients while the underlying evidence is inaccessible. These are different functions and should be analyzed separately. Storage answers the question of where the information survives. Notification answers the question of how people learn that action may be required. Activation answers the question of when the process should begin. Treating all three as one mechanism can create hidden dependencies.

A layered system might therefore contain a preservation layer, an awareness layer, a verification layer, and an access layer. Preservation keeps the information intact. Awareness ensures that relevant people know when circumstances have changed. Verification helps distinguish genuine emergencies from technical or human errors. Access determines how authorized recipients obtain the material. Each layer can have different failure modes. Separating them makes it possible to strengthen one without unnecessarily exposing the others.

Verification is especially important because absence of communication is not proof of death or wrongdoing. A missed check-in can result from travel, illness, technical failure, distraction, loss of connectivity, or many other ordinary events. A robust system should therefore distinguish between an anomaly and a confirmed emergency. The distinction can be implemented through staged procedures rather than immediate irreversible action. An initial failure might create an internal alert. A prolonged failure could initiate a second verification pathway. Only after predefined conditions are satisfied should the system move toward a consequential action.

The architecture should also contain a way to stop or modify an activation process when new information appears. This is the principle of reversibility. Not every stage of a contingency process needs to be irreversible. A reminder can be cancelled. A custodian can confirm that the creator is safe. A professional reviewer can determine that the material should not yet be released. Once information has been publicly distributed, however, meaningful reversal becomes extremely difficult. The system should therefore place the most consequential actions behind the strongest verification layers. Irreversibility should increase the evidentiary threshold rather than decrease it.

Physical and digital systems can reinforce one another particularly well in this respect. A physical archive can preserve original evidence independently of online infrastructure. A digital archive can provide geographically distributed copies. A human custodian can interpret ambiguous circumstances. An automated system can provide regular reminders. A professional intermediary can evaluate legal or evidentiary implications. Each component compensates for weaknesses in another. The resulting system is not invulnerable, but it is less likely to fail catastrophically from one event.

The concept of multiple repositories is especially important for valuable or sensitive information. A single repository concentrates both information and risk. If the location is discovered, destroyed, compromised, or rendered inaccessible, the entire archive is affected. Separate repositories can reduce that concentration. But repositories should not necessarily contain identical information. Depending on the threat model, it may be appropriate for one location to preserve originals, another to preserve encrypted digital copies, and another to preserve only the documentation necessary to recover the system. Functional separation can reduce both physical and informational concentration.

There is also a case for separating evidence from identifying information. An archive may contain documents that establish a claim while also containing the names, addresses, communications, or personal information of people who contributed to the investigation. If everything is stored together, unauthorized access exposes all of it simultaneously. Segmentation can reduce that risk. The evidentiary material can be preserved independently from sensitive identity information where practical. Such separation also allows different disclosure decisions to be made for different categories of information.

The same logic applies to decoys, except that the term should be treated carefully. A system should not rely upon deceptive mechanisms merely because they sound sophisticated. A misleading or unnecessary component can create confusion for legitimate custodians. The useful principle is not deception but compartmentalization. A person who compromises one part of the system should not automatically gain access to every other part. This can be achieved through independent authentication, segmented storage, restricted permissions, and separate custodians without introducing unnecessary false information.

Maintenance remains one of the most important layers because every long-lived system decays. A service that exists today may disappear tomorrow. A trusted contact may change their circumstances. A storage device may fail. A password may be forgotten. A legal arrangement may become outdated. A file format may become obsolete. The system should therefore have a review cycle in which its critical assumptions are examined and its components verified. A dead man's switch that was perfectly designed five years ago may be poorly designed today if nobody has maintained it.

Testing should be performed at several levels. The creator can verify that backups can actually be opened and that important files remain intact. Custodians can verify that they understand their roles without necessarily accessing sensitive content. Recovery procedures can be reviewed to determine whether credentials and instructions remain valid. Communication mechanisms can be checked for continued operation. The objective is not merely to prove that the system works under ideal conditions. It is to discover where it fails under realistic conditions. Every test should produce information that can improve the architecture.

A useful test is to imagine the disappearance of each major component one at a time. What happens if the primary storage location disappears? What happens if the main custodian cannot be reached? What happens if the primary account becomes inaccessible? What happens if the creator misses several scheduled confirmations? What happens if the communication channel fails? What happens if an attacker gains access to one layer? The architecture should be evaluated against these scenarios. If any one answer is "everything is lost," that component represents a significant single point of failure.

More difficult is the possibility of correlated failure. Two or more components can sometimes fail because of the same underlying event. A regional disaster can affect multiple physical locations. A widespread cloud outage can affect several services that depend upon the same infrastructure. A compromised password can expose several accounts. A legal action can affect several related custodians. Correlated failure is why apparent redundancy can be misleading. The designer must ask whether apparently separate components are actually independent.

This principle can be extended to people. If all custodians are close friends from the same professional environment, they may share the same assumptions, pressures, or vulnerabilities. If every decision depends upon one organization, an institutional failure can affect the entire system. Diversity of custody can therefore include diversity of perspective. Different custodians may notice different problems. One may identify a technical issue that another overlooks. Another may recognize a legal complication. Another may question whether disclosure is ethically justified. Resilience can come from diversity of judgment as well as diversity of storage.

Professional review can form another protective layer. Certain information may have legal, journalistic, scientific, or security implications that a private individual cannot properly evaluate. A lawyer can advise on legal exposure. A qualified journalist can assess whether material meets publication standards. A relevant scientific expert can examine technical evidence. The purpose is not to transfer responsibility blindly to professionals. It is to introduce specialized judgment before an irreversible decision is made. A layered architecture can therefore include people whose role is evaluation rather than custody.

The question of legal jurisdiction becomes increasingly important as systems become geographically distributed. A document stored in one jurisdiction may be governed differently from one stored in another. A digital service may have terms that determine how accounts are handled after death. Privacy laws may restrict disclosure of certain personal information. Evidence obtained through questionable means may create additional complications. The technical architecture cannot resolve these questions. Legal review should therefore be treated as one of the layers rather than something considered only after activation.

Ethical review is similarly important. The fact that information is true does not automatically mean that every detail should be released to everyone. A disclosure could expose innocent people, reveal private information, compromise legitimate investigations, or create unnecessary danger. A resilient system should therefore distinguish preservation from publication. Preserving evidence does not require immediately publishing it. In many cases, the responsible pathway may involve controlled review followed by selective disclosure. This distinction can make the system both more credible and more protective.

There is also a psychological benefit to layered protection. A person living with sensitive information may experience significant anxiety when they believe that everything depends upon their continued ability to act. Knowing that information has been preserved through several independent mechanisms can reduce the sense that one mistake will destroy the entire plan. But this psychological benefit must not become false reassurance. A contingency system is not a guarantee of personal safety. Its purpose is to improve information continuity, not to encourage someone to take unnecessary risks because they believe they are protected.

A sophisticated system should therefore avoid becoming an excuse for confrontation. The existence of a dead man's switch does not make a person invulnerable, and it does not guarantee that a threat will be deterred. It can create a degree of informational resilience, but physical safety remains a separate concern. The safest architecture is generally one that reduces unnecessary exposure rather than encouraging dramatic tests of the system. Information protection should complement sensible personal-security and legal strategies rather than replace them.

The ultimate measure of resilience is graceful degradation. If one layer fails, the system should lose some capability but not collapse entirely. If the primary custodian disappears, another pathway should remain. If one repository is destroyed, another should survive. If one communication channel stops working, another should provide awareness. If one credential becomes inaccessible, a legitimate recovery pathway should exist. If an automated mechanism malfunctions, the system should have a human or independent verification layer. Graceful degradation transforms redundancy from a collection of backups into an actual architecture.

This principle also clarifies why simplicity matters. Every layer must earn its place. An unnecessary component increases maintenance requirements and can create new failure modes. The best architecture is not the one containing the greatest number of technologies. It is the one in which every important risk has a reasonable countermeasure and every critical dependency has an alternative. The system should be understandable enough that its creator and legitimate custodians can explain how it works. Complexity without purpose is not resilience. It is another form of fragility.

Ultimately, designing for survival means accepting that uncertainty cannot be eliminated. Nobody can predict every event that may occur after a contingency system is created. Nobody can guarantee that every service will remain operational, every custodian will remain available, or every legal circumstance will remain unchanged. What can be done is to distribute dependency. Information can be separated across locations. Authority can be divided among appropriate custodians. Access can be protected through independent mechanisms. Physical and digital systems can support one another. Verification can stand between an initial failure and an irreversible disclosure.

The dead man's switch is therefore best understood not as a single trigger but as an architecture of continuity. Its strength comes from the relationships among its components. Storage preserves information. Redundancy preserves storage. Distributed custody preserves human responsibility. Authentication preserves controlled access. Verification preserves judgment. Geographic separation preserves independence from local catastrophe.

Maintenance preserves the system itself. When these layers are deliberately connected, the disappearance or failure of one component does not necessarily become the disappearance of the truth it was meant to protect.

The next problem is more fundamental still. Once an information-preservation system has multiple layers, the creator must decide exactly what belongs inside those layers and what should remain outside them. Evidence, personal records, source identities, photographs, recordings, classified material, correspondence, interpretations, and raw data do not carry identical risks or identical evidentiary value. Protecting everything equally can create unnecessary complexity and unnecessary danger. The architecture must therefore be matched to the information. The next chapter examines that question by asking what kinds of data deserve protection in the first place and how sensitive material can be classified before it enters the system.

Resources

1. NIST Cybersecurity Framework 2.0[1] — provides a comprehensive framework for managing cybersecurity risk through identification, protection, detection, response, and recovery.

2. NIST Special Publication 800-53, Security and Privacy Controls for Information Systems and Organizations[2] — particularly relevant to contingency planning, access control, separation of duties, least privilege, auditability, system integrity, and recovery.

3. NIST Special Publication 800-34, Contingency Planning Guide for Federal Information Systems[3] — provides established guidance on contingency planning, alternate storage, backup, recovery, and operational resilience.

4. NIST Special Publication 800-57, Recommendation for Key Management — authoritative resource for cryptographic key protection, backup, recovery, and lifecycle management.

5. NIST Digital Identity Guidelines[4] — addresses authentication, identity assurance, authenticators, and recovery mechanisms relevant to continuity of authorized access.

6. NIST Special Publication 800-207, Zero Trust Architecture[5] — useful for understanding the principle that access should not depend upon implicit trust and should be continuously evaluated.

7. CISA Cross-Sector Cybersecurity Performance Goals[6] — practical recommendations concerning backups, authentication, incident response, recovery, and cybersecurity resilience.

8. National Archives — Digital Preservation — authoritative archival guidance concerning authenticity, integrity, accessibility, preservation, and long-term management of digital records.

9. Library of Congress — Digital Preservation[7] — resources on preserving digital information, managing technological change, sustaining formats, and maintaining long-term access.

---

1. https://www.nist.gov/cyberframework?utm_source=chatgpt.com

2. https://csrc.nist.gov/publications/detail/sp/800-53/rev-5/final?utm_source=chatgpt.com

3. https://csrc.nist.gov/publications/detail/sp/800-34/rev-1/final?utm_source=chatgpt.com

4. https://pages.nist.gov/800-63-4/?utm_source=chatgpt.com

5. https://csrc.nist.gov/publications/detail/sp/800-207/final?utm_source=chatgpt.com

6. https://www.cisa.gov/cross-sector-cybersecurity-performance-goals?utm_source=chatgpt.com

7. https://www.loc.gov/preservation/digital/?utm_source=chatgpt.com

10. ISO/IEC 27001 — Information Security Management Systems[8] — international standard for systematic information-security risk management.

11. ISO 22301 — Security and Resilience, Business Continuity Management Systems[9] — international framework for business continuity and organizational resilience during disruption.

12. Electronic Frontier Foundation — Surveillance Self-Defense[10] — practical resources on threat modeling, secure communications, authentication, device security, and information protection.

13. Committee to Protect Journalists — Safety Kit[11] — guidance relevant to risk assessment, source protection, physical safety, digital security, and contingency planning.

14. Adi Shamir, "How to Share a Secret," *Communications of the ACM*, Vol. 22, No. 11, 1979 — foundational paper introducing secret-sharing techniques in which reconstruction can require cooperation among multiple participants.

15. Leslie Lamport, Robert Shostak, and Marshall Pease, "The Byzantine Generals Problem," *ACM Transactions on Programming Languages and Systems*, Vol. 4, No. 3, 1982 — foundational research on distributed agreement and resilience in systems containing unreliable or compromised components.

16. Ross Anderson, *Security Engineering: A Guide to Building Dependable Distributed Systems*, 3rd ed., Wiley, 2020 — comprehensive treatment of dependable systems, security architecture, human factors, distributed systems, and failure analysis.

17. Bruce Schneier, *Beyond Fear: Thinking Sensibly About Security in an Uncertain World*, Copernicus Books, 2003 — examines security through threat modeling, tradeoffs, incentives, and realistic evaluation of protective measures.

18. Bruce Schneier, *Secrets and Lies: Digital Security in a Networked World*, Wiley, 2000 — examines the interaction between technology, people, procedures, authentication, and organizational security.

19. Nancy G. Leveson, *Engineering a Safer World: Systems Thinking Applied to Safety*, MIT Press, 2011 — systems-engineering analysis of complex failures, unsafe interactions, and designing systems around constraints and resilience.

20. Charles B. Perrow, *Normal Accidents: Living with High-Risk Technologies*, Princeton University Press, 1999 — influential analysis of interacting failures and the difficulty of predicting failures in complex systems.

21. Nancy G. Leveson, "A New Accident Model for Engineering Safer Systems," *Safety Science*, Vol. 42, No. 4, 2004 — influential systems approach emphasizing interactions and organizational conditions rather than isolated component failure.

22. Karl E. Weick and Kathleen M. Sutcliffe, *Managing the Unexpected: Sustained Performance in a Complex World*, 3rd ed., Wiley, 2015 — important work on high-reliability organizations, resilience, anomaly detection, and responding effectively to unexpected events.

---

8. https://www.iso.org/isoiec-27001-information-security.html?utm_source=chatgpt.com

9. https://www.iso.org/standard/75106.html?utm_source=chatgpt.com

10. https://ssd.eff.org/?utm_source=chatgpt.com

11. https://cpj.org/safety-kit/?utm_source=chatgpt.com

23. Internet Engineering Task Force — RFC 4949, Internet Security Glossary[12] — technical reference for concepts including confidentiality, integrity, authentication, availability, and security architecture.

24. SRE Book — Site Reliability Engineering, Google[13] — useful technical background on reliability engineering, monitoring, redundancy, incident response, and designing systems that continue operating despite failures.

25. CISA Resources and Tools[14] — government resources covering cybersecurity resilience, incident response, recovery, and infrastructure protection.

---

12. https://www.rfc-editor.org/rfc/rfc4949?utm_source=chatgpt.com

13. https://sre.google/sre-book/table-of-contents/?utm_source=chatgpt.com

14. https://www.cisa.gov/resources-tools/resources?utm_source=chatgpt.com

What Is Worth Protecting?

The most important decision in a dead man's switch is made before any file is encrypted, any document is placed in a vault, or any automated mechanism is activated. It is the decision about what deserves to survive. People who believe they possess dangerous or important information can easily confuse evidence with suspicion, documentation with interpretation, and firsthand knowledge with something they have heard from another person. If everything is treated as equally significant, the archive quickly becomes overloaded with material whose relevance cannot be established. Worse, genuinely important evidence can become buried beneath speculation and noise. A serious information-preservation system therefore begins by asking a deceptively simple question: what exactly do you have, and what makes it worth protecting?

Evidence has value because it can support or challenge a proposition through information that is capable of being examined. That does not mean every piece of evidence is conclusive. A photograph can be authentic but misinterpreted. A document can be genuine but incomplete. A witness can be sincere but mistaken. A recording can accurately capture words while leaving out the circumstances surrounding them. Scientific data can be technically valid while being interpreted incorrectly. The purpose of preservation is therefore not to declare the material true before anyone examines it. It is to preserve the material in a condition that allows competent people to examine it later.

This distinction becomes crucial when the stakes are high. Someone may possess information suggesting corruption, criminal conduct, institutional abuse, corporate wrongdoing, intelligence activity, scientific misconduct, or another serious matter. The information may be extremely important, but its importance does not automatically establish its accuracy. A responsible archive preserves the underlying material rather than simply preserving the conclusion drawn from it. Instead of recording only "this proves X," the archive should preserve the document, recording, photograph, dataset, communication, or firsthand account that led the creator to believe X. That approach allows later investigators to reach their own conclusions.

The difference between evidence and speculation is particularly important because extraordinary claims often attract extraordinary amounts of commentary. A person may receive an anonymous message, hear a rumor from a colleague, discover an unexplained financial transaction, or encounter a document whose origin is uncertain. Each may justify further investigation, but none should automatically be elevated to established fact. Preserving such material can still be worthwhile if its uncertain status is clearly documented. The danger comes when uncertain information becomes indistinguishable from verified information. Once that happens, the archive itself can become misleading.

A useful way to think about evidence is to consider several dimensions at once. One concerns provenance: where did the information come from? Another concerns integrity: has it been altered since it was obtained? A third concerns context: what circumstances surround the information? A fourth concerns corroboration: can independent material support or challenge it? A fifth concerns relevance: does it actually bear upon the issue being investigated? These questions do not produce an automatic verdict. They provide a disciplined framework for preserving material so that its later evaluation is possible.

Provenance is particularly important because information without a known origin is difficult to evaluate. A document found anonymously on a computer has a different evidentiary status from a document obtained directly from the organization that created it. A photograph taken by a known witness has a different provenance from an image downloaded from an unknown website. A financial spreadsheet generated by an identifiable accounting system differs from an unexplained spreadsheet sent by an anonymous source. The provenance does not determine truth by itself. It establishes the beginning of the chain through which authenticity and meaning can be investigated.

Documents are among the most obvious forms of evidence that a dead man's switch might preserve. They can include contracts, memoranda, letters, reports, internal communications, invoices, meeting records, handwritten notes, government records, corporate materials, scientific papers, and administrative files. Their value depends heavily upon authenticity and context. A single page may appear incriminating while being misleading if preceding or subsequent pages are missing. A memorandum may describe a proposal that was never implemented. An internal email may reflect one person's opinion rather than an institutional decision. Preserving surrounding documentation can therefore be as important as preserving the apparently significant document itself.

Correspondence deserves particular attention because communications often reveal chronology. Emails, letters, text messages, messaging records, and other communications can establish who knew what, when they knew it, what they discussed, and how their understanding changed over time. Yet communications are also easy to misunderstand when separated from their context. A short message may refer to a conversation that occurred elsewhere. A sarcastic comment can appear literal when read without the surrounding exchange. An attachment may contain the information that gives the message meaning. Preserving the conversation as completely as reasonably possible can therefore be more valuable than preserving isolated quotations.

Photographs present a different evidentiary problem. An image can preserve details that a written account cannot, including physical conditions, locations, objects, injuries, documents, or events. But digital photographs also contain information that may be invisible in the image itself. Original files can contain metadata concerning the device, date, time, or other technical characteristics, although such metadata should not automatically be treated as definitive proof. Images can also be edited, cropped, compressed, re-encoded, or stripped of metadata. A preservation system should therefore distinguish between an original file, a derivative copy, and an edited or annotated version.

Video and audio recordings can be even richer because they preserve sequences rather than isolated moments. A recording may capture speech, behavior, environmental sounds, physical surroundings, or interactions between people. Yet recordings can also be deceptively incomplete. A camera has a field of view. A microphone has a limited range. A recording begins at one moment and ends at another. Missing material can be as important as recorded material. Preserving the original recording together with information about how, when, and where it was created can substantially improve its later evidentiary value.

Testimony is another important category, but testimony must be understood differently from documentary evidence. A witness provides an account based upon perception, memory, inference, or information received from others. A sincere witness can still be wrong. Human memory is reconstructive rather than a perfect recording of events, and recollection can change over time. This does not make testimony worthless. Courts, journalists, historians, investigators, and researchers routinely rely upon witness accounts while assessing their reliability in context. A dead man's switch should therefore preserve testimony carefully without presenting every assertion as independently verified fact.

Firsthand knowledge should be distinguished from hearsay. Someone saying "I personally saw this happen" is making a different kind of claim from "someone told me this happened." The second statement may still be important, particularly if it identifies a potential witness or investigative lead. But its evidentiary status is different.

Preserving that distinction prevents an information archive from unintentionally upgrading rumor into firsthand evidence. The creator should record what they personally know, what they were told, what they inferred, and what they merely suspect. These categories can coexist within the same archive as long as they remain clearly separated.

Financial records can provide particularly powerful forms of documentation because transactions often leave structured traces. Bank records, invoices, accounting entries, tax documents, corporate filings, procurement records, property records, and payment histories can establish relationships and chronology. They can also reveal patterns that individual documents do not make obvious. But financial information is frequently complex and easy to misinterpret. A payment may have a legitimate explanation that is not apparent from the transaction itself. A company name may represent a subsidiary rather than the organization initially suspected. A suspicious pattern deserves investigation, not automatic conclusions.

Scientific data presents another important category. Laboratory notebooks, raw measurements, instrument outputs, sample records, datasets, experimental protocols, calibration information, correspondence, and analysis files can become critical when allegations concern scientific misconduct, technological discoveries, environmental hazards, or disputed research. Raw data is particularly important because published conclusions often depend upon processing and interpretation. If only the final graph survives, later investigators may have difficulty determining how it was produced. Preserving the underlying data and methodology can allow independent analysis.

Metadata is frequently overlooked because it is not always visible to ordinary users. File creation dates, modification information, device identifiers, geolocation data, software information, communication headers, and other technical details can sometimes provide useful context. Metadata can help establish relationships between files or reconstruct aspects of a digital timeline. But metadata should not be treated as infallible. It can be altered, lost during copying, generated incorrectly, or interpreted without sufficient understanding of the underlying system. Metadata is evidence about evidence. It can strengthen an investigation without necessarily settling it.

Chronology is one of the most powerful organizing principles for an archive. Important events rarely exist in isolation. A document may become significant because of something that happened before it. A communication may matter because it preceded a particular decision. A financial transaction may acquire meaning because of what occurred afterward. Building a reliable timeline can therefore reveal relationships that are invisible when materials are stored as disconnected files. The timeline itself should be distinguished from the underlying evidence, because it represents an interpretation of the sequence rather than the events themselves.

Originals deserve special protection whenever possible. An original document, raw data file, original photograph, or uncompressed recording may contain information that disappears when a derivative copy is created. Compression, conversion, editing, scanning, and transcription can all introduce changes. Copies remain valuable because redundancy protects against loss, but the existence of copies should not lead to unnecessary destruction of originals. A preservation system should ideally retain the original form while also creating accessible working copies. This allows investigators to examine the material without repeatedly handling the most important version.

Integrity is closely related to preservation. An archive needs some method of determining whether material has changed. Digital systems can use cryptographic hashes and other integrity mechanisms to compare files over time. Physical documents can be protected through controlled custody, documentation, and preservation practices. Neither approach proves that the material was truthful when originally created. Integrity answers a narrower question: has the preserved object remained consistent with the version that was originally archived? That distinction becomes extremely important when the material may eventually be scrutinized in a legal, journalistic, scientific, or historical context.

Chain of custody adds another layer. It concerns the documented history of possession and handling of evidence. If a document passes from a source to an investigator, then to a lawyer, then to a journalist, each transition can potentially affect how the material is evaluated. A strong chain-of-custody record does not magically make evidence true. It provides information about how the evidence was handled. This can help later reviewers determine whether contamination, alteration, substitution, or other problems may have occurred. The more consequential the material, the more important careful custody becomes.

Context may be the most commonly lost element in modern information storage. A file can survive while the circumstances surrounding it disappear. Who created it? Why was it created? What did the author know at the time? Was it preliminary or final? Was the photograph taken before or after a particular event? Was the recording complete? Was the spreadsheet generated automatically or manually? Without answers to such questions, an apparently important piece of information can become almost impossible to interpret correctly.

For this reason, preservation should include explanatory documentation, but that documentation must be clearly distinguished from the evidence itself. A creator might write a note explaining why they believe a particular document matters. That note can be extremely useful. But it is an interpretation, not the document's independent proof. Future investigators should be able to see both. Separating observation from interpretation protects the archive against the creator's own assumptions. It also makes the archive more credible because it allows others to disagree with the conclusions while still evaluating the underlying material.

Corroboration is another central principle. A single source may be mistaken, incomplete, or deceptive. Independent evidence can strengthen confidence when it points toward the same conclusion. A witness account supported by contemporaneous documents has a different evidentiary profile from an unsupported allegation. A photograph accompanied by independent location records can provide more context than the photograph alone. A financial claim supported by accounting records, communications, and external documentation may be more persuasive than one isolated transaction. Corroboration does not guarantee truth, but it can substantially improve the quality of an investigation.

Independence itself must be examined carefully. Ten websites repeating the same claim do not necessarily constitute ten independent sources if they all copied the same original report. Five witnesses who discussed the event together before giving their accounts may not provide the same degree of independent corroboration as witnesses who independently recorded their observations. Likewise, multiple digital copies generated from one original are redundant copies, not independent evidence. The archive should therefore preserve information about relationships among sources. Knowing that two pieces of evidence are connected can be as important as knowing that they appear to agree.

The distinction between preservation and publication becomes particularly important when dealing with sensitive material. A creator may have strong reasons to preserve evidence without wanting every detail immediately exposed. An archive can contain information that is important for investigators but dangerous for innocent individuals if published indiscriminately. Personal addresses, medical information, identities of confidential sources, financial account information, or private correspondence may have legitimate reasons for restricted handling. Preservation should therefore not automatically mean public disclosure. The dead man's switch is a mechanism for continuity, not an instruction to ignore privacy.

This is especially important when information concerns other people. A creator may possess evidence because someone trusted them with a confidential communication. They may hold photographs containing bystanders. They may have records concerning employees, clients, patients, colleagues, or family members. Those individuals may have nothing to do with the wrongdoing under investigation. Releasing their information unnecessarily can create a second injustice while attempting to expose the first. A responsible archive therefore distinguishes between information necessary to establish the underlying claim and information that merely happens to accompany it.

Classified or restricted information introduces still greater complexity. Government classification systems exist for reasons that can include national security, intelligence protection, diplomatic interests, military capabilities, and protection of sensitive sources and methods. The existence of a classification marking does not automatically establish that every restriction is justified, nor does it automatically establish that disclosure is lawful or unlawful. Classification status is a factual circumstance that should be recorded accurately. Decisions about disclosure can require specialized legal and professional advice. A dead man's switch should not substitute personal judgment for that expertise.

The same principle applies to proprietary corporate information. Trade secrets, confidential business information, customer records, intellectual property, and internal communications can sometimes reveal genuine misconduct. They can also contain unrelated proprietary material belonging to innocent parties. Preserving everything indiscriminately may create unnecessary exposure. A more disciplined approach is to preserve the material necessary to establish the relevant facts while minimizing unrelated information. This is not merely a legal precaution. It improves the evidentiary quality of the archive by reducing irrelevant material.

Scientific evidence requires similar discipline. Raw observations should be distinguished from statistical interpretations. Experimental results should be distinguished from hypotheses. A researcher's suspicion that an experiment demonstrates something is not equivalent to the experimental result itself. A dataset should ideally be accompanied by information concerning how it was collected, processed, and analyzed. This enables later researchers to reproduce or challenge the interpretation. The archive becomes valuable not because it dictates a conclusion but because it preserves the ability to investigate.

One particularly important category is negative evidence, or information showing that something did not occur as claimed. Absence can be difficult to interpret because missing evidence may result from many causes. Nevertheless, records showing that a particular event was not documented, a transaction did not occur, or a timeline conflicts with a claim can be important. Preserving contradictory material is therefore part of responsible evidence management. An archive that contains only information supporting the creator's theory is vulnerable to confirmation bias. A credible archive should preserve information that challenges its own conclusions.

Confirmation bias is a significant threat when people preserve information about events they already believe to be true. Once a person becomes convinced that a particular institution or individual is responsible for wrongdoing, ambiguous evidence may begin to appear supportive. Contradictory information may be dismissed or ignored. The archive can then become a record of belief rather than a record of evidence. The best defense is deliberate separation between observations and interpretations. Preserving inconvenient evidence can ultimately strengthen the credibility of the entire collection.

There is also the problem of forged or planted evidence. An archive can contain material that appears highly convincing while having been deliberately created to mislead. Digital technology makes manipulation easier in some respects, particularly with images, audio, documents, and metadata. That does not mean genuine evidence should be dismissed simply because manipulation is possible. It means authenticity should be treated as a question requiring examination. Original files, provenance records, independent corroboration, technical analysis, and contextual evidence can all contribute to that evaluation.

The rise of synthetic media makes this problem increasingly important. Artificial intelligence can generate or alter images, audio, video, and text with increasing sophistication. Future investigators may encounter evidence whose origin is difficult to determine simply by looking at it. This makes provenance and preservation more important rather than less. Knowing where a file came from, how it was obtained, and whether an original version exists can become crucial. The archive of the future will increasingly need to preserve not only content but evidence about the history of that content.

A good evidence archive should therefore preserve uncertainty honestly. If the creator does not know whether a document is authentic, the archive should say so. If a photograph's location is uncertain, that uncertainty should remain visible. If a witness account is secondhand, it should not be rewritten as firsthand knowledge. If a conclusion is only a hypothesis, it should be labeled as such. Uncertainty is not necessarily weakness. An archive that accurately records what is unknown can be more credible than one that pretends to possess certainty it does not have.

The same discipline applies to dates. Exact dates are often treated as more authoritative than they deserve to be. A file timestamp may reflect the time a document was copied rather than created. A photograph's embedded date may depend upon a camera clock that was incorrectly configured. A witness may remember an event occurring "in the summer" rather than on a particular day. Preserving approximate dates as approximate is better than manufacturing false precision. Chronological accuracy depends upon recognizing the limitations of the underlying information.

Naming conventions and organization also matter. An archive containing thousands of files with meaningless names can become practically unusable. A consistent structure can preserve relationships among documents without altering their contents. Original files should generally remain distinguishable from copies, edited versions, transcripts, summaries, and analytical notes. The purpose is not bureaucratic perfection. It is to ensure that someone unfamiliar with the material can understand what they are looking at. A dead man's switch must assume that its future users may know far less about the archive than its creator did.

Documentation should also explain what is missing. If an important email thread has an attachment that cannot be located, that absence should be recorded. If a video begins after the event of greatest interest, the archive should say so. If a document references another document that is unavailable, that relationship should be preserved in the notes. Missing information can itself become an investigative lead. Concealing gaps creates the false impression of completeness. A transparent archive shows both what exists and what does not.

The value of preservation increases when multiple forms of evidence converge. A photograph may establish physical conditions. A contemporaneous message may establish timing. A financial record may establish a transaction. A witness may explain what happened. A scientific record may establish the technical context. Each piece answers a different question. Together they can create a more complete evidentiary picture than any single item could provide.

This is why a dead man's switch should not be thought of as a container for secrets. It is better understood as a container for future inquiry. The creator may believe they understand what the evidence means, but the person who eventually receives it may reach a different conclusion. That possibility is healthy. The purpose of preservation is to keep the underlying information available for examination rather than freezing one person's interpretation as permanent truth. A strong archive allows later investigators to challenge, refine, corroborate, or reject the original interpretation.

The question of worth should also include consequences. Some information may be historically fascinating but have little practical importance. Other information may be highly consequential but extremely sensitive. A creator should consider whether preserving a particular item contributes meaningfully to understanding the central issue. They should also consider whether the material creates unnecessary risks for unrelated people. The most valuable archive is not necessarily the largest. It is the archive in which important information can be found, understood, authenticated, and responsibly evaluated.

Ultimately, what deserves protection is information whose loss would materially impair the ability to establish, investigate, understand, or challenge an important claim. That may include original documents, photographs, recordings, financial records, scientific datasets, correspondence, testimony, metadata, physical objects, and other records. But the value of each item depends upon provenance, integrity, context, relevance, and corroboration. Speculation can sometimes deserve preservation as a lead, but it should never be disguised as established evidence. Interpretation can provide useful guidance, but it should remain distinguishable from the underlying record. The goal is to preserve the evidence and preserve the uncertainty surrounding it when uncertainty genuinely exists.

The dead man's switch becomes meaningful only when the information inside it can survive scrutiny after its creator is gone. A dramatic allegation without supporting material may attract attention but collapse under examination. A carefully preserved collection of original documents, authenticated records, corroborating communications, contextual notes, and transparent uncertainties can do something far more powerful: it can give future investigators something they can actually work with. That is the real purpose of information survival. The objective is not merely to make sure that a secret escapes. It is to make sure that whatever deserves to be known does not disappear, become corrupted, or become impossible to evaluate when the person who knew about it is no longer there to explain it.

Resources

1. Federal Rules of Evidence — Rule 901: Authenticating or Identifying Evidence[1] — useful legal reference concerning authentication and establishing that evidence is what its proponent claims it to be.

2. Federal Rules of Evidence — Rule 803: Exceptions to the Rule Against Hearsay[2] — provides context for the complex treatment of hearsay and recorded information in U.S. federal courts.

3. National Archives — Digital Preservation — authoritative resources concerning preservation, authenticity, integrity, metadata, and continued accessibility of digital records.

4. Library of Congress — Digital Preservation[3] — extensive guidance concerning long-term preservation of digital materials, including formats, storage, metadata, and sustainability.

5. Library of Congress — Sustainability of Digital Formats[4] — information concerning characteristics affecting the long-term preservation and usability of digital files.

---

1. https://www.law.cornell.edu/rules/fre/rule_901?utm_source=chatgpt.com

2. https://www.law.cornell.edu/rules/fre/rule_803?utm_source=chatgpt.com

3. https://www.loc.gov/preservation/digital/?utm_source=chatgpt.com

4. https://www.loc.gov/preservation/digital/formats/?utm_source=chatgpt.com

6. NIST Cybersecurity Framework 2.0[5] — framework addressing information security risks, asset identification, protection, detection, response, and recovery.

7. NIST Special Publication 800-53 — Security and Privacy Controls[6] — relevant to access control, auditability, system integrity, configuration management, contingency planning, and protection of information.

8. NIST Special Publication 800-88 — Guidelines for Media Sanitization[7] — provides guidance concerning the handling and disposition of information-bearing media.

9. Internet Engineering Task Force — RFC 4949, Internet Security Glossary[8] — technical reference for terminology involving integrity, authentication, confidentiality, availability, and information security.

10. ISO 15489 — Information and Documentation: Records Management[9] — international records-management framework concerning the creation, capture, management, and preservation of reliable records.

11. ISO 23081 — Information and Documentation: Metadata for Records[10] — relevant to metadata management and the contextual information required to understand records.

12. Scientific Working Group on Digital Evidence — SWGDE Resources[11] — professional resources concerning digital evidence, forensic handling, preservation, and examination.

13. National Institute of Justice — Electronic Crime and Digital Evidence — government resource concerning digital evidence and forensic considerations.

14. Federal Bureau of Investigation — Handbook of Forensic Services[12] — federal forensic reference covering evidence handling, documentation, preservation, and examination.

15. Innocence Project — Understanding Wrongful Convictions and Evidence[13] — useful background on eyewitness error, forensic evidence, misconduct, and the consequences of unreliable evidence.

16. Elizabeth F. Loftus, *Eyewitness Testimony*, Harvard University Press, 1979 — foundational work on eyewitness memory, recollection, and the reliability limitations of human testimony.

17. Daniel L. Schacter, *The Seven Sins of Memory: How the Mind Forgets and Remembers*, Houghton Mifflin, 2001 — influential examination of memory distortion, reconstruction, and the limitations of human recollection.

18. National Academies — Strengthening Forensic Science in the United States[14] — landmark examination of forensic-science reliability, validation, standards, and interpretation.

---

5. https://www.nist.gov/cyberframework?utm_source=chatgpt.com

6. https://csrc.nist.gov/publications/detail/sp/800-53/rev-5/final?utm_source=chatgpt.com

7. https://csrc.nist.gov/publications/detail/sp/800-88/rev-1/final?utm_source=chatgpt.com

8. https://www.rfc-editor.org/rfc/rfc4949?utm_source=chatgpt.com

9. https://www.iso.org/standard/62542.html?utm_source=chatgpt.com

10. https://www.iso.org/standard/81610.html?utm_source=chatgpt.com

11. https://www.swgde.org/?utm_source=chatgpt.com

12. https://www.fbi.gov/file-repository/handbook-of-forensic-services-pdf.pdf?utm_source=chatgpt.com

13. https://innocenceproject.org/?utm_source=chatgpt.com

14. https://nap.nationalacademies.org/catalog/12589/strengthening-forensic-science-in-the-united-states-a-path-forward?utm_source=chatgpt.com

19. National Academies — Reproducibility and Replicability in Science[15] — important resource concerning the distinction between reproducibility, replicability, data, methods, and scientific reliability.

20. Committee to Protect Journalists — Safety Kit[16] — practical guidance concerning source protection, documentation, digital security, physical safety, and risk assessment for investigative work.

21. Reporters Without Borders — Journalism Trust Initiative — resources concerning journalistic reliability, transparency, verification, and professional standards.

22. Society of Professional Journalists — Code of Ethics[17] — useful framework for verification, minimizing harm, accountability, and distinguishing reliable reporting from unsupported claims.

23. International Council on Archives[18] — international archival perspective on authenticity, preservation, provenance, records management, and long-term accessibility.

24. UNESCO — Memory of the World Programme[19] — international preservation framework emphasizing documentary heritage, accessibility, authenticity, and the importance of protecting significant records.

25. Bruce Schneier, *Secrets and Lies: Digital Security in a Networked World*, Wiley, 2000 — useful background on information security, threat assessment, authentication, and the relationship between technical safeguards and human behavior.

15. https://nap.nationalacademies.org/catalog/25303/reproducibility-and-replicability-in-science?utm_source=chatgpt.com

16. https://cpj.org/safety-kit/?utm_source=chatgpt.com

17. https://www.spj.org/ethicscode.asp?utm_source=chatgpt.com

18. https://www.ica.org/?utm_source=chatgpt.com

19. https://www.unesco.org/en/memory-world?utm_source=chatgpt.com

The Evidence Vault: Documents, Photos, Video, and Testimony

An evidence vault sounds like something out of a spy novel, a hidden room containing boxes of documents, photographs, recordings, and secrets waiting for someone to discover them after the person who collected them has disappeared. In reality, the most important evidence vaults are often much less dramatic, because their value comes not from secrecy alone but from disciplined preservation. A collection can contain extraordinary information and still become practically useless if nobody can determine where the material came from, whether it has been altered, when it was created, or what circumstances surrounded it. The central challenge is therefore not simply keeping evidence safe from destruction. It is keeping evidence sufficiently intact and contextualized that another person can eventually understand and evaluate it.

This distinction matters because evidence is not merely information. Evidence is information placed within a framework of provenance, context, chronology, authenticity, and relevance. A photograph without a reliable account of its origin may be interesting but difficult to authenticate. A document without surrounding correspondence may be impossible to interpret. A recording without information about its source and circumstances may leave crucial questions unanswered. A witness statement without a record of when and how it was obtained can become difficult to evaluate later. The evidence vault must therefore preserve relationships as carefully as it preserves individual objects.

The first principle is preservation of the original whenever possible. An original document may contain handwriting, paper characteristics, signatures, annotations, stamps, folds, or other physical details that disappear in a transcription. An original photograph may contain technical information that is absent from a screenshot or compressed copy. An original video file may contain properties that disappear when the recording is uploaded to another platform. An original dataset may contain information that is lost when someone exports a simplified spreadsheet. Copies are valuable because they provide redundancy and accessibility, but they should not automatically replace the original.

Digital evidence creates an especially complicated preservation problem because copying is both extraordinarily easy and potentially transformative. A file can be duplicated perfectly at the binary level, yet it can also be opened, edited, converted, compressed, renamed, or re-encoded in ways that change its properties. Some ordinary applications automatically modify metadata when a file is opened or exported. Some platforms strip information during upload. Some messaging services convert photographs and videos into new formats. Consequently, the existence of a visually identical copy does not necessarily mean that every technical characteristic of the original has survived.

For this reason, an evidence vault should distinguish between originals, preservation copies, working copies, and analytical products. The original is the material as initially obtained or created, subject to whatever limitations are known about its authenticity. A preservation copy is a controlled duplicate intended to protect against loss. A working copy is used for ordinary examination and analysis. An analytical product might be a transcript, enhancement, translation, summary, frame extraction, or other derivative. These categories should remain identifiable. Otherwise, years later, someone may mistake an edited working file for the original evidence.

Documents require similar discipline. A single page can be important, but its significance often depends upon what surrounds it. A memorandum may refer to an attachment that is missing. A contract may contain amendments on later pages. An email may be understandable only when the preceding and subsequent messages are available. A handwritten note may appear incriminating until its date and circumstances are established. The vault should therefore preserve relevant surrounding material rather than extracting only the most dramatic passages. Context protects evidence from being transformed into misleading fragments.

Chronology is one of the most powerful tools for creating that context. When information is collected over time, dates can establish relationships between events that are otherwise difficult to see. A communication before a meeting can mean something different from the same communication afterward. A financial transaction may become significant only when placed alongside a contract or corporate decision. A photograph may establish physical conditions at a particular moment. A sequence of recordings may reveal changes that a single recording cannot. Chronology does not prove causation, but it gives later investigators a structure within which causation can be examined.

Chronological records must themselves be handled carefully. File timestamps can be useful, but they do not always represent the moment an event occurred. A file may have been copied from another device, causing its filesystem timestamps to change. A camera clock may have been incorrectly configured. An email may show the time according to a particular server or time zone. A document may have been modified after its original creation. The responsible approach is therefore to preserve timestamps while recording what they actually represent, rather than automatically treating every timestamp as an unquestionable historical fact.

Metadata can become particularly valuable here. Digital photographs, documents, recordings, emails, and other files may contain technical information about their creation and handling. Depending on the format and system, this can include dates, software information, device information, file characteristics, location information, or communication headers. Such information can help investigators establish relationships among files. But metadata should not be regarded as an independent guarantee of authenticity. It can be incomplete, modified, stripped, or generated by systems that behave differently than the user assumes. Metadata is one evidentiary layer among several.

A disciplined evidence vault therefore records provenance. Provenance means the history or origin of a record and the circumstances through which it came into the collection. If a document was supplied by a source, the vault should preserve whatever information can responsibly be recorded about how it was obtained. If a photograph was taken by the creator, that fact is relevant. If a recording was received from another person, the distinction should remain visible. If a file was downloaded from an online source, that circumstance should be recorded rather than allowing the file to appear as though it originated with the person preserving it.

The same principle applies to testimony. A witness statement is not simply a block of text. It represents an account given by a particular person at a particular time under particular circumstances. The vault should preserve the original statement when possible, along with the date, circumstances, and identity information appropriate to the sensitivity of the case. If the statement was subsequently edited, summarized, translated, or transcribed, those versions should be distinguishable from the original. The objective is to preserve the witness's account without silently changing it through the preservation process.

Human testimony deserves special caution because memory is not a static recording of experience. People can sincerely remember events incorrectly, especially when substantial time has passed. Memories can be influenced by later conversations, media coverage, questioning, expectations, and subsequent experiences. None of this means that witnesses are inherently unreliable. It means that testimony should be evaluated as testimony. A responsible evidence vault preserves what the witness actually said rather than unconsciously improving the story over time.

This makes contemporaneous records particularly useful. Notes created close to the time of an event may preserve details that later recollection loses. Emails, diaries, messages, photographs, receipts, calendars, recordings, and other contemporaneous materials can help establish what someone believed or observed at the time. They do not necessarily prove that the person's interpretation was correct. They can nevertheless provide an important temporal anchor. When later testimony corresponds with earlier records created independently of the later investigation, the overall evidentiary picture may become stronger.

The vault should also preserve contradictions. This can feel uncomfortable because someone creating a dead man's switch may have a strong belief about what happened. Yet evidence that challenges that belief can be extremely important. A contradictory document may reveal a mistake in the original theory. A witness may remember an event differently. A timestamp may conflict with the assumed chronology. A financial record may provide an alternative explanation. Preserving these contradictions makes the archive more intellectually honest and gives future investigators the opportunity to test the original interpretation rather than merely inherit it.

Chain of custody provides another essential layer. In its simplest form, chain of custody is a record of who possessed evidence, when they possessed it, and what happened to it during that period. The exact requirements vary depending upon the legal and professional context. Nevertheless, the underlying principle is universal: evidence becomes easier to evaluate when its history is documented. If nobody can explain how a file moved from one person to another, questions about alteration or substitution may arise. A documented history cannot prove authenticity by itself, but it reduces uncertainty about handling.

Digital chain of custody can involve technical measures as well as human documentation. Cryptographic hashes, for example, can provide a way of determining whether a digital file remains identical to a previously recorded version. If the same file produces the same hash under the same algorithm, that can provide useful evidence of file integrity. A changed hash indicates that something about the file has changed, although it does not necessarily explain why. Hashes therefore complement rather than replace provenance and custody records. They answer an integrity question rather than the much broader question of whether the content itself is truthful.

Physical evidence presents different challenges. Paper can deteriorate through moisture, heat, light, mold, handling, and chemical processes. Photographic prints can fade. Magnetic media can degrade. Optical media can become unreadable. Older storage technologies can become difficult to access as hardware disappears. Preservation therefore requires attention to the physical characteristics of the materials involved. A vault should not merely be secure today. It should remain usable tomorrow.

This is where redundancy becomes essential. An important document should not depend upon a single physical copy. A significant digital file should not exist on only one drive. A crucial recording should not depend upon a single cloud account. But redundancy should be designed carefully because copies can inherit the same weaknesses. Ten drives stored in one building are vulnerable to the same fire. Several accounts using identical credentials can be compromised together. Multiple copies on one platform can disappear through a single account failure. Meaningful redundancy requires some degree of independence.

The evidence vault can therefore benefit from geographically separated preservation. One repository might be physical while another is digital. One copy might be held by the creator while another is maintained by an appropriate independent custodian. Another might be preserved through a professional organization or archival service where appropriate. Geographic separation reduces the possibility that one localized event destroys every copy. Yet it also creates legal and logistical considerations, especially when information crosses national boundaries. The principle should be applied thoughtfully rather than mechanically.

Accessibility is the other side of preservation. Information that nobody can retrieve is functionally unavailable. A highly secure archive may fail if its access credentials disappear with its creator. An encrypted collection may become useless if the recovery mechanism is not preserved. A physical vault may be inaccessible if nobody knows that it exists or how legitimate access is established. Security therefore cannot be measured solely by how difficult it is to enter. A successful evidence vault must make authorized future access possible while preventing unauthorized access.

This is particularly important for long-term archives because people naturally disappear from the system. A creator may die. A trusted colleague may move away. A lawyer may retire. A storage provider may discontinue a service. A password may be forgotten. A device may fail. A legal arrangement may change. The vault should therefore be designed around succession rather than assuming that the original creator will remain available indefinitely. Preservation is fundamentally a problem of continuity across time.

One of the most useful practices is maintaining an inventory. An inventory does not need to expose sensitive content. It can simply establish what categories of material exist, where they are preserved, what their general importance is, and what dependencies affect access. The inventory becomes a map of the archive. Without such a map, future custodians may not know whether they have received the complete collection. They may discover a folder but have no idea whether another repository exists. They may find a hard drive but not know whether it contains original evidence or a working copy.

The inventory should also identify gaps. If a recording is known to exist but cannot currently be located, that fact matters. If a document is referenced but missing, the absence should be recorded. If a photograph has been preserved only as a compressed copy because the original was lost, that limitation should be stated. An archive that openly documents its weaknesses is more useful than one that pretends to be complete. Future investigators can then distinguish between evidence that does not exist and evidence that has simply not yet been recovered.

The same principle applies to translations and transcriptions. A transcription can make a recording much easier to search and understand, but it is not the recording itself. A translation can make foreign-language material accessible, but translation inevitably involves interpretation. The original should therefore be retained whenever possible. Derived text can accompany it as an aid. This allows later reviewers to return to the underlying material if questions arise concerning wording or meaning.

Photographs deserve particular treatment because modern digital images can exist in many versions. The original camera file may differ from an edited image, a screenshot, a social-media copy, and a printed version. Each can have different evidentiary characteristics. An edited version may be useful for highlighting a feature, but it should not silently replace the original. Cropping can remove contextual information. Compression can remove technical information. Filters can alter visual characteristics. The archive should therefore preserve the original and clearly label derivative versions.

Video presents an even more obvious version of the same problem. A short clip may be extracted from a longer recording. A platform may re-encode the file. A person may add subtitles or commentary. Someone may slow down or enhance selected frames. Each transformation can be useful for analysis while changing the object being analyzed. The original recording should therefore remain identifiable. Analytical versions can be created without pretending that they are equivalent to the source file. This distinction becomes increasingly important as synthetic media and sophisticated editing tools become more widespread.

Audio evidence has similar concerns. Background sounds may establish location or circumstances. Voices may provide important information, but voice identification is a specialized forensic task rather than something that should be assumed from casual familiarity. Editing can alter the apparent sequence of speech. Compression can remove information. Transcription can introduce errors. The safest archival principle is to preserve the original recording alongside any cleaned, enhanced, translated, or transcribed versions.

Physical documents can also be transformed by digitization. Scanning creates a highly useful preservation and access copy, but it can omit characteristics visible only in the original. Paper texture, ink differences, pressure marks, watermarks, physical alterations, and other features may not be captured adequately. Digitization should therefore be viewed as an additional preservation layer rather than an automatic substitute for the original. Where originals have genuine evidentiary significance, they should be preserved appropriately. The digital copy provides accessibility and redundancy.

Another important category is source identity. The person who supplied evidence may themselves be vulnerable. Revealing their identity can expose them to retaliation, harassment, legal consequences, or other risks. This creates a tension between evidentiary provenance and source protection. A future investigator may need to know where material came from, but public disclosure of that identity may not be necessary. Sensitive identifying information can therefore require its own protection layer. The evidence vault should preserve enough information for legitimate evaluation while limiting unnecessary exposure.

This is one reason compartmentalization can be useful. The evidence itself and the identifying information associated with its source do not always need to be stored in the same place or made available to the same people. Separation can reduce the consequences of a compromise. It can also allow material to be evaluated without immediately exposing individuals. The precise arrangement depends upon the legal and ethical circumstances. What matters is recognizing that the archive contains different kinds of information with different protection requirements.

Legal considerations become unavoidable when an archive contains confidential communications, privileged material, classified information, personal data, trade secrets, or evidence obtained under unusual circumstances. The person preserving the material may not know which rules apply. Different jurisdictions can impose different obligations. Some materials may be protected by privilege while others are not. Some information may be lawful to possess but unlawful to disclose publicly. The evidence vault should therefore preserve information responsibly while recognizing that preservation and publication are separate decisions.

The temptation to make the vault completely secret should also be resisted. Absolute secrecy can create a continuity problem. If nobody knows that the archive exists, it may disappear with the person who created it. If only one person knows how to access it, that person becomes a single point of failure. If the location is known to everyone, however, security may be compromised. The objective is controlled discoverability. Appropriate people should know enough to preserve continuity without giving unauthorized parties unnecessary access.

This is where the architecture developed in earlier chapters becomes relevant. Multiple repositories protect against physical destruction. Distributed custody protects against dependence upon one person. Separate authentication protects against unauthorized access. Verification protects against premature activation. Documentation protects against contextual loss. Professional review can provide legal, journalistic, scientific, or technical expertise. No single layer is sufficient by itself. The evidence vault becomes resilient because several layers reinforce one another.

Testing is essential because assumptions about preservation often prove wrong when challenged. A backup that has never been restored is an assumption, not a demonstrated recovery capability. A storage device that has not been examined for years may already be failing. A password believed to be correct may not work after a service changes its authentication requirements. A custodian who agreed to help several years earlier may no longer be available. Periodic verification reveals these problems while they can still be corrected. A dead man's switch should not discover its own weaknesses only after its creator is gone.

Long-term preservation also requires technological migration. File formats change. Storage media become obsolete. Software disappears. Hardware interfaces become unavailable. A file preserved perfectly on a medium that nobody can read is not a successful archive. Digital preservation therefore involves monitoring technological change and, where appropriate, migrating information into sustainable formats while retaining the original when feasible. Every migration should itself be documented. The history of the file becomes part of the archive's provenance.

The same principle applies to passwords and access credentials, although sensitive credentials should never be casually embedded in ordinary documentation. The problem is one of controlled succession. Someone must eventually be able to authenticate legitimate access without giving unauthorized people an easy route into the archive. The solution may involve professional custodians, carefully structured recovery mechanisms, or other security arrangements appropriate to the circumstances. What matters is that the access problem is deliberately designed rather than left to memory. A vault without a recovery pathway can become a tomb.

The most important discipline, however, is intellectual rather than technical. The creator should resist the temptation to treat the vault as a monument to their own interpretation. The purpose is not to ensure that future readers agree with the creator. It is to ensure that future readers can examine what the creator knew, what they believed, what they could document, and what remained uncertain. That means preserving contradictions, acknowledging gaps, and separating original evidence from commentary. It also means resisting unnecessary embellishment. An archive gains credibility when it shows its work.

A well-designed evidence vault consequently becomes something more than a storage system. It becomes a historical record of how information was obtained, preserved, interpreted, and transferred. Documents retain their origins. Photographs retain their technical and contextual history. Recordings retain their original forms. Testimony retains the circumstances under which it was given. Copies provide redundancy without silently replacing originals. Metadata, chronology, and custody records provide the connective tissue that allows individual pieces to become a coherent body of evidence.

The deepest purpose of such preservation is continuity. A person may disappear, but the information they possessed does not necessarily have to disappear with them. If the evidence is preserved with sufficient integrity and context, another person can eventually examine it without relying entirely upon the creator's memory or interpretation. That future investigator might confirm the original conclusions, challenge them, or discover something the creator never recognized. All three outcomes are legitimate because the purpose of preservation is inquiry rather than predetermined judgment.

The evidence vault is therefore the heart of the dead man's switch. The trigger, the communication system, the storage architecture, and the custodians all exist for one reason: to prevent important information from being lost while ensuring that it can eventually be evaluated responsibly. Documents must remain connected to their origins. Photographs and recordings must retain their original forms where possible. Testimony must remain distinguishable from interpretation. Chronology, provenance, metadata, and chain of custody must survive alongside the evidence itself. When those principles are respected, the archive becomes more than a collection of secrets; it becomes a durable record capable of surviving the person who created it.

The next challenge is protecting that record against a different kind of danger: the danger created by the evidence's sensitivity. Some information can be damaging if stolen, exposed, misunderstood, or released without context. The problem is therefore no longer simply how to preserve evidence, but how to preserve it while protecting the people and interests connected to it. That requires understanding encryption, access control, secure storage, and the difference between confidentiality and availability. The following chapters turn to the technical problem of keeping sensitive information protected without making it impossible for legitimate recipients to recover.

Resources

1. National Archives — Digital Preservation — authoritative guidance concerning the preservation, authenticity, integrity, and continued accessibility of digital records.

2. Library of Congress — Digital Preservation[1] — resources concerning preservation planning, digital formats, metadata, storage, and long-term accessibility.

3. Library of Congress — Sustainability of Digital Formats[2] — detailed information about characteristics affecting the long-term preservation of digital files.

4. NIST Special Publication 800-88 — Guidelines for Media Sanitization[3] — useful technical reference for information-bearing media and lifecycle considerations.

5. NIST Special Publication 800-57 — Recommendation for Key Management — authoritative resource concerning cryptographic key management, protection, backup, and recovery.

6. NIST Cybersecurity Framework 2.0[4] — framework for identifying, protecting, detecting, responding to, and recovering from information-security risks.

7. NIST Special Publication 800-53 — Security and Privacy Controls[5] — comprehensive catalog of controls relevant to access, auditability, integrity, authentication, contingency planning, and information protection.

8. Scientific Working Group on Digital Evidence[6] — professional guidance and best practices concerning digital evidence collection, preservation, examination, and reporting.

9. National Institute of Justice — Electronic Crime and Digital Evidence — government resource explaining important concepts surrounding digital evidence and forensic examination.

---

1. https://www.loc.gov/preservation/digital/?utm_source=chatgpt.com

2. https://www.loc.gov/preservation/digital/formats/?utm_source=chatgpt.com

3. https://csrc.nist.gov/publications/detail/sp/800-88/rev-1/final?utm_source=chatgpt.com

4. https://www.nist.gov/cyberframework?utm_source=chatgpt.com

5. https://csrc.nist.gov/publications/detail/sp/800-53/rev-5/final?utm_source=chatgpt.com

6. https://www.swgde.org/?utm_source=chatgpt.com

10. Federal Bureau of Investigation — Handbook of Forensic Services[7] — reference covering evidence handling, documentation, preservation, and forensic examination.

11. Federal Rules of Evidence — Rule 901: Authenticating or Identifying Evidence[8] — useful legal reference concerning authentication of evidence.

12. Federal Rules of Evidence — Rule 902: Evidence That Is Self-Authenticating[9] — provides additional context concerning authentication of certain categories of documentary and electronic evidence.

13. Federal Rules of Evidence — Rule 803[10] — reference concerning exceptions to the hearsay rule and the treatment of certain recorded information.

14. ISO 15489 — Information and Documentation: Records Management[11] — international framework concerning reliable records, provenance, capture, management, and preservation.

15. ISO 23081 — Information and Documentation: Metadata for Records[12] — international guidance concerning metadata and contextual information associated with records.

16. International Organization for Standardization — ISO 14721, Open Archival Information System (OAIS)[13] — foundational archival model for long-term preservation and access to digital information.

17. Digital Preservation Coalition — Digital Preservation Handbook[14] — extensive professional guidance on digital preservation, storage, metadata, integrity, migration, and continuity.

18. Internet Engineering Task Force — RFC 4949, Internet Security Glossary[15] — technical reference for concepts including integrity, authentication, confidentiality, and availability.

19. Electronic Frontier Foundation — Surveillance Self-Defense[16] — practical information-security guidance covering authentication, secure storage, threat modeling, and protection of sensitive information.

20. Committee to Protect Journalists — Safety Kit[17] — guidance relevant to source protection, evidence handling, digital security, and contingency planning.

21. Elizabeth F. Loftus, *Eyewitness Testimony*, Harvard University Press, 1979 — foundational research on eyewitness memory and the limitations of human recollection.

---

7. https://www.fbi.gov/file-repository/handbook-of-forensic-services-pdf.pdf?utm_source=chatgpt.com

8. https://www.law.cornell.edu/rules/fre/rule_901?utm_source=chatgpt.com

9. https://www.law.cornell.edu/rules/fre/rule_902?utm_source=chatgpt.com

10. https://www.law.cornell.edu/rules/fre/rule_803?utm_source=chatgpt.com

11. https://www.iso.org/standard/62542.html?utm_source=chatgpt.com

12. https://www.iso.org/standard/81610.html?utm_source=chatgpt.com

13. https://www.iso.org/standard/57284.html?utm_source=chatgpt.com

14. https://www.dpconline.org/handbook?utm_source=chatgpt.com

15. https://www.rfc-editor.org/rfc/rfc4949?utm_source=chatgpt.com

16. https://ssd.eff.org/?utm_source=chatgpt.com

17. https://cpj.org/safety-kit/?utm_source=chatgpt.com

22. Daniel L. Schacter, *The Seven Sins of Memory: How the Mind Forgets and Remembers*, Houghton Mifflin, 2001 — important work on memory distortion, reconstruction, and recall.

23. National Academies — Strengthening Forensic Science in the United States[18] — landmark assessment of forensic-science reliability, standards, validation, and interpretation.

24. National Academies — Reproducibility and Replicability in Science[19] — useful for understanding the importance of preserving underlying data, methods, and analytical context.

25. Bruce Schneier, *Security Engineering: A Guide to Building Dependable Distributed Systems*, 3rd ed., Wiley, 2020 — comprehensive treatment of dependable systems, security architecture, human factors, and failure analysis.

18. https://nap.nationalacademies.org/catalog/12589/strengthening-forensic-science-in-the-united-states-a-path-forward?utm_source=chatgpt.com

19. https://nap.nationalacademies.org/catalog/25303/reproducibility-and-replicability-in-science?utm_source=chatgpt.com

Encryption and the Protection of Sensitive Information

Once important evidence has been preserved, another problem immediately appears: preservation without protection can create a new vulnerability. A carefully assembled archive containing documents, photographs, recordings, financial records, testimony, and correspondence may become more dangerous to its owner and sources precisely because it concentrates valuable information in one place. Anyone who gains unauthorized access may acquire not merely a collection of files but a map of relationships, identities, allegations, communications, and potentially sensitive evidence. Encryption exists partly to address this problem by transforming readable information into a form that is intended to be unintelligible without the appropriate cryptographic means of access. Yet understanding encryption requires moving beyond the popular idea that it is simply a digital lock, because encryption is only one component of a larger security architecture.

At its most basic level, encryption converts plaintext into ciphertext using a mathematical process controlled by a cryptographic key. The ciphertext is designed to reveal little useful information to someone who does not possess the appropriate means of decryption. Modern cryptography is based on mathematical algorithms that have been extensively studied rather than on the secrecy of the algorithm itself. In well-designed systems, the secret is normally the key. This distinction is important because a system should not depend upon keeping the underlying encryption method mysterious. Security should instead depend upon strong, properly implemented cryptographic algorithms and effective protection of the keys that control them.

The concept can be illustrated without becoming technical. Imagine that a document is placed inside a container that has been transformed by a mathematical mechanism, and only someone possessing the correct key can restore it to readable form. The strength of that protection depends on the cryptographic design, the key, the implementation, and the circumstances surrounding its use. If the key is stolen, the encryption may provide no meaningful protection against the person who possesses it. If the encryption is poorly implemented, vulnerabilities may exist even when the underlying mathematics is strong. If the information is exposed before encryption or after decryption, encryption cannot retroactively protect it.

This is the first principle that anyone designing a dead man's switch should understand: encryption protects data, not necessarily the person using it. It can protect an encrypted archive from someone who obtains the storage device. It can help protect communications while they are being transmitted. It can reduce the consequences of a lost laptop or misplaced drive. But it cannot prevent someone from coercing a person into revealing a password. It cannot determine whether the person requesting access is trustworthy. It cannot correct a malicious alteration made before the information was encrypted. It cannot prevent an authorized recipient from copying the decrypted information and distributing it. Encryption is therefore a powerful layer, not a complete security system.

Confidentiality is the protection most people associate with encryption. Confidentiality means preventing unauthorized parties from learning protected information. But sensitive evidence also requires integrity and availability. Integrity concerns whether information has been altered without authorization. Availability concerns whether authorized users can actually obtain the information when they need it. A perfectly confidential archive that has been corrupted beyond recovery is not useful. An intact archive that nobody can access is equally problematic. Effective information security therefore considers confidentiality, integrity, and availability together.

Authentication is related but distinct from encryption. Encryption asks whether information can be understood without the necessary cryptographic capability. Authentication asks who or what is requesting access and whether that identity can be trusted. A person may possess the correct password while still not being the legitimate person intended to use the account. Conversely, a system may successfully authenticate someone but then transmit information without adequate encryption. Strong security requires both concepts. The distinction becomes particularly important in a dead man's switch because future access must be restricted to appropriate recipients.

Passwords are one of the oldest and most familiar forms of authentication, but they are also one of the most persistent sources of weakness. People reuse passwords, choose predictable combinations, write them in insecure locations, share them through ordinary channels, or forget them entirely. A sophisticated encryption system can therefore be undermined by a weak human credential. The strength of a password depends on factors including its length, unpredictability, uniqueness, and how the system stores and verifies it. Modern security practice increasingly encourages password managers, strong unique credentials, and additional authentication factors rather than relying on one memorable password.

A password should also not automatically be confused with an encryption key. They can be related, but they are conceptually different. A password is generally a human-selected secret used for authentication or to derive cryptographic material. A cryptographic key is data used directly by a cryptographic algorithm. Modern systems may derive keys from passwords using specialized key-derivation functions designed to make guessing more expensive. This distinction matters because protecting a password and protecting a cryptographic key can involve different requirements. Losing either one at the wrong stage can make protected information inaccessible.

Key management is therefore one of the most important subjects in encryption. The strongest encryption in the world cannot help if the key is lost. Consider an encrypted archive created by someone who is later unable to communicate. If the only decryption key exists in their memory and nobody else has a legitimate recovery pathway, the archive may remain permanently inaccessible. This creates an important tension between security and continuity. The key must be protected strongly enough that unauthorized people cannot obtain it, while a legitimate succession mechanism must exist if the creator becomes unavailable.

This is where the design of a dead man's switch intersects with the principles established in earlier chapters. The evidence can be distributed across multiple repositories while access information is distributed separately. Different custodians can hold different components of a recovery process where appropriate. A professional intermediary can maintain instructions without necessarily possessing every piece of sensitive evidence. The precise design should depend upon the threat model and legal circumstances. What matters is that key recovery is treated as an explicit architectural problem rather than an afterthought.

Cryptographic systems can also use asymmetric encryption, often called public-key cryptography. In a simplified explanation, one key can be made publicly available while another corresponding key remains private. Information encrypted appropriately with one part of the key pair can be processed using the other under the rules of the particular cryptographic system. Public-key systems have become foundational to secure internet communications, digital signatures, identity systems, and secure key exchange. Their importance lies partly in reducing the need for two parties to have already shared the same secret before communicating securely.

Digital signatures demonstrate another important capability of cryptography. Encryption is primarily concerned with confidentiality, whereas digital signatures can help establish authenticity and integrity. A digital signature can allow a recipient to verify that data was signed using the corresponding private key and that the signed content has not changed since signing, assuming the underlying system and key remain trustworthy. This can be valuable when preserving evidence because the archive may need to demonstrate that a file has remained unchanged. A signature does not prove that the underlying statement is true. It helps establish something narrower: the relationship between a particular signer and a particular digital object.

Cryptographic hashing provides another useful integrity mechanism. A cryptographic hash function produces a fixed-length value derived from the contents of a file or other input. Even a small change to the input will normally produce a different hash value. Recording a hash can therefore provide a practical way to detect whether a file has changed since the hash was created. Hashing is not encryption because a hash is not intended to be decrypted back into the original data. It is better understood as a mathematical fingerprint of the input. For evidence preservation, that distinction is crucial.

A hash does not prove that the original file was authentic or truthful. If someone creates a fraudulent document and hashes it, the hash can demonstrate that the fraudulent document has not changed since hashing. The integrity mechanism has worked perfectly while the underlying content remains false. This illustrates a broader lesson about security technology: technical integrity and factual truth are separate questions. Cryptography can help preserve what exists. It cannot determine whether what exists deserves to be believed.

Secure communications introduce another layer of complexity. When sensitive information travels from one person to another, there are multiple points at which it may be exposed. The device sending the information may be compromised. The communication channel may be vulnerable. The recipient's device may be insecure. The information may be copied after receipt. Authentication may fail. Metadata may reveal information even when message content is protected. End-to-end encryption can substantially improve confidentiality in appropriate circumstances by ensuring that message content is encrypted on the sender's device and decrypted on the intended recipient's device. But the security of the endpoints remains important.

This is why the phrase "encrypted" should never be treated as a complete security assessment. An encrypted message can still be exposed through a compromised device. An encrypted archive can still be copied after legitimate decryption. A secure communication channel can still connect the wrong people. An encrypted backup can still be deleted. A protected account can still be taken over through social engineering. Security is therefore a chain. The weakest important link can determine the practical outcome.

Access control determines who is permitted to interact with protected information. In a large organization, access may be divided according to roles, responsibilities, and levels of authorization. The same principle can apply to a personal evidence archive. Not everyone involved in preservation needs access to everything. One person might maintain a repository without having authority to publish it. Another might be able to review a subset of material. A professional intermediary might be responsible for determining whether predefined conditions have been met. Limiting access according to legitimate need reduces the consequences of compromise.

The principle of least privilege is particularly useful here. A person or system should generally have only the access necessary to perform its legitimate function. If someone merely needs to maintain a backup, they may not need unrestricted access to every document. If someone needs to verify the existence of an archive, they may not need to read its contents. If someone is responsible for evaluating a disclosure request, they may not need control over every storage system. Least privilege does not eliminate insider risk, but it limits the amount of damage that can result from one compromised account or person.

Multi-factor authentication can provide another layer. Instead of relying solely upon something a person knows, such as a password, authentication can incorporate something they possess or something associated with a verified characteristic. The important principle is that compromising one factor should not automatically compromise the entire account. Different authentication methods have different strengths and weaknesses. Security-conscious users should therefore consider the recovery process as carefully as the initial authentication process. A system that is secure until the recovery procedure is invoked may possess a hidden weakness.

Recovery mechanisms deserve special attention in dead man's switch systems because the ordinary account holder may eventually become unavailable. Many services provide account-recovery procedures intended for ordinary users who forget credentials. Those mechanisms can be useful, but they can also become an attack surface. A recovery email account may itself be compromised. A telephone number may change ownership. Security questions may be guessable. Customer-support procedures may be vulnerable to social engineering. The strongest protection can therefore be undermined by the weakest recovery pathway.

The problem becomes even more significant when information must survive for years. People change devices. They replace telephone numbers. They move between countries. Services change policies. Encryption software is updated. File formats evolve. Accounts are closed. A recovery mechanism that works today may not work a decade from now. Long-term information protection therefore requires periodic review. Keys, credentials, backups, software dependencies, and access arrangements should be treated as living components rather than permanent objects. The system must evolve without losing track of its original evidence.

Backups are an essential complement to encryption. Encryption can prevent unauthorized access, but it does not protect against accidental deletion, hardware failure, corruption, ransomware, or physical destruction unless protected copies also exist. A backup that is stored in exactly the same place as the primary copy provides limited protection against local disaster. A backup that remains permanently connected to the same compromised system may also be vulnerable to the same attack. Effective resilience therefore considers where backups exist, how independently they are protected, and whether they can actually be restored.

Encryption should generally be applied to sensitive backups as well. Otherwise, the primary archive may be strongly protected while its backup represents an easily accessible copy. This is an example of a common security failure in which attention is concentrated on the main system while secondary copies are neglected. The same information may exist on laptops, phones, removable drives, cloud accounts, email attachments, and temporary working directories. An evidence inventory should therefore consider the entire information lifecycle. Protecting one copy while leaving several others exposed can create a false sense of security.

Cloud storage illustrates the distinction between convenience and control. Cloud services can provide geographic redundancy, automated synchronization, availability across devices, and professional infrastructure. These advantages can be extremely useful for information preservation. But cloud storage also introduces dependence on third parties, account credentials, service availability, access policies, and network connectivity. The user may not control every aspect of the underlying infrastructure. Encryption can reduce some of these risks, particularly when strong client-side or end-to-end encryption is used appropriately, but the exact security model depends upon the service.

A particularly important distinction is between encryption performed by a service provider and encryption performed before information reaches that provider. In some systems, the provider may manage the encryption keys and be able to decrypt stored information under defined circumstances. In other systems, the user or an application may control the keys so that the provider cannot ordinarily read the protected content. These architectures have different tradeoffs concerning convenience, recovery, trust, and access. Users should understand which model they are actually using rather than assuming that the word "encrypted" means the same thing everywhere.

Physical storage remains relevant even in a highly digital world. External drives, removable media, printed records, optical media, and other physical repositories can provide independence from online services. They can also introduce their own risks. Devices can fail. Media can deteriorate. Physical objects can be lost or stolen. Old interfaces can disappear. A drive preserved for ten years may eventually require hardware or software that is no longer readily available. Physical protection and technological migration therefore belong together.

A secure archive also needs to distinguish between protecting information from unauthorized access and protecting it from its own owner. Someone may accidentally overwrite an original file, delete an important folder, or synchronize a damaged version across multiple devices. Access controls and versioned backups can reduce these risks. The objective is not merely preventing malicious outsiders from reaching the evidence. It is preventing ordinary human mistakes from destroying it. In many real-world systems, accidental actions are at least as important to resilience as deliberate attacks.

Threat modeling provides a useful framework for deciding how much protection is appropriate. A person preserving ordinary personal documents does not face the same threat environment as an investigative journalist protecting a confidential source or a researcher preserving sensitive proprietary data. Security measures should therefore be matched to realistic threats. Excessive complexity can create its own risks if users cannot operate the system correctly. Insufficient protection can expose highly sensitive information. The right design is the one that addresses the credible threats without becoming so cumbersome that it fails through human error.

Threat modeling also helps separate dramatic fears from practical risks. Someone may worry about an exceptionally sophisticated attacker while leaving an account protected by a reused password. They may invest in complex cryptographic systems while neglecting backups. They may encrypt a laptop while leaving sensitive information in an unprotected email account. They may create an elaborate recovery system that nobody understands. Security is improved not by choosing the most impressive technology but by identifying the actual paths through which information could be lost or exposed.

Social engineering deserves particular attention because it attacks people rather than mathematical algorithms. An attacker may attempt to persuade someone to reveal credentials, approve access, open a malicious attachment, or bypass an established procedure. Strong encryption cannot prevent a legitimate user from voluntarily giving an attacker the information needed to defeat it. Education, verification procedures, limited privileges, and cautious handling of unexpected requests can therefore be as important as cryptographic strength. The human layer remains part of the security system.

Coercion presents an even more difficult problem. Encryption assumes that the person controlling the key can keep it secret. If that person is compelled to reveal it, the cryptographic protection may no longer help. This does not make encryption useless. It simply demonstrates that encryption addresses unauthorized technical access rather than every possible form of access. Physical safety, legal advice, organizational safeguards, and personal security are separate considerations. A dead man's switch should never encourage someone to believe that encryption makes them physically untouchable.

The same limitation applies to endpoint security. Suppose an evidence archive is strongly encrypted while stored on a computer. If malware gains control of that computer while the archive is open, the attacker may be able to access the decrypted information. Encryption protects data while it remains encrypted. Once legitimate access converts it back into readable form, endpoint security becomes critical. This is why secure operating systems, software updates, device protections, authentication, and cautious application use remain relevant even when encryption is extremely strong.

The relationship between encryption and evidence integrity is equally important. Encryption can prevent unauthorized people from reading a file, but it does not necessarily reveal whether the file has changed. Integrity mechanisms such as cryptographic hashes and digital signatures can address that question. Proper archival procedures can add another layer by documenting when the file was acquired, where it came from, and how it was handled. Together, these measures can create a stronger evidentiary record. None of them independently establishes that the content is true.

Long-term protection also requires documenting the system itself. Future custodians need to know what technology was used, what categories of data exist, how legitimate access is established, and which dependencies must remain functional. This documentation must itself be protected because a detailed map of the security architecture can become sensitive information. The objective is controlled documentation. Enough information should exist to permit legitimate continuity, but not so much that an unauthorized reader receives a convenient blueprint for defeating the system.

The architecture should also account for the possibility that the creator becomes incapacitated rather than dead. A dead man's switch is often discussed as though death were the only trigger, but the same continuity problem can arise through serious illness, imprisonment, disappearance, loss of communication, or cognitive incapacity. If encryption keys and access procedures depend completely upon the creator, any of these circumstances can create a failure. Designing legitimate succession pathways can therefore make the system useful beyond its most dramatic scenario. The emphasis should remain on continuity and controlled access rather than automatic disclosure at the first sign of disruption.

There is another subtle danger: encryption can make information appear more secure than it really is. A person may believe that because a folder is encrypted, the information inside it is protected everywhere. Yet unencrypted copies may exist in temporary folders, email accounts, cloud synchronization directories, browser caches, messaging applications, thumbnails, backups, or other locations. The security of the system must therefore be evaluated across the entire lifecycle of the information. Where information is created, edited, transmitted, stored, copied, analyzed, and eventually disclosed can all affect its exposure. Encryption is one control within that lifecycle, not a universal cloak.

The same principle applies to communication. End-to-end encrypted messaging can protect the content of a conversation from many forms of interception, but the devices themselves may still reveal information. Notifications can expose message content. Contact lists can reveal relationships. Backups may follow different security rules from the live messages. Screenshots can create uncontrolled copies. Recipients can preserve or forward messages. Metadata can sometimes reveal patterns even when content remains confidential. Secure communication therefore requires understanding the complete system rather than focusing exclusively on the encryption label.

For an evidence-preservation system, the ideal objective is controlled survivability. The information should remain available to legitimate recipients under predefined conditions while remaining inaccessible to unauthorized parties. That means balancing several competing requirements. Security must be strong enough to resist credible threats. Recovery must be possible if the creator becomes unavailable. Evidence must remain intact. Backups must exist.

Custody must be documented. Access must be limited. The system must also remain understandable enough to be maintained over time.

The most important lesson is therefore that encryption should never be considered in isolation. It is a tool for protecting confidentiality and, when combined with related cryptographic mechanisms, can contribute to integrity and authentication. It cannot establish the truth of a document. It cannot guarantee that the correct person will receive the key. It cannot protect an already compromised device. It cannot prevent coercion. It cannot compensate for the absence of backups. It cannot decide whether disclosure is ethically or legally justified. Those questions belong to the larger architecture of the dead man's switch.

A properly designed information-preservation system treats encryption as one layer among many. Original evidence is preserved separately from working copies. Backups protect against loss. Authentication restricts access. Cryptographic integrity mechanisms help detect alteration. Distributed custody reduces dependence upon one person. Recovery arrangements address the possibility that the creator becomes unavailable. Documentation preserves the knowledge required to maintain continuity. Professional advice can address legal and ethical questions. Each layer handles a different failure mode, and the system becomes stronger because no single layer is expected to solve every problem.

Ultimately, encryption is valuable because information has value even before anyone decides what that information means. A document can expose corruption, a photograph can establish a physical fact, a recording can preserve testimony, and a dataset can reveal a scientific result. If such material is destroyed or exposed prematurely, the opportunity for responsible investigation may disappear. Encryption provides a way to reduce one category of risk while preserving the possibility of future access. Its greatest strength is not that it makes information untouchable, but that it can help preserve control over who gets to examine it and when.

That leads directly to the next problem. Even perfectly encrypted information has to live somewhere, and the storage environment can determine whether the evidence survives at all. Cloud systems offer convenience and geographic redundancy but introduce third-party dependence. Local drives provide control but can fail, be stolen, or become obsolete. Physical archives can preserve originals but require careful environmental protection. The next chapter therefore examines cloud storage, its advantages, its weaknesses, and the difficult question of how much control a person should surrender to an outside service when the information being protected may one day become critically important.

Resources

1. NIST Cryptographic Standards and Guidelines[1] — authoritative U.S. government resources concerning cryptographic algorithms, protocols, key management, digital signatures, and related standards.

2. NIST Special Publication 800-57 — Recommendation for Key Management — foundational guidance on cryptographic key generation, storage, protection, backup, recovery, and lifecycle management.

3. NIST Special Publication 800-63-4 — Digital Identity Guidelines[2] — authoritative guidance on authentication, authenticators, identity assurance, and account recovery.

---

1. https://csrc.nist.gov/projects/cryptographic-standards-and-guidelines?utm_source=chatgpt.com

2. https://pages.nist.gov/800-63-4/?utm_source=chatgpt.com

4. NIST Special Publication 800-53 — Security and Privacy Controls[3] — comprehensive security-control framework covering access control, authentication, least privilege, auditability, contingency planning, and system integrity.

5. NIST Cybersecurity Framework 2.0[4] — risk-management framework covering identification, protection, detection, response, and recovery.

6. NIST Special Publication 800-61 — Computer Security Incident Handling Guide[5] — guidance concerning preparation, detection, analysis, containment, recovery, and lessons learned following security incidents.

7. NIST FIPS 180-4 — Secure Hash Standard[6] — establishes the SHA-2 family of secure hash algorithms used for integrity verification and related cryptographic applications.

8. NIST FIPS 186-5 — Digital Signature Standard[7] — federal standard concerning digital signatures and cryptographic authentication of digital information.

9. NIST FIPS 197 — Advanced Encryption Standard (AES)[8] — specifies AES, one of the principal modern symmetric encryption standards.

10. NIST Special Publication 800-38A — Recommendation for Block Cipher Modes of Operation[9] — technical reference concerning secure use of block ciphers in various operational modes.

11. NIST Special Publication 800-132 — Recommendation for Password-Based Key Derivation — addresses deriving cryptographic keys from passwords and related security considerations.

12. Internet Engineering Task Force — RFC 8446: The Transport Layer Security Protocol Version 1.3[10] — foundational technical specification for modern TLS-secured internet communications.

13. Internet Engineering Task Force — RFC 9106: Argon2 Memory-Hard Function[11] — technical standard concerning Argon2, a password-hashing and key-derivation function designed to resist certain password-guessing attacks.

14. OWASP Authentication Cheat Sheet[12] — practical security guidance on authentication, passwords, multi-factor authentication, and session security.

15. OWASP Password Storage Cheat Sheet[13] — technical guidance concerning secure password storage and modern password-hashing practices.

---

3. https://csrc.nist.gov/publications/detail/sp/800-53/rev-5/final?utm_source=chatgpt.com
4. https://www.nist.gov/cyberframework?utm_source=chatgpt.com
5. https://csrc.nist.gov/publications/detail/sp/800-61/rev-2/final?utm_source=chatgpt.com
6. https://csrc.nist.gov/publications/detail/fips/180/4/final?utm_source=chatgpt.com
7. https://csrc.nist.gov/publications/detail/fips/186/5/final?utm_source=chatgpt.com
8. https://csrc.nist.gov/publications/detail/fips/197/final?utm_source=chatgpt.com
9. https://csrc.nist.gov/publications/detail/sp/800-38a/final?utm_source=chatgpt.com
10. https://www.rfc-editor.org/rfc/rfc8446?utm_source=chatgpt.com
11. https://www.rfc-editor.org/rfc/rfc9106?utm_source=chatgpt.com
12. https://cheatsheetseries.owasp.org/cheatsheets/Authentication_Cheat_Sheet.html?utm_source=chatgpt.com
13. https://cheatsheetseries.owasp.org/cheatsheets/Password_Storage_Cheat_Sheet.html?utm_source=chatgpt.com

16. Electronic Frontier Foundation — Surveillance Self-Defense[14] — accessible guidance concerning threat modeling, device security, encryption, authentication, and secure communications.

17. Signal — Encryption and Security Information[15] — useful technical background on end-to-end encrypted communications and the security model behind modern encrypted messaging.

18. Cloud Security Alliance[16] — resources concerning cloud security, identity, access management, encryption, governance, and risks associated with cloud environments.

19. ISO/IEC 27001 — Information Security Management Systems[17] — international framework for systematic information-security risk management.

20. ISO/IEC 27002 — Information Security Controls[18] — guidance concerning practical information-security controls, access management, cryptography, operations, and protection of information assets.

21. CISA — Cybersecurity Best Practices[19] — government guidance concerning backups, authentication, ransomware resilience, and protection against common cybersecurity threats.

22. Bruce Schneier, *Applied Cryptography: Protocols, Algorithms, and Source Code in C*, 2nd ed., Wiley, 1996 — influential technical reference covering cryptographic concepts, algorithms, protocols, and practical security considerations.

23. Ross Anderson, *Security Engineering: A Guide to Building Dependable Distributed Systems*, 3rd ed., Wiley, 2020 — comprehensive examination of security architecture, human factors, dependable systems, authentication, access control, and failure modes.

24. Whitfield Diffie and Martin E. Hellman, "New Directions in Cryptography," *IEEE Transactions on Information Theory*, Vol. 22, No. 6, 1976 — landmark paper introducing concepts underlying modern public-key cryptography and secure key exchange.

25. Claude E. Shannon, "Communication Theory of Secrecy Systems," *Bell System Technical Journal*, Vol. 28, No. 4, 1949 — foundational mathematical treatment of secrecy systems and information-theoretic principles underlying modern cryptography.

---

14. https://ssd.eff.org/?utm_source=chatgpt.com

15. https://signal.org/?utm_source=chatgpt.com

16. https://cloudsecurityalliance.org/?utm_source=chatgpt.com

17. https://www.iso.org/isoiec-27001-information-security.html?utm_source=chatgpt.com

18. https://www.iso.org/standard/75652.html?utm_source=chatgpt.com

19. https://www.cisa.gov/stopransomware/ransomware-guide?utm_source=chatgpt.com

Cloud Storage, Offline Archives, and Distributed Custody

The moment sensitive information is preserved, another question becomes unavoidable: where does it live? A dead man's switch may depend upon documents, photographs, recordings, testimony, financial records, correspondence, and other evidence surviving for months or even years, yet every storage medium has a failure point. A hard drive can die, a cloud account can be locked, a building can burn, a password can be lost, or an entire service can disappear. Even information that appears perfectly protected can become inaccessible if the technology required to retrieve it no longer exists. The real objective, therefore, is not to discover a storage system that can never fail, because no such system exists, but to construct an architecture in which one failure does not destroy everything.

This is the fundamental principle of redundancy. Redundancy means maintaining more than one means of preserving something important so that the failure of one component does not result in total loss. In ordinary life, redundancy is often invisible because it is built into systems we take for granted. Banks maintain multiple copies of financial information, data centers use redundant infrastructure, and professional archives employ preservation strategies designed around anticipated failure. A personal evidence archive deserves the same conceptual discipline when the consequences of losing the information could be substantial. The key is not simply having multiple copies, but having copies whose vulnerabilities are sufficiently independent that the same event is unlikely to destroy all of them.

Cloud storage is attractive because it appears to solve several problems simultaneously. Information can be stored remotely, synchronized between devices, backed up automatically, and accessed from different locations. Large cloud providers can maintain sophisticated physical infrastructure that would be impractical for an individual to reproduce. Geographic distribution can also provide resilience against a localized disaster. If a computer is destroyed, the information may remain available through another device. If a local building is damaged, a remote copy may survive. These advantages make cloud storage an important component of many modern preservation strategies.

But convenience should not be confused with control. When information is stored through a cloud provider, the preservation system becomes dependent upon an outside organization, its infrastructure, its policies, its account-management procedures, and its continued operation. The provider may change its terms of service, discontinue a product, restrict an account, experience an outage, or become subject to legal demands. Even a highly reliable company remains a third party operating outside the direct control of the person who owns the information. Cloud storage therefore transfers some risks rather than eliminating them. It can be an excellent layer of redundancy, but it should rarely be mistaken for the entire architecture.

Account access represents one of the most obvious cloud vulnerabilities. An archive can remain physically intact on remote servers while becoming practically inaccessible because the legitimate account holder can no longer authenticate. Passwords may be forgotten, authentication devices may be lost, recovery addresses may become unavailable, or security procedures may change. The person who created the archive may also die or become incapacitated without leaving a legitimate mechanism through which an authorized successor can obtain access. This creates a paradox in which information is extremely durable technically but fragile administratively. A resilient system must therefore consider not only where the data resides but how legitimate access will survive the creator.

Cloud synchronization introduces another subtle risk. Synchronization is designed to make information consistent across devices, but consistency is not always the same thing as preservation. If an important file is accidentally deleted or corrupted and the change propagates automatically, multiple synchronized devices may acquire the same damaged state. Similarly, ransomware or malicious software can potentially affect connected systems and synchronized storage. Version history and protected backups can mitigate some of these risks, but they must be configured and tested. Automatic duplication is not automatically independent backup.

The distinction between synchronization and backup is therefore crucial. Synchronization attempts to keep multiple locations aligned. Backup attempts to preserve recoverable historical states so that information can be restored after loss or corruption. If a person deletes a file accidentally, synchronization may faithfully reproduce the deletion. A properly designed backup may retain an earlier version. If ransomware encrypts accessible files, a protected backup may provide a recovery path. The two functions complement one another but should not be treated as interchangeable. A dead man's switch concerned with long-term evidence preservation needs to understand this difference.

Offline archives provide a different form of protection. An offline copy is not continuously connected to the network and therefore is less exposed to many online attacks. External storage devices, removable media, archival drives, and appropriately preserved physical records can provide an important barrier between the evidence and threats that operate through network connectivity. If a malicious program compromises an online system, an offline archive may remain untouched. If an account is hijacked, the offline copy may remain available. This separation can be extremely valuable. But offline does not mean invulnerable.

Physical storage introduces its own failure modes. A hard drive can suffer mechanical failure. Flash storage can experience degradation or controller failure. Optical media can become unreadable. Magnetic media can deteriorate or become difficult to access. Physical documents can be damaged by water, fire, humidity, insects, mold, or careless handling. A storage device can be stolen or simply forgotten in a drawer. An archive may therefore be offline yet still poorly preserved. The correct question is not whether a copy is offline, but whether it is protected against the specific threats likely to affect it.

Technological obsolescence is one of the least dramatic but most important threats to long-term archives. A storage medium can survive physically while the equipment required to read it becomes unavailable. Interfaces change. File formats become unsupported. Software disappears. Encryption standards evolve. A computer capable of reading an old device may eventually become difficult to obtain. Professional archivists therefore treat preservation as an active process rather than assuming that storing an object today guarantees access decades later. Digital information needs a strategy for technological continuity. Preservation is not the same thing as simply putting a hard drive in a safe.

This is why periodic verification matters. A stored device should eventually be checked to determine whether it remains readable and whether the files remain intact. Cryptographic hashes can help verify that digital content has not changed unexpectedly. Test restorations can determine whether backups can actually be recovered. File inventories can reveal missing objects. Documentation can establish which formats and software dependencies exist. These checks transform preservation from an assumption into a demonstrated capability. A backup that has never been tested is a promise rather than proof.

Offline storage can also become a single point of failure if every offline copy is kept in one place. Imagine an archive containing three identical drives, all stored in the same room. Technically there are three copies, but operationally they may behave like one. A fire, flood, burglary, or other localized event could destroy all three simultaneously. Meaningful redundancy requires some independence in location, medium, or custody. The objective is to avoid correlated failure. Three copies vulnerable to the same event provide much less protection than three copies exposed to different risks.

Geographic separation is therefore one of the most powerful forms of redundancy. A local archive can protect against network failure while a geographically remote archive can protect against local disaster. A professional repository in another location can add another layer. A carefully controlled cloud archive can provide remote availability. The precise arrangement depends upon the sensitivity of the information and the realistic threat environment. The broader principle is straightforward: if one event can reach every copy at once, the system has not achieved genuine independence.

Distributed custody extends this concept from geography to people. Instead of one individual controlling every component, different trusted parties can hold different elements of the preservation system. One person might possess a physical archive. Another might maintain a separate copy. A professional intermediary might hold instructions or a recovery mechanism. A legal representative might possess documents establishing authority. This structure can reduce the danger that one person's death, disappearance, compromise, or error destroys the entire system. It can also reduce the likelihood that one compromised individual can immediately access everything.

Distributed custody, however, is not automatically safer. Every additional person introduces another potential failure point. A custodian may become unavailable, lose the material, mishandle it, betray the trust placed in them, or simply misunderstand their responsibilities. Someone may also be targeted specifically because they are known to possess part of the archive. The system must therefore balance distribution against complexity. The goal is not to involve as many people as possible. It is to create enough independence that no single failure becomes catastrophic.

This is where compartmentalization becomes valuable. Different custodians do not necessarily need complete copies of everything. Information can sometimes be divided according to legitimate access requirements, sensitivity, or function. One custodian might preserve a collection without knowing its entire interpretation. Another might maintain access instructions without possessing the evidence itself. A third might be responsible for verifying a predefined condition. Such arrangements can reduce the consequences of a compromise. They can also make unauthorized reconstruction of the entire archive more difficult.

Yet excessive fragmentation can create its own problem. If an archive is divided into too many pieces, future recovery may become impractical. The creator may understand the architecture perfectly while alive but leave successors unable to reconstruct it. People may forget which custodian holds which component. A custodian may disappear. Instructions may become ambiguous. The system can become so secure that legitimate access becomes impossible. This is one of the recurring tensions in security engineering: every barrier introduced against unauthorized access can potentially become another barrier against authorized recovery.

The ideal architecture therefore seeks controlled recoverability. A legitimate future custodian should be able to understand what exists, establish their authority, and recover the information without requiring the creator to explain everything personally. At the same time, an unauthorized person should not be able to discover the entire archive simply by finding one password or one device. This balance requires documentation, authentication, redundancy, and carefully considered custody arrangements. It also requires testing. The creator should know whether the system actually works before relying upon it.

Cloud and offline storage can complement one another precisely because their failure modes differ. Cloud storage may provide remote availability, automated replication, and convenient access. Offline storage can provide isolation from network attacks and independence from a particular service provider. A physical archive can preserve originals that should not exist only as digital copies. Distributed custody can protect against dependence upon a single person. Each layer addresses a different class of failure. The strength of the architecture comes from their differences rather than their similarities.

Consider a simple conceptual model. The primary working archive might exist in an encrypted digital environment. A protected backup could exist offline. Another copy could be maintained at a geographically separate location. Selected originals might be preserved physically under appropriate conditions. Access information could be handled separately from the evidence itself. A designated custodian could know how legitimate succession is established. None of these components needs to be perfect. Their purpose is to ensure that the failure of one does not automatically eliminate every route to recovery.

The architecture should also distinguish between preservation copies and disclosure copies. The complete archive may contain information that should never be released indiscriminately. Some material may identify innocent individuals, expose personal information, reveal confidential sources, or create legal complications. A disclosure package may therefore need to be assembled separately from the preservation archive. The preservation archive retains the full evidentiary record. A future authorized reviewer can then determine what can appropriately be released. This prevents the dead man's switch from turning every piece of preserved information into an automatic public disclosure.

The difference between storage and publication is especially important. A person may want evidence to survive without necessarily wanting every detail published immediately. Preservation protects the possibility of future investigation. Publication creates consequences in the outside world. The two decisions can therefore be separated. An archive can remain confidential while a designated reviewer evaluates whether disclosure is warranted. This distinction provides an additional layer of ethical and legal control.

Cloud providers also vary considerably in their security architectures. Some services may encrypt data at rest while retaining the ability to manage the encryption keys. Others may provide stronger client-side or end-to-end encryption models in which the provider has less ability to access content. These distinctions matter. The word "encrypted" alone does not reveal who controls the keys or under what circumstances data can be decrypted. Anyone building a sensitive archive should understand the provider's actual security model rather than relying on marketing terminology.

The same caution applies to cloud redundancy. A provider may operate multiple data centers, but that does not necessarily mean a user's account is immune to deletion, administrative error, credential compromise, or service-level failure. Infrastructure redundancy protects against some physical and technical problems. It does not automatically protect against every account-level or user-level problem. A cloud archive should therefore be considered one layer within a broader preservation strategy. The provider's redundancy and the user's redundancy are different things.

Offline archives also require an access strategy. A drive locked inside a safe may survive for years, but future custodians need to know that it exists. They may need compatible hardware, appropriate software, and legitimate decryption credentials. If the drive is encrypted, the key must survive independently enough to remain available to authorized users. If the physical archive is located somewhere unfamiliar, access instructions may be necessary. Again, the principle is controlled recoverability. Security is useful only if legitimate access remains possible.

The storage environment itself matters. Physical archives should be protected from environmental conditions that accelerate deterioration. Digital devices should be stored appropriately for their medium and periodically assessed. Original paper documents may require archival-quality storage materials. Magnetic and optical media may have different preservation requirements. The exact method should reflect the medium. There is no universal "safe place" that works equally well for every kind of evidence.

Documentation becomes increasingly important as the architecture grows more complex. A future custodian should be able to determine what repositories exist, what each contains, which copies are original or derivative, when they were last verified, and what dependencies affect access. The documentation should not itself become an unnecessary security vulnerability. Sensitive credentials and highly detailed technical information should be handled appropriately. But the existence and purpose of each preservation layer must be sufficiently documented to prevent the archive from becoming an archaeological puzzle.

One useful way to think about distributed custody is as a continuity network. The original creator is one node. Storage repositories are other nodes. Custodians, professional intermediaries, legal representatives, and authorized recipients can become additional nodes. The system is resilient when there are multiple legitimate pathways between the evidence and its eventual authorized recovery. If every pathway passes through one person, one device, one building, or one company, the network contains a critical bottleneck. Removing that bottleneck increases resilience.

This does not mean that information should be distributed indiscriminately. Sensitive evidence can become more vulnerable as the number of copies and custodians increases. Every additional copy represents another opportunity for accidental exposure. Every additional custodian represents another human risk. Redundancy must therefore be selective. The objective is to create independent protection without creating unnecessary proliferation. In security engineering, more is not always better. Better-designed independence is better.

The dead man's switch introduces another consideration: the possibility that the creator may deliberately become unreachable. A system that depends upon continuous interaction with the creator must distinguish between temporary silence and genuine incapacity. Cloud services may continue operating automatically, while physical custodians may need explicit instructions. A distributed architecture can allow different components to continue functioning independently. But the conditions under which those components should act must be clear. Storage redundancy and trigger logic are related but should not be confused.

For example, the existence of multiple copies does not mean that every copy should automatically be released when a check-in is missed. Preservation and activation are separate functions. The archive should first ensure that information survives. The trigger mechanism should then determine whether predefined conditions for disclosure have actually been met. This separation reduces the risk that a storage failure is mistaken for a personal emergency. It also reduces the possibility that a technical malfunction causes premature disclosure. A resilient dead man's switch therefore needs both resilient storage and resilient decision logic.

Testing the complete architecture is one of the most important practices and one of the easiest to neglect. A creator may know that a file exists in the cloud, that another copy is on a drive, and that a third copy is held elsewhere. But can those copies actually be recovered? Can the encrypted archive be opened using the legitimate recovery process? Can a successor understand the documentation? Can an original file be distinguished from a derivative? Can the archive survive if one custodian becomes unavailable? These questions should be answered before the system is needed rather than after a crisis begins.

Testing should also include failure scenarios. What happens if the primary device fails? What happens if the cloud account becomes inaccessible? What happens if one custodian disappears? What happens if a password is lost? What happens if the storage medium becomes unreadable? What happens if the creator cannot communicate for an extended period? What happens if a copy is discovered by an unauthorized person? These are not exercises in pessimism. They are exercises in engineering. A safety system becomes trustworthy by demonstrating how it behaves when something goes wrong.

The concept of graceful degradation is particularly useful. A well-designed system should ideally continue functioning in a reduced form when individual components fail. If one backup disappears, another remains. If one custodian becomes unavailable, another legitimate pathway survives. If a cloud service experiences an outage, an offline archive remains. If one storage device becomes corrupted, a verified copy can replace it. Graceful degradation prevents minor failures from becoming total failures. It is one of the strongest arguments for layered architecture.

There is also a philosophical dimension to redundancy. A dead man's switch is ultimately an attempt to extend human agency beyond the point at which ordinary agency may become impossible. The creator cannot control the future, but they can influence the probability that information survives into it. Storage architecture becomes the physical expression of that intention. Every independent copy represents another chance for the record to survive. Every documented recovery path represents another bridge between the past and the future. Redundancy is therefore not technological excess. It is continuity planning.

Yet redundancy should never become an excuse for indiscriminate duplication. Sensitive information can harm innocent people if exposed. Copies can escape. Custodians can make mistakes. Devices can be stolen. Cloud accounts can be compromised. The more copies that exist, the greater the number of places that require protection. The correct objective is therefore not maximum replication but resilient replication. Every additional copy should serve a clear purpose. If it does not materially improve resilience, it may simply enlarge the attack surface.

The most effective architecture often combines different types of independence. Geographic independence protects against local disaster. Technological independence protects against dependence upon one storage medium. Organizational independence protects against dependence upon one institution. Human independence protects against dependence upon one custodian. Cryptographic independence can protect against dependence upon one access mechanism. Together, these forms of independence create a much stronger system than simply purchasing more storage. The deeper principle is diversification of failure modes.

This approach also changes how we think about the phrase "backup." A backup is not merely a second copy. A useful backup is a recoverable copy whose integrity can be verified and whose existence is sufficiently independent from the original that the same failure is unlikely to destroy both. It must also remain accessible to legitimate future custodians. If the backup shares every weakness of the primary, it provides limited additional protection. The value of redundancy lies in independence. Two identical vulnerabilities are not equivalent to two independent safeguards.

Cloud storage, offline archives, and distributed custody therefore should not be viewed as competing ideologies. They are complementary tools. Cloud systems can provide accessibility and remote infrastructure. Offline archives can provide isolation and independence from network threats. Physical preservation can protect original materials. Distributed custody can reduce dependence upon one individual. Geographic separation can protect against localized catastrophe. Encryption can protect confidentiality. Authentication can protect access. Verification can protect integrity. The architecture becomes robust when these capabilities are combined deliberately.

The final measure of success is deceptively simple: if something goes wrong, does the evidence survive? If a device fails, can another copy be recovered? If the creator disappears, can an authorized successor eventually locate and access the archive? If a cloud account becomes unavailable, does another route exist? If one custodian is compromised, does the entire collection become exposed? If technology changes, can the files still be read? If a document is challenged, can its provenance and history be demonstrated? These questions transform an abstract idea about a dead man's switch into a practical discipline of information resilience.

The strongest evidence archive is therefore not the one protected by the most exotic technology. It is the one whose designer has anticipated ordinary failure. Hardware will fail. People will forget. Organizations will change. Services will disappear. Files will become corrupted. Buildings will suffer disasters. Accounts will be compromised. The system should assume these things can happen and remain functional despite them. That is the essence of redundancy: not believing that failure can be prevented everywhere, but ensuring that failure in one place does not become failure everywhere.

A dead man's switch ultimately depends upon continuity. The evidence must survive the person who gathered it, the technology they initially used, the place where they lived, the people they trusted, and the services they relied upon. Cloud storage can provide one layer of that continuity. Offline archives can provide another. Distributed custody can provide another. None is sufficient by itself, but together they can create a preservation architecture capable of surviving substantial disruption. The objective is not technological perfection. It is survivability.

That survivability now brings us to another difficult question: what happens when the archive contains information that should not simply be released in its entirety? Preserving evidence is only half the problem. Eventually someone may have to decide which documents, photographs, recordings, and testimony should be disclosed, to whom, and under what circumstances. The next stage of the dead man's switch therefore moves from preservation architecture toward human judgment, examining how information can be prepared for responsible release without destroying context, exposing innocent people, or turning a carefully preserved evidentiary record into an uncontrolled information dump.

Resources

1. National Archives — Digital Preservation — authoritative guidance on preserving digital records and maintaining their accessibility over time.

2. Library of Congress — Digital Preservation[1] — extensive resources on digital preservation, storage, sustainability, metadata, and long-term access.

3. Library of Congress — Sustainability of Digital Formats[2] — information concerning file-format sustainability and the technological characteristics relevant to long-term preservation.

4. NIST Cybersecurity Framework 2.0[3] — framework addressing cybersecurity risk management, including protection, detection, response, and recovery.

5. NIST Special Publication 800-34 — Contingency Planning Guide for Federal Information Systems[4] — guidance concerning contingency planning, system recovery, alternate processing, and continuity.

1. https://www.loc.gov/preservation/digital/?utm_source=chatgpt.com
2. https://www.loc.gov/preservation/digital/formats/?utm_source=chatgpt.com
3. https://www.nist.gov/cyberframework?utm_source=chatgpt.com

6. NIST Special Publication 800-53 — Security and Privacy Controls[5] — comprehensive controls concerning contingency planning, access control, system integrity, auditability, and information protection.

7. NIST Special Publication 800-57 — Recommendation for Key Management — guidance concerning cryptographic-key lifecycle, protection, backup, recovery, and management.

8. NIST Special Publication 800-88 — Guidelines for Media Sanitization[6] — useful reference concerning information-bearing media and lifecycle management.

9. CISA — Cybersecurity Performance Goals[7] — practical cybersecurity recommendations emphasizing resilience, authentication, backups, and recovery.

10. CISA — StopRansomware Guide[8] — government guidance concerning protected backups, recovery, ransomware resilience, and separation of backup systems.

11. Digital Preservation Coalition — Digital Preservation Handbook[9] — professional guidance covering storage, preservation planning, format migration, metadata, integrity, and organizational continuity.

12. ISO 14721 — Open Archival Information System (OAIS)[10] — foundational international archival model for preserving and providing continued access to digital information.

13. ISO 15489 — Records Management[11] — international standard concerning the reliable creation, capture, management, preservation, and disposition of records.

14. ISO/IEC 27001 — Information Security Management Systems[12] — international framework for managing information-security risks systematically.

15. ISO/IEC 27002 — Information Security Controls[13] — guidance concerning practical controls for information security, access management, cryptography, and operational resilience.

16. Cloud Security Alliance[14] — research and guidance concerning cloud architecture, storage, identity, security controls, and cloud-specific risks.

17. National Institute of Standards and Technology — Cloud Computing Program — NIST resources concerning cloud computing architectures, interoperability, security, and deployment models.

---

4. https://csrc.nist.gov/publications/detail/sp/800-34/rev-1/final?utm_source=chatgpt.com

5. https://csrc.nist.gov/publications/detail/sp/800-53/rev-5/final?utm_source=chatgpt.com

6. https://csrc.nist.gov/publications/detail/sp/800-88/rev-1/final?utm_source=chatgpt.com

7. https://www.cisa.gov/cybersecurity-performance-goals-cpgs?utm_source=chatgpt.com

8. https://www.cisa.gov/stopransomware/ransomware-guide?utm_source=chatgpt.com

9. https://www.dpconline.org/handbook?utm_source=chatgpt.com

10. https://www.iso.org/standard/57284.html?utm_source=chatgpt.com

11. https://www.iso.org/standard/62542.html?utm_source=chatgpt.com

12. https://www.iso.org/isoiec-27001-information-security.html?utm_source=chatgpt.com

13. https://www.iso.org/standard/75652.html?utm_source=chatgpt.com

14. https://cloudsecurityalliance.org/?utm_source=chatgpt.com

18. Internet Engineering Task Force — RFC 4949, Internet Security Glossary[15] — technical definitions for security concepts including availability, integrity, authentication, confidentiality, and threat.

19. OWASP — Threat Modeling[16] — practical security guidance on identifying assets, threats, vulnerabilities, and mitigations.

20. Electronic Frontier Foundation — Surveillance Self-Defense[17] — accessible guidance concerning threat modeling, backups, secure storage, authentication, encryption, and device security.

21. Federal Emergency Management Agency — Continuity Resource Toolkit — resources illustrating broader continuity principles applicable to planning for disruption and recovery.

22. National Archives — Records Management Guidance[18] — government guidance on maintaining reliable records and ensuring their continued usability.

23. Ross Anderson, *Security Engineering: A Guide to Building Dependable Distributed Systems*, 3rd ed., Wiley, 2020 — major reference on dependable systems, security architecture, human factors, distributed systems, and failure analysis.

24. Bruce Schneier, *Secrets and Lies: Digital Security in a Networked World*, Wiley, 2000 — influential discussion of security as a system involving technology, people, incentives, and organizational processes.

25. Bruce Schneier, *Applied Cryptography: Protocols, Algorithms, and Source Code in C*, 2nd ed., Wiley, 1996 — foundational reference for cryptography, secure systems, protocols, and the practical limitations of cryptographic protection.

---

15. https://www.rfc-editor.org/rfc/rfc4949?utm_source=chatgpt.com

16. https://owasp.org/www-community/Threat_Modeling?utm_source=chatgpt.com

17. https://ssd.eff.org/?utm_source=chatgpt.com

18. https://www.archives.gov/records-mgmt?utm_source=chatgpt.com

Hidden Information

Encryption addresses the problem of someone obtaining information and being unable to understand it, but another problem exists before encryption even begins: what if someone discovers that the information exists? The distinction is subtle but important because the visibility of information can itself create risk. A file clearly labeled "CONFIDENTIAL EVIDENCE," for example, immediately announces its importance to anyone who encounters it, even if the contents are strongly encrypted. Throughout history, people have therefore developed methods for concealing messages, separating information into compartments, disguising sensitive material, or creating apparently ordinary objects that contain something more significant beneath the surface. Modern information security continues this tradition, although the methods have changed dramatically with the arrival of computers, networks, digital media, and enormous quantities of easily copied data.

The technical term steganography comes from the Greek words associated with covered or concealed writing, and its central idea is different from conventional encryption. An encrypted message openly announces that protected information exists, even though its contents may be unreadable. A steganographic approach attempts to conceal the existence of the message itself by embedding information within another apparently ordinary carrier. Historically, examples have included hidden writing, concealed markings, and messages incorporated into seemingly innocent materials. The carrier can be a physical object, an image, a document, or, in digital environments, various forms of electronic data. The underlying concept is therefore not new, even though digital technology has greatly expanded the number of possible carriers.

The distinction between secrecy of existence and secrecy of content is useful throughout this book. If an investigator discovers an encrypted file named "archive," they already know something potentially important exists. If the same information is stored in a manner that does not obviously identify its significance, the discovery process becomes different. This does not necessarily make the information secure. Concealment can fail, and sophisticated analysis can sometimes identify anomalies that reveal hidden content. But concealment can reduce casual discovery and may add another layer to a broader security architecture. As with encryption, its value depends upon the threat being considered.

Digital steganography has attracted considerable attention because ordinary multimedia files can contain enormous quantities of data. Images, audio, video, and other digital objects contain structured information that can sometimes be manipulated without producing immediately obvious visual or auditory changes. Researchers have developed techniques for embedding additional information into such carriers. The general concept is mathematically and technically sophisticated, but the principle remains relatively simple: modify aspects of an existing digital object so that additional information is represented within it. The challenge is maintaining the carrier's apparent normality while preserving the hidden information reliably.

The existence of digital steganography does not mean that any unusual photograph or strangely formatted file contains a secret message. This distinction is important because the subject is easily surrounded by speculation. Digital files naturally contain metadata, compression artifacts, encoding variations, formatting irregularities, and other characteristics that can appear unusual without indicating deliberate concealment. Determining whether a file actually contains hidden information requires analysis rather than intuition. The same evidence-first approach used throughout this book should therefore apply here. Suspicion is not proof.

Steganalysis is the corresponding field concerned with detecting potentially hidden information. Analysts can examine statistical properties, file structures, metadata, unusual patterns, and other characteristics for indications that a carrier has been manipulated. No detection method is universally successful because steganographic techniques vary widely. Some forms of concealment may leave detectable statistical traces, while others can be much more difficult to identify. The contest between concealment and detection is therefore dynamic. Whenever one technique becomes easier to detect, researchers may develop alternatives designed to reduce those detectable characteristics.

The security value of steganography is consequently difficult to measure in isolation. If the presence of hidden information itself would create danger, concealment may provide an additional layer. But if the hidden information is discovered, the fact that concealment was attempted may attract greater attention. An investigator who finds a deliberately manipulated file may reasonably ask why it was manipulated. Concealment can therefore create both protection and suspicion. This is another example of why security measures should be evaluated in the context of a specific threat model rather than treated as inherently beneficial.

Within a dead man's switch, the more useful concept may often be compartmentalization rather than elaborate concealment. Compartmentalization means dividing information, access, responsibilities, or knowledge so that no single component necessarily reveals the entire system. It is a principle that appears across intelligence organizations, military structures, cybersecurity, corporate security, and ordinary organizational practice. Someone may have access to one part of a project without having access to all of it. The purpose is to limit the consequences of compromise. If one account or person is compromised, the attacker should ideally obtain only what that component legitimately needs to contain.

Compartmentalization begins with a simple question: who actually needs to know what? That question can be surprisingly difficult because people often distribute information according to convenience rather than security. A creator may send the complete archive to one trusted friend because doing so is easier than designing a more sophisticated structure. The friend then becomes a single point of failure. If the person loses the device, is compromised, changes their relationship with the creator, or simply makes a mistake, the entire archive may be affected. Dividing responsibility can reduce this dependency.

However, compartmentalization must be designed carefully because excessive fragmentation can make legitimate recovery impossible. If evidence is divided into dozens of pieces and nobody knows how the pieces relate to one another, the archive may survive technically while becoming useless operationally. A future custodian might possess several fragments without understanding their significance. Another person might hold the missing context. A third might have the authentication information required to connect the components. The architecture therefore needs enough documentation to support legitimate reconstruction without unnecessarily revealing everything to every participant.

This creates an interesting tension between secrecy and usability. Strong compartmentalization limits exposure by restricting knowledge, but strong compartmentalization also increases complexity. Complexity creates opportunities for human error. A person may forget where something is stored, misunderstand their role, or lose track of which version is authoritative. The designer must therefore decide what information truly needs to be separated and what information can safely remain together. Good security architecture is often less about maximizing barriers than about placing barriers where they actually reduce risk.

The principle can be applied to the evidence itself. Not every document in an archive necessarily deserves the same level of protection. Some material may be public and independently verifiable. Other material may contain private information. Some records may identify confidential sources. Other documents may reveal the existence of an investigation without revealing its conclusions. Treating everything as equally sensitive can create unnecessary complexity. Classifying information according to its sensitivity and function allows protection measures to be proportionate.

Information compartmentalization can also separate identity from content. An archive might contain evidence concerning an event without unnecessarily exposing the identity of every person associated with it. Where legally and ethically appropriate, identifying information can be handled separately from the evidentiary material. This does not mean altering the evidence. It means controlling access to different categories of information. Such separation can reduce unnecessary exposure of innocent individuals. It can also make later review more disciplined because a person examining the substantive evidence does not automatically receive every associated personal detail.

The same principle applies to source protection. Investigative journalism provides a well-known example because journalists may possess information from confidential sources whose identities require protection. A source's identity can be separated from the material they provide, with controlled access to the relationship between the two. This does not make the source invulnerable, and legal systems differ concerning protections and disclosure obligations. But the architectural principle remains valuable. Sensitive relationships should not necessarily be exposed simply because the underlying evidence must be preserved.

Decoys introduce another concept. A decoy is material designed to appear significant or authentic while diverting attention from something else. In physical security, decoys have long been used to confuse observers about the location or importance of protected assets. In information security, the concept can appear in various forms, including deliberately misleading but non-harmful information or systems designed to attract unauthorized attention. Defensive cybersecurity also uses related concepts such as honeypots, which are systems intentionally configured to attract and observe unauthorized activity. These applications demonstrate that deception can sometimes be used defensively.

Yet decoys are particularly problematic in an evidence archive because deliberately false material can contaminate the evidentiary environment. If a future investigator cannot immediately distinguish genuine evidence from decoy material, the credibility of the entire archive may be compromised. A person receiving a collection after the creator's death may not know which files are authentic and which were intentionally placed there. This creates a serious provenance problem. A dead man's switch should therefore prioritize evidentiary clarity over theatrical secrecy. If defensive decoys are used at all, their status and handling should be documented through a secure, legitimate mechanism.

The distinction between a decoy and an ordinary working file is also important. Digital archives naturally contain duplicates, temporary files, obsolete drafts, thumbnails, exported versions, and unrelated material. These objects can look mysterious to someone who encounters the archive without context. They are not necessarily decoys. Proper archival discipline should therefore establish which materials are authoritative and which are derivative or incidental. File naming, metadata, manifests, hashes, and preservation documentation can help future custodians understand the collection. The objective is to make the evidentiary record intelligible rather than deliberately confusing.

Layered information architecture provides another approach. Instead of treating an archive as one enormous collection with one universal access mechanism, information can be organized into layers based on sensitivity and purpose. A publicly releasable summary might occupy one layer. Supporting documentation might occupy another. Highly sensitive source material could reside in a more restricted layer. Access instructions and recovery information could be handled separately. The structure resembles the layered security model used in many other domains. Different layers can have different custodians, controls, and disclosure conditions.

Layering also helps address the problem of premature disclosure. Imagine an archive containing evidence that is potentially important but also includes personal information about unrelated individuals. Releasing everything automatically could create unnecessary harm. A layered structure could allow a responsible reviewer to examine the core evidence first, determine what is substantiated, and then decide which supporting materials are appropriate for release. This preserves the possibility of disclosure without turning the dead man's switch into an indiscriminate publishing machine. Preservation and publication remain separate decisions.

A layered archive can also preserve context. Evidence rarely speaks entirely for itself. A photograph may require a date, location, provenance, and explanation of how it was obtained. A recording may require information about who created it and whether the file is complete. A document may depend upon surrounding correspondence. If these elements are separated without a mechanism for reconnecting them, the evidentiary value can decline. Compartmentalization should therefore separate sensitive components while preserving their relationships. Security should not destroy meaning.

Metadata plays an important role in this architecture. Metadata can describe when a file was created, modified, acquired, or processed, depending upon the system generating it. It can identify file types, software, devices, locations, and other contextual information. Metadata can help establish relationships between objects and can support archival management. But metadata can also reveal sensitive information. A photograph may contain location information. A document may contain an author's name. A file may reveal the software and device used to create it. Protecting content while ignoring metadata can therefore expose information that the creator intended to conceal.

This is one reason that information security must distinguish between content and context. Sometimes the most revealing information is not what a file says but what its existence implies. A folder containing records from a particular organization may reveal that an investigation is underway. A photograph's timestamp may establish that someone was present at a location. A communications log may reveal relationships even if the message content is encrypted. Metadata and contextual information can therefore be sensitive in their own right. An effective archive should identify these secondary information flows rather than treating them as harmless technical details.

The idea of information architecture becomes especially important when evidence is expected to survive for many years. Future recipients may not understand the original software environment or the creator's assumptions. A carefully structured archive can communicate relationships through manifests, documentation, identifiers, and preservation records. The architecture becomes a kind of map. The evidence remains the territory, while the metadata and documentation explain how the pieces relate. Without the map, a future investigator may possess the territory without understanding how to navigate it.

Compartmentalization can also be applied to authentication. Rather than allowing one credential to unlock every component, different layers can require different forms of authorization. This can reduce the consequences of a compromised credential. It can also establish different levels of access for different recipients. A person responsible for maintaining an archive may not require the ability to publish it. A reviewer may need access to evidence without control over the preservation infrastructure. A legal representative may need authority to make certain decisions without possessing every file. Separation of authority can therefore be as important as separation of information.

The principle of separation of duties is closely related. In organizational security, separation of duties attempts to prevent one individual from exercising unchecked control over a sensitive process. Different responsibilities are divided among different people or systems. In the context of a dead man's switch, this might mean that no single participant can both retrieve the complete archive and independently authorize its public release. Such structures can reduce the risk of accidental or malicious action. They can also provide a form of institutional accountability.

But once again, complexity has to be controlled. Every additional authentication requirement, custodian, repository, or procedural step creates another opportunity for failure. A system that requires five people to coordinate may be secure in theory but unusable if those people are unavailable at the critical moment. A future custodian may be unable to determine which sequence of approvals is required. A legal condition may have changed. A technology may have disappeared. Resilience therefore requires simplicity wherever simplicity can be achieved without sacrificing meaningful protection.

The most useful question is not "How hidden can this information become?" but "What failure are we trying to prevent?" If the concern is casual discovery, modest concealment may be appropriate. If the concern is unauthorized reading, encryption is more relevant. If the concern is one custodian being compromised, compartmentalization may be useful. If the concern is accidental deletion, independent backups matter more. If the concern is premature publication, layered access and review procedures may be more appropriate. Different threats require different controls. Combining unrelated techniques simply because they sound sophisticated can create unnecessary complexity without producing meaningful security.

The concept of threat modeling therefore returns once again. An archive should begin with its assets and realistic threats. Who might want the information? What could they gain from it? What access might they possess? Are they likely to be technically sophisticated? Could they obtain physical access? Could they influence a custodian? Could they compel disclosure through legal means? Could they exploit ordinary human error? These questions determine whether concealment, encryption, compartmentalization, or other measures are appropriate. Security becomes more rational when it begins with a defined threat rather than with a fascination for technology.

Historical steganography demonstrates another important lesson: concealment methods evolve in response to detection. What appears invisible to one generation may become recognizable to another. The same is true of digital techniques. Software improves. Analytical tools become more capable. File formats change. Statistical detection methods become more sophisticated. A concealment method that appears effective today may not provide the same protection years later. Long-term preservation should therefore never depend entirely upon the assumption that hidden information will remain hidden indefinitely.

For this reason, concealed information should not be treated as the only copy. If a critical archive depends upon one hidden representation, discovering or corrupting that representation could destroy the system. The original evidence should remain preserved through conventional archival methods appropriate to its sensitivity. Concealment, where legitimately used, should be an additional layer rather than the foundation. This mirrors the larger principle of redundancy. Security should survive the failure of any single technique.

There is also a profound difference between concealment and destruction. A hidden archive continues to preserve information. A destroyed archive does not. This distinction matters ethically as well as technically. The objective of a dead man's switch is normally to preserve the possibility that important information will eventually reach appropriate people. Concealment should therefore serve continuity rather than become an excuse for eliminating records. The preservation objective remains primary.

Decoys require even greater caution because they can create false narratives. If a future investigator discovers a convincing but fabricated document alongside genuine evidence, they may waste enormous resources investigating something that never happened. Worse, the fabricated material may cast doubt upon the authentic material. A single deliberately misleading artifact can therefore damage the credibility of an entire archive. Any legitimate defensive use of decoy concepts should be separated clearly from the evidentiary record. Authentic evidence should never depend upon the recipient correctly guessing which files are real.

This principle is especially important when dealing with allegations of institutional wrongdoing. An archive that contains serious accusations must be capable of surviving scrutiny. Investigators, journalists, lawyers, regulators, or other legitimate reviewers may ask where the evidence originated, whether it has been altered, and whether its supporting documentation is complete. A confusing archive makes those questions harder to answer. A carefully structured archive makes them easier. Credibility depends not only upon possessing evidence but upon demonstrating how the evidence came into existence and how it was preserved.

The best information architecture therefore resembles a carefully designed archive rather than a maze. Sensitive information can be separated. Access can be restricted. Certain components can be distributed. Metadata can be preserved. Encryption can protect content. Backups can provide redundancy. But the relationships among the pieces should remain understandable to legitimate custodians. The creator should be able to explain the architecture to a future investigator without requiring that investigator to reverse-engineer a puzzle. Security should protect evidence while preserving its evidentiary meaning.

There is another reason to avoid unnecessary obscurity: succession. The creator of a dead man's switch may understand every hidden folder, every unusual filename, every storage location, and every relationship between different components. Future custodians will not possess that intuitive knowledge. They need explicit documentation. If the creator becomes unavailable, the archive should not become a mystery box. A well-designed succession system therefore separates the protection of information from the concealment of the architecture itself. Legitimate successors should have enough information to recover the archive responsibly.

The concept of compartmentalization can also extend beyond technology into human relationships. A journalist may know the identity of a source without revealing it to every colleague. A lawyer may maintain confidential client information separately from public case materials. An investigator may preserve raw evidence independently from analytical conclusions. A scientist may separate research data from personal identifiers. These arrangements are not inherently secretive in a sinister sense. They are ordinary methods of protecting sensitive information while maintaining professional responsibilities.

Ultimately, hidden information presents a paradox. The more effectively something is concealed, the harder it may become for legitimate people to discover and use it. The less it is concealed, the greater the risk of unauthorized discovery. The solution is not to choose absolute secrecy or absolute transparency. It is to determine what needs to be hidden, from whom, for how long, and under what conditions legitimate access should become possible.

Those questions transform concealment from an abstract technique into an information-governance problem. That is where a responsible dead man's switch should operate.

Steganography, decoys, and compartmentalization therefore belong within the broader architecture of information resilience, but none should be mistaken for a universal solution. Steganography can conceal the existence of information but may be detectable. Decoys can divert attention but may contaminate an evidentiary environment. Compartmentalization can reduce the consequences of compromise but can also create complexity. Layered architectures can separate information according to sensitivity but require careful documentation. Each technique has advantages and failure modes. The strongest system is the one that understands both.

The deeper lesson is that information security is ultimately about controlling relationships: who knows that information exists, who can read it, who can alter it, who can authenticate it, who can release it, and who can recover it when the creator is gone. Encryption addresses one part of that problem. Storage addresses another. Redundancy addresses another. Compartmentalization addresses another. Evidence preservation addresses another. None is sufficient independently. The architecture succeeds when these layers reinforce one another without creating unnecessary obstacles to legitimate recovery.

A dead man's switch is therefore not simply a hidden message waiting to emerge. It is a carefully constructed continuity system in which information may need to remain confidential until a legitimate future decision can be made. The objective is not secrecy for its own sake. It is controlled survival. The information should survive the loss of the person who created it while remaining protected from premature discovery, unauthorized alteration, and irresponsible disclosure. Concealment can contribute to that objective, but only when it is subordinate to preservation, provenance, and recoverability.

The next problem follows naturally from this one. Even if sensitive information is securely stored, concealed, distributed, and protected against unauthorized access, someone must eventually possess the authority to retrieve it. The system therefore moves from the question of how information is protected to the more human question of who should become its guardian. Choosing those recipients may ultimately be more difficult than choosing the technology itself, because every custodian represents both a potential safeguard and a potential point of failure.

Resources

1. NIST Special Publication 800-53 — Security and Privacy Controls[1] — authoritative guidance covering access control, separation of duties, least privilege, system integrity, and information protection.

2. NIST Cybersecurity Framework 2.0[2] — framework for identifying, protecting, detecting, responding to, and recovering from cybersecurity risks.

3. NIST Special Publication 800-57 — Recommendation for Key Management — guidance on cryptographic keys, their lifecycle, protection, storage, and recovery.

4. NIST Special Publication 800-88 — Guidelines for Media Sanitization[3] — relevant to managing information-bearing media and controlling residual information.

1. https://csrc.nist.gov/publications/detail/sp/800-53/rev-5/final?utm_source=chatgpt.com

2. https://www.nist.gov/cyberframework?utm_source=chatgpt.com

3. https://csrc.nist.gov/publications/detail/sp/800-88/rev-1/final?utm_source=chatgpt.com

5. NIST Special Publication 800-61 — Computer Security Incident Handling Guide[4] — guidance concerning security incidents, preparation, detection, analysis, containment, and recovery.

6. OWASP Threat Modeling[5] — practical framework for identifying assets, threats, vulnerabilities, and appropriate security controls.

7. OWASP Access Control Cheat Sheet[6] — practical guidance on authorization, least privilege, and access-control architecture.

8. Electronic Frontier Foundation — Surveillance Self-Defense[7] — accessible resources concerning threat modeling, encryption, authentication, secure storage, and privacy.

9. National Archives — Digital Preservation — authoritative resources concerning long-term preservation, digital records, authenticity, and accessibility.

10. Library of Congress — Digital Preservation[8] — extensive preservation resources concerning digital objects, metadata, storage, formats, and long-term access.

11. Library of Congress — Sustainability of Digital Formats[9] — resources on file formats, sustainability, technical characteristics, and long-term digital preservation.

12. Digital Preservation Coalition — Digital Preservation Handbook[10] — professional guidance concerning digital preservation, metadata, storage, integrity, and technological change.

13. ISO 14721 — Open Archival Information System (OAIS)[11] — international reference model for preserving information and maintaining long-term access to digital objects.

14. ISO 15489 — Records Management[12] — international standard addressing reliable records creation, management, preservation, and authenticity.

15. Internet Engineering Task Force — RFC 4949, Internet Security Glossary[13] — technical definitions for security concepts including confidentiality, integrity, authentication, access control, and threats.

16. Neil F. Johnson and Sushil Jajodia, "Exploring Steganography: Seeing the Unseen," *Computer*, Vol. 31, No. 2, 1998 — influential technical discussion of steganography and methods for concealing information within digital media.

---

4. https://csrc.nist.gov/publications/detail/sp/800-61/rev-2/final?utm_source=chatgpt.com

5. https://owasp.org/www-community/Threat_Modeling?utm_source=chatgpt.com

6. https://cheatsheetseries.owasp.org/cheatsheets/Authorization_Cheat_Sheet.html?utm_source=chatgpt.com

7. https://ssd.eff.org/?utm_source=chatgpt.com

8. https://www.loc.gov/preservation/digital/?utm_source=chatgpt.com

9. https://www.loc.gov/preservation/digital/formats/?utm_source=chatgpt.com

10. https://www.dpconline.org/handbook?utm_source=chatgpt.com

11. https://www.iso.org/standard/57284.html?utm_source=chatgpt.com

12. https://www.iso.org/standard/62542.html?utm_source=chatgpt.com

13. https://www.rfc-editor.org/rfc/rfc4949?utm_source=chatgpt.com

17. Jessica Fridrich, *Steganography in Digital Media: Principles, Algorithms, and Applications*, Cambridge University Press, 2009 — major academic reference examining digital steganography, detection, and analysis.

18. Ross Anderson, *Security Engineering: A Guide to Building Dependable Distributed Systems*, 3rd ed., Wiley, 2020 — comprehensive treatment of security architecture, compartmentalization, access control, human factors, and dependable systems.

19. Bruce Schneier, *Secrets and Lies: Digital Security in a Networked World*, Wiley, 2000 — influential examination of security as a combination of technology, people, processes, and organizational design.

20. Bruce Schneier, *Applied Cryptography: Protocols, Algorithms, and Source Code in C*, 2nd ed., Wiley, 1996 — foundational reference for cryptographic principles and the distinction between cryptographic protection and broader security architecture.

21. Claude E. Shannon, "Communication Theory of Secrecy Systems," *Bell System Technical Journal*, Vol. 28, No. 4, 1949 — foundational theoretical work on secrecy, information, and cryptographic systems.

22. National Institute of Standards and Technology — Privacy Framework[14] — useful for considering the risks of exposing personal and contextual information within sensitive archives.

23. CISA — Cybersecurity Resources[15] — government resources concerning layered security, access protection, threat awareness, and resilience.

24. SANS Institute — Information Security Resources[16] — educational material concerning defense-in-depth, access control, threat modeling, and information security architecture.

25. MITRE ATT&CK[17] — knowledge base documenting adversary behaviors and techniques, useful for understanding how attackers may attempt to discover, access, collect, and exfiltrate protected information.

14. https://www.nist.gov/privacy-framework?utm_source=chatgpt.com

15. https://www.cisa.gov/topics/cybersecurity-best-practices?utm_source=chatgpt.com

16. https://www.sans.org/white-papers/?utm_source=chatgpt.com

17. https://attack.mitre.org/?utm_source=chatgpt.com

The Password Problem: Keys, Access, and Digital Inheritance

There is a paradox at the center of every serious information-preservation system: protection can become a form of destruction if nobody legitimate can eventually unlock what has been protected. A person may spend enormous effort encrypting documents, securing devices, creating redundant archives, and restricting access, only to discover that the system depends upon a password that exists only in their memory. If that person dies, disappears, becomes incapacitated, or simply loses the ability to communicate, the information may remain perfectly intact while becoming effectively unreachable. The problem is particularly important for a dead man's switch because the entire purpose of the system is continuity beyond the creator. Security must therefore accomplish two apparently conflicting objectives at once: preventing unauthorized access today and enabling legitimate access tomorrow.

Passwords are often the first point at which this conflict becomes visible. Most people encounter passwords as credentials used to authenticate themselves to websites, applications, computers, and other services. In a sensitive archive, however, passwords can serve several different roles, and confusing those roles can create weaknesses. A password may authenticate a user to an online account, unlock a device, protect a password manager, or contribute to the generation of an encryption key. Each situation has different consequences if the password is lost. The phrase "I have encrypted it" therefore tells us very little until we know how the encryption is controlled and how legitimate future access is supposed to occur.

A useful starting point is to separate authentication from encryption. Authentication is fundamentally about establishing that someone is authorized to access a system. Encryption is about transforming information so that it cannot ordinarily be understood without the appropriate cryptographic capability. These functions often interact, but they are not identical. A password used to log into an account may not itself be the encryption key protecting the underlying files. Conversely, a cryptographic key may be stored or unlocked through an authentication mechanism. Understanding these distinctions becomes critical when planning for digital inheritance.

The simplest password system creates an obvious succession problem. One person knows the password, and nobody else does. While the creator remains available, this may appear secure. Once the creator disappears, however, the security boundary becomes an obstacle to legitimate recovery. A family member, lawyer, journalist, or other authorized recipient may know that an archive exists but have no way to access it. In some circumstances, the service provider may have a recovery process. In others, strong encryption may mean that even the provider cannot recover the information. The stronger the cryptographic design, the more important the recovery architecture becomes.

This is why password management should be treated as part of continuity planning rather than as a minor administrative task. A sensitive archive can contain dozens of credentials, devices, repositories, authentication factors, and recovery mechanisms. Losing one critical credential may break the chain. The creator may remember the password to the primary account but forget the secondary account that contains the backup. They may have a recovery code stored on a device that has failed. They may use multi-factor authentication tied to a telephone number that is no longer active. The system can therefore fail through a small administrative weakness even when its principal encryption remains strong.

Password managers can reduce some of this complexity by allowing a person to maintain many unique credentials under a central protected system. Instead of memorizing dozens of passwords, the user generally needs to remember or otherwise securely access one primary credential or authentication mechanism. This can significantly improve password hygiene because unique, difficult-to-guess credentials can be used for individual services. But it also creates concentration risk. If the password manager becomes inaccessible, the person may lose access to many accounts simultaneously. The master credential therefore becomes a particularly important component of the overall continuity architecture.

The master credential problem illustrates a broader principle: every system has something that ultimately controls access. Sometimes it is a password. Sometimes it is a cryptographic key. Sometimes it is a hardware authenticator. Sometimes it is a combination of factors. Sometimes it is a recovery mechanism maintained by a service provider. Identifying that ultimate control point is essential. A person cannot properly plan digital inheritance without knowing what actually stands between a future legitimate custodian and the protected information.

Cryptographic keys deserve special attention because they are not simply longer passwords. A key is information used by a cryptographic algorithm to perform operations such as encryption, decryption, signing, or authentication. Modern cryptographic systems may generate keys randomly rather than having people invent them. The security of the resulting system depends heavily on how those keys are generated, stored, protected, backed up, and eventually destroyed. If a key is stolen, an attacker may gain access to protected information. If a key is permanently lost, legitimate users may be unable to recover it. Key management is therefore a lifecycle problem.

Digital inheritance adds another dimension because digital assets rarely consist of a single file sitting on a single computer. A modern person's digital environment may contain email accounts, cloud storage, photographs, financial records, correspondence, research, intellectual property, websites, domain registrations, social-media accounts, password managers, encrypted drives, cryptocurrency holdings, and private archives. Each may have different ownership rules and different recovery mechanisms. Some may be governed by contracts. Some may be governed by law. Some may be protected by encryption that no third party can bypass. Others may depend on the policies of a service provider. Digital inheritance is therefore more complicated than simply leaving someone a list of passwords.

The legal status of digital accounts can also differ from the status of physical property. A person may own a computer while not necessarily possessing unrestricted rights to transfer every account or digital service associated with it. Terms of service can impose restrictions. Privacy laws may affect access to communications. Intellectual-property rights may apply to particular materials. Financial services may have specialized succession procedures. Cryptocurrency can present additional technical and legal complications because control may depend directly upon cryptographic credentials. Anyone designing a serious succession system should therefore distinguish technical access from legal authority.

This distinction is particularly important for a dead man's switch because possession of a password does not automatically create legitimate authority. A person might technically be able to access someone else's account while having no legal right to do so. Conversely, someone may have legal authority but lack the technical means to exercise it. The two systems must therefore be coordinated. Technical succession should not be designed in a vacuum. Where valuable, sensitive, or legally significant information is involved, professional legal advice may be appropriate.

There is also an important difference between transferring ordinary digital property and transferring confidential information. A family member may reasonably need access to personal photographs or financial documents after someone's death. That does not necessarily mean the same family member should automatically receive confidential source material, protected communications, sensitive research, or evidence involving third parties. Digital inheritance should therefore be categorized. Different classes of information may require different custodians and different access conditions. A single universal password may be convenient, but convenience can create unacceptable exposure.

One solution is to separate access into layers. The creator might maintain ordinary personal digital assets separately from highly sensitive evidence. Family members could receive legitimate access to one category while professional custodians handle another. A lawyer might retain instructions concerning legally sensitive material. A journalist or investigative organization might become the appropriate recipient for information involving public-interest reporting. This architecture prevents the death of the creator from automatically collapsing every boundary between personal, professional, confidential, and evidentiary information.

The idea of inheritance can therefore be expanded beyond ownership. What is being inherited may be responsibility rather than property. A person entrusted with a sensitive archive is not necessarily receiving the right to use it for personal purposes. They may instead become a custodian whose responsibility is to preserve it until specific conditions are satisfied. This distinction is essential. A dead man's switch should ideally transfer stewardship according to predefined rules rather than simply transferring unrestricted possession. Custody and ownership are not always the same thing.

Authentication factors complicate succession further. Modern systems increasingly use combinations of passwords, authentication applications, hardware security keys, biometric characteristics, recovery codes, and trusted devices. Multi-factor authentication can significantly improve security while the creator is alive. But some factors are inherently difficult to transfer. A biometric characteristic cannot simply be handed to another person. A trusted device may be destroyed or inaccessible. A hardware security key can be lost. A recovery code may exist only on a piece of paper in a locked drawer. A succession plan must therefore identify which factors are transferable, which are replaceable, and which depend upon provider-specific recovery procedures.

Biometrics illustrate a particularly important limitation. A fingerprint, facial characteristic, or other biometric factor can help authenticate the original user, but biometric data should not be treated as a conventional secret. Unlike a password, a person cannot simply replace their fingerprint if biometric information is compromised. For inheritance purposes, biometrics also create an obvious problem: they are designed to identify the individual rather than a successor. A system that depends exclusively upon the creator's biometric authentication may therefore become inaccessible after death. Biometric security and digital inheritance must be considered separately.

Recovery codes can sometimes provide an alternative route, but they create their own security problem. A recovery code is effectively a secondary credential. If stored insecurely, it can undermine the primary security system. If stored too securely, it may become impossible for a legitimate successor to locate it. The same balancing problem appears repeatedly. The objective is not to hide every access mechanism from everyone. The objective is to ensure that unauthorized people cannot obtain them while legitimate successors can obtain them under appropriate conditions.

This is where distributed custody can become useful. A recovery process does not necessarily have to exist in one complete object. Different components can be entrusted to separate legitimate parties where appropriate. One custodian might know where the archive exists. Another might hold a recovery credential. A third might have authority to determine whether the conditions for access have been satisfied. Such arrangements can reduce dependence upon one individual. They can also reduce the damage caused by the compromise of any single component. But distribution increases complexity and should therefore be used only when its benefits justify the additional administrative burden.

The concept resembles a safe-deposit arrangement in which no single person necessarily controls every stage of access. The analogy is imperfect because digital systems behave differently from physical locks, but the underlying principle is useful. A sensitive asset can require multiple legitimate conditions before access becomes possible. This can protect against both premature access and unilateral misuse. However, every additional condition creates another opportunity for failure. The architecture must therefore be tested from the perspective of the future successor, not just the present creator.

A common mistake is to assume that because a password has been written down, the succession problem has been solved. The paper may be lost, destroyed, stolen, or discovered by an unauthorized person. The password may have changed since the paper was created. The account may require a second factor that is unavailable. The service may have closed. The encrypted archive may use a different key. The written instructions may not identify which password belongs to which system. Digital inheritance therefore requires more than credentials. It requires an accurate map of the digital environment and the dependencies necessary to navigate it.

A useful inventory can identify the major categories of digital assets without exposing the actual credentials in ordinary documentation. The inventory can establish that an account exists, what purpose it serves, what kind of authentication it uses, where recovery information is maintained, and who should become responsible for it. Sensitive credentials can then be protected separately. This separation reduces the consequences if the inventory itself is discovered. It also helps future custodians understand the architecture without receiving unrestricted access to everything immediately.

The archive should also distinguish between credentials and instructions. A password alone does not tell a future custodian what to do with it. Instructions can establish the intended purpose, conditions of use, relevant legal considerations, and identity of the authorized recipient. The instructions should be sufficiently clear to prevent guesswork. At the same time, they should not expose sensitive credentials unnecessarily. This creates an information architecture in which knowledge about the system and the means of accessing the system are related but distinct.

Digital inheritance also raises the issue of succession timing. Should access become available immediately upon death? Should there be a waiting period? Should independent evidence of death or incapacity be required? Should a lawyer or other professional verify the condition? Should the information be released only after multiple parties agree? These are not purely technical questions. They involve personal wishes, legal requirements, ethical considerations, and the nature of the information being protected. Technology can implement conditions, but it cannot decide whether those conditions are morally or legally appropriate.

The same problem exists when the creator disappears without confirmation of death. A dead man's switch cannot automatically know the difference between death, voluntary absence, hospitalization, imprisonment, travel, technical failure, and deliberate silence unless additional information exists. This is why earlier chapters emphasized trigger design. Access inheritance must be connected to a carefully defined continuity process. Otherwise, an ordinary technical failure could be interpreted as a catastrophic event. The result could be premature disclosure.

This is also why grace periods and multiple forms of verification can matter. A missed check-in should not necessarily be treated as definitive evidence that a person has died. The system may allow time for technical problems to be resolved. It may attempt secondary contact through legitimate channels. It may require independent confirmation before a highly sensitive archive becomes accessible. Such safeguards reduce false positives. In a system designed to protect both people and information, avoiding premature activation is as important as ensuring eventual activation.

The relationship between passwords and encryption keys becomes particularly important when information is stored offline. Suppose a person maintains an encrypted external drive as the ultimate archive. The drive can survive a cloud-service failure, account closure, or cyberattack. But if the encryption key is inaccessible, the physical drive may be nothing more than an expensive container. The creator must therefore preserve a legitimate recovery mechanism. That mechanism must itself be protected. This creates a chain of dependencies in which each component must remain available to the authorized successor.

The chain can be represented conceptually as evidence, storage, encryption, key, authentication, authorization, and recovery. Each layer answers a different question. Where is the information? Is it intact? Can it be decrypted? Who possesses the key? Who is requesting access? Are they authorized? What happens if the normal method fails? If any link is overlooked, the system may fail despite the strength of the others. Digital inheritance is therefore fundamentally an exercise in dependency management.

There is also a temporal problem. A succession system may work perfectly when created but fail years later because the technology changes. A password manager may alter its inheritance features. A cloud provider may discontinue a service. A hardware authenticator may stop functioning. An old encrypted archive may depend upon obsolete software. The person who created the system may have forgotten how it works. Long-term digital inheritance therefore requires periodic maintenance. It is not enough to create the system once and assume that it will remain valid indefinitely.

Periodic testing is one of the strongest defenses against this problem. The creator or authorized custodian can verify that backups remain readable, credentials remain valid, recovery procedures remain understandable, and important documentation remains accurate. Testing should be conducted carefully so that it does not accidentally trigger the very disclosure mechanism being tested. The purpose is to demonstrate continuity without creating unnecessary exposure. A system that has never been tested should be treated with caution. The existence of a plan is not evidence that the plan works.

Digital inheritance also involves the problem of changing relationships. A person who is trusted today may not be trusted ten years from now. Family circumstances change. Friendships end. Professional relationships move on. Lawyers retire. Organizations merge or dissolve. A custodian may become compromised or simply lose interest. The identity of the trusted recipient should therefore not be treated as permanently fixed. The architecture needs a mechanism for legitimate updates. Otherwise, yesterday's trusted person may become tomorrow's vulnerability.

This is where revocation becomes important. If a person loses their custodial role, access should ideally be capable of being removed or replaced. In some systems this can be straightforward. In others, especially with offline archives or copies already distributed, revocation may be difficult or impossible. The designer should therefore consider what happens when a custodian must be replaced. Can their credentials be changed? Can their copy be recovered? Can access permissions be revoked? Can a new custodian assume responsibility without reconstructing the entire system? These questions belong in the original architecture rather than being postponed until a crisis occurs.

The problem becomes especially difficult when the information has already been distributed. A person may have received an encrypted archive and then ceased to be trusted. If they possess the necessary key, revocation may no longer be technically possible. This is one reason to avoid giving unrestricted access when limited custody would accomplish the same purpose. Distribution should be based upon function and necessity. The fewer unnecessary complete copies that exist, the more manageable future changes can become. Again, redundancy must be balanced against exposure.

Cryptocurrency illustrates the extreme version of digital inheritance because control over some digital assets can depend directly upon possession of private cryptographic keys. There may be no traditional customer-support department capable of resetting access in the way a conventional website can. Losing the key can mean losing control permanently. Transferring the key, however, can transfer the asset. The inheritance problem therefore becomes both a security problem and an estate-planning problem. This example demonstrates why technical architecture and legal planning sometimes need to operate together.

The same logic applies to intellectual property. A writer, scientist, inventor, researcher, or entrepreneur may possess years of work inside digital systems that are protected by credentials. If the creator dies unexpectedly, heirs or professional successors may know that the material exists but be unable to retrieve it. Worse, they may retrieve only fragments while losing access to the systems containing the contextual information that explains them. Digital inheritance should therefore preserve not just files but the relationships among files, accounts, software, metadata, and supporting documentation.

For a dead man's switch, the most important distinction is between access and disclosure. A future custodian may need access to determine whether disclosure conditions have been met, but that does not mean they should immediately publish everything they discover. The archive can remain encrypted until a legitimate succession event occurs. Once access is granted, a separate decision process can determine what should be disclosed. This layered approach reduces the danger that inheritance becomes synonymous with automatic publication. The creator's intention can therefore survive without turning every future custodian into an unrestricted publisher.

There is also a psychological element to digital inheritance. People often postpone the task because thinking about their own death or incapacitation is uncomfortable. They assume that someone will "figure it out" later. But digital systems are designed around authentication and authorization, not around the emotional expectations of families. A grieving relative may know that important information exists and still have no lawful or technical means of accessing it. A professional investigator may know that evidence was preserved but have no credentials. The absence of a continuity plan can therefore defeat the purpose of years of careful preservation.

This is why digital inheritance should be treated as part of responsible information stewardship rather than as a morbid administrative exercise. People preserve wills, property records, insurance information, and other important documents because they recognize that circumstances can change suddenly. Digital information deserves similar attention. The difference is that digital systems often contain invisible dependencies. A physical filing cabinet can be opened by someone who has the key. A digitally encrypted archive may require several independent elements before legitimate access is possible. Those dependencies must be deliberately mapped.

The strongest approach is therefore neither "give someone all the passwords" nor "tell nobody anything." Both extremes create obvious weaknesses. Giving one person everything creates a concentrated point of compromise. Telling nobody anything creates a concentrated point of failure. The more resilient approach is controlled succession, in which responsibility, credentials, evidence, and authority are arranged so that legitimate continuity remains possible without creating unnecessary exposure. The precise architecture should reflect the sensitivity of the information and the credible threats involved. There is no universal inheritance design.

The deeper lesson is that security and inheritance are not opposites. Properly designed, they reinforce one another. Strong authentication protects the archive while the creator is alive. Secure key management protects the underlying encryption. Distributed recovery arrangements can preserve legitimate access. Documentation can explain the architecture. Legal planning can establish authority. Redundant storage can ensure that access remains possible if one repository fails. The result is not a weaker security system but a more complete one.

A dead man's switch ultimately succeeds only if information can cross the boundary between one person's control and another person's legitimate custody. That transition must be designed rather than assumed. Passwords must remain available through appropriate recovery mechanisms. Encryption keys must survive without becoming publicly exposed. Authentication systems must account for the possibility that the original user will no longer be present. Custodians must understand their responsibilities. The legal and ethical status of access must be clear. The system must also be tested while the creator is still capable of correcting it.

The password problem therefore turns out to be much larger than passwords. It is really a problem of continuity, authority, dependency, and trust. A forgotten password is merely the simplest expression of a much deeper failure: the inability to transfer control safely when the original controller is gone. The same principle applies to encryption keys, authentication devices, cloud accounts, offline archives, and distributed evidence repositories. Every protected system needs a legitimate answer to the question of what happens when its creator can no longer operate it. If there is no answer, protection can become permanent isolation.

The objective of digital inheritance is not to make everything accessible after death. It is to make the right things accessible to the right people under the right conditions. Some information may belong with family. Some may require professional custody. Some may need legal review. Some may need to remain confidential. Some may eventually warrant public disclosure. The architecture should preserve those distinctions rather than erase them. A dead man's switch should therefore be understood as a controlled transition of information stewardship, not merely an automated mechanism for releasing secrets.

In the end, the most secure archive is not necessarily the one that is hardest to open. It is the one that is hardest for unauthorized people to open while remaining reliably accessible to the people who are legitimately supposed to inherit responsibility for it. That balance is difficult because security, usability, continuity, privacy, and legal authority pull in different directions. But it is precisely that tension that makes the design problem worth taking seriously. A dead man's switch is ultimately a promise that important information will not disappear simply because its creator does. Keeping that promise requires more than storing the evidence. It requires ensuring that someone trustworthy can eventually reach it.

Resources

1. NIST Special Publication 800-57 — Recommendation for Key Management — authoritative guidance on cryptographic-key generation, storage, protection, backup, recovery, and lifecycle management.

2. NIST Special Publication 800-63-4 — Digital Identity Guidelines[1] — comprehensive guidance concerning authentication, authenticators, identity assurance, and recovery processes.

3. NIST Special Publication 800-53 — Security and Privacy Controls[2] — security controls concerning access management, least privilege, authentication, contingency planning, system integrity, and accountability.

4. NIST Cybersecurity Framework 2.0[3] — framework for identifying, protecting, detecting, responding to, and recovering from cybersecurity risks.

1. https://pages.nist.gov/800-63-4/?utm_source=chatgpt.com

2. https://csrc.nist.gov/publications/detail/sp/800-53/rev-5/final?utm_source=chatgpt.com

5. NIST Special Publication 800-63B — Authentication and Authenticator Management[4] — detailed guidance concerning passwords, authenticators, multi-factor authentication, recovery, and authentication assurance.

6. NIST Special Publication 800-132 — Recommendation for Password-Based Key Derivation — technical guidance concerning the derivation of cryptographic keys from passwords.

7. NIST Special Publication 800-88 — Guidelines for Media Sanitization[5] — guidance relevant to digital-media lifecycle management and information protection.

8. CISA — Secure Our World[6] — government guidance concerning strong passwords, multi-factor authentication, software updates, and phishing resistance.

9. CISA — Cybersecurity Performance Goals[7] — practical recommendations concerning authentication, backups, access control, and resilience.

10. OWASP Authentication Cheat Sheet[8] — practical guidance on authentication architecture, password practices, multi-factor authentication, and account recovery.

11. OWASP Password Storage Cheat Sheet[9] — guidance concerning password protection and modern password-hashing practices.

12. Electronic Frontier Foundation — Surveillance Self-Defense[10] — accessible resources covering passwords, encryption, authentication, device security, backups, and threat modeling.

13. National Archives — Digital Preservation — authoritative resources concerning long-term digital preservation, accessibility, and continuity.

14. Library of Congress — Digital Preservation[11] — extensive resources concerning digital objects, preservation, metadata, storage, and long-term accessibility.

15. ISO/IEC 27001 — Information Security Management Systems[12] — international framework for systematic information-security risk management.

16. ISO/IEC 27002 — Information Security Controls[13] — guidance concerning access management, cryptography, information protection, and organizational security controls.

---

3. https://www.nist.gov/cyberframework?utm_source=chatgpt.com

4. https://pages.nist.gov/800-63-4/sp800-63b.html?utm_source=chatgpt.com

5. https://csrc.nist.gov/publications/detail/sp/800-88/rev-1/final?utm_source=chatgpt.com

6. https://www.cisa.gov/secure-our-world?utm_source=chatgpt.com

7. https://www.cisa.gov/cybersecurity-performance-goals-cpgs?utm_source=chatgpt.com

8. https://cheatsheetseries.owasp.org/cheatsheets/Authentication_Cheat_Sheet.html?utm_source=chatgpt.com

9. https://cheatsheetseries.owasp.org/cheatsheets/Password_Storage_Cheat_Sheet.html?utm_source=chatgpt.com

10. https://ssd.eff.org/?utm_source=chatgpt.com

11. https://www.loc.gov/preservation/digital/?utm_source=chatgpt.com

12. https://www.iso.org/isoiec-27001-information-security.html?utm_source=chatgpt.com

13. https://www.iso.org/standard/75652.html?utm_source=chatgpt.com

17. ISO 15489 — Records Management[14] — international standard addressing reliable records management, authenticity, preservation, and continued usability.

18. ISO 14721 — Open Archival Information System (OAIS)[15] — foundational archival model concerning preservation and continued access to digital information.

19. National Institute of Standards and Technology — Privacy Framework[16] — useful framework for managing privacy risks associated with personal and sensitive information.

20. Internet Engineering Task Force — RFC 4949, Internet Security Glossary[17] — technical definitions of authentication, authorization, confidentiality, integrity, availability, and related security concepts.

21. Ross Anderson, *Security Engineering: A Guide to Building Dependable Distributed Systems*, 3rd ed., Wiley, 2020 — comprehensive examination of security architecture, human factors, authentication, access control, dependable systems, and failure modes.

22. Bruce Schneier, *Secrets and Lies: Digital Security in a Networked World*, Wiley, 2000 — influential analysis of security as a combination of technology, people, processes, and organizational design.

23. Bruce Schneier, *Applied Cryptography: Protocols, Algorithms, and Source Code in C*, 2nd ed., Wiley, 1996 — foundational reference covering cryptographic systems, key management, authentication, and security architecture.

24. Digital Preservation Coalition — Digital Preservation Handbook[18] — professional guidance concerning preservation planning, storage, metadata, integrity, technological change, and long-term access.

25. Internet Engineering Task Force — RFC 9106: Argon2 Memory-Hard Function[19] — technical standard concerning Argon2, a modern password-hashing and key-derivation function designed to make certain password-guessing attacks more expensive.

---

14. https://www.iso.org/standard/62542.html?utm_source=chatgpt.com

15. https://www.iso.org/standard/57284.html?utm_source=chatgpt.com

16. https://www.nist.gov/privacy-framework?utm_source=chatgpt.com

17. https://www.rfc-editor.org/rfc/rfc4949?utm_source=chatgpt.com

18. https://www.dpconline.org/handbook?utm_source=chatgpt.com

19. https://www.rfc-editor.org/rfc/rfc9106?utm_source=chatgpt.com

Choosing the Guardians of the Information

Every dead man's switch eventually arrives at the same human question: who should receive the information if the person who created it can no longer protect it? Technology can encrypt a file, distribute copies, monitor a deadline, and transmit a message, but none of those mechanisms can independently determine whether the person receiving the material is trustworthy or capable of handling it responsibly. The recipient may become the final guardian between important evidence and the outside world, which means that choosing that person can be more consequential than choosing the storage system itself. A beautifully engineered archive can fail if the person who inherits it panics, leaks it prematurely, destroys it, ignores it, or becomes compromised. The guardian is therefore not merely a recipient but a critical component of the architecture.

The word guardian is useful because it emphasizes responsibility rather than possession. Someone entrusted with sensitive information does not necessarily become its owner, publisher, investigator, or judge. Their responsibility may simply be to preserve it, verify the circumstances under which it was received, and transfer it to an appropriate authority or institution. In some cases, that authority might be a lawyer. In others, it could be an investigative journalist, regulator, court, professional organization, or family representative. The appropriate destination depends upon the nature of the information and the legitimate purpose for which it was preserved. A guardian's first duty is therefore not necessarily to release information but to protect its integrity until a responsible decision can be made.

This distinction immediately changes how recipients should be evaluated. Friendship alone is not enough. Family loyalty alone is not enough. Professional prestige alone is not enough. Technical expertise alone is not enough. A suitable guardian needs a combination of characteristics appropriate to the information they are being asked to protect. The more sensitive the archive, the more important it becomes to examine those characteristics deliberately rather than relying on instinct or emotional attachment.

Reliability is perhaps the most obvious quality, but reliability is more complicated than simply believing someone is a good person. A reliable custodian must demonstrate that they can follow instructions, maintain confidentiality, respond when required, and remain dependable during stressful circumstances. Someone who frequently loses documents, forgets commitments, ignores communications, or acts impulsively may be a poor guardian even if they are deeply loyal. Reliability is demonstrated through behavior over time. It is not created by assigning someone a title.

Independence is equally important. A recipient may be extremely trustworthy but still have interests that conflict with the information they receive. Imagine an archive containing evidence implicating an organization that employs the proposed guardian. The person might genuinely care about the creator while simultaneously fearing the consequences of exposing their employer. Another recipient might have financial interests connected to the subject of the evidence. Someone else might have a close personal relationship with an individual whose reputation could be damaged. These conflicts do not automatically make a person dishonest, but they introduce pressures that must be recognized.

Independence does not mean emotional detachment. In fact, a person who has no relationship whatsoever with the creator may have little motivation to carry out the intended responsibility. The objective is not to find a person who feels nothing. It is to find someone whose relationship does not prevent them from exercising sound judgment. A close friend might be an excellent guardian if they can remain disciplined. A distant professional might be a poor choice if they have strong interests that conflict with the archive. The question is always whether the person's incentives align with responsible stewardship.

Legal exposure is another factor that is often underestimated. Sensitive information may involve allegations, confidential communications, personal data, trade secrets, national-security information, copyrighted material, or evidence relevant to criminal or civil proceedings. A person who receives such information may face legal obligations or risks that they did not anticipate. They may be subject to subpoenas, court orders, professional confidentiality rules, contractual obligations, or other legal constraints. The guardian should therefore understand that receiving information can itself create consequences. Where the material is legally sensitive, professional legal advice can be essential.

This does not mean that a lawyer is automatically the best guardian. Lawyers have professional duties and operate within legal frameworks that may impose restrictions on how information can be handled. Their involvement can be valuable precisely because they understand those frameworks, but their role should be defined clearly. A lawyer may be best positioned to preserve certain materials, assess legal exposure, or coordinate with appropriate authorities. In another case, a journalist may be better positioned to evaluate public-interest information. The correct choice depends upon the nature of the archive rather than the prestige of the profession.

Technical competence also matters, particularly when the information is encrypted or distributed across multiple repositories. A guardian who cannot operate the relevant systems may be unable to recover the evidence when required. They may misunderstand encryption, accidentally overwrite files, lose credentials, or expose sensitive material through insecure practices. Technical competence does not require the guardian to be a cybersecurity expert. It does require sufficient understanding to follow the preservation and access procedures correctly. If specialist knowledge is necessary, the architecture should provide access to that expertise rather than assuming the guardian will somehow acquire it during a crisis.

Personal relationships create another layer of complexity. A spouse, sibling, parent, child, or close friend may have powerful emotional reasons to protect the creator's wishes. Those same emotions can also interfere with judgment. A grieving relative may struggle to distinguish the creator's instructions from their own feelings about what should happen. They may fear reputational damage to the family. They may decide that disclosure would dishonor the deceased. Conversely, they may become determined to expose everything regardless of context. Family members can be excellent custodians, but their emotional proximity should be considered rather than ignored.

The same principle applies to professional allies. A journalist may have a professional commitment to investigating matters of public interest but may also have editorial policies that restrict what can be published. An investigator may be highly capable but may have jurisdictional limitations. An activist organization may have a strong public-interest mission but may approach the evidence through a particular ideological framework. A scientific colleague may understand the technical material better than anyone else but may have professional interests affected by its publication. No recipient exists outside a network of incentives.

The evaluation of a guardian therefore resembles a risk assessment. The relevant question is not whether a person is "good" or "bad." Human beings are more complicated than that binary. The question is what pressures they might experience, what authority they possess, what capabilities they have, and how they are likely to behave under those circumstances. Someone may be highly reliable in ordinary life but respond unpredictably under legal pressure. Another may be calm during crises but careless with confidential material. A third may be exceptionally competent but have a conflict of interest. Good selection examines the whole profile.

One useful concept is single-point failure. If the entire archive depends upon one person, that person becomes a single point of failure. They can be unavailable, compromised, persuaded, threatened, legally constrained, or simply mistaken. The previous chapters examined technological redundancy, but human redundancy is equally important. Two independent custodians may provide greater resilience than one exceptionally trusted individual. The objective is not to create a committee for its own sake. It is to prevent the failure of one person from destroying the entire continuity plan.

Multiple guardians, however, introduce coordination problems. If everyone has equal authority, disagreements can prevent action. One person may believe disclosure is justified while another believes it is premature. If unanimity is required, one uncooperative guardian can effectively block the system. If a simple majority controls, a minority may feel that sensitive information has been released against the creator's intentions. The architecture therefore needs clear roles. Distribution of responsibility is useful only when decision authority is understandable.

The identity of the guardian can also be separated from possession of the complete archive. One person might hold information about where the evidence is stored. Another might possess a cryptographic key. A third might have instructions concerning the circumstances under which access should occur. This reduces the risk that any one person has unrestricted control. It also means that compromising one guardian does not necessarily compromise everything. Such arrangements must be carefully documented, however, because fragmentation can become a failure point if the successors do not understand how the components fit together.

The principle of least privilege is relevant here. A guardian should receive only the level of access necessary to perform their assigned responsibility. If someone merely needs to verify that an archive exists, they may not need access to its contents. If someone needs to preserve encrypted files, they may not need the decryption key. If someone is responsible for legal review, they may not need access to unrelated personal information. Limiting unnecessary access reduces the consequences of mistakes and compromises. It also clarifies accountability because each person has a defined role.

The guardian should also understand the difference between authenticity and interpretation. A custodian may be responsible for preserving an original recording without being qualified to determine whether the recording proves the allegation attached to it. Those are different tasks. The custodian protects the integrity of the evidence. An investigator evaluates its meaning. A journalist may assess public interest. A court may determine admissibility and legal significance. Separating these functions can prevent a guardian from accidentally transforming preservation into premature judgment.

This is particularly important when the archive contains allegations of wrongdoing. A person who receives emotionally compelling evidence may immediately conclude that the underlying claim is proven. But evidence can be incomplete, misleading, manipulated, or misunderstood. A guardian should therefore preserve the distinction between what is documented and what is alleged. The archive should contain provenance and context wherever possible. A responsible recipient should resist the temptation to become an advocate before determining what the material actually establishes.

The creator's own biases must also be considered. A dead man's switch may preserve information because its creator genuinely believes that they possess important evidence. That belief may be justified. It may also be mistaken. A person under severe pressure can interpret ambiguous events as evidence of a larger pattern. A person deeply committed to a cause may select material that confirms their expectations. A responsible guardian should therefore be prepared to evaluate the evidence independently. Preserving a creator's claim does not require automatically accepting the creator's interpretation.

This is where independent verification becomes valuable. If a guardian receives a document alleging misconduct, they may seek corroborating records, independent witnesses, authenticated originals, or other evidence. They may compare timestamps, metadata, correspondence, financial records, or publicly available documentation. The objective is not necessarily to conduct a complete investigation personally. It is to avoid treating an archive as self-authenticating simply because it was left behind with instructions to publish it. The more serious the allegation, the more important independent scrutiny becomes.

A guardian also needs the ability to resist pressure. This does not necessarily mean physical danger. Pressure can be social, professional, financial, legal, or psychological. A person may be threatened with dismissal, litigation, reputational damage, loss of relationships, or public criticism. They may be offered incentives to surrender the material. They may be told that the information is false or that releasing it would cause harm. The guardian must therefore have sufficient independence and emotional stability to make decisions according to evidence and legitimate instructions rather than immediate pressure.

This raises the difficult question of whether the guardian themselves could become a target. In sensitive cases, the answer may be yes, although the level of risk varies enormously. A person holding evidence concerning organized crime may face a very different threat environment from someone preserving evidence of corporate misconduct. The system should therefore avoid creating unnecessary concentrations of sensitive information. Where appropriate, distributed custody can mean that no single guardian possesses everything. This reduces both practical and personal risk.

Geographical separation can sometimes reinforce that principle. Guardians located in different jurisdictions may not be exposed to identical legal or institutional pressures. But geographical distribution does not automatically create safety. Different jurisdictions have different laws, enforcement capabilities, privacy protections, and procedures for cross-border information. International distribution can introduce additional complexity rather than simply adding protection. The choice should therefore be based upon the actual threat environment and legal context.

The guardian's relationship to the creator's family can also influence outcomes. Family members may expect to control the information because they believe they have inherited the creator's property. A professional guardian may believe that the creator's instructions take precedence over family preferences. Conflict can emerge immediately. This is another reason that the creator should distinguish personal property from sensitive information and clearly document the intended responsibilities. Ambiguity invites disputes. A well-defined succession architecture reduces the possibility that the first major decision becomes an argument over authority.

There is also the question of age and continuity. A guardian who is highly suitable today may not remain suitable indefinitely. They may become elderly, develop health limitations, retire, move to another country, change professions, or lose contact with the creator's network. The system should therefore have succession mechanisms for guardians themselves. A guardian may need to designate an approved successor. Alternatively, a professional institution may provide continuity that an individual cannot. Long-term information systems must account for the mortality and changing circumstances of the custodians as well as the creator.

This creates a recursive problem. If the dead man's switch protects information beyond the creator's lifetime, who protects the guardians? A system designed around one person simply transfers the original vulnerability to another person. True resilience requires continuity beyond individual personalities. That might mean multiple custodians, institutional repositories, professional intermediaries, or clearly documented succession procedures. The precise solution depends upon the circumstances. The underlying principle is universal: the system should not depend indefinitely upon one human being remaining available and trustworthy.

Institutional guardians can offer advantages because organizations may have established procedures, professional obligations, secure infrastructure, and continuity across personnel changes. A reputable archive, legal practice, investigative organization, or other institution may be able to preserve information more reliably than an individual. But institutions have vulnerabilities of their own. Organizations can change leadership, merge, close, become politically pressured, or alter their policies. Institutional trust therefore requires the same scrutiny as personal trust. A famous name is not a substitute for understanding who actually controls the information.

Anonymous custodians introduce another possibility but also significant difficulties. An anonymous person may reduce the risk that an attacker can easily identify every component of the system. Yet anonymity can make accountability difficult. If something goes wrong, there may be no reliable mechanism for resolving the problem. The creator may also have limited ability to evaluate the person's character or competence. Anonymity is therefore not inherently synonymous with security. It can be useful in some architectures, but it should never be treated as a guarantee of trustworthiness.

The concept of trust itself deserves careful examination. Trust is often described as a personal feeling, but information security treats trust as a relationship involving assumptions, permissions, and controls. You may trust someone to hold a sealed envelope without trusting them to read its contents. You may trust a lawyer to preserve confidential material without trusting them to publish it. You may trust a journalist to investigate evidence without trusting them to accept every claim contained within it. Trust can therefore be granular. The most resilient system defines precisely what each person is trusted to do.

This approach also allows trust to be tested. Rather than giving a new guardian unrestricted access immediately, the system can assign limited responsibilities first. Someone might demonstrate that they can preserve an archive without altering it. Another might demonstrate that they understand the recovery process. A professional recipient might review the legal instructions before receiving the underlying evidence. These staged relationships can reduce uncertainty. They also make it easier to identify weaknesses before a genuine emergency occurs.

The creator should also consider what happens if a guardian refuses the responsibility. This possibility is often ignored because people assume that someone who is trusted today will automatically agree to carry the burden tomorrow. But receiving sensitive information can be frightening. A person may have family responsibilities, professional restrictions, or personal reasons for declining. The system should therefore not depend upon an unwilling participant. Alternative guardians or institutions may need to exist. Consent matters because an unwilling custodian can become an immediate point of failure.

Another problem is overexposure. A creator may be tempted to tell many people about the existence of the dead man's switch because doing so seems to provide additional protection. In reality, every additional person who knows sensitive details increases the number of possible leaks. There is a difference between distributed custody and indiscriminate distribution. Redundancy should create resilience without turning confidentiality into a lottery. The number of participants should therefore be justified by the architecture rather than by fear.

The same principle applies to the information given to each guardian. A person may need to know that they are responsible for a particular task without knowing every detail of the underlying evidence. Another may need to know where a repository exists but not possess the key required to open it. Another may hold a key without knowing what it unlocks. This type of controlled knowledge can reduce the damage caused by compromise. But again, the architecture must remain comprehensible to authorized successors.

Documentation becomes crucial because human memory is unreliable. The creator may believe that a trusted person will remember an informal conversation about what to do after their death. Years later, the person may remember the broad intention but forget the specific instructions. Written documentation can establish responsibilities and reduce ambiguity. It should distinguish between factual instructions and personal preferences. Where legal authority is involved, the documentation should also be consistent with applicable legal arrangements.

The guardian should ideally know how to recognize an authentic activation event. If they receive a message claiming that the creator has died, they should not necessarily assume that the message itself is proof. Authentication of the trigger is essential. Otherwise, an attacker could imitate the activation process and persuade the guardian to release information prematurely. This is another example of why the human layer and technical layer cannot be separated completely. The guardian needs a reliable way to distinguish legitimate instructions from manipulation.

Social engineering is particularly relevant here. An attacker may contact a guardian while pretending to be the creator, a lawyer, a police officer, a family member, or another authorized person. They may claim that an emergency exists and demand immediate action. They may exploit fear or urgency. A guardian who understands the architecture should know that legitimate instructions have defined authentication procedures. Urgency should not automatically override verification. In sensitive information systems, pressure is often itself a warning sign.

The guardian also needs to understand when not to act. This may be the most difficult responsibility of all. If the system activates because a check-in was missed, the guardian should determine whether the trigger has actually satisfied the predefined conditions. If the information appears incomplete, they may need to preserve it rather than release it. If a legal restriction applies, they may need professional advice. If the evidence appears fraudulent, they may need independent verification. Responsible guardianship includes restraint.

The choice of guardian therefore becomes a form of governance. The creator establishes rules. The guardian operates within those rules. Professional or institutional authorities may evaluate the evidence. Ultimately, the public or a legal system may determine its significance. The dead man's switch should not attempt to collapse all these functions into one person. Its purpose is continuity, not the creation of a private court of final judgment.

There is an important ethical dimension to this architecture. A creator may believe that every piece of information should become public if they die. But sensitive archives can contain information about innocent people who never consented to publication. They can expose private medical, financial, or personal information. They can identify confidential sources. They can reveal security-sensitive information unrelated to the creator's original objective. A guardian therefore needs enough discretion and guidance to distinguish the legitimate public-interest core from unnecessary collateral exposure. "Release everything" is simple, but simplicity is not always responsible.

This is where the creator's instructions should be specific about objectives rather than merely outcomes. Instead of saying only that all material should be published, the instructions can explain what the archive is intended to accomplish. Is the objective to expose corruption? Preserve evidence? Protect a source? Ensure that a scientific discovery survives? Document wrongdoing? Establish a historical record? Different objectives lead to different decisions about what should ultimately be disclosed. The guardian becomes better equipped to exercise judgment when they understand the purpose behind the system.

The best guardian is therefore not necessarily the person who promises absolute obedience. Blind obedience can be dangerous when circumstances change or evidence turns out to be incomplete. A better guardian understands the creator's objectives while retaining the ability to recognize fraud, legal complications, technical failures, and unintended consequences. The system should preserve the creator's intentions without eliminating responsible judgment. This is especially important because no contingency plan can predict every future circumstance.

Ultimately, choosing a guardian requires a sober assessment of human strengths and weaknesses. Reliability matters. Independence matters. Technical competence matters. Legal awareness matters. Emotional stability matters. Continuity matters. So does the ability to resist pressure without becoming reckless. These characteristics rarely exist perfectly in one person, which is why distributed responsibility can sometimes produce a stronger system than reliance upon a single trusted individual.

The deeper lesson is that trust should be designed rather than merely assumed. A creator should ask not only, "Do I trust this person?" but also, "What exactly am I trusting them to do?" The second question produces a much more useful answer. Someone may be trusted to preserve a file but not publish it. Someone else may be trusted to verify a death but not access the evidence. Another may be trusted to conduct legal review. Another may be trusted to communicate with the media. When responsibilities are clearly defined, trust becomes a controlled relationship rather than a vague emotional judgment.

A dead man's switch is ultimately a bridge between one person's knowledge and the future. The creator cannot know exactly who will stand on the other side of that bridge when the time comes. They can, however, influence how that person is selected, what authority they possess, what information they receive, and what safeguards surround their decisions. The strongest architecture therefore does not merely ask whether someone is trustworthy. It asks whether the system remains safe if that person's judgment is imperfect. That is the standard by which guardians should be chosen.

The final responsibility belongs not to the person who creates the archive but to the architecture that remains after they are gone. A guardian should never have to guess what the creator intended, discover the entire system through trial and error, or decide alone whether a sensitive allegation is true. The system should provide context, provenance, authority, verification procedures, and appropriate alternatives. Human judgment will always remain necessary, but good design can prevent that judgment from becoming an impossible burden. In the end, the best guardian is not simply a person you trust with the truth. It is a person placed within a structure that gives the truth its best chance of surviving responsibly.

Resources

1. NIST Cybersecurity Framework 2.0[1] — provides a widely used framework for identifying, protecting, detecting, responding to, and recovering from cybersecurity risks.

2. NIST Special Publication 800-53 — Security and Privacy Controls[2] — includes controls relating to access enforcement, least privilege, separation of duties, accountability, contingency planning, and personnel security.

1. https://www.nist.gov/cyberframework?utm_source=chatgpt.com

2. https://csrc.nist.gov/publications/detail/sp/800-53/rev-5/final?utm_source=chatgpt.com

3. NIST Special Publication 800-61 — Computer Security Incident Handling Guide[3] — relevant to incident preparation, response, communication, and recovery responsibilities.

4. NIST Special Publication 800-63-4 — Digital Identity Guidelines[4] — provides guidance on identity proofing, authentication, authenticators, and establishing confidence in digital identities.

5. NIST Special Publication 800-57 — Recommendation for Key Management — addresses cryptographic-key management, custody, protection, recovery, and lifecycle responsibilities.

6. NIST Special Publication 800-30 — Guide for Conducting Risk Assessments[5] — useful for evaluating threats, vulnerabilities, likelihood, impact, and risk in selecting custodians and security controls.

7. NIST Privacy Framework[6] — provides a framework for identifying and managing privacy risks associated with sensitive information.

8. CISA Cybersecurity Performance Goals[7] — practical recommendations concerning access control, authentication, backups, and organizational resilience.

9. OWASP Threat Modeling[8] — useful methodology for identifying assets, actors, attack surfaces, threats, and appropriate mitigations.

10. OWASP Authorization Cheat Sheet[9] — guidance on least privilege, access control, role separation, and authorization design.

11. OWASP Authentication Cheat Sheet[10] — guidance concerning authentication, identity verification, recovery, and resistance to account compromise.

12. Electronic Frontier Foundation — Surveillance Self-Defense[11] — practical educational resources concerning threat modeling, authentication, encryption, secure communications, and protecting sensitive information.

13. National Archives — Digital Preservation — authoritative material concerning digital records, authenticity, preservation, and long-term access.

14. Library of Congress — Digital Preservation[12] — resources concerning digital preservation, metadata, file integrity, formats, and continuity.

15. ISO 15489 — Records Management[13] — international standard concerning reliable records management, authenticity, integrity, and preservation.

---

3. https://csrc.nist.gov/publications/detail/sp/800-61/rev-2/final?utm_source=chatgpt.com

4. https://pages.nist.gov/800-63-4/?utm_source=chatgpt.com

5. https://csrc.nist.gov/publications/detail/sp/800-30/rev-1/final?utm_source=chatgpt.com

6. https://www.nist.gov/privacy-framework?utm_source=chatgpt.com

7. https://www.cisa.gov/cybersecurity-performance-goals-cpgs?utm_source=chatgpt.com

8. https://owasp.org/www-community/Threat_Modeling?utm_source=chatgpt.com

9. https://cheatsheetseries.owasp.org/cheatsheets/Authorization_Cheat_Sheet.html?utm_source=chatgpt.com

10. https://cheatsheetseries.owasp.org/cheatsheets/Authentication_Cheat_Sheet.html?utm_source=chatgpt.com

11. https://ssd.eff.org/?utm_source=chatgpt.com

12. https://www.loc.gov/preservation/digital/?utm_source=chatgpt.com

16. ISO 27001 — Information Security Management Systems[14] — internationally recognized framework for managing information-security risks through organizational controls and governance.

17. ISO 27002 — Information Security Controls[15] — guidance on information-security controls, including access management, cryptography, human-resource security, and operational safeguards.

18. Ross Anderson, *Security Engineering: A Guide to Building Dependable Distributed Systems*, 3rd ed., Wiley, 2020 — extensive treatment of trust, security architecture, human factors, access control, organizational vulnerabilities, and dependable systems.

19. Bruce Schneier, *Secrets and Lies: Digital Security in a Networked World*, Wiley, 2000 — influential analysis of security as a combination of technology, people, processes, incentives, and institutional behavior.

20. Bruce Schneier, *Liars and Outliers: Enabling the Trust That Society Needs to Thrive*, Wiley, 2012 — examination of trust, social pressure, incentives, cooperation, and the mechanisms societies use to manage unreliable behavior.

21. Association of Certified Fraud Examiners — Fraud Risk Management Resources[16] — useful material concerning conflicts of interest, fraud risk, organizational controls, and human vulnerabilities.

22. U.S. Securities and Exchange Commission — Whistleblower Program[17] — official resources illustrating the institutional and legal context surrounding whistleblowers and the handling of sensitive information.

23. U.S. Department of Justice — Justice Manual — official reference for federal legal and prosecutorial policies relevant to sensitive information and investigative matters.

24. Society of Professional Journalists — Code of Ethics[18] — relevant ethical framework for journalists evaluating information, minimizing harm, acting independently, and seeking truth.

25. Reuters Handbook of Journalism[19] — professional standards concerning verification, accuracy, independence, source protection, and responsible publication.

26. Committee to Protect Journalists — Safety Resources[20] — practical resources concerning source protection, journalist security, risk assessment, and threats faced by people handling sensitive information.

---

13. https://www.iso.org/standard/62542.html?utm_source=chatgpt.com

14. https://www.iso.org/isoiec-27001-information-security.html?utm_source=chatgpt.com

15. https://www.iso.org/standard/75652.html?utm_source=chatgpt.com

16. https://www.acfe.com/fraud-resources.aspx?utm_source=chatgpt.com

17. https://www.sec.gov/whistleblower?utm_source=chatgpt.com

18. https://www.spj.org/ethicscode.asp?utm_source=chatgpt.com

19. https://reutersagency.com/en/about/standards-values/?utm_source=chatgpt.com

20. https://cpj.org/safety-kit/?utm_source=chatgpt.com

Family, Friends, Lawyers, and Professional Intermediaries

The easiest person to trust with something important is often the person we already know, love, and believe would stand beside us when everyone else walked away. That instinct has obvious value, particularly when the information being protected concerns a deeply personal experience, a family history, evidence of wrongdoing, or circumstances that outsiders might not immediately understand. Yet the qualities that make someone emotionally close to the creator can also make them unsuitable for certain responsibilities after a crisis occurs. Grief can distort judgment, loyalty can become secrecy, fear can become paralysis, and personal interests can collide with the public interest. Professional custodians present a different set of advantages because they may bring legal knowledge, investigative experience, institutional procedures, technical competence, or editorial independence. The central question is therefore not whether family or professionals are better guardians, but which person or combination of people is best suited to each specific responsibility.

Family members have one enormous advantage over almost every professional intermediary: they may understand the person behind the information. A spouse, sibling, parent, or adult child may know the creator's values, fears, motivations, relationships, and intentions in ways that an outsider never could. If the creator has spent years explaining why particular information matters, a close relative may understand the context immediately. That knowledge can be invaluable when instructions are incomplete. At the same time, intimate knowledge can become a liability when emotional attachment overwhelms independent judgment.

A family member may believe that protecting the creator means protecting their reputation at all costs. If the archive contains embarrassing information, accusations against powerful people, or evidence that could attract unwanted attention, relatives may decide that silence is the safest form of loyalty. They may also fear consequences for themselves. The creator's death does not necessarily eliminate the risks associated with the information. Instead, those risks may be transferred to the surviving family. A relative who understands this may deliberately choose not to activate a mechanism even when the creator clearly intended disclosure.

There is an opposite possibility as well. A grieving relative may become determined to expose everything because they believe the creator was wronged. Emotion can produce excessive disclosure just as easily as excessive secrecy. Material that was intended for careful legal or journalistic review may suddenly be published without context. Private information about innocent people may be exposed alongside the central evidence. Unverified allegations may be presented as established fact. The family member may believe they are honoring the creator while unintentionally damaging the credibility of the very evidence they were meant to protect.

This is why emotional loyalty should never be confused with operational competence. A person can love the creator deeply and still be the wrong person to manage encrypted files, preserve evidence, authenticate documents, or communicate with investigative institutions. The opposite is equally true. A technically competent professional may be able to preserve the archive perfectly while misunderstanding why certain distinctions matter to the creator. The strongest arrangements recognize that different people possess different forms of competence. The system should assign responsibilities accordingly.

Friends occupy an interesting position between family and professional intermediaries. A close friend may be emotionally connected enough to understand the creator while maintaining greater independence than a spouse or immediate relative. A friend may also be more willing to challenge the creator's assumptions. Yet friendship can create its own conflicts. Friends may share financial interests, professional relationships, political commitments, or social networks with the people implicated by the information. They may also underestimate the seriousness of the responsibility because they perceive themselves as helping a friend rather than managing potentially consequential evidence.

The informality of friendship can become particularly dangerous when the information requires formal handling. A friend may store documents on a personal computer, forward material through ordinary email, copy files to an unencrypted device, or discuss the existence of the archive with other people. None of these actions necessarily arise from bad intentions. They may simply reflect a lack of familiarity with information-security practices. The friend may believe that possession is enough. In reality, sensitive information often requires preservation, access control, provenance management, and careful documentation.

Lawyers occupy a different category because their professional relationship is structured by legal and ethical duties. Depending upon the jurisdiction and circumstances, a lawyer may be subject to obligations concerning confidentiality, conflicts of interest, competence, client property, records, and communication. These obligations can make legal professionals valuable custodians for certain categories of sensitive information. They may also understand the consequences of releasing particular documents and can help distinguish between evidence that can safely be disclosed and material that may create unnecessary legal exposure. However, a lawyer's professional obligations also mean that they cannot simply function as an unrestricted publication mechanism.

This distinction is essential. A person may imagine that giving everything to a lawyer guarantees eventual public disclosure. It does not. Lawyers are not merely neutral storage facilities, and their professional duties can impose limits on what they may do with information. A lawyer may advise against publication, seek clarification, preserve material, communicate with authorities, or take another lawful course depending upon the circumstances. The creator should therefore understand the actual professional relationship rather than assuming that a lawyer will automatically carry out every instruction.

The selection of a lawyer also requires attention to conflicts of interest. A lawyer employed by an organization implicated in the evidence may be an inappropriate custodian. A lawyer with existing relationships to relevant parties may have professional restrictions. A lawyer may also lack expertise in the particular subject matter. The mere possession of a legal qualification does not make someone an appropriate guardian of every kind of sensitive information. The relevant question is whether the lawyer can act independently and competently within the applicable professional framework.

There can also be a difference between a lawyer who represents the creator and a lawyer who represents an heir or another recipient after the creator's death. Those relationships can involve different interests. A family member may consult their own attorney concerning inherited material, while the creator's attorney may have separate obligations arising from the original representation. Confusing these roles can create serious misunderstandings. The succession plan should therefore identify the intended professional relationship as clearly as possible. Where the legal position is complicated, specialized estate or information-law advice may be necessary.

Professional journalists represent another potential category of intermediary. An investigative journalist may have expertise in evaluating sources, corroborating claims, protecting confidential informants, and determining whether information meets editorial standards. News organizations may also possess secure systems and legal resources that an individual friend does not. This can make journalism an appropriate destination for evidence involving matters of significant public interest. But journalists also operate under editorial judgment. They are not obligated to publish everything they receive merely because a source demands it.

That independence is actually one of the strengths of the professional intermediary model. If the archive contains material that is incomplete or questionable, an experienced journalist may investigate rather than immediately publish. They may seek corroboration, identify contradictions, authenticate records, and consult relevant parties. This can protect both the public and the creator's reputation. It also creates a valuable distinction between preserving evidence and making allegations. A responsible intermediary should be willing to say that something requires further verification.

Investigators and researchers can serve similar functions. A professional investigator may know how to establish timelines, interview witnesses, locate corroborating records, and identify inconsistencies. A researcher may understand specialized technical evidence that a general journalist or family member cannot interpret. An archivist may understand preservation and provenance better than anyone else involved. Each professional brings a particular competence. The best custodian is often the person whose skills match the nature of the material.

This leads to a broader principle: custodianship should be divided according to function. A family member might hold the creator's personal instructions. A lawyer might hold legally sensitive documentation. A journalist might evaluate evidence concerning public wrongdoing. A technical specialist might maintain encrypted repositories. A professional archivist might preserve original records. These roles can overlap, but they do not need to be identical. Separating responsibilities reduces the pressure placed upon any one individual and allows each participant to operate within their area of competence.

Such separation can also reduce conflicts of interest. If the person deciding whether information is authentic is the same person who benefits from its publication, the system has an obvious vulnerability. If the person holding the archive is also the person accused by the archive, the conflict is even more severe. Independent custody creates a degree of institutional friction. That friction can slow the process, but in sensitive situations a degree of friction is desirable. It gives the system an opportunity to catch mistakes before irreversible disclosure occurs.

The danger, however, is that too many intermediaries can create paralysis. If five people must agree before anything happens, one person's absence can prevent the system from functioning. If every professional insists that another person should make the decision, responsibility can disappear into procedural uncertainty. A dead man's switch should therefore establish clear authority. Each participant should know what they are expected to do, what they are not authorized to do, and what happens if another participant is unavailable. Complexity should serve resilience rather than become an excuse for inaction.

Professional intermediaries can also become unavailable. Lawyers retire or change firms. Journalists change organizations. Investigative organizations close. Researchers move institutions. A professional relationship that appears permanent may not actually be permanent. This is why the succession architecture must include continuity planning. The system should not depend upon a specific individual remaining in the same position for decades. Institutional arrangements can help, but institutions themselves must be evaluated for continuity.

Family systems have the same problem. A child who is an appropriate guardian at forty may become an inappropriate guardian at seventy. A spouse may remarry. A sibling may move abroad. A family relationship may deteriorate. The person who was once trusted may become estranged. The architecture should therefore allow legitimate guardians to be replaced. Trust should be renewable rather than permanent. Otherwise, the system becomes frozen in the circumstances that existed when it was created.

The question of confidentiality also differs between personal and professional custodians. A family member may feel morally obligated to tell other relatives what they know. A friend may confide in a spouse. A professional may have formal confidentiality obligations. The distinction is important because sensitive information can spread through informal conversations long before anyone realizes that a disclosure has occurred. Once information is copied or repeated, control becomes increasingly difficult. The creator should therefore understand the confidentiality environment surrounding each proposed custodian.

The same principle applies to digital communication. A family member may receive sensitive files through an ordinary messaging application because it is convenient. A lawyer may use a professional document system. A journalist may have specialized secure communication procedures. A technical custodian may use encrypted storage and controlled access. The method of transfer should match the sensitivity of the information. Convenience should not be allowed to determine the security architecture.

A particularly dangerous assumption is that professional status automatically creates security. A lawyer can be phished. A journalist can lose a device. A professional investigator can have an account compromised. An institution can suffer a data breach. Human beings remain human regardless of their occupation. Professional intermediaries reduce certain risks but do not eliminate them. Technical and procedural safeguards remain necessary.

The same applies to family. Being related to someone does not automatically make a person careless or trustworthy. Many family members can be exceptionally disciplined guardians. Some may have professional backgrounds that make them better custodians than outside experts. The mistake is not trusting family. The mistake is selecting family solely because they are family. Relationship should be one factor among many. Competence, independence, reliability, and ability to withstand pressure remain important.

There is also a question of motivation. A family member may be motivated by love and loyalty. A lawyer may be motivated by professional responsibility. A journalist may be motivated by public interest and editorial standards. An investigator may be motivated by the pursuit of facts. An archivist may be motivated by preservation. None of these motivations is inherently superior. The important issue is whether the motivation is compatible with the purpose of the archive. A person whose incentives point in the opposite direction may become a vulnerability even if they are otherwise highly capable.

The creator should also consider whether the guardian can distinguish personal wishes from objective evidence. A close relative may know exactly what the creator wanted to happen but may not know whether the information supports the creator's conclusions. A journalist may understand evidence but know little about the creator's personal intentions. A lawyer may understand legal consequences but lack technical expertise. This is another reason to divide the functions. The person who knows the creator best does not necessarily need to be the person who determines what the evidence proves.

The distinction between intention and evidence is fundamental. The creator can establish instructions concerning what should happen to information. The guardian must still preserve the distinction between those instructions and the factual status of the material itself. If the creator writes, "This proves corruption," the statement is evidence of what the creator believed, not independent proof that corruption occurred. The archive should preserve the claim without automatically treating it as established fact. Professional review can then evaluate the underlying material.

A sophisticated system can therefore use what might be called a chain of custody among people. The creator establishes the archive. A custodian preserves it. A professional intermediary authenticates or evaluates it. Another authority may determine whether publication is justified. Each transition should be documented. This resembles evidentiary procedures used in legal and investigative contexts, although a private information archive does not automatically possess formal evidentiary status merely because it uses such procedures. The purpose is to reduce uncertainty about what happened to the material after it left the creator's hands.

Documentation becomes particularly important when multiple custodians are involved. The record should establish who received what, when they received it, under what authority, and what actions they were permitted to take. This does not require creating an elaborate bureaucracy. It requires enough information to reconstruct the history of the archive. If a document is altered, duplicated, or moved, the custodian should ideally be able to explain what happened. Provenance can be damaged by innocent handling just as easily as by deliberate manipulation.

Professional intermediaries can be especially valuable in this respect because they may already work within documented procedures. Law firms, news organizations, archives, laboratories, and investigative institutions often have established protocols for handling sensitive information. But the creator should still understand those procedures before relying upon them. An institution may have excellent systems for one category of information and poor systems for another. Institutional reputation should therefore be evaluated alongside actual practices.

There is also the issue of jurisdiction. A professional custodian in one country may operate under very different legal rules from someone in another. Privacy laws, disclosure obligations, national-security laws, professional duties, and evidentiary procedures vary. International distribution may sometimes provide resilience, but it can also create legal conflicts. A guardian should understand the jurisdiction in which they operate. The creator should not assume that a professional intermediary can simply ignore local law because the information is important.

Family members may face jurisdictional problems as well. If the creator lives in one country and the family lives in another, the process of accessing accounts, transferring property, or handling sensitive records may become complicated. Digital service providers may apply their own policies in addition to local law. Cross-border succession can therefore require specialized legal advice. The dead man's switch should not be designed around assumptions about universal digital access. Geography still matters even in a networked world.

A further consideration is financial pressure. Maintaining a sensitive archive can involve costs for legal services, secure storage, professional review, travel, or technical infrastructure. A family member may not have the resources to maintain the system. A professional intermediary may have institutional funding but may also have policies governing what resources can be committed. The creator should consider who will pay for long-term custody. A system that cannot be maintained financially may eventually fail even if its technical architecture is sound.

The possibility of intimidation must also be considered carefully. Anyone holding sensitive information may experience pressure, although the nature and severity of that pressure depend entirely upon the circumstances. Family members can be pressured through threats against relationships or livelihoods. Professionals can face litigation, reputational attacks, employment consequences, or institutional pressure. The correct response is not to assume that every custodian will become a target. It is to recognize that pressure is a potential failure mode and build reasonable safeguards against it.

This is where independent custodians can become especially useful. If a family member is the only person who knows about the archive, pressure on that person can end the system. If a lawyer, journalist, or other independent professional also possesses a relevant component, the system has greater resilience. The arrangement should remain proportionate, however. Excessive distribution can create unnecessary exposure. The objective is independent continuity, not maximum publicity.

One of the most effective approaches may therefore be a hybrid model. A family member can preserve knowledge of the creator's intentions. A lawyer can hold legally sensitive instructions. A professional journalist or investigative organization can receive information appropriate for public-interest review. A technical custodian can maintain encrypted archives. Each person receives only what they need to perform their role. If one participant fails, the others can preserve enough of the architecture to prevent total collapse.

Such a model also respects the emotional realities of death. Family members should not necessarily be forced to become investigators, publishers, or cybersecurity specialists while grieving. Professional intermediaries can absorb responsibilities that would otherwise become overwhelming. At the same time, professionals should not be expected to understand every personal nuance that matters to the creator. The combination allows emotional continuity and professional competence to coexist. The system becomes stronger precisely because different people contribute different forms of knowledge.

There is an ethical advantage to this separation as well. Sensitive information may contain material that affects people who are not responsible for the underlying wrongdoing. Family members may instinctively protect relatives. Journalists may focus on public interest. Lawyers may focus on legal obligations. Investigators may focus on factual verification. These perspectives can conflict, but the conflict can be constructive. Responsible disclosure often requires more than one perspective before irreversible publication occurs.

The creator should also resist the temptation to select a guardian based entirely on fear. Someone who is extremely cautious may seem attractive because they are unlikely to disclose information prematurely. But excessive caution can be just as dangerous as recklessness if the archive exists precisely because important information must eventually survive. Conversely, someone who promises to "publish everything immediately" may appear courageous while actually creating serious evidentiary and legal problems. The correct guardian is neither the most fearful nor the most aggressive. It is the person capable of disciplined action under uncertainty.

Trust should therefore be evaluated against scenarios rather than personalities. Ask how the person would respond if the creator died unexpectedly. Ask how they would respond if the archive contained information they found personally offensive. Ask how they would respond if the information implicated someone they knew. Ask how they would respond if a lawyer advised caution. Ask how they would respond if a journalist questioned the evidence. Ask how they would respond if someone demanded immediate publication. The goal is not to predict every reaction. It is to identify vulnerabilities before the system depends upon them.

A guardian should also be capable of saying, "I do not know." That may be one of the most valuable qualities in the entire system. Someone who recognizes uncertainty is more likely to seek expert advice, verify evidence, and avoid premature conclusions. Someone who believes they understand everything may become dangerously confident. Sensitive information often involves incomplete records and competing interpretations. Intellectual humility is therefore a practical security characteristic.

Professional intermediaries can provide another advantage through institutional memory. If a journalist leaves a news organization, another journalist may inherit the responsibility. If a lawyer retires, another attorney may assume the matter. If an archive employs multiple preservation specialists, continuity does not depend entirely upon one individual. This institutional continuity can be valuable for information intended to survive decades. Yet the creator should still ensure that the institution understands the nature of the arrangement. A document sent to an institution does not automatically become part of its permanent preservation system.

The creator should also avoid confusing fame with suitability. A prominent lawyer may be too busy to provide meaningful attention. A famous journalist may receive more information than they can investigate. A large institution may have procedures that are poorly suited to unusual material. A respected friend may still lack technical competence. Smaller, less prestigious organizations may sometimes provide better custodial attention. The appropriate standard is capability and fit. Reputation is evidence of something, but it is not proof of suitability.

The most resilient arrangements often contain both personal and professional dimensions. The personal custodian preserves the human meaning of the information. The professional custodian preserves its procedural integrity. One understands why the creator cared. The other understands how sensitive information should be handled. One may provide continuity of intention. The other may provide continuity of process. Together, these functions can compensate for one another's weaknesses.

This arrangement also creates a useful safeguard against misunderstanding the creator's wishes. A family member can explain the context of an instruction. A professional can evaluate whether the proposed action is lawful and appropriate. If they disagree, the disagreement can trigger further review rather than unilateral action. That is precisely the kind of friction that can protect a sensitive system. A dead man's switch should not be designed to eliminate every disagreement. It should be designed so that disagreement does not automatically destroy the archive.

Ultimately, the question of who should receive the truth cannot be answered by choosing between family and professionals as competing categories. The more useful question is what the truth requires from the person entrusted with it. Does it require emotional understanding? Legal expertise? Technical competence? Investigative independence? Archival discipline? Public-interest judgment? Sometimes one person may possess several of these qualities. More often, different people will possess different strengths. A carefully designed system assigns responsibilities accordingly.

The deepest lesson is that trust is not a single commodity. You can trust someone with your memories without trusting them with your evidence. You can trust someone with your evidence without trusting them to decide whether it should be published. You can trust someone to preserve information without trusting them to interpret it. You can trust a professional to follow legal procedures without expecting them to understand your personal motivations. Once trust is divided into specific responsibilities, the problem becomes much easier to design.

A dead man's switch is ultimately an exercise in transferring responsibility under circumstances in which the original decision-maker may no longer be present. Family can provide loyalty. Friends can provide familiarity. Lawyers can provide legal structure. Journalists can provide investigative judgment. Technical specialists can provide security expertise. Archivists can provide preservation discipline. The strongest systems do not pretend that one category can perform every function. They build a chain of guardians in which each participant is trusted for a defined reason, operates within defined boundaries, and contributes to the survival of information without unnecessarily controlling its entire destiny.

The final measure of a guardian is therefore not how much they love the creator or how impressive their professional credentials may be. It is whether they can carry responsibility without allowing emotion, fear, convenience, ambition, or personal interest to corrupt that responsibility. The right guardian knows when to preserve, when to verify, when to seek advice, when to resist pressure, and when the evidence genuinely justifies the next step. The creator cannot guarantee that such a person will always make the perfect decision. What they can do is build a system in which no single imperfect decision has to determine the fate of everything.

That is the real purpose of choosing guardians. It is not simply to find someone who will inherit a secret. It is to create a human structure capable of carrying sensitive knowledge safely across time. When the personal and professional dimensions are properly balanced, the creator's information can survive without being either buried forever or released recklessly. The archive remains protected, the evidence remains distinguishable from speculation, and legitimate custodians retain the ability to act when circumstances require it. In that sense, the best guardian is not merely the person who can be trusted with the truth, but the person who understands why the truth must be handled carefully before it is finally revealed.

Resources

1. American Bar Association — Model Rules of Professional Conduct[1] — foundational professional framework concerning lawyers' duties, confidentiality, conflicts of interest, competence, and responsibilities to clients.

2. American Bar Association — Rule 1.6: Confidentiality of Information[2] — addresses lawyers' duties concerning confidential client information, subject to the rules and exceptions applicable in the relevant jurisdiction.

3. American Bar Association — Rule 1.7: Conflict of Interest: Current Clients[3] — relevant to evaluating whether a lawyer can act independently when competing interests are present.

4. American Bar Association — Rule 1.1: Competence[4] — establishes the professional competence standard relevant to legal custodianship.

5. Society of Professional Journalists — Code of Ethics[5] — professional principles concerning seeking truth, minimizing harm, acting independently, and remaining accountable.

6. Reuters — Trust Principles and Journalistic Standards[6] — professional standards emphasizing accuracy, independence, freedom from bias, and reliable reporting.

7. Associated Press — News Values and Principles[7] — standards concerning accuracy, fairness, independence, sourcing, and editorial responsibility.

8. Committee to Protect Journalists — Safety Kit[8] — resources concerning risk assessment, source protection, digital security, and physical and legal risks faced by journalists and their sources.

1. https://www.americanbar.org/groups/professional_responsibility/publications/model_rules_of_professional_conduct/?utm_source=chatgpt.com
2. https://www.americanbar.org/groups/professional_responsibility/publications/model_rules_of_professional_conduct/rule_1_6_confidentiality_of_information/?utm_source=chatgpt.com
3. https://www.americanbar.org/groups/professional_responsibility/publications/model_rules_of_professional_conduct/rule_1_7_conflict_of_interest_current_clients/?utm_source=chatgpt.com
4. https://www.americanbar.org/groups/professional_responsibility/publications/model_rules_of_professional_conduct/rule_1_1_competence/?utm_source=chatgpt.com
5. https://www.spj.org/ethicscode.asp?utm_source=chatgpt.com
6. https://reutersagency.com/en/about/standards-values/?utm_source=chatgpt.com
7. https://www.ap.org/about/news-values-and-principles/?utm_source=chatgpt.com
8. https://cpj.org/safety-kit/?utm_source=chatgpt.com

9. Electronic Frontier Foundation — Surveillance Self-Defense[9] — practical guidance on threat modeling, secure communication, encryption, device security, and protecting sensitive information.

10. NIST Cybersecurity Framework 2.0[10] — framework for identifying, protecting, detecting, responding to, and recovering from cybersecurity risks.

11. NIST Special Publication 800-53 — Security and Privacy Controls[11] — includes controls relevant to least privilege, separation of duties, access enforcement, accountability, personnel security, and contingency planning.

12. NIST Special Publication 800-30 — Guide for Conducting Risk Assessments[12] — provides a systematic methodology for identifying threats, vulnerabilities, likelihood, impact, and risk.

13. NIST Special Publication 800-57 — Recommendation for Key Management — authoritative guidance on cryptographic-key protection, custody, recovery, and lifecycle management.

14. ISO/IEC 27001 — Information Security Management Systems[13] — international framework for information-security governance and risk management.

15. ISO/IEC 27002 — Information Security Controls[14] — guidance concerning access control, information protection, cryptography, organizational security, and human factors.

16. ISO 15489 — Records Management[15] — international standard concerning records authenticity, integrity, reliability, and preservation.

17. ISO 14721 — Open Archival Information System Reference Model[16] — establishes a conceptual framework for long-term preservation and continued access to digital information.

18. National Archives — Digital Preservation — resources concerning digital records, preservation, authenticity, and continued accessibility.

19. Library of Congress — Digital Preservation[17] — resources on preserving digital materials, metadata, file formats, integrity, and long-term access.

20. Ross Anderson, *Security Engineering: A Guide to Building Dependable Distributed Systems*, 3rd ed., Wiley, 2020 — comprehensive treatment of security architecture, human behavior, trust, access control, institutional vulnerabilities, and dependable systems.

21. Bruce Schneier, *Liars and Outliers: Enabling the Trust That Society Needs to Thrive*, Wiley, 2012 — examination of trust, incentives, social pressure, cooperation, and mechanisms for managing unreliable behavior.

---

9. https://ssd.eff.org/?utm_source=chatgpt.com

10. https://www.nist.gov/cyberframework?utm_source=chatgpt.com

11. https://csrc.nist.gov/publications/detail/sp/800-53/rev-5/final?utm_source=chatgpt.com

12. https://csrc.nist.gov/publications/detail/sp/800-30/rev-1/final?utm_source=chatgpt.com

13. https://www.iso.org/isoiec-27001-information-security.html?utm_source=chatgpt.com

14. https://www.iso.org/standard/75652.html?utm_source=chatgpt.com

15. https://www.iso.org/standard/62542.html?utm_source=chatgpt.com

16. https://www.iso.org/standard/57284.html?utm_source=chatgpt.com

17. https://www.loc.gov/preservation/digital/?utm_source=chatgpt.com

22. Bruce Schneier, *Secrets and Lies: Digital Security in a Networked World*, Wiley, 2000 — analysis of information security as an interaction between technology, people, processes, and institutional structures.

23. U.S. Securities and Exchange Commission — Whistleblower Program[18] — official example of institutional structures for receiving sensitive information from people reporting potential wrongdoing.

24. U.S. Department of Justice — Justice Manual — official reference for federal legal and prosecutorial policies relevant to sensitive information, investigations, and legal decision-making.

25. National Institute of Standards and Technology — Privacy Framework[19] — framework for identifying and managing privacy risks associated with sensitive personal information.

26. Digital Preservation Coalition — Digital Preservation Handbook[20] — professional guidance on preservation planning, storage, integrity, metadata, technological change, and long-term access.

---

18. https://www.sec.gov/whistleblower?utm_source=chatgpt.com

19. https://www.nist.gov/privacy-framework?utm_source=chatgpt.com

20. https://www.dpconline.org/handbook?utm_source=chatgpt.com

Journalists, Investigators, and the Power of Independent Publication

There is a moment in the life of sensitive information when preservation may no longer be enough, yet publication may still be premature. A document can be stored securely for years without anyone determining what it means, whether it is authentic, or whether it supports the claim attached to it. A witness can make a serious allegation without possessing the evidence necessary to establish it. A recording can appear compelling while lacking the context required to understand what happened before or after it was made. This is where journalists and professional investigators can occupy an important position between private custody and public disclosure. Their value is not simply that they can publish information, but that responsible professionals can subject information to scrutiny before deciding whether publication or further investigation is justified.

Investigative journalism is fundamentally different from simply receiving a leak and putting it online. Serious investigative reporting generally involves assessing the reliability of sources, examining documents, seeking corroboration, contacting relevant subjects, establishing chronology, and determining whether the available evidence supports the conclusions being drawn. The process can be slow precisely because the consequences of error can be significant. A journalist may receive material that appears explosive but discover that important details are missing. They may find that an apparently authentic document has been altered, misunderstood, or taken out of context. The discipline of investigation exists partly to prevent the excitement of a discovery from becoming a substitute for verification.

This makes professional journalism potentially valuable to a dead man's switch. The creator may possess information that they believe is important but lack the resources, time, expertise, or independence to investigate it fully. A trusted journalist or investigative organization may have access to researchers, editors, lawyers, technical specialists, and established publication procedures. Those resources can transform an archive from a collection of claims into material that can be independently assessed. The journalist does not become the unquestioning voice of the deceased. Instead, the journalist becomes another layer of scrutiny between the creator's interpretation and the public.

That distinction is critical because the creator may be wrong. A dead man's switch is not a truth machine. Its existence demonstrates that someone believed certain information was important enough to preserve or disclose. It does not establish the accuracy of every allegation contained within the archive. A responsible journalist must therefore be willing to investigate the creator's claims rather than simply inherit them. The strongest evidence is evidence that can survive scrutiny from people who did not begin with the same assumptions as the person who collected it.

Source protection is another reason professional journalism can matter. A person who provides sensitive information may face professional, social, legal, or other consequences if their identity becomes known. Journalists often develop procedures for handling confidential sources and may have technical and organizational resources unavailable to private individuals. But source protection is not absolute, and the legal environment differs across jurisdictions. A journalist cannot simply promise that a source's identity can never be discovered. The nature of the publication, the jurisdiction involved, applicable law, and the organization's own policies all affect what protection can realistically be provided.

A dead man's switch can therefore create a complicated relationship between source protection and posthumous disclosure. The creator may want their identity revealed after death, or they may want certain material published without identifying other people involved. A journalist must evaluate those instructions against professional obligations and legal realities. The creator's wishes matter, but they do not automatically override the journalist's responsibilities. Publication decisions remain editorial decisions. This independence is one of the defining characteristics of professional journalism.

Independent publication also creates an important distinction between custody and credibility. If a journalist receives an archive, the fact that the journalist possesses it does not make the archive true. What changes is the opportunity for independent evaluation. The journalist may compare the documents with public records, obtain additional records, interview witnesses, consult experts, examine technical metadata, and reconstruct events. Each independent confirmation can strengthen confidence. Each contradiction can weaken the original claim. The process is cumulative rather than magical.

Documentary evidence often becomes particularly important during such investigations. A single document may establish little by itself. A series of records can establish chronology, relationships, transactions, communications, or institutional decisions. Emails may corroborate meeting records. Financial documents may corroborate claims about transactions. Photographs may establish that a person or object was present at a particular location. Official records may contradict or confirm testimony. The strength of an investigative archive often lies not in one spectacular item but in the convergence of multiple independent sources.

This is why chronology is so valuable. Human memory can be imperfect, particularly when events occurred years earlier. A witness may remember the general sequence correctly while misremembering dates or details. Documentary records can provide an external framework against which testimony can be compared. If a witness says an event occurred on a particular date, records from that period may confirm whether the relevant people were present. Chronology does not automatically prove a claim, but it can expose inconsistencies and identify questions that require further investigation.

Metadata can sometimes contribute to this process. Digital photographs, recordings, documents, and other files may contain information about creation, modification, location, software, or other characteristics, depending upon the format and how the files were handled. Metadata can be useful but should not be treated as infallible. It can be altered, stripped, generated incorrectly, or interpreted improperly. Professional investigators therefore treat metadata as one potential source of corroboration rather than as an unquestionable fingerprint of authenticity. Its value increases when it agrees with independent evidence.

The original file can also matter greatly. A screenshot of a document is not necessarily equivalent to the original document. A compressed video copied through multiple systems may contain less information than the original recording. A photograph downloaded from a social-media platform may have lost important metadata. A forwarded message may not preserve the complete context of the original communication. Investigators therefore have strong reasons to seek original material where legitimately available. Preservation begins before analysis because every transformation can potentially affect evidentiary value.

The concept of provenance becomes central here. Provenance concerns the history of an item: where it came from, who possessed it, how it was transferred, and what happened to it afterward. A document with a clear and credible history may be more persuasive than an identical document whose origins are impossible to establish. This does not mean that anonymous or uncertain material is worthless. It means that uncertainty about provenance becomes part of the assessment. Responsible investigators record what they know and what they cannot establish.

Corroboration is the next layer. If one source makes a claim, independent evidence can determine whether that claim is consistent with reality. The strongest corroboration comes from sources that are genuinely independent rather than from multiple copies of the same original allegation. Ten websites repeating one anonymous claim do not create ten independent sources. Ten documents generated from one manipulated file do not create ten independent records. Investigative rigor requires attention to the independence of evidence, not merely its quantity.

Professional journalists also have an important advantage in knowing how to ask questions of people who are implicated by the evidence. A subject may deny an allegation. They may provide documents that challenge it. They may explain an apparently suspicious event. They may identify an error in the original material. Contacting the subject can therefore strengthen a story when done appropriately, even if the subject refuses to comment. It gives the investigation an opportunity to test its own assumptions. The goal is not simply to obtain a denial but to expose the evidence to another perspective.

There are circumstances, however, in which contacting a subject may create risks. It can alert someone who might destroy evidence. It can endanger a source. It can compromise an ongoing investigation. It can create legal or personal risks. Professional organizations therefore make these decisions according to the circumstances rather than following a single universal rule. This illustrates another important point about independent publication: responsible journalism involves judgment. Procedures provide structure, but they do not eliminate the need for careful decisions.

Editorial review can provide another layer of protection. An investigative reporter working alone may become deeply invested in a story after months of research. An editor who was not involved in every discovery can ask uncomfortable questions. Where did this document come from? How do we know this person is telling the truth? What alternative explanation exists? Have we independently confirmed this detail? Are we exposing innocent people unnecessarily? Such questions can be frustrating during an investigation, but they can prevent serious errors.

Legal review can serve a similar function. News organizations sometimes consult lawyers before publishing material that carries significant legal risk. The purpose is not necessarily to eliminate controversy. It is to identify potential legal problems and determine whether the available evidence supports the publication. Defamation law, privacy law, copyright, confidentiality obligations, national-security restrictions, and other legal issues can vary substantially between jurisdictions. Professional legal review can therefore help identify risks that a private individual may not recognize.

None of this makes professional journalism infallible. Journalists make mistakes. News organizations have biases, commercial pressures, editorial cultures, and institutional interests. Reporters can misunderstand technical evidence. Editors can reject important stories. Organizations can publish inaccurate material. Some outlets have stronger standards than others. Independent publication is therefore not synonymous with objective truth. It is a mechanism that, when practiced responsibly, can provide additional layers of scrutiny and accountability.

The same caution applies to professional investigators. An investigator may have excellent training but approach a case with assumptions. They may become attached to a theory. They may prioritize evidence that confirms their hypothesis. They may overlook alternative explanations. Professional methodology reduces these risks but cannot eliminate human cognitive bias. Good investigators therefore distinguish between hypothesis and evidence. They test explanations rather than merely collecting material that supports their preferred conclusion.

This is particularly important when a dead man's switch contains a narrative about a conspiracy. Conspiratorial explanations can sometimes describe real coordinated wrongdoing, but the existence of coordination cannot be assumed simply because several events appear connected. Investigators should ask whether there is direct evidence of coordination, whether independent mechanisms can explain the observations, and whether the apparent connections survive scrutiny. The same standard should apply regardless of how extraordinary the claim may seem. Neither automatic belief nor automatic dismissal constitutes rigorous investigation.

The creator may also deliberately include unverified theories in an archive because they want future investigators to consider them. That is legitimate as an investigative lead, but the material should be labeled appropriately. A hypothesis is not the same thing as a finding. A witness statement is not the same thing as corroborated fact. A photograph is not automatically evidence of what someone claims it depicts. A document is not automatically authentic merely because it appears official. The guardian and the investigator must preserve these distinctions.

This is where a structured archive can become extremely valuable. Instead of presenting everything as one continuous narrative, the creator can preserve source documents, supporting records, testimony, correspondence, and personal interpretations separately. The investigator can then reconstruct the argument without having to accept the creator's conclusions. This separation protects the evidentiary value of the material. It also makes it easier to identify what is missing. An archive that distinguishes evidence from interpretation is more useful to independent reviewers.

Journalists also understand the importance of protecting source material from unnecessary alteration. Original documents can be preserved while working copies are used for analysis. Recordings can be duplicated without modifying the originals. Researchers can maintain notes showing when material was received and from whom. Secure storage can protect sensitive material from unauthorized access. These practices do not magically establish authenticity, but they preserve the conditions under which authenticity can later be evaluated.

The concept of chain of custody is especially relevant when evidence may eventually become part of legal proceedings. Private individuals should not assume that simply preserving a file establishes a formal legal chain of custody. Legal standards vary, and admissibility depends upon jurisdiction and circumstances. Nevertheless, maintaining a documented history of possession can improve credibility. It can show that the material was not casually altered or repeatedly transferred without explanation. Professional investigators and journalists often recognize this distinction even when their work is not itself a courtroom proceeding.

The relationship between journalist and source also requires careful handling. A source may expect the journalist to publish everything. The journalist may conclude that only a fraction of the material is relevant. The source may believe that certain documents speak for themselves. The journalist may discover that they require context or corroboration. These disagreements are normal. Professional independence requires the journalist to retain editorial control rather than becoming an agent of the source.

That independence can frustrate creators of dead man's switches. A creator may believe that the whole purpose of the system is to guarantee publication. They may therefore expect the journalist to act automatically when a trigger occurs. But professional journalists cannot responsibly promise to publish material simply because a mechanical or digital condition has been satisfied. They must evaluate the information. They may publish part of it, investigate it further, refer it to another authority, or decline to publish it. The dead man's switch can deliver information, but it cannot legitimately eliminate editorial judgment.

This is one reason the concept of independent publication is so important. Independence means that the recipient is not simply executing the creator's wishes. The recipient is evaluating whether the material deserves public dissemination according to professional standards. That may mean publication. It may also mean rejection. The creator's objective is therefore best understood as preserving an opportunity for scrutiny rather than guaranteeing a predetermined outcome. Such an arrangement can protect the public from both suppressed information and irresponsible disclosure.

Professional investigators can similarly provide an intermediate stage before publication. They may establish whether a claim deserves further attention. They may identify corroborating witnesses. They may discover that apparently unrelated records are actually connected. They may also discover that a claim is unsupported. This ability to investigate without immediately publishing can be particularly valuable. It allows evidence to be tested while reducing unnecessary public harm.

There is another advantage to professional intermediaries: they can recognize the difference between information that is newsworthy and information that is merely sensational. Not everything shocking is important. Not everything secret is evidence of wrongdoing. Not every allegation deserves public attention. Professional editorial judgment attempts to evaluate significance, relevance, public interest, credibility, and potential harm. The standards differ among organizations, but the underlying problem is universal. A responsible publication should justify why the information matters.

The public-interest test can become especially important when disclosure could harm innocent people. An archive might contain the names of family members, private individuals, confidential sources, medical information, financial records, or personal communications. Publishing such material may add little to the public understanding of the underlying issue. Professional journalists often consider whether sensitive details are necessary to tell the story. This principle of minimizing unnecessary harm can coexist with aggressive investigation. Strong journalism does not require indiscriminate exposure.

The same consideration applies to classified or security-sensitive information. A document may be genuine and still not be appropriate for unrestricted publication. It may reveal operational details, personal information, security vulnerabilities, or other material whose disclosure creates risks unrelated to the public interest. Journalists may seek legal advice and assess the necessity of publication. The existence of public interest does not automatically resolve every competing concern. Responsible publication involves balancing competing consequences.

A dead man's switch should therefore avoid defining success solely as "everything gets released." The more sophisticated definition is that important information reaches an appropriate independent decision-maker who can evaluate it under circumstances in which the original creator is unavailable. Sometimes the correct outcome will be publication. Sometimes it will be further investigation. Sometimes it will be referral to a competent authority. Sometimes it will be preservation without publication. The system succeeds when information survives and receives responsible consideration.

The relationship between the creator and journalist should also be established with realistic expectations. The creator can explain the significance of the archive, identify potential sources, provide background, and document their concerns. They cannot ethically dictate the final editorial conclusion. A journalist who agrees to publish regardless of what the evidence shows has surrendered the independence that makes the relationship valuable. The strongest arrangement allows the journalist to disagree with the creator. That possibility is evidence that the journalist remains an independent evaluator rather than an extension of the dead man's switch.

The same principle applies to anonymous publication platforms. Digital technology can make it possible to distribute documents rapidly and widely without traditional editorial intermediaries. This can be valuable when conventional institutions are compromised or inaccessible. It can also remove important layers of verification. An anonymous upload can contain genuine evidence, manipulated material, stolen private information, fabricated documents, or a mixture of all four. Distribution is not verification. The wider the audience, the greater the potential consequences of error.

This distinction has become even more important in an era of synthetic media. Photographs, audio, video, documents, and online identities can be manipulated with increasing sophistication. Investigators can no longer rely solely upon the apparent realism of digital material. Provenance, source history, independent corroboration, technical examination, and contextual evidence become increasingly important. A dead man's switch designed around the assumption that a digital file is self-authenticating is therefore increasingly fragile. The archive must preserve evidence in a form that permits future examination.

Artificial intelligence introduces another complication because it can assist both investigators and fabricators. Automated systems can help search large document collections, identify patterns, transcribe recordings, translate material, compare records, and organize evidence. They can also generate convincing synthetic content or produce misleading summaries. Professional users must therefore understand the difference between computational assistance and evidentiary proof. An AI-generated analysis is not independent evidence merely because it is technically sophisticated. Human verification remains essential.

Journalists and investigators can also serve as bridges between specialized domains. A creator may possess scientific material they understand deeply but lack the ability to communicate its significance to the public. A journalist can consult independent scientists. A technical investigator can examine the underlying data. A lawyer can assess the legal implications. The resulting investigation can translate specialized evidence without relying solely upon the creator's interpretation. This multidisciplinary process can be one of the strongest reasons to involve professionals.

The power of independent publication therefore comes from the combination of independence and infrastructure. A professional organization may have editors, researchers, legal counsel, secure systems, and established relationships with experts. None of these guarantees truth. Together, however, they can create conditions in which truth claims are subjected to more scrutiny than they would receive inside a private archive. This is particularly important when the creator is emotionally involved in the subject. Distance can expose assumptions that proximity hides.

Yet professional independence can also create a painful possibility: the journalist may decide not to publish. The creator may regard that as failure. It may actually be responsible judgment. If the evidence cannot be authenticated, the allegation cannot be corroborated, or publication would cause disproportionate harm, refusal may be justified. The purpose of a serious dead man's switch should therefore not be to force professionals to abandon their standards. It should be to ensure that the information reaches people capable of applying those standards.

There is also a powerful psychological advantage in knowing that information has been placed with an independent professional. The creator may feel less pressure to maintain the archive personally. The guardian may know that someone else can evaluate the evidence. The existence of a credible external recipient can also make it more difficult for information to disappear quietly. But this deterrent effect should not be exaggerated. A person who creates a dead man's switch should not assume that the existence of an archive guarantees protection. Its actual value depends upon whether the archive can be accessed, authenticated, evaluated, and responsibly acted upon.

The ideal professional recipient is therefore not necessarily the most famous journalist or largest organization. It is the recipient whose expertise, independence, security practices, legal resources, and editorial standards fit the nature of the information. A scientific archive may require a publication with technical expertise. A corruption investigation may require investigative journalists familiar with financial records. A national-security matter may require professionals experienced in handling classified or legally restricted information. A human-rights archive may require investigators familiar with documentation and witness protection. Suitability matters more than prestige.

The creator should also recognize that professional organizations can change. A journalist may leave. An editor may retire. A publication may be sold. A nonprofit may lose funding. A newsroom may change its editorial direction. The archive should therefore not depend entirely upon one individual or institution remaining unchanged. Multiple professional contacts can provide continuity, provided that distribution is controlled and justified. The objective is to preserve access without creating uncontrolled exposure.

The deeper lesson is that publication is not the opposite of secrecy. Between total secrecy and unrestricted public release lies an entire ecosystem of responsible information handling. Journalists, investigators, lawyers, archivists, researchers, and technical specialists can occupy different positions within that ecosystem. Their roles can overlap, but each can contribute a different form of scrutiny. The dead man's switch becomes stronger when it recognizes these distinctions. The ultimate goal is not simply to make information public but to give important information a credible path toward independent evaluation.

A well-designed archive can therefore reach a professional recipient in stages. The initial material may establish that the archive exists. A second layer may provide instructions and context. A third may contain the underlying evidence. Another may contain authentication information. Professional investigators can then determine what can be verified. Editors can evaluate public interest and potential harm. Lawyers can assess legal constraints. Only after these stages have occurred does publication become a considered outcome rather than an automatic reaction.

This layered model also protects the creator from their own assumptions. If the creator's interpretation is incorrect, independent investigators have an opportunity to discover that before publication. If the creator is correct, corroboration can strengthen the case. If the evidence is incomplete, further investigation may fill the gaps. If the information is genuine but too dangerous to publish in its raw form, professionals can determine whether a safer form of disclosure is possible. The archive therefore becomes the beginning of an investigation rather than the conclusion of one.

Ultimately, journalists and investigators matter because truth rarely arrives in a perfectly packaged form. It arrives as fragments: a document, a recording, a witness, a transaction, a photograph, an unexplained event, an email, a laboratory result, or a pattern that demands explanation. The professional task is to determine how those fragments fit together without forcing them into a predetermined narrative. That requires skepticism, persistence, corroboration, and the willingness to abandon a theory when the evidence does not support it. A dead man's switch can preserve the fragments, but independent professionals may be better positioned to determine what those fragments actually mean.

The power of independent publication therefore lies less in the act of publishing than in the process that precedes it. Verification creates credibility. Corroboration creates confidence. Editorial review creates accountability. Legal review identifies constraints. Source protection can preserve the flow of information. Independent investigation can challenge the assumptions of both the source and the public. When these functions operate properly, a private archive can become the starting point for a responsible public record.

A dead man's switch should never be confused with proof. It is a mechanism for continuity. It ensures that information has a path beyond the person who originally possessed it. What happens after that information reaches an independent journalist or investigator is a separate question, and that separation is precisely what gives professional intermediaries their value. They can examine what the creator believed without being required to believe it themselves. They can preserve what is important without automatically publishing what is unnecessary. They can expose wrongdoing while still demanding evidence.

The final safeguard is therefore independence itself. A guardian who is too emotionally attached may protect the information into silence. A recipient who is too eager to publish may destroy credibility through premature disclosure. A professional intermediary who can remain independent can occupy the difficult middle ground between those extremes. Their responsibility is to ask what happened, what can be demonstrated, what remains uncertain, who may be harmed, and whether the public interest justifies disclosure. When a dead man's switch places important information into such hands, it does not guarantee that the truth will emerge, but it gives the truth something essential: an opportunity to be tested.

Resources

1. Society of Professional Journalists — Code of Ethics[1] — establishes widely cited journalistic principles concerning seeking truth, verifying information, minimizing harm, acting independently, and remaining accountable.

2. Reuters — Trust Principles and Journalistic Standards[2] — professional standards emphasizing accuracy, independence, freedom from bias, and reliable reporting.

3. Associated Press — News Values and Principles[3] — standards concerning accuracy, fairness, independence, sourcing, verification, and editorial responsibility.

4. Committee to Protect Journalists — Safety Kit[4] — practical resources concerning journalist safety, source protection, digital security, risk assessment, and legal threats.

5. Reporters Without Borders — Handbook for Journalists — resources addressing journalistic safety, source protection, digital security, and working with sensitive information.

6. Freedom of the Press Foundation — Digital Security Training[5] — practical resources for journalists and sources concerning secure communications, authentication, encryption, and digital threat models.

---

1. https://www.spj.org/ethicscode.asp?utm_source=chatgpt.com

2. https://reutersagency.com/en/about/standards-values/?utm_source=chatgpt.com

3. https://www.ap.org/about/news-values-and-principles/?utm_source=chatgpt.com

4. https://cpj.org/safety-kit/?utm_source=chatgpt.com

5. https://freedom.press/training/?utm_source=chatgpt.com

7. Electronic Frontier Foundation — Surveillance Self-Defense[6] — accessible guidance on threat modeling, encryption, secure communications, account security, and protection of sensitive sources.

8. National Institute of Standards and Technology — Cybersecurity Framework 2.0[7] — framework for managing cybersecurity risks, including identification, protection, detection, response, and recovery.

9. NIST Special Publication 800-53 — Security and Privacy Controls[8] — detailed security and privacy controls relevant to access management, system integrity, accountability, and information protection.

10. NIST Special Publication 800-61 — Computer Security Incident Handling Guide[9] — guidance concerning preparation, incident response, evidence handling, communication, and recovery.

11. National Archives — Digital Preservation — authoritative material concerning preservation, authenticity, accessibility, and management of digital records.

12. Library of Congress — Digital Preservation[10] — resources concerning preservation of digital materials, metadata, file formats, integrity, and long-term access.

13. ISO 15489 — Records Management[11] — international standard addressing reliable records, authenticity, integrity, preservation, and management.

14. ISO 14721 — Open Archival Information System Reference Model[12] — framework for long-term digital preservation and continued access to information.

15. U.S. National Archives — Digital Records Management[13] — federal guidance concerning the management, preservation, and accessibility of government records.

16. Kovach, Bill, and Tom Rosenstiel, *The Elements of Journalism: What Newspeople Should Know and the Public Should Expect*, Crown Publishers, 2001 — influential examination of journalistic verification, independence, accountability, and the relationship between journalism and truth.

17. Kovach, Bill, and Tom Rosenstiel, *Blur: How to Know What's True in the Age of Information Overload*, Bloomsbury, 2010 — examination of verification, evidence, information overload, and evaluating claims in modern media environments.

18. Philip Meyer, *Precision Journalism: A Reporter's Introduction to Social Science Methods*, Rowman & Littlefield, 2002 — influential work on applying systematic research methods, quantitative analysis, and evidence-based reasoning to investigative journalism.

---

6. https://ssd.eff.org/?utm_source=chatgpt.com

7. https://www.nist.gov/cyberframework?utm_source=chatgpt.com

8. https://csrc.nist.gov/publications/detail/sp/800-53/rev-5/final?utm_source=chatgpt.com

9. https://csrc.nist.gov/publications/detail/sp/800-61/rev-2/final?utm_source=chatgpt.com

10. https://www.loc.gov/preservation/digital/?utm_source=chatgpt.com

11. https://www.iso.org/standard/62542.html?utm_source=chatgpt.com

12. https://www.iso.org/standard/57284.html?utm_source=chatgpt.com

13. https://www.archives.gov/records-mgmt?utm_source=chatgpt.com

19. Steve Weinberg, *The Reporter's Handbook: An Investigator's Guide to Documents and Techniques*, St. Martin's Press, 1996 — practical reference concerning documentary investigation, public records, source development, and investigative reporting.

20. Brant Houston, *Computer-Assisted Reporting: A Practical Guide*, Bedford/St. Martin's, 2004 — reference on investigative research, databases, documents, verification, and analytical methods.

21. International Fact-Checking Network — Code of Principles — standards emphasizing nonpartisanship, transparency of sources and methodology, corrections, and evidence-based fact-checking.

22. Bellingcat — Online Investigation Toolkit[14] — open-source investigative resources covering verification, geolocation, image analysis, social-media research, and digital investigation methods.

23. Berkeley Protocol on Digital Open Source Investigations — methodological framework for collecting, preserving, verifying, and analyzing digital open-source information in human-rights investigations.

24. United Nations — Berkeley Protocol on Digital Open Source Investigations — authoritative human-rights framework concerning ethical and methodological standards for digital investigations.

25. First Draft — Essential Guide to Verifying Online Information — resources concerning verification of digital content, sources, imagery, and online claims.

26. Poynter Institute — International Fact-Checking Network[15] — professional resources concerning fact-checking methodology, transparency, corrections, and verification.

27. U.S. Securities and Exchange Commission — Whistleblower Program[16] — official example of institutional channels for receiving and evaluating information concerning potential wrongdoing.

28. U.S. Department of Justice — Justice Manual — official reference for federal legal and prosecutorial policies relevant to investigations, evidence, disclosure, and sensitive information.

---

14. https://bellingcat.gitbook.io/toolkit?utm_source=chatgpt.com

15. https://www.poynter.org/ifcn/?utm_source=chatgpt.com

16. https://www.sec.gov/whistleblower?utm_source=chatgpt.com

International Protection and Distributed Truth

Information has always been vulnerable to geography because power itself is often geographic. A government can control records within its territory, a court can issue orders within its jurisdiction, a company can control servers under its authority, and an institution can restrict access to material held inside its own systems. The internet changed the speed at which information crosses borders, but it did not eliminate the legal and political significance of those borders. A person attempting to protect sensitive information may therefore face a fundamental question: what happens if the entire protection system depends upon one country, one institution, or one legal environment? International distribution offers one possible answer by creating multiple points of custody, but it replaces some single-jurisdiction risks with the complexity of coordinating across different jurisdictions. The objective is not to make information untouchable, but to prevent one point of failure from having complete control over whether the information survives.

The concept of distributed protection is straightforward even when its implementation can become complicated. Instead of placing an entire archive in one location, different components can exist under the control of different people or institutions. One jurisdiction might hold original records. Another might hold encrypted copies. A third might contain instructions concerning access. A fourth might provide an independent investigative contact. No single participant necessarily possesses the entire picture. If one repository disappears, the remaining components can preserve continuity. This is essentially the same redundancy principle used elsewhere in resilient systems, but geography introduces another layer of independence.

Geographic distribution can be useful because institutions do not all experience the same risks simultaneously. A local political crisis may affect one jurisdiction while leaving another relatively stable. A court order may apply in one country but have no direct effect elsewhere. A company operating under one regulatory system may not control infrastructure maintained by an unrelated organization in another country. A journalist working in one jurisdiction may face pressures that would not exist in another. None of these differences guarantees safety. They simply create opportunities for risk diversification.

However, the phrase "outside the jurisdiction" should never be treated as synonymous with "outside legal reach." International law is complex, and countries cooperate through treaties, mutual legal assistance mechanisms, law-enforcement cooperation, diplomatic channels, sanctions regimes, and other arrangements. Companies may also operate across multiple jurisdictions and may be subject to obligations in several countries. A person cannot reasonably assume that placing a file on a foreign server makes it immune from lawful access or investigation. The practical legal environment must be evaluated according to the particular circumstances.

Jurisdiction matters because legal authority is not merely a question of where a server sits. It can involve the residence or nationality of the people involved, the location of relevant events, the corporate domicile of a service provider, the location of affected individuals, contractual relationships, and applicable international agreements. A cloud provider may have infrastructure in several countries while being legally headquartered somewhere else. A journalist may work for an international organization while physically residing in another country. A lawyer may have obligations under the law of a particular jurisdiction even when the client is elsewhere. Geography is therefore one variable in a larger legal system.

For the creator of a dead man's switch, this creates a practical distinction between geographic redundancy and legal redundancy. Geographic redundancy means that information physically exists in different locations. Legal redundancy means that custody and decision-making are not entirely subject to one legal environment. The two concepts can overlap but are not identical. Ten copies stored in ten data centers belonging to the same company may provide geographic redundancy while providing little institutional diversity. Conversely, several independent organizations in different countries may provide meaningful institutional diversity even if their technical infrastructure overlaps. The strongest systems consider both dimensions.

International organizations can sometimes provide valuable alternatives to private custody. Human-rights organizations, investigative networks, academic institutions, archival bodies, and press organizations may have established procedures for handling sensitive information. Their mandates and capabilities differ substantially, however. A human-rights organization may specialize in documenting abuses. An investigative newsroom may focus on corruption or organized crime. An academic institution may preserve research data. An archive may prioritize long-term preservation. The suitability of an organization depends upon what the information actually is and what outcome the creator intends.

Independent investigative networks are particularly interesting because they can combine expertise across borders. Modern investigations frequently involve records from multiple countries. Financial transactions may pass through several jurisdictions. Corporations may maintain subsidiaries internationally. Government officials may travel across borders. Digital communications can be routed through infrastructure located in multiple countries. A journalist working alone may struggle to investigate such matters. An international investigative network can sometimes divide research among specialists who understand different languages, records systems, and legal environments.

One important example of this model is the International Consortium of Investigative Journalists, which has demonstrated how journalists from different countries can collaborate on complex cross-border investigations. Its work illustrates a principle relevant to dead man's switches: information can become more difficult to suppress when independent organizations in different jurisdictions possess overlapping knowledge. A local institution may face pressure that another institution can resist. A story that depends upon one reporter can disappear when that reporter is silenced or leaves. A network distributes investigative capacity as well as information.

This does not mean that international journalism is immune from pressure. Journalists can face threats in almost every country, and organizations can face lawsuits, regulatory restrictions, political pressure, hacking, financial difficulties, or internal disputes. International collaboration reduces certain risks while introducing others. Communication itself becomes more complicated. Participants may have different security practices and different assumptions about confidentiality. The more people involved, the greater the need for clear protocols.

The same principle applies to lawyers. A lawyer in one jurisdiction may understand local law but have limited ability to advise on another country's legal system. An international matter may require multiple legal professionals with different areas of expertise. This can be expensive and complicated. It can also be valuable because no single lawyer should be expected to understand every relevant jurisdiction. Legal diversification can therefore mirror information diversification.

Foreign lawyers may also have different professional obligations concerning confidentiality, reporting, disclosure, and client relationships. These differences matter. A creator who assumes that a foreign attorney will provide exactly the same protections as a domestic attorney may be mistaken. Professional privilege and confidentiality are legal concepts whose scope varies by jurisdiction. Before relying upon an international professional intermediary, the actual legal relationship should be understood.

Independent investigators can provide another form of cross-border resilience. An investigator may be able to examine public records, corporate structures, property records, court filings, customs data, satellite imagery, or other information distributed across countries. Modern open-source investigation has made it possible for researchers to reconstruct events without relying entirely upon government-controlled sources. This can be particularly useful when official records are incomplete or contested. Yet open-source investigation must still distinguish between information that is publicly accessible and information that has been independently verified.

International distribution also raises the issue of language. A document preserved in one country may be useless to a recipient who cannot understand it. A witness statement may require translation. A legal instruction may have different meanings when translated. Technical terminology can be distorted across languages. For a long-term archive, preserving original-language material alongside accurate translations can therefore be important. The translation itself should be regarded as an interpretation of the original, not necessarily as a replacement for it.

Time zones create a surprisingly practical problem. A crisis can develop rapidly, yet the people responsible for responding may be asleep, traveling, or unreachable. A geographically distributed system should therefore not depend upon everyone being simultaneously available. Clear succession arrangements can reduce this vulnerability. Automated notification can alert custodians, while independent human participants can decide what action is appropriate. The objective is continuity rather than instantaneous action at all costs.

International distribution also creates potential problems with authentication. A recipient in another country may have no way to know whether a document genuinely originated from the claimed source. This makes provenance even more important. The creator should preserve original records, acquisition histories, timestamps where meaningful, relevant contextual material, and other information that can help establish authenticity. Multiple copies of an uncertain document do not transform it into an authenticated document. Distribution preserves information; it does not prove it.

One of the strongest principles in distributed preservation is that copies should be meaningfully independent. If every copy is generated from the same corrupted archive, the corruption is simply reproduced. If every copy is maintained by the same administrator, a single compromise can affect all of them. If every custodian receives the same password, one compromised credential may expose everything. Independence therefore needs to exist at several levels. The technical system, human custody, authentication mechanisms, and institutional relationships should be considered separately.

This is where the idea of compartmentalization becomes useful. A distributed archive does not necessarily require every participant to possess every document. One custodian might hold evidence while another holds the instructions needed to interpret it. Another may know the identity of a source. Another may have the means to authenticate the archive. This can reduce the consequences of compromising one participant. It can also protect innocent people whose identities do not need to be exposed to everyone involved.

Compartmentalization, however, must be balanced against recoverability. If too little information is shared, the system may become impossible to reconstruct after the creator's death. A person may possess an encrypted archive without possessing the key. Another may possess the key without knowing what it unlocks. A third may know the purpose but have no access to the relevant accounts. Excessive fragmentation can therefore create a system that is theoretically secure but practically useless. The architecture must preserve enough information at each stage for legitimate custodians to perform their responsibilities.

International distribution also raises the problem of cultural and institutional differences. What constitutes an appropriate disclosure in one country may be viewed differently elsewhere. Journalistic standards differ. Privacy expectations differ. Legal concepts differ. Public attitudes toward government secrecy differ. A creator should not assume that an international recipient will share the same understanding of what should happen. Clear instructions can help, but they cannot eliminate these differences. Ultimately, the professional intermediary must operate within their own ethical and legal framework.

This becomes especially important when information concerns national security. Material that exposes government misconduct may be of legitimate public interest, but it may also contain information whose publication could cause genuine harm. A foreign recipient may face pressure to publish because the material concerns another country's government. Yet the ethical problem does not disappear simply because the recipient is outside the country involved. Responsible investigators must still consider whether publication is justified, whether sensitive operational details can be removed, and whether innocent individuals could be endangered. International distance does not eliminate ethical responsibility.

The same principle applies to corporate secrets. A company headquartered in one country may have operations around the world. Information about fraud, environmental damage, regulatory violations, or internal misconduct may cross several jurisdictions. A foreign journalist may be able to investigate the matter independently. But the publication can still expose private individuals, trade secrets, confidential customer information, or unrelated proprietary material. The existence of wrongdoing does not automatically justify publication of everything contained within an archive. Evidence must still be separated from unnecessary collateral information.

Financial information presents another layer of complexity. International banking systems operate across multiple regulatory environments, and records can be distributed among institutions and jurisdictions. Investigators may need to understand corporate ownership structures, beneficial ownership records, financial transfers, tax arrangements, and regulatory filings. Cross-border financial investigations can therefore require specialized expertise. A private creator should not assume that possession of financial documents automatically establishes the meaning of a transaction. Financial evidence often requires contextual interpretation.

Human-rights investigations provide another important example of international evidence preservation. Witnesses may be located in different countries. Events may occur in areas where official records are unreliable or inaccessible. Digital evidence may be collected by people who are not professional investigators. International organizations have therefore developed methodologies for documenting and preserving information from conflict zones and other difficult environments. These methods emphasize provenance, verification, source protection, contextual information, and responsible handling. Such principles are broadly relevant to any sensitive archive.

Digital evidence has also made international collaboration increasingly possible. A photograph uploaded from one country can be analyzed by a researcher in another. Satellite imagery can be examined remotely. Public records can be compared across jurisdictions. Databases can reveal connections that are invisible within a single national system. The internet has therefore created an unprecedented investigative environment. Yet it has also created unprecedented opportunities for misinformation, manipulation, impersonation, and synthetic evidence.

The rise of artificial intelligence intensifies this problem. A convincing synthetic photograph may circulate internationally within minutes. A fabricated document may be translated into multiple languages. An artificial voice may imitate a real person. A false narrative can be repeated by automated accounts across several countries.

International distribution can amplify false information just as effectively as true information. The more distributed the archive, the more important provenance and independent corroboration become.

Cryptographic systems can provide another form of cross-border resilience. Properly implemented encryption can allow information to remain inaccessible to unauthorized parties even when physical custody changes. Cryptographic signatures can help establish whether a file has changed after signing, depending upon how the system is implemented and whether the signing keys remain secure. Hashes can help detect modifications to digital files. These technologies can be useful, but they are not substitutes for sound governance. A cryptographically protected false document remains a false document. Technology can protect integrity without establishing truth.

International storage providers can also create misunderstandings. A company may advertise global availability, but its terms of service, account policies, legal obligations, and response procedures still govern the practical relationship. A foreign data center does not necessarily mean that the provider is independent of the country in which its parent company operates. A distributed cloud architecture can therefore appear more independent than it actually is. The creator should distinguish between technical distribution and institutional independence.

This distinction is central to the architecture of a serious dead man's switch. If all components ultimately depend upon one company, one email provider, one authentication service, or one administrator, then the system may have a hidden single point of failure. It may look distributed because the files exist in several locations while remaining operationally dependent upon one external service. Resilience requires identifying these hidden dependencies. The question is not simply, "How many copies exist?" but "How many independent paths exist from the information to a legitimate recipient?"

The same reasoning applies to governments. A creator may believe that placing information in another country protects it from their own government. That may be partially true in some circumstances, but the foreign government has its own interests. It may cooperate with the original government. It may have laws permitting access. It may have political relationships that change over time. No government should automatically be treated as a permanent neutral guardian. The objective is diversification, not faith in a particular state.

International non-governmental organizations can sometimes provide another layer of independence. Organizations such as human-rights groups, press-freedom organizations, archival institutions, and investigative networks may operate with mandates that cross national boundaries. Their independence varies, and their resources are not unlimited. Some may have particular areas of expertise and may decline material outside their mandate. Their involvement should therefore be based on suitability rather than the assumption that an international organization is inherently safer.

The concept of distributed truth also has a philosophical dimension. When information exists only in one person's possession, the person's death can erase not only the information but also the possibility of independent verification. When evidence exists across multiple independent custodians, it becomes harder for any single actor to rewrite the historical record. This does not mean that distributed information is automatically true. It means that the record becomes more difficult to erase completely. Multiple independent records can preserve competing perspectives until future investigators can determine what happened.

That distinction between preserving a record and establishing truth is crucial. A distributed archive should not become a distributed rumor. If unverified allegations are replicated across ten countries, the allegations remain unverified. Repetition can create the appearance of consensus without creating evidence. Independent custodians should therefore preserve the distinction between original evidence, testimony, interpretation, and subsequent reporting. The archive's integrity depends upon maintaining those categories over time.

International cooperation can also provide an important safeguard against premature disclosure. If one custodian believes information should be released immediately while another believes further investigation is required, the disagreement can trigger review. Cross-border collaboration can create additional opportunities to test the evidence. This can slow the process, but delay is not always a failure. In sensitive matters, a few additional days of verification may prevent years of damage caused by an incorrect publication.

The opposite problem must also be recognized. Excessive hesitation can become another form of suppression. If every custodian waits for another organization to act, nothing happens. A distributed system therefore needs clearly defined responsibilities. Someone must know who evaluates the evidence. Someone must know who can authorize publication or referral. Someone must know how to contact the next person if a primary custodian becomes unavailable. Distribution without responsibility is simply confusion.

This is why succession planning becomes particularly important internationally. People move. Organizations merge. Websites disappear. Laws change. Governments change. Contact information becomes obsolete. An archive designed to survive for decades cannot depend upon a static list of names and email addresses. The system should include mechanisms for reviewing custodians and updating relationships while preserving appropriate security. Long-term resilience requires maintenance.

The creator should also recognize the difference between emergency protection and permanent preservation. An emergency system may need to ensure that information survives a sudden disappearance. A permanent archive may need to remain accessible for decades. These are different engineering problems. Emergency systems prioritize rapid continuity. Long-term archives prioritize format migration, institutional continuity, metadata preservation, authentication, and periodic review. A dead man's switch may need both capabilities if the creator expects the information to remain relevant for a long period.

Geographic distribution can also protect against physical disasters. Fire, flood, earthquakes, war, equipment failure, and other events can destroy local archives. Copies stored in geographically separate locations reduce the probability that one event will destroy everything. Professional archival systems often use geographic redundancy for precisely this reason. Yet physical separation should be combined with integrity checking and recovery testing. A backup that cannot be restored is not a reliable backup. Resilience must be demonstrated rather than assumed.

Testing is therefore essential. A creator may believe that several custodians have access, only to discover that one account has been closed. A password may no longer work. An encrypted file may be unreadable because the required software has disappeared. A custodian may have forgotten the arrangement. A professional organization may have changed its policies. Periodic review can identify these failures while the creator is still alive and able to correct them. A dead man's switch that is never tested is essentially a hypothesis about future reliability.

International systems also require attention to data-protection law. Personal information may be subject to privacy regulations that restrict collection, transfer, storage, or disclosure. The rules differ substantially across jurisdictions. A creator should therefore avoid assuming that international distribution automatically creates a legal safe harbor. In some cases, moving personal information across borders may create additional obligations. Professional legal advice can be particularly important when the archive contains information about third parties.

The ethical treatment of innocent people is another central concern. An archive created to expose corruption may contain private information about employees who were merely witnesses. A scientific archive may contain research participants' personal data. A political archive may contain family information unrelated to the alleged wrongdoing. International distribution increases the number of people who may potentially encounter that information. Compartmentalization and selective disclosure can therefore be as important as encryption. Protecting the truth should not require unnecessary exposure of people who are not responsible for the conduct under investigation.

There is also a danger in assuming that foreign recipients will always be more courageous. Professionals in another country may be subject to their own political pressures, legal risks, or institutional vulnerabilities. They may have little reason to prioritize a creator's objectives. They may also misunderstand local context. International independence is valuable because it creates another perspective, not because foreign actors are inherently more trustworthy. The same standards of competence, independence, integrity, and suitability must apply.

The strongest international arrangements therefore resemble a network rather than a hierarchy. No single institution is necessarily the master custodian. Instead, different participants possess defined responsibilities and overlapping knowledge. One may preserve. One may investigate. One may authenticate. One may provide legal advice. One may publish. Another may maintain a long-term archive. This creates resilience because the system does not collapse simply because one institution fails.

Such a network must nevertheless remain understandable. Complexity can become its own vulnerability. If the creator cannot explain the system, future custodians may not be able to reconstruct it. If the instructions require a dozen complicated dependencies, one missing component can stop the entire process. Simplicity should therefore be treated as a security feature. The architecture should be as distributed as necessary but no more complicated than necessary.

The ultimate purpose of international protection is not to evade legitimate law. It is to prevent information from disappearing simply because one institution controls one repository. A creator who has evidence of serious wrongdoing should understand the distinction between lawful preservation and unlawful disclosure. International custody may provide resilience, but it does not grant immunity from law. The objective is to create legitimate avenues through which evidence can survive, be independently assessed, and, where appropriate, reach the institutions or public audiences capable of acting upon it.

This makes international distribution particularly powerful when combined with professional independence. A journalist in one country can collaborate with another journalist elsewhere. A lawyer can advise on local legal issues while another lawyer considers cross-border implications. An investigator can compare records from multiple jurisdictions. An archive can preserve material independently of the organization that originally collected it. Each layer contributes a different form of resilience. None needs to control everything.

The most important principle is therefore independence without fragmentation. Information should be distributed enough that one failure cannot destroy it, but organized enough that legitimate custodians can reconstruct and evaluate it. Evidence should be protected without becoming inaccessible. Jurisdictional diversity should reduce concentration of risk without creating unrealistic assumptions about immunity. International collaboration should increase investigative capacity without replacing skepticism. And public disclosure should remain a considered decision rather than an automatic consequence of geographic distribution.

A dead man's switch becomes considerably stronger when it recognizes that the world is not governed by one system. Governments differ. Laws differ. Institutions differ. Professional standards differ. Technical infrastructures differ. These differences create vulnerabilities, but they also create opportunities for resilience. A system that depends upon one country, one company, one lawyer, one journalist, or one server can fail through a single point of pressure. A carefully constructed network of independent custodians can make total disappearance considerably more difficult.

Ultimately, distributed truth is not about hiding information beyond the reach of authority. It is about ensuring that no single authority, institution, accident, technical failure, or individual decision automatically determines whether important evidence survives. The information can move across borders while retaining its provenance. Independent professionals can examine it without inheriting the creator's assumptions. Multiple repositories can preserve it without every participant receiving everything. And different jurisdictions can provide alternative paths for investigation when one path becomes unavailable.

The creator's greatest protection is therefore not secrecy alone, and it is not geographic distance alone. It is resilience created by independent custody, careful preservation, professional scrutiny, and legitimate pathways toward disclosure. When those elements work together, the dead man's switch becomes more than a private contingency mechanism. It becomes a distributed architecture for preserving the possibility that evidence will survive its creator. The truth may still have to fight its way into public view, but it is no longer dependent upon one person, one institution, or one jurisdiction for its existence.

Resources

1. International Consortium of Investigative Journalists[1] — international investigative network demonstrating cross-border collaboration among journalists investigating complex global matters.

2. Organized Crime and Corruption Reporting Project[2] — international investigative journalism network focused on cross-border corruption and organized crime investigations.

3. Global Investigative Journalism Network[3] — international association providing investigative-journalism resources, training, networking, and research.

4. Committee to Protect Journalists — Safety Kit[4] — resources concerning physical, digital, and legal risks faced by journalists and their sources internationally.

5. Reporters Without Borders[5] — international press-freedom organization documenting threats to journalism and providing resources for journalists working in difficult environments.

6. Freedom of the Press Foundation[6] — nonprofit organization providing digital-security resources and tools for journalists and sources.

---

1. https://www.icij.org/?utm_source=chatgpt.com

2. https://www.occrp.org/?utm_source=chatgpt.com

3. https://gijn.org/?utm_source=chatgpt.com

4. https://cpj.org/safety-kit/?utm_source=chatgpt.com

5. https://rsf.org/?utm_source=chatgpt.com

6. https://freedom.press/?utm_source=chatgpt.com

7. Electronic Frontier Foundation — Surveillance Self-Defense[7] — practical guidance concerning threat modeling, encryption, secure communications, account security, and protection of sensitive information.

8. Berkeley Protocol on Digital Open Source Investigations — methodological framework for collecting, preserving, verifying, and analyzing digital information for investigations.

9. Office of the United Nations High Commissioner for Human Rights — Berkeley Protocol — internationally recognized guidance concerning responsible digital open-source investigations.

10. International Committee of the Red Cross — International Humanitarian Law Database[8] — authoritative resource for understanding the international legal framework relevant to armed conflict and humanitarian protection.

11. United Nations Office on Drugs and Crime — Mutual Legal Assistance — resources concerning international cooperation and mutual legal assistance in criminal matters.

12. United Nations — Convention against Transnational Organized Crime[9] — international framework addressing cooperation against transnational organized crime.

13. Council of Europe — Convention on Cybercrime[10] — major international framework concerning cybercrime, electronic evidence, and international cooperation.

14. Council of Europe — Data Protection Convention 108[11] — international framework concerning protection of personal data and cross-border data processing.

15. European Commission — General Data Protection Regulation[12] — official European Union resource concerning data protection, processing, individual rights, and international data transfers.

16. NIST Cybersecurity Framework 2.0[13] — framework for identifying and managing cybersecurity risks, including resilience and recovery.

17. NIST Special Publication 800-53[14] — security and privacy controls relevant to access management, separation of duties, accountability, contingency planning, and system resilience.

18. NIST Special Publication 800-57 — Key Management — guidance on cryptographic keys, key protection, recovery, and lifecycle management.

19. ISO/IEC 27001 — Information Security Management Systems[15] — international information-security management framework emphasizing risk management and organizational controls.

---

7. https://ssd.eff.org/?utm_source=chatgpt.com

8. https://ihl-databases.icrc.org/en/ihl-treaties?utm_source=chatgpt.com

9. https://www.unodc.org/unodc/en/organized-crime/intro/UNTOC.html?utm_source=chatgpt.com

10. https://www.coe.int/en/web/cybercrime/the-budapest-convention?utm_source=chatgpt.com

11. https://www.coe.int/en/web/data-protection/convention108-and-protocol?utm_source=chatgpt.com

12. https://commission.europa.eu/law/law-topic/data-protection/data-protection-eu_en?utm_source=chatgpt.com

13. https://www.nist.gov/cyberframework?utm_source=chatgpt.com

14. https://csrc.nist.gov/publications/detail/sp/800-53/rev-5/final?utm_source=chatgpt.com

15. https://www.iso.org/isoiec-27001-information-security.html?utm_source=chatgpt.com

20. ISO/IEC 27002 — Information Security Controls[16] — international guidance covering access control, cryptography, organizational security, and information protection.

21. ISO 15489 — Records Management[17] — international standard concerning authenticity, integrity, reliability, and preservation of records.

22. ISO 14721 — Open Archival Information System Reference Model[18] — conceptual framework for long-term preservation and continued accessibility of digital information.

23. National Archives — Digital Preservation — guidance concerning long-term preservation, authenticity, accessibility, and management of digital records.

24. Library of Congress — Digital Preservation[19] — extensive resources concerning preservation of digital materials, metadata, file formats, and long-term access.

25. Internet Engineering Task Force — RFC 5280: Internet X.509 Public Key Infrastructure Certificate and CRL Profile[20] — technical standard relevant to digital certificates and public-key infrastructure.

26. Internet Engineering Task Force — RFC 4880: OpenPGP Message Format[21] — technical specification for OpenPGP message formats and cryptographic protection.

27. United Nations Office on Drugs and Crime — Witness Protection[22] — resources concerning witness protection and the challenges of protecting people involved in investigations.

28. International Association of Prosecutors[23] — international professional network relevant to cross-border prosecutorial cooperation and professional standards.

29. International Council on Archives[24] — international archival organization providing professional principles and resources for preservation and access to records.

30. Digital Preservation Coalition — Digital Preservation Handbook[25] — professional guidance on long-term digital preservation, storage, integrity, metadata, and organizational continuity.

---

16. https://www.iso.org/standard/75652.html?utm_source=chatgpt.com

17. https://www.iso.org/standard/62542.html?utm_source=chatgpt.com

18. https://www.iso.org/standard/57284.html?utm_source=chatgpt.com

19. https://www.loc.gov/preservation/digital/?utm_source=chatgpt.com

20. https://www.rfc-editor.org/rfc/rfc5280?utm_source=chatgpt.com

21. https://www.rfc-editor.org/rfc/rfc4880?utm_source=chatgpt.com

22. https://www.unodc.org/unodc/en/organized-crime/witness-protection.html?utm_source=chatgpt.com

23. https://www.iap-association.org/?utm_source=chatgpt.com

24. https://www.ica.org/?utm_source=chatgpt.com

25. https://www.dpconline.org/handbook?utm_source=chatgpt.com

The Technology of Delayed Disclosure

The most dramatic moment in any dead man's switch is the moment when nothing appears to happen and then, suddenly, something does. A period of silence ends with an email, a notification, a document becoming accessible, or an instruction reaching someone who did not expect to receive it. From the outside, this can look almost magical, as though a machine has been waiting patiently for its creator to disappear. In reality, delayed disclosure is a systems problem involving authentication, scheduling, communication infrastructure, human judgment, data preservation, and failure management. Every automated release mechanism depends upon assumptions about time, identity, connectivity, availability, and the meaning of silence. Understanding those assumptions is more important than choosing any particular technology.

The basic concept is deceptively simple. Information is placed somewhere, a condition is established, and the system is expected to release or transmit something if that condition is satisfied. The condition might involve a missed confirmation, the expiration of a scheduled event, an explicit instruction, or some other predefined circumstance. The technology then performs an action without requiring the creator to be physically present at that moment. This can reduce dependence on human memory and can preserve continuity when the creator becomes unavailable. But automation also creates a fundamental danger: machines execute conditions, not intentions.

That distinction should remain at the center of every discussion about delayed disclosure. A human being can understand that someone missed a check-in because they were traveling, hospitalized, unable to access an account, or deliberately changing their plans. A simple automated system may see only the absence of a required signal. If the system interprets silence as death, it may activate when no emergency exists. If it interprets silence as irrelevant, it may fail when an emergency actually occurs. The challenge is therefore not merely creating an automated action but defining the condition under which that action is justified.

Email is one of the most obvious technologies for delayed disclosure because it is familiar, widely available, and capable of transmitting both messages and attachments. A person can maintain instructions for recipients, communicate with a designated custodian, or use scheduled messages as part of a broader contingency system. Email also has the advantage of being understandable to ordinary users rather than requiring specialized infrastructure. Yet email depends upon accounts, passwords, providers, network connectivity, and continued operation of the relevant services. An email address that works today may not remain accessible indefinitely.

Email also creates an important distinction between message transmission and information preservation. Sending an email is relatively straightforward. Ensuring that the recipient can still access the account, recognize the message as legitimate, open any protected attachments, and understand what should happen next is considerably more difficult. A message containing an encrypted archive is not useful if the recipient cannot obtain the necessary decryption key. A link to a private repository is not useful if the account has expired. A beautifully designed automated message can therefore fail at the final step. The system must be considered from the perspective of the recipient rather than merely the sender.

Scheduled delivery introduces another variation. Instead of waiting for a missed check-in, a message can be prepared for delivery at a future time. This creates a simple form of temporal redundancy because the creator's intention is encoded before the event occurs. But scheduled delivery has its own weaknesses. The message may be sent even if circumstances change. The account may be inaccessible. The service may discontinue the feature. The recipient may change their address. The device or application responsible for scheduling may fail. A scheduled message is therefore only one component of a larger continuity system.

Some systems reverse the logic by requiring periodic confirmation. Rather than instructing a service to release information at a predetermined time, the creator periodically signals that everything remains normal. If confirmations stop, a process begins. This model is conceptually closer to a traditional dead man's switch because continued human action suppresses the release condition. It can be useful because it accommodates uncertainty about when an emergency might occur. But it also introduces false positives. People miss appointments, forget passwords, lose phones, travel without connectivity, become busy, or simply decide that the system is no longer necessary.

A robust design therefore requires a grace period. Silence should not necessarily produce immediate disclosure. A missed confirmation can initiate a warning phase during which the creator is given opportunities to respond. A secondary contact may be notified. A second confirmation may be requested. The system may require multiple independent conditions before proceeding. These mechanisms do not eliminate uncertainty, but they can reduce the probability that ordinary human error becomes irreversible public disclosure. Time itself becomes a safety mechanism.

The concept of delayed disclosure is therefore closely connected to escalation. A system can move through progressively more serious stages rather than jumping directly from normal operation to public release. An initial missed check-in might generate a private reminder. A second failure might notify a trusted custodian. A longer period of unexplained silence might trigger professional review. Only under a separately defined condition might the archive become eligible for wider disclosure. This layered approach recognizes that uncertainty increases the need for human review rather than eliminating it.

Encrypted communication adds another dimension. Encryption can protect information while it is transmitted or stored, depending upon the technology and configuration used. It can reduce the risk that unauthorized parties will understand intercepted communications. But encryption does not determine who should receive the information or whether the information itself is true. It protects confidentiality and, in some systems, integrity and authenticity. It does not automatically solve the problems of identity, judgment, provenance, or authorization. A secure channel can transmit a false claim just as effectively as a true one.

Authentication becomes particularly important when delayed disclosure is involved. The recipient needs some reasonable basis for determining that a message genuinely originated from the expected source or system. Without authentication, an attacker might attempt to imitate the creator or trigger false disclosure. Digital signatures, authenticated accounts, cryptographic keys, and other mechanisms can contribute to identity assurance. Each mechanism has limitations, and key management becomes crucial. A cryptographic system is only as reliable as the procedures surrounding the keys.

Key management may be one of the least glamorous and most important parts of delayed disclosure. Encryption can make an archive inaccessible to unauthorized people, but it can also make the archive inaccessible to legitimate recipients if the keys are lost. A dead man's switch therefore faces a paradox: the stronger the protection against unauthorized access, the greater the importance of reliable authorized access. If the creator is the only person who understands the key structure, the system may die with the creator. If too many people possess the keys, confidentiality may be weakened. The design problem is to create controlled continuity.

This is where secret-sharing concepts can become relevant. Cryptographic systems can sometimes divide control among several participants so that no single participant possesses the entire authorization mechanism. Such approaches can reduce dependence on one individual. They can also create more complicated recovery procedures. The fundamental principle is that access can be distributed without necessarily distributing the entire underlying information. The technical details vary, but the conceptual goal is consistent: prevent both unilateral compromise and total dependence upon one person.

Third-party custodial services introduce another possibility. A specialized provider may offer mechanisms for storing information, managing access, maintaining backups, or initiating a release under defined conditions. Such services can reduce the burden on an individual who does not want to maintain the technical infrastructure personally. They may also have professional security procedures and redundancy that individuals cannot easily reproduce. But the provider becomes another point of trust. The creator must consider what happens if the company fails, changes ownership, changes its terms, loses access, experiences a breach, or simply ceases operating.

The problem of institutional continuity is frequently underestimated. Technology companies disappear. Products are discontinued. Applications are abandoned. Websites change. APIs are retired. Authentication systems are replaced. A system that works perfectly today can become unusable years later without anyone maliciously interfering with it. Long-term information protection therefore requires periodic review. The creator must consider not only whether the mechanism functions now but whether it has a plausible path toward continued operation. Technological longevity is never guaranteed.

Cloud infrastructure presents a similar issue. Cloud services can provide geographic redundancy, automatic backups, scalability, and convenient access. They can be extremely useful for preserving information. Yet the creator is relying upon an external provider's infrastructure, policies, authentication systems, and legal obligations. A cloud account can also become inaccessible if credentials are lost or if security systems identify suspicious activity. Cloud storage should therefore be regarded as one layer of an architecture rather than as the architecture itself. The principle of redundancy remains more important than loyalty to any particular platform.

Decentralized technologies attempt to address some of these dependencies by distributing records across networks rather than placing complete control in one organization. Blockchain systems are an example of this broader category. They can create tamper-evident records and can automate certain conditions through programmable logic. In principle, this can reduce reliance on a central intermediary. But decentralization does not eliminate trust; it moves trust to other components such as software, protocols, cryptographic assumptions, network participants, interfaces, and external data sources. A decentralized system can still fail or behave differently from what its creator expected.

Smart contracts illustrate this problem clearly. A smart contract can execute predefined logic on a blockchain network. If certain technical conditions are satisfied, the contract can perform an action according to its programming. This can be useful for automation. But a smart contract cannot independently determine whether a person has died, disappeared, been coerced, or changed their mind. Those conditions are external facts. The system must rely upon some mechanism for representing them. That mechanism becomes another point where uncertainty and trust enter the design.

The problem is sometimes called the oracle problem in decentralized computing. A blockchain can reliably determine what has been recorded within its own system, but it cannot automatically know whether an external event has occurred. If a smart contract is supposed to respond to a person's death, someone or something must provide the relevant information. If that information is wrong, delayed, manipulated, or unavailable, the automated logic may produce the wrong outcome. Decentralization therefore does not eliminate the need for trusted inputs. It simply changes where those inputs originate.

Artificial intelligence introduces another possible layer of automation. An AI system might monitor communications, analyze patterns, classify documents, identify unusual account activity, or assist with determining whether a predefined condition appears to have occurred. Such systems can process information at a scale that humans cannot easily match. They can also produce false positives and false negatives. An AI model does not possess independent knowledge of reality merely because it can recognize patterns. For irreversible actions, automated inference should therefore be treated cautiously.

This is particularly important when the trigger depends upon ambiguous human circumstances. Suppose a person stops communicating for an extended period. An automated system might interpret that as evidence of an emergency. But silence can have countless explanations. The person may be traveling, deliberately withdrawing from communication, suffering equipment failure, or simply abandoning the system. An AI might estimate probabilities, but probability is not proof of death or coercion. A high-stakes disclosure system should therefore distinguish between an automated signal and a verified event.

Biometric systems create another interesting possibility. A device could theoretically use biometric authentication to determine whether a person is present or capable of authorizing an action. Yet biometric information has significant limitations. Fingerprints, faces, voices, and other biometric characteristics can sometimes be copied, spoofed, altered by circumstances, or rendered unusable. Unlike a password, a biometric characteristic cannot simply be replaced if compromised. Biometric activation should therefore be regarded as one factor among several rather than as an infallible identity mechanism.

Location data presents similar complications. A system may know where a device was last connected or where a person was apparently located. That does not establish what happened to the person. GPS signals can be unavailable or inaccurate. Devices can be lost, damaged, stolen, or deliberately left behind. A geographic trigger can therefore provide useful context without providing definitive proof. Location is evidence about a device, not necessarily evidence about the human being associated with it.

One of the most important principles in automated disclosure is fail-safe versus fail-secure design. A system designed to fail open may release information when a technical failure occurs. A system designed to fail closed may preserve confidentiality when something goes wrong. Neither approach is universally correct. The appropriate behavior depends upon the nature of the information and the consequences of an incorrect release. Highly sensitive personal information may require a bias toward withholding, while evidence of an imminent threat may create arguments for rapid notification. The architecture must be matched to the consequences.

This is why the phrase "foolproof trigger" should be treated skeptically. There is no technological trigger that can guarantee perfect interpretation of complex human circumstances. A mechanism can be made more reliable, more redundant, and more resistant to accidental activation. It cannot eliminate uncertainty from the real world. The best system therefore acknowledges uncertainty rather than pretending it does not exist. Designing around known failure modes is more realistic than searching for an imaginary perfect trigger.

Delayed disclosure can also be vulnerable to adversaries. Someone who knows that a dead man's switch exists may attempt to gain access to the creator's accounts. They may try to disable notifications. They may attempt to impersonate the creator. They may interfere with devices or communication channels. They may seek to discover where information is stored. Security therefore requires thinking about the system from the perspective of an attacker as well as the perspective of the creator. Threat modeling becomes essential.

Threat modeling does not require assuming that every person is an adversary. It requires identifying plausible threats and determining which protections are proportionate. A system protecting ordinary personal records may require very different safeguards from one protecting evidence of organized wrongdoing. The potential adversary's capabilities matter. So do the consequences of compromise. A realistic system begins with these questions rather than with a particular technology. Technology should serve the threat model, not define it.

Another important consideration is availability. A highly secure archive that cannot be reached when needed has failed in a different way. Encryption, authentication, access controls, and physical security can all reduce unauthorized access while increasing the possibility of legitimate lockout. This is why recovery mechanisms matter. A trusted recipient may need a documented path to regain access if a device is lost or an account is compromised. Recovery itself must be protected, because an insecure recovery channel can undermine the entire system.

Testing is therefore indispensable. A creator should not wait for the worst possible moment to discover that an automated process no longer works. Scheduled messages should be tested. Recipient addresses should be verified. Backup archives should be checked. Encryption keys should be tested through controlled recovery procedures. Custodians should understand their responsibilities. Technology should be updated when necessary. A dead man's switch is not a one-time construction project; it is a system that requires maintenance.

This maintenance creates a paradox of its own. The more frequently the system is changed, the more opportunities there are for introducing new errors. The less frequently it is reviewed, the greater the risk that it becomes obsolete. The solution is controlled review rather than constant tinkering. Major changes should be documented. Critical dependencies should be known. Old systems should not be abandoned until replacements have been verified. Continuity requires disciplined change management.

Third-party custodians also raise questions about incentives. A company may have an excellent security reputation today but encounter financial problems tomorrow. A service may promise long-term availability without being able to guarantee it. Terms of service can change. Ownership can change. Legal obligations can change. A provider that was once ideal may become unsuitable. The creator should therefore understand what is actually being promised rather than relying on marketing language.

The same caution applies to decentralized services. "Decentralized" can mean many different things. A network may distribute data while relying upon centralized websites for access. A blockchain may be decentralized while its most convenient wallet or interface is controlled by one company. A token-based system may depend upon centralized exchanges. A smart contract may be autonomous while its external data source is not. Understanding the actual architecture matters more than the label attached to it.

Delayed disclosure also has to account for the recipient's technological capabilities. A highly sophisticated encryption system may be useless to a family member who has never worked with encrypted archives. A decentralized system may be incomprehensible to a journalist. A technical archive may require specialized software. A recipient who cannot use the system becomes an accidental point of failure. Accessibility is therefore part of security. The intended recipient must be capable of carrying out the next step.

Documentation can make an enormous difference. The system should have enough information for legitimate custodians to understand what they are receiving and what the next stage requires. Yet documentation should not expose secrets unnecessarily. This creates another balancing problem between clarity and confidentiality. The answer is often layered documentation, in which general instructions are separated from sensitive credentials or keys. Each layer serves a different purpose. Good documentation reduces dependence upon the creator's memory.

The timing of disclosure can also influence its impact. Immediate release may generate attention but provide little opportunity for verification. Delayed release can allow investigators to examine material before it becomes public. In some circumstances, that delay may be beneficial. In others, delay could allow evidence to disappear or ongoing harm to continue. There is no universally correct timing. The appropriate schedule depends upon the nature of the information, the urgency of the threat, and the intended recipient.

This is why delayed disclosure should not automatically mean public disclosure. A system might first notify a lawyer. It might alert a journalist. It might inform a trusted investigator. It might release a verification package rather than the full archive. It might tell a custodian where the evidence is stored. These intermediate steps create opportunities for human judgment. The most responsible system is often one that separates activation from publication.

A particularly useful conceptual distinction is between notification and release. Notification tells someone that a condition has occurred or that an archive requires attention. Release makes the underlying information accessible. These actions do not have to happen simultaneously. A notification can trigger a human review before the evidence is disclosed. This can substantially reduce the risk of accidental publication. It also makes the system more flexible when circumstances are ambiguous.

Another distinction is between access and dissemination. Giving one investigator access to an archive is very different from publishing that archive to millions of people. The consequences are different. The legal and ethical considerations are different. The technological controls are different. A sophisticated dead man's switch should therefore avoid treating them as the same event. The system can be designed so that escalation occurs gradually.

This layered approach also creates opportunities for corroboration. An investigator who receives the archive can independently examine it. A journalist can contact sources. A lawyer can evaluate legal risks. A technical specialist can analyze files. Only after these steps can a decision be made about wider disclosure. The technology therefore becomes an information-routing mechanism rather than an automatic publishing machine. That distinction may be the difference between responsible protection and reckless exposure.

The creator should also consider what happens if the system activates incorrectly. Can the process be stopped? Can a custodian suspend publication? Can an erroneous message be withdrawn? Can an exposed password be invalidated? Can recipients be warned that material was released in error? These questions should be answered before the system is needed. Once sensitive information has been publicly released, technical recovery may be impossible. Prevention and controlled escalation are therefore much more valuable than attempting to repair an irreversible mistake.

The opposite failure also deserves attention. What if the creator dies and nothing happens? What if the scheduled message fails? What if the account is locked? What if the provider shuts down? What if the recipient misses the notification? What if the encryption key is lost? A system that has no alternative path may fail silently. This is why redundancy must exist not only in storage but also in communication and activation. Multiple independent pathways can reduce the chance that one technical failure destroys the intended continuity.

The most resilient systems therefore resemble layered safety architectures. One layer may monitor normal status. Another may provide warnings. Another may preserve the evidence. Another may authenticate the creator's identity. Another may notify a human custodian. Another may permit controlled access. Another may provide independent archival continuity. Each layer compensates for weaknesses elsewhere. No individual component has to be perfect if the overall architecture can tolerate reasonable failure.

This approach also reduces the temptation to rely upon exotic technology merely because it appears sophisticated. A simple, well-understood mechanism can be more reliable than a complex system that its creator barely understands. Technology should be judged by whether it solves the actual problem. A sophisticated decentralized protocol that no recipient understands may be less useful than a conventional archive with carefully maintained independent custodians. Complexity should have a purpose. Otherwise, complexity becomes another form of fragility.

The future will almost certainly produce more powerful mechanisms for delayed disclosure. Artificial intelligence will become better at analyzing patterns. Cryptographic systems will evolve. Distributed networks will become more accessible. Authentication technologies will improve. Automated agents may eventually coordinate complicated information-preservation tasks. These developments will increase capability, but they will not remove the fundamental human problem. Someone must still decide what information deserves protection, what conditions justify disclosure, and what consequences are acceptable.

The central principle is therefore remarkably old-fashioned: technology should remain subordinate to judgment. Automation can reduce forgetfulness. Encryption can reduce unauthorized access. Redundancy can reduce the consequences of failure. Distributed systems can reduce dependence upon one institution. Scheduled communication can preserve continuity. None of these technologies can determine what the truth is. None can decide whether a person genuinely intended a disclosure under every conceivable future circumstance.

A dead man's switch becomes stronger when its technological components are treated as servants rather than authorities. The machine should preserve the creator's ability to communicate beyond the point at which communication is possible. It should not pretend to know more than the creator, the evidence, or the surrounding circumstances allow. The safest architecture recognizes uncertainty and creates opportunities for correction. It distinguishes notification from release, evidence from interpretation, and activation from publication.

Delayed disclosure is therefore best understood not as a single technological trick but as a chain of dependencies. The creator must remain identifiable. The condition must be recognized. The system must remain operational. The information must remain accessible. The recipient must be reachable. The archive must be interpretable. The evidence must remain intact. And, when the consequences justify it, a human being must still decide what should happen next.

That final human element may be the most important safeguard of all. Machines are exceptionally good at repeating predefined instructions. Humans are capable of understanding context, ambiguity, proportionality, and consequences. A responsible dead man's switch uses the strengths of both. Technology keeps the information alive when its creator cannot. Independent people determine what the information means and whether it should be acted upon. Between those two functions lies the difference between automated disclosure and responsible continuity.

The ultimate achievement of delayed disclosure is therefore not the ability to make a file appear after a period of silence. It is the ability to preserve a credible path from the creator's intention to a future decision-maker without allowing one technical failure, one lost password, one unavailable person, or one compromised institution to destroy that path. When designed properly, the technology does not guarantee an outcome. It guarantees an opportunity. And in the uncertain world for which a dead man's switch is created, preserving that opportunity may be the most important form of protection technology can provide.

Resources

1. National Institute of Standards and Technology — Cybersecurity Framework 2.0[1] — framework for identifying, protecting against, detecting, responding to, and recovering from cybersecurity risks.

2. NIST Special Publication 800-57 — Recommendation for Key Management — authoritative guidance on cryptographic key management, protection, recovery, and lifecycle considerations.

3. NIST Special Publication 800-63 — Digital Identity Guidelines[2] — guidance concerning digital identity, authentication, identity assurance, and secure authentication mechanisms.

4. NIST Special Publication 800-61 — Computer Security Incident Handling Guide[3] — guidance concerning preparation, detection, response, and recovery from information-security incidents.

5. NIST Special Publication 800-53 — Security and Privacy Controls[4] — comprehensive catalog of security and privacy controls, including access control, contingency planning, identification, authentication, and system integrity.

6. NIST Special Publication 800-34 — Contingency Planning Guide for Federal Information Systems[5] — guidance concerning contingency planning, recovery, redundancy, and maintaining critical information systems.

7. Internet Engineering Task Force — RFC 5321: Simple Mail Transfer Protocol[6] — foundational technical specification for Internet email transport.

8. Internet Engineering Task Force — RFC 5322: Internet Message Format[7] — technical specification describing the format of Internet messages.

9. Internet Engineering Task Force — RFC 8446: TLS 1.3[8] — current major Internet standard defining Transport Layer Security version 1.3 for protecting communications.

10. Internet Engineering Task Force — RFC 4880: OpenPGP Message Format[9] — technical specification for OpenPGP-based encrypted and digitally signed messaging.

11. Internet Engineering Task Force — RFC 9580: OpenPGP[10] — modern OpenPGP specification concerning encryption, signatures, authentication, and message protection.

---

1. https://www.nist.gov/cyberframework?utm_source=chatgpt.com

2. https://pages.nist.gov/800-63-4/?utm_source=chatgpt.com

3. https://csrc.nist.gov/publications/detail/sp/800-61/rev-2/final?utm_source=chatgpt.com

4. https://csrc.nist.gov/publications/detail/sp/800-53/rev-5/final?utm_source=chatgpt.com

5. https://csrc.nist.gov/publications/detail/sp/800-34/rev-1/final?utm_source=chatgpt.com

6. https://www.rfc-editor.org/rfc/rfc5321?utm_source=chatgpt.com

7. https://www.rfc-editor.org/rfc/rfc5322?utm_source=chatgpt.com

8. https://www.rfc-editor.org/rfc/rfc8446?utm_source=chatgpt.com

9. https://www.rfc-editor.org/rfc/rfc4880?utm_source=chatgpt.com

12. Electronic Frontier Foundation — Surveillance Self-Defense[11] — accessible guidance on threat modeling, encryption, authentication, secure communications, and protecting sensitive information.

13. Freedom of the Press Foundation — Digital Security Training[12] — practical resources for journalists and sources concerning secure communications and digital security.

14. Cloud Security Alliance[13] — research and guidance concerning cloud security, identity, access control, data protection, and cloud-specific risks.

15. ISO/IEC 27001 — Information Security Management Systems[14] — international framework for managing information-security risks and organizational controls.

16. ISO/IEC 27002 — Information Security Controls[15] — guidance concerning security controls including access management, cryptography, operational security, and resilience.

17. ISO 22301 — Security and Resilience: Business Continuity Management Systems[16] — international standard concerning continuity, disruption planning, recovery, and organizational resilience.

18. Internet Engineering Task Force — RFC 6962: Certificate Transparency[17] — technical work relevant to publicly auditable records and detection of unauthorized certificate issuance.

19. Ethereum Documentation — Smart Contracts[18] — technical documentation explaining programmable blockchain contracts and their operational characteristics.

20. Ethereum Documentation — Oracles[19] — explanation of how blockchain systems obtain information from external sources and the resulting trust considerations.

21. National Institute of Standards and Technology — Blockchain Technology Overview[20] — technical overview of blockchain architecture, distributed ledgers, consensus, and associated security considerations.

22. NIST Cybersecurity Practice Guide — Blockchain and Distributed Ledger Technology[21] — research concerning distributed-ledger architectures and their security implications.

23. NIST Privacy Framework[22] — framework for identifying and managing privacy risks associated with information processing.

---

10. https://www.rfc-editor.org/rfc/rfc9580?utm_source=chatgpt.com

11. https://ssd.eff.org/?utm_source=chatgpt.com

12. https://freedom.press/training/?utm_source=chatgpt.com

13. https://cloudsecurityalliance.org/?utm_source=chatgpt.com

14. https://www.iso.org/isoiec-27001-information-security.html?utm_source=chatgpt.com

15. https://www.iso.org/standard/75652.html?utm_source=chatgpt.com

16. https://www.iso.org/standard/75106.html?utm_source=chatgpt.com

17. https://www.rfc-editor.org/rfc/rfc6962?utm_source=chatgpt.com

18. https://ethereum.org/en/developers/docs/smart-contracts/?utm_source=chatgpt.com

19. https://ethereum.org/en/developers/docs/oracles/?utm_source=chatgpt.com

20. https://www.nist.gov/publications/blockchain-technology-overview?utm_source=chatgpt.com

21. https://www.nist.gov/publications/blockchain-technology-overview?utm_source=chatgpt.com

22. https://www.nist.gov/privacy-framework?utm_source=chatgpt.com

24. National Archives — Digital Preservation — authoritative resources concerning preservation, accessibility, authenticity, and long-term management of digital information.

25. Library of Congress — Digital Preservation[23] — resources concerning sustainable digital preservation, file formats, metadata, storage, and continued access.

26. Digital Preservation Coalition — Digital Preservation Handbook[24] — professional guidance on digital preservation, integrity, storage, organizational continuity, and technological change.

27. Open Web Application Security Project — Threat Modeling[25] — practical security methodology for identifying assets, threats, vulnerabilities, and mitigations.

28. CISA — Cybersecurity Best Practices[26] — U.S. government guidance concerning authentication, account protection, resilience, incident preparedness, and cybersecurity risk reduction.

29. CISA — Secure by Design[27] — principles emphasizing that security and resilience should be incorporated into system design rather than added only after deployment.

30. IETF RFC 6973 — Privacy Considerations for Internet Protocols[28] — framework for identifying and considering privacy threats in Internet protocol design.

---

23. https://www.loc.gov/preservation/digital/?utm_source=chatgpt.com

24. https://www.dpconline.org/handbook?utm_source=chatgpt.com

25. https://owasp.org/www-community/Threat_Modeling?utm_source=chatgpt.com

26. https://www.cisa.gov/topics/cybersecurity-best-practices?utm_source=chatgpt.com

27. https://www.cisa.gov/securebydesign?utm_source=chatgpt.com

28. https://www.rfc-editor.org/rfc/rfc6973?utm_source=chatgpt.com

Blockchain, Smart Contracts, and the Decentralization of Trust

Blockchain entered public consciousness with promises that sounded almost tailor-made for the dead man's switch: information could be recorded without a central authority, transactions could be governed by code, and systems could continue operating even when no single institution remained in control. For someone concerned about the survival of sensitive information, the attraction is obvious. A conventional archive depends upon organizations, administrators, passwords, servers, and legal jurisdictions, whereas a distributed ledger appears to offer something structurally different. Yet the reality is considerably more nuanced because blockchains do not eliminate trust so much as redistribute it among protocols, cryptographic keys, software, network participants, interfaces, and external data sources. A blockchain can make certain records difficult to alter without making every surrounding component trustworthy. Understanding that distinction is essential if decentralized technology is to be incorporated responsibly into a dead man's switch.

At its simplest, a blockchain is a distributed ledger in which participants maintain records according to a defined protocol. Rather than relying exclusively upon one central database administrator, a network can maintain synchronized copies and use a consensus mechanism to determine which transactions are accepted into the ledger. The precise architecture differs substantially between blockchain networks, and the word itself covers a wide range of systems. Some are public and permissionless, while others are private or permissioned. Some emphasize financial transactions, while others support programmable applications. The important point for information preservation is that the ledger provides a particular kind of persistence and agreement about what has been recorded.

That persistence is valuable, but it needs to be described accurately. A blockchain can provide strong evidence that particular data or a representation of data was recorded at a particular point in the history of a network, depending upon the architecture and the evidence available. It can also make subsequent alteration detectable or difficult without controlling sufficient network resources or cryptographic authority. What it does not automatically establish is that the underlying information was true when it was recorded. A fabricated document can be hashed and recorded. A false photograph can have its fingerprint placed on a blockchain. The ledger may preserve evidence that something was recorded, but it does not transform that something into truth.

This distinction between integrity and truth is one of the most important concepts in decentralized information systems. Integrity concerns whether information has been altered in an unauthorized or undetected manner. Authenticity concerns whether information genuinely came from the claimed source. Truth concerns whether the information accurately represents reality. A cryptographic hash can be extremely useful for detecting changes to a file, while a digital signature can help establish that a particular key signed it. Neither mechanism independently proves that the person controlling the key was honest or that the underlying claim was correct. Blockchain technology is powerful precisely because it can address certain technical questions without pretending to answer every human one.

For a dead man's switch, one potentially useful application is the preservation of cryptographic fingerprints of evidence. Instead of placing the complete sensitive archive on a public ledger, a creator could theoretically record a cryptographic digest associated with a document or collection. If the underlying file is later presented to investigators, the digest can be recalculated and compared with the previously recorded value. A matching result can provide evidence that the file has not changed since the relevant digest was created. This can be useful for establishing continuity. It does not, by itself, establish when the underlying evidence was originally created or whether it was genuine.

This distinction becomes particularly important when discussing timestamps. Blockchain records can provide evidence associated with the ordering of transactions on a particular network. That can be useful in demonstrating that a particular digital fingerprint existed no later than a certain point in the ledger's history. But a blockchain timestamp should not automatically be described as an absolute proof of when the underlying event occurred. A document could have existed for years before its hash was recorded. Conversely, the act of recording a hash does not prove that the document's contents accurately describe events occurring before the recording. Temporal evidence must therefore be interpreted in context.

The technology becomes more interesting when programmable logic enters the picture. Smart contracts are programs deployed on certain blockchain networks that execute according to their programmed rules. They can store state, receive transactions, and perform predefined actions when their conditions are satisfied. This creates the possibility of automating certain aspects of a dead man's switch. A system could, for example, maintain a state indicating whether a particular condition has been satisfied. If the required transaction or authorization does not occur within a specified period, the program could change its state or permit another action. The crucial limitation is that the smart contract knows only what its code and available inputs tell it.

This is where the apparent simplicity of the dead man's switch encounters the complexity of the real world. A human being can say, "If I die, release this information," but a smart contract cannot independently observe death. It cannot examine a hospital record in the ordinary sense. It cannot interview family members. It cannot understand whether a person has been kidnapped, voluntarily disappeared, lost access to a device, or deliberately stopped communicating. The blockchain can execute logic perfectly while still receiving an incorrect representation of reality. Automation therefore shifts the problem from "Can the system execute the rule?" to "Who or what determines whether the rule's condition has actually occurred?"

This is the oracle problem. Blockchain networks are generally designed to reach agreement about information within their own environments, but many useful applications depend upon facts originating outside the network. An oracle is a mechanism that supplies external information to a smart contract. The information might concern a price, a date, an event, or another real-world condition. In the context of a dead man's switch, the external condition might be a verified death, an authenticated instruction, or a series of missed confirmations. The smart contract can then act on the information it receives. But the reliability of the resulting action depends partly upon the reliability of the information source.

Multiple oracles can reduce dependence upon a single source, but they do not eliminate the underlying problem. Suppose several independent systems report that a particular event occurred. Their agreement may increase confidence, but they could still share common dependencies. They might rely on the same underlying database. They might use similar assumptions. They might inherit errors from the same source. Decentralization is therefore a matter of degree. Counting the number of participants without examining their actual independence can create a misleading impression of resilience.

The same problem appears at the level of blockchain networks themselves. A network may contain thousands of participants, yet users often interact with it through a relatively small number of wallets, exchanges, websites, application interfaces, or infrastructure providers. The underlying ledger may be decentralized while the surrounding user experience is highly centralized. If a creator loses access to the interface, the existence of the blockchain does not automatically solve the problem. If a recipient does not understand how to interact with the network, decentralization becomes irrelevant to them. The architecture must therefore be evaluated as a complete system rather than by looking only at the ledger.

Cryptocurrency wallets illustrate this issue particularly well. Control over blockchain assets or permissions commonly depends upon cryptographic keys or seed phrases. Whoever controls the relevant credentials may be able to perform actions permitted by the system. This provides strong user sovereignty but also creates an unforgiving recovery problem. If the creator dies without providing an appropriate and secure inheritance mechanism, the information or assets may remain inaccessible. If the credentials are widely distributed, unauthorized access becomes more likely. The dead man's switch therefore encounters the same central problem discussed earlier in this book: security and recoverability must be balanced.

Cryptographic keys should consequently be treated as assets requiring lifecycle management rather than as magical passwords. Keys can be lost, copied, exposed, revoked, replaced, or rendered inaccessible by changes in technology. Some systems support sophisticated arrangements for multiple authorization participants, while simpler systems rely upon a single secret. The appropriate model depends upon the consequences of compromise and the importance of continuity. A creator should understand exactly what a particular key controls before placing it at the center of a contingency system. A key that controls everything may create an unacceptable single point of failure.

One possible conceptual approach is threshold authorization. In such an arrangement, several independent parties can collectively authorize an action without any one party possessing complete unilateral control. Cryptographic secret-sharing techniques can also divide a secret into components such that a predefined number of components are required for reconstruction. These approaches can reduce dependence upon a single custodian. They can also make the system more difficult to recover if too many participants become unavailable. Again, the principle is not maximum complexity but appropriate resilience.

Smart contracts can also be designed with time-based conditions. A contract may recognize that a certain period has elapsed and permit a predefined action after that interval. This sounds attractive for a dead man's switch because time is measurable and does not require a human interpretation. Yet time alone does not establish why the period elapsed. A person may have missed a check-in because of travel, illness, technical failure, or a change of circumstances. The contract can reliably determine that a condition in its own environment has occurred. It cannot reliably determine what that condition means unless additional information is introduced.

This creates a distinction between temporal automation and contextual automation. Temporal automation asks whether enough time has passed. Contextual automation asks what happened during that time and why. Blockchains are much better suited to the first question than the second. A creator could establish a time-dependent mechanism, but doing so safely may require additional human or technical verification before irreversible disclosure occurs. A missed deadline can therefore be treated as a signal rather than as conclusive proof. The system can escalate rather than immediately publish.

The difference between a trigger and a release is particularly important here. A blockchain mechanism might record that a creator has failed to perform a required action. That does not necessarily mean the underlying archive should instantly become public. Instead, the event could authorize a trusted custodian to investigate. Another condition might then be required before disclosure. A third condition could authorize publication. This layered structure allows decentralized technology to provide automation without assigning it unlimited authority. The blockchain becomes one component of a broader decision architecture.

Another possible use is decentralized storage, although blockchain and decentralized storage should not be confused. A blockchain is generally not an efficient place to store large collections of documents, photographs, and video because ledger storage can be expensive, constrained, or technically inappropriate for substantial data.

Separate distributed storage systems can store the actual content while a blockchain records identifiers, hashes, permissions, or references. This creates a hybrid architecture in which the blockchain provides a durable coordination or integrity layer while another system provides the bulk data storage. Such designs can be powerful but introduce additional dependencies.

Decentralized storage also raises the question of persistence. A file may be distributed across multiple nodes, but that does not necessarily mean it will remain available forever. Networks depend upon participants, incentives, software, hardware, and protocols. A system may be technically decentralized while experiencing declining participation over time. A file may remain referenced while becoming difficult to retrieve. Long-term preservation therefore requires more than initial distribution. It requires mechanisms for continued availability, verification, migration, and recovery.

The distinction between permanence and availability deserves particular attention. A record can remain technically present in a ledger while becoming practically difficult for ordinary people to use. A blockchain can preserve a transaction history while the tools necessary to interpret it change. Software libraries can become obsolete. Interfaces can disappear. Cryptographic algorithms can become outdated. Network rules can evolve. A serious archive therefore needs a preservation strategy extending beyond the initial technology. Long-term information survival is an archival problem as much as a blockchain problem.

Public blockchains also introduce privacy concerns that can be overlooked by enthusiasts. Information recorded on a public ledger may be visible indefinitely. Even if the underlying document is not placed directly on-chain, associated metadata, transaction relationships, addresses, timestamps, and other information may reveal patterns. A creator who wants to protect sensitive information should therefore distinguish between transparency of the ledger and confidentiality of the evidence. Public verifiability can be valuable, but permanent public records can also create permanent privacy consequences. "Immutable" is not automatically synonymous with "safe."

Anonymity is similarly easy to exaggerate. Many blockchain systems allow participants to operate under pseudonymous addresses rather than conventional names. Pseudonymity can provide some separation between an address and a real-world identity. But transactions can create durable records that may be analyzed through blockchain data, external information, exchange records, device information, and other sources. The fact that an address does not display a person's name does not make the person unknowable. Anonymity is a much stronger claim than pseudonymity.

For a dead man's switch, this distinction matters because the creator may want both confidentiality and credible attribution. A completely anonymous archive may be difficult for recipients to authenticate. A completely public archive may expose sensitive information prematurely. A carefully designed system can instead separate identity evidence from the substantive archive. Cryptographic signatures, independent witnesses, legal records, and corroborating evidence can contribute to attribution without necessarily making the entire archive public. Again, compartmentalization becomes a valuable principle.

Decentralization can also be misunderstood as independence from governments. A blockchain network may operate without a single central administrator, but the people and organizations using it remain subject to laws. Exchanges can be regulated. Service providers can be compelled to provide information where legally required. Developers and infrastructure providers can operate within particular jurisdictions. Users can be identified through ordinary investigative methods. A decentralized network therefore changes the architecture of control without abolishing the legal environment surrounding its participants.

The same applies to censorship resistance. Some blockchain systems are deliberately designed to make unauthorized alteration or unilateral deletion difficult. This can be valuable for preserving records. But censorship resistance does not mean universal immunity from intervention. Access points can be blocked. Websites can be removed. Users can be prosecuted. Devices can be seized. Services can be regulated. The underlying network may remain operational while practical access becomes difficult. The distinction between protocol-level resilience and real-world accessibility is critical.

One of the strongest legitimate applications of blockchain in a dead man's switch may therefore be evidentiary rather than custodial. Instead of attempting to make the entire disclosure system depend upon a blockchain, the technology can provide a tamper-evident reference layer. A creator could preserve sensitive material elsewhere while recording cryptographic commitments that allow later investigators to test whether a particular archive corresponds to an earlier commitment. This can contribute to provenance without requiring sensitive material to become publicly visible. It also reduces the amount of information exposed to the blockchain itself.

Digital signatures can complement this approach. A signature can provide evidence that a holder of a particular private key approved or signed a document or message. If the key's ownership and security are well established, this can strengthen attribution. But again, a signature proves control of a key, not necessarily the identity or honesty of the person behind it. Key compromise is another concern. If someone obtains a private key, they may be able to create apparently legitimate signatures. Authentication therefore depends upon the entire lifecycle of the credential.

The concept of a decentralized identity system offers another potential avenue. Rather than relying entirely upon usernames and passwords controlled by centralized providers, emerging identity architectures attempt to give individuals greater control over verifiable credentials. Such systems can potentially help recipients establish that particular claims or credentials originated from recognized issuers. However, these technologies remain dependent upon standards, wallets, issuers, key management, and ecosystem adoption. They should be evaluated as evolving infrastructure rather than as a universal replacement for conventional identity systems.

Smart contracts can also create conditional access mechanisms. A creator could theoretically define a sequence of permissions under which different participants receive different capabilities at different stages. The attraction is obvious because the rules are encoded into software rather than left entirely to a human intermediary. Yet software rules can contain bugs. A programmer can misunderstand the intended condition. An attacker can exploit an unforeseen interaction. A contract may be difficult or impossible to modify once deployed. Code can therefore become a form of institutional rigidity.

This introduces the broader principle that immutable code is not necessarily desirable code. Immutability is useful when the objective is to prevent unauthorized alteration. It becomes problematic when an error needs correction. Traditional institutions can sometimes revise procedures when circumstances change. A rigid smart contract may continue executing obsolete logic indefinitely. For a dead man's switch, this could be especially dangerous because the creator's intentions may evolve over years. A system should therefore distinguish between what must be immutable and what must remain updateable under controlled authorization.

Governance becomes unavoidable at this point. Who decides when the system should change? Who can replace an obsolete key? Who can modify a recipient? Who can suspend a release after evidence of fraud? Who can respond if the original creator changes their mind? A decentralized system still needs governance even when it does not have a conventional central administrator. Governance can be encoded in software, distributed among participants, or handled through external processes. The question is not whether governance exists but where it resides.

A particularly serious concern is the possibility of coercion. If a person is forced to surrender a password, private key, device, or other credential, the system may interpret that action as legitimate. Cryptography cannot necessarily distinguish voluntary authorization from authorization obtained under duress. More sophisticated authentication architectures can introduce additional factors or delayed confirmation, but the human problem remains. A dead man's switch designed for high-risk circumstances must therefore consider coercion as distinct from simple unauthorized access. The existence of a valid cryptographic signature does not necessarily tell us why it was produced.

The same problem applies to automated agents. An AI-controlled system might monitor whether a person appears active and make recommendations about whether an activation condition has occurred. This could reduce administrative burdens. But AI systems can misunderstand unusual behavior, generate false conclusions, or inherit biases from their training and data. The consequences of an incorrect activation may be irreversible. AI can therefore assist with triage and anomaly detection without necessarily being granted unilateral authority to release sensitive information. Human review remains especially valuable when the consequences are substantial.

There is also a philosophical danger in treating code as law. Software executes precisely what it has been programmed to execute, but human intentions are rarely as precise as software conditions. A person may say, "Release this information if I disappear," while meaning, "Release it if I am unlawfully detained and cannot communicate." Those are not the same condition. The first might be triggered by voluntary disappearance. The second requires contextual judgment. Translating natural language into code therefore creates interpretive choices. Those choices can become hidden assumptions within the system.

The safest use of smart contracts may consequently be in narrowly defined functions. A contract might record authorization. It might enforce a predetermined time delay. It might distribute a cryptographic capability among predefined participants. It might preserve a tamper-evident event history. These functions are relatively well suited to deterministic software. The contract should be less responsible for interpreting complex human circumstances. The closer a condition comes to requiring judgment about intent, coercion, death, or public interest, the stronger the argument for human intervention.

Blockchain technology can nevertheless contribute something genuinely valuable to the architecture of a dead man's switch: distributed verification. If several independent parties can examine the same cryptographic record, they may be able to determine whether information has changed. If an archive's existence can be demonstrated independently of the creator's continued control over a single server, its evidentiary resilience can increase. If a predefined transaction or authorization can be independently verified, disputes over what the system recorded can become easier to resolve. These are real capabilities. They do not require exaggerated claims about technological liberation.

The most useful way to think about blockchain is therefore as a specialized tool for particular trust problems. It can reduce dependence upon a central database in certain circumstances. It can create durable records. It can automate deterministic rules. It can make unauthorized alteration more difficult or detectable. It can distribute verification across network participants. These properties can be valuable in information-preservation systems. But none of them means that the technology has eliminated trust.

Trust has simply moved. We now have to trust the cryptographic primitives, the software implementation, the network's consensus assumptions, the key-management procedures, the external data sources, the interfaces, and the people who operate surrounding infrastructure. If the archive depends upon a third-party oracle, we must assess that oracle. If it depends upon a wallet, we must assess the wallet. If it depends upon a cloud service for the underlying documents, we must assess that service. Decentralization is therefore better understood as redistribution of trust than as abolition of trust.

This perspective also prevents a common mistake: believing that more decentralization is automatically better. There are circumstances in which centralization provides valuable accountability. A professional archive may have preservation standards. A law firm may have established confidentiality obligations. An investigative newsroom may have editorial review. A court may provide procedural safeguards. A blockchain may provide excellent technical integrity but poor contextual judgment. The best architecture may therefore combine centralized institutions and decentralized technologies rather than choosing one ideology over the other.

A hybrid system can assign each component to the environment best suited to it. Sensitive evidence might remain encrypted in professional or offline custody. Cryptographic fingerprints could be recorded on a distributed ledger. Independent custodians could hold different authorization components. A legal representative could review the circumstances surrounding activation. An investigative organization could assess the evidence. A blockchain could provide a durable record of selected system events. Such an architecture uses decentralization where it provides genuine value without pretending that every problem is technological.

This is ultimately the mature view of blockchain and the dead man's switch. The technology can strengthen certain layers of resilience, but it cannot replace evidence, judgment, law, or human responsibility. A blockchain can remember that something was recorded. A smart contract can execute a rule. A cryptographic signature can help establish that a key approved a message. A decentralized network can reduce reliance upon one administrator. None of these capabilities determines whether a disclosure is morally justified or factually correct.

The dead man's switch is therefore unlikely to be transformed by blockchain into an autonomous machine that perfectly knows when its creator has died and releases the truth without human involvement. The more realistic future is more interesting. Distributed ledgers, smart contracts, cryptographic credentials, decentralized storage, and automated agents may become individual components within sophisticated continuity systems. Each component can perform a narrow function while human custodians retain responsibility for interpretation and consequential decisions. The result is not the elimination of trust but the deliberate distribution of it.

In that sense, blockchain's greatest contribution may not be secrecy at all. It may be memory. A system capable of preserving verifiable records beyond the lifespan of a particular institution can help ensure that evidence of existence, authorization, or integrity is not dependent upon one database administrator. When combined with independent archives and professional investigation, that capability can make historical records harder to rewrite. But memory is only valuable when the record is preserved accurately and interpreted honestly. A permanent record of a falsehood is still a falsehood.

The responsible creator should therefore approach decentralized technology with neither blind enthusiasm nor reflexive skepticism. The correct question is not whether blockchain is revolutionary. The correct question is what specific failure it prevents, what new dependency it introduces, and whether the trade-off is justified. If it provides a useful integrity layer, use it for that purpose. If it provides unnecessary complexity, do not add it merely because it sounds sophisticated. If a conventional professional custodian is better suited to a particular responsibility, there is no virtue in replacing that institution with code.

The dead man's switch ultimately depends upon a chain of trust extending from the creator into the future. Blockchain can strengthen some links in that chain. Smart contracts can automate some decisions. Cryptography can protect some communications and establish some forms of integrity. Distributed networks can prevent certain forms of unilateral control. But the chain still contains human beings, legal systems, evidence, institutions, and judgment. The real achievement is not creating a system that trusts nobody. It is creating a system in which no single point of trust becomes powerful enough to determine whether the information survives.

Resources

1. NIST — Blockchain Technology Overview[1] — foundational technical overview of blockchain architecture, distributed ledgers, consensus, and associated limitations.

2. NIST — Blockchain and Related Technologies[2] — NIST research and resources concerning blockchain and distributed ledger technologies.

3. Ethereum Documentation — Introduction to Smart Contracts[3] — technical explanation of smart contracts, their execution environment, and their limitations.

4. Ethereum Documentation — Oracles[4] — explanation of how external information enters blockchain systems and why external data creates additional trust assumptions.

5. Ethereum Documentation — Decentralized Storage[5] — overview of storage considerations surrounding blockchain-based applications.

6. National Institute of Standards and Technology — Digital Identity Guidelines[6] — authoritative guidance concerning identity proofing, authentication, and digital credentials.

7. NIST Special Publication 800-57 — Recommendation for Key Management — guidance on cryptographic keys, their protection, lifecycle, backup, recovery, and compromise.

8. NIST Special Publication 800-63B — Authentication and Authenticator Management[7] — technical guidance concerning authentication mechanisms and authenticator management.

9. Internet Engineering Task Force — RFC 6962: Certificate Transparency[8] — technical work illustrating the use of append-only, publicly auditable records to detect unauthorized changes.

10. Internet Engineering Task Force — RFC 9162: Certificate Transparency Version 2.0[9] — updated specification for publicly auditable append-only logs and cryptographic verification.

---

1. https://www.nist.gov/publications/blockchain-technology-overview?utm_source=chatgpt.com

2. https://www.nist.gov/blockchain?utm_source=chatgpt.com

3. https://ethereum.org/en/developers/docs/smart-contracts/?utm_source=chatgpt.com

4. https://ethereum.org/en/developers/docs/oracles/?utm_source=chatgpt.com

5. https://ethereum.org/en/developers/docs/storage/?utm_source=chatgpt.com

6. https://pages.nist.gov/800-63-4/?utm_source=chatgpt.com

7. https://pages.nist.gov/800-63-4/sp800-63b.html?utm_source=chatgpt.com

8. https://www.rfc-editor.org/rfc/rfc6962?utm_source=chatgpt.com

9. https://www.rfc-editor.org/rfc/rfc9162?utm_source=chatgpt.com

11. Bitcoin Developer Documentation — Blockchain Data[10] — technical documentation explaining Bitcoin's blockchain structure and transaction history.

12. Bitcoin Developer Documentation — Transactions[11] — explanation of transaction structure, signatures, and cryptographic authorization.

13. Bitcoin Developer Documentation — Wallets[12] — technical discussion of wallets and key management concepts relevant to decentralized systems.

14. Cloud Security Alliance — Blockchain and Distributed Ledger Technology Resources[13] — research addressing blockchain security, decentralized systems, and associated risks.

15. OWASP — Smart Contract Security[14] — security research concerning vulnerabilities that can affect smart-contract implementations.

16. OWASP — Threat Modeling[15] — methodology for identifying assets, adversaries, attack surfaces, and system weaknesses.

17. ENISA — Blockchain Technology and Security[16] — European Union cybersecurity research concerning blockchain security and associated risks.

18. ENISA — Distributed Ledger Technology and Cybersecurity[17] — European cybersecurity resources relevant to distributed technologies and trust architectures.

19. ISO — Blockchain and Distributed Ledger Technologies[18] — international standards work concerning blockchain and distributed ledger technology.

20. ISO/TC 307 — Blockchain and Distributed Ledger Technologies[19] — international standardization work covering terminology, architecture, security, privacy, identity, and interoperability.

21. National Archives — Digital Preservation — guidance relevant to the long-term preservation and accessibility of digital information.

22. Library of Congress — Digital Preservation[20] — research and guidance on digital preservation, file formats, metadata, and long-term accessibility.

---

10. https://developer.bitcoin.org/devguide/block_chain.html?utm_source=chatgpt.com

11. https://developer.bitcoin.org/devguide/transactions.html?utm_source=chatgpt.com

12. https://developer.bitcoin.org/devguide/wallets.html?utm_source=chatgpt.com

13. https://cloudsecurityalliance.org/research/working-groups/blockchain?utm_source=chatgpt.com

14. https://owasp.org/www-project-smart-contract-top-10/?utm_source=chatgpt.com

15. https://owasp.org/www-community/Threat_Modeling?utm_source=chatgpt.com

16. https://www.enisa.europa.eu/publications/blockchain-security?utm_source=chatgpt.com

17. https://www.enisa.europa.eu/?utm_source=chatgpt.com

18. https://www.iso.org/committee/6266604.html?utm_source=chatgpt.com

19. https://www.iso.org/committee/6266604.html?utm_source=chatgpt.com

20. https://www.loc.gov/preservation/digital/?utm_source=chatgpt.com

23. Digital Preservation Coalition — Digital Preservation Handbook[21] — professional guidance concerning digital preservation, storage, integrity, and technological obsolescence.

24. W3C — Verifiable Credentials Data Model[22] — technical standard for expressing digitally verifiable credentials and associated claims.

25. W3C — Decentralized Identifiers (DIDs)[23] — technical specification for decentralized identifiers and identity-related architectures.

26. NIST — Privacy Framework[24] — framework for identifying and managing privacy risks associated with information systems.

27. NIST — Cybersecurity Framework 2.0[25] — framework for managing cybersecurity risks, including governance, protection, detection, response, and recovery.

28. CISA — Secure by Design[26] — principles emphasizing security and resilience as properties that should be incorporated into system architecture.

29. Electronic Frontier Foundation — Surveillance Self-Defense[27] — practical resources concerning encryption, authentication, threat modeling, and protection of sensitive communications.

30. Berkeley Protocol on Digital Open Source Investigations — methodological framework for collecting, preserving, verifying, and analyzing digital evidence, particularly relevant when blockchain records are used as one component of a broader evidentiary chain.

---

21. https://www.dpconline.org/handbook?utm_source=chatgpt.com

22. https://www.w3.org/TR/vc-data-model/?utm_source=chatgpt.com

23. https://www.w3.org/TR/did-core/?utm_source=chatgpt.com

24. https://www.nist.gov/privacy-framework?utm_source=chatgpt.com

25. https://www.nist.gov/cyberframework?utm_source=chatgpt.com

26. https://www.cisa.gov/securebydesign?utm_source=chatgpt.com

27. https://ssd.eff.org/?utm_source=chatgpt.com

The Failure Problem: What Happens When the Switch Doesn't Work?

The most important question about a dead man's switch is not how elegantly it can be activated, but what happens when it fails. Every system designed to preserve information after its creator becomes unavailable contains assumptions about electricity, networks, passwords, software, storage, people, timing, and human behavior, and every one of those assumptions can eventually be wrong. A mechanism may be technically impressive and still fail because a battery dies, an account is locked, a recipient cannot be reached, or nobody remembers how the system was supposed to operate. The danger is particularly acute because failure may remain invisible until the exact moment when the system is needed. A dead man's switch therefore has to be designed not merely as an activation mechanism but as a failure-management system. Its reliability depends less upon eliminating every possible failure than upon ensuring that one failure does not destroy the entire chain of protection.

This principle is familiar in safety engineering, aviation, medicine, communications, and critical infrastructure. Engineers rarely assume that a component will operate perfectly forever, because real systems experience faults, degradation, human mistakes, environmental changes, software defects, and unexpected interactions. Instead, important systems are designed with fault tolerance, monitoring, redundancy, maintenance procedures, and recovery mechanisms. The same philosophy applies to information continuity. A creator who possesses information important enough to justify a dead man's switch should assume that something will eventually go wrong. The relevant question then becomes whether the architecture can absorb that failure without losing the evidence or triggering an unintended disclosure. Reliability begins with accepting imperfection.

One of the simplest failure modes is loss of power. A laptop may be left unused until its battery is completely discharged. A phone may become damaged. A physical device may depend upon batteries that eventually leak or expire. A home server may lose electricity. A network device may stop functioning after a power interruption. These failures sound mundane compared with the dramatic circumstances for which a dead man's switch is created, but mundane failures are precisely the ones that can defeat sophisticated plans. The system does not care why the hardware stopped working. If the mechanism depends upon that hardware, the mechanism may simply stop.

Hardware failure introduces another category of risk. Storage drives can fail without warning, memory cards can become corrupted, devices can suffer physical damage, and older interfaces can become obsolete. Solid-state storage is not magically permanent, while mechanical drives have their own failure characteristics. A device stored for years may also become unreadable because the hardware needed to connect it is no longer available. Digital preservation therefore requires thinking beyond the question of whether a file exists. The real question is whether the file will remain accessible, interpretable, and verifiable when someone eventually needs it.

Passwords create an equally serious problem because they combine security with human memory. A strong password can prevent unauthorized access, but if the creator is the only person who knows it, the same protection can prevent legitimate access after death or incapacitation. Password managers can reduce the burden of remembering numerous credentials, but the manager itself becomes another critical dependency. Recovery codes, master credentials, authentication devices, and account-recovery procedures must all be considered. A dead man's switch can therefore fail even when the underlying evidence remains perfectly intact. The information survives physically while becoming inaccessible operationally.

Multifactor authentication can complicate this problem further. Modern security systems may require a password plus a hardware security key, authenticator application, trusted device, biometric factor, or recovery code. These controls can substantially improve account security by making stolen passwords less useful. Yet they can also create additional failure points when the legitimate owner disappears. A recipient may possess the password but not the security key. The security key may exist but be locked behind another credential. The authenticator may reside on a damaged phone. Recovery codes may have been printed but lost. Security mechanisms must therefore be designed with legitimate recovery in mind.

Account lockout is another overlooked problem. Providers may detect unusual activity and temporarily restrict an account. A recipient attempting to access a system after the creator's death may trigger additional security controls because the access pattern is unfamiliar. Some services may require identity verification that only the original account holder can complete. Others may have formal procedures for deceased users that vary considerably between providers and jurisdictions. A system that assumes an account will remain permanently accessible is therefore making an assumption about a third party's policies. That assumption may eventually become false.

Service shutdown presents an even more fundamental problem. Companies fail, applications disappear, products are discontinued, and services change their technical architecture. A creator may establish an automated disclosure system that works perfectly for several years before the provider announces that the service is being retired. If nobody notices, the system can quietly become useless. This is one reason why long-term digital preservation requires periodic review rather than one-time setup. A system that is never tested may be a system that no longer exists. Technological continuity must be actively maintained.

Software updates can produce subtler failures. A provider may change an authentication mechanism. An operating system may stop supporting an old application. An encryption library may become obsolete. A file format may become difficult to open. An automated integration may break because an application programming interface has changed. None of these events requires malicious interference. The system simply drifts away from the environment in which it was originally created. Long-lived information systems must therefore anticipate technological obsolescence. Preservation is partly the discipline of moving information forward without destroying its evidentiary integrity.

Corrupted files create another challenge because corruption may remain invisible until access is attempted. A file may appear to exist while portions of its underlying data have become unreadable. A backup may faithfully reproduce a corrupted file, creating multiple copies of the same damaged evidence. This is why redundancy should not mean merely making duplicates. Good preservation involves independent copies, verification, and periodic integrity checking. If the same error propagates through every backup, apparent redundancy provides little protection. True resilience requires some degree of independence between copies.

The difference between redundancy and duplication is therefore fundamental. If five copies of an archive are stored on the same failing device, there are not five independent safety nets. If five copies are stored through the same account and protected by the same password, they may all disappear when that credential becomes inaccessible. If five recipients depend upon one cloud provider, they may all be affected by the same service outage. Redundancy becomes meaningful when failures are sufficiently independent. Independence can involve different storage media, different locations, different providers, different custodians, and different access mechanisms.

Yet redundancy introduces its own management problems. More copies mean more opportunities for outdated versions to circulate. More custodians mean more people who might mishandle sensitive information. More credentials mean more secrets to protect. More systems mean more maintenance. More geographic locations mean more complexity. A poorly designed redundant architecture can therefore become harder to secure than the original system. The goal is not maximum duplication. The goal is sufficient diversity to prevent common failures from producing catastrophic loss.

False triggers are perhaps the most dangerous failure mode because the system may work exactly as designed while producing the wrong result. Imagine a mechanism that interprets a missed check-in as evidence that the creator is no longer able to communicate. The creator travels somewhere without reliable Internet access, loses a phone, or becomes temporarily unable to access an account. The system interprets the silence as activation. If the resulting action is merely a reminder, the consequences may be minor. If the system immediately releases sensitive information publicly, the consequences may be irreversible.

This is why a missed signal should not automatically be treated as proof of death or disappearance. Silence is an ambiguous event. It has many possible causes. A sophisticated system should distinguish between a trigger condition and a confirmed circumstance. A trigger can begin an escalation process without immediately producing the final consequence. This allows time for correction. It also recognizes that humans sometimes fail to follow their own procedures.

Grace periods are therefore more than a convenience. They are a form of error tolerance. A system can provide an opportunity for the creator or a designated custodian to cancel or verify an activation before irreversible disclosure occurs. The longer the grace period, the greater the opportunity to correct accidental triggers, but the greater the delay if an actual emergency has occurred. The appropriate balance depends upon the nature of the information and the urgency involved. There is no universal interval that makes every system safe.

Conditional logic can also reduce false activation. Instead of requiring one condition, a system can require several independent conditions before progressing. For example, a missed confirmation might generate a warning, while a second condition might be required before a custodian is notified. Another condition could be required before access is granted. The advantage is that a single failure is less likely to cause catastrophic consequences. The disadvantage is additional complexity. Every added condition is another component that can fail.

Human error remains one of the most persistent sources of failure. People forget. They misunderstand instructions. They change devices. They mistype addresses. They misplace recovery codes. They fail to update contact information. They assume someone else has checked the system. They create elaborate procedures and then become too busy to maintain them. None of these mistakes reflects stupidity. They reflect the ordinary limitations of human attention. A serious safety architecture must therefore assume that competent people will occasionally make ordinary mistakes.

The problem becomes more severe when instructions are written for a future recipient who does not share the creator's background. The creator may know exactly what every folder means. They may understand the significance of cryptographic keys, filenames, timestamps, or obscure references. A future custodian may see only an apparently confusing collection of files. This is why documentation is itself part of preservation. The system needs enough contextual information to explain what the recipient has received without exposing unnecessary secrets. A perfectly preserved archive can still fail if nobody understands it.

Recipient failure can also occur because the recipient is simply unavailable. A family member may move. A journalist may retire. A lawyer may change firms. An investigator may die. An organization may dissolve. An email address may disappear. A telephone number may be reassigned. A recipient who was highly reliable when selected may become unreliable through no fault of their own. Long-term systems must therefore account for turnover. The identity of a custodian should not necessarily remain fixed forever if the surrounding circumstances change.

This makes succession planning important. A creator can conceptually distinguish between a primary recipient and a secondary recipient, allowing responsibility to move if the first person becomes unavailable. Professional organizations may already have internal succession procedures, while individuals may need to establish their own. The underlying principle is simple: a contingency plan should itself have a contingency plan. If one person becomes the only gateway to the information, the system has created a new single point of failure. A dead man's switch should not merely transfer dependence from the creator to one substitute.

Legal and institutional changes can also disrupt a system. A service provider may change its policies. A custodian may become subject to a legal order. A company may be acquired. An organization may change its mission. A government may enact new requirements affecting data storage or disclosure. A system created under one legal environment may eventually operate under another. This does not mean that every future legal change can be predicted. It means that long-term planning should recognize law as an evolving dependency rather than a fixed background condition.

Compromise is another failure mode. An attacker may obtain access to an account, discover the existence of the archive, steal credentials, or manipulate the mechanism responsible for activation. The objective may be to obtain the information before disclosure, prevent disclosure, or trigger disclosure at an advantageous moment. A system designed only around accidental failure may therefore remain vulnerable to deliberate interference. Threat modeling should consider both availability and confidentiality. Protecting the information means protecting the system that controls access to it.

Compromise can also occur through trusted insiders. A custodian may misuse their authority. A recipient may disclose information prematurely. Someone close to the creator may pressure a custodian. A professional intermediary may have a conflict of interest. This is why distributing responsibility can sometimes be preferable to concentrating it. No individual should necessarily possess more authority than their role requires. The principle of least privilege, widely used in cybersecurity, is relevant here because limiting unnecessary access can reduce the consequences of compromise.

Decoy information introduces a different category of complexity. A creator may attempt to conceal the existence of the genuine archive by maintaining false locations or harmless material. This can theoretically complicate unauthorized discovery. But decoys can also confuse legitimate recipients. If the creator dies without explaining the architecture, custodians may waste time investigating false leads while the genuine information remains inaccessible. A defensive mechanism that depends upon the creator personally explaining its deception may fail precisely when the creator is unavailable. Complexity must therefore be balanced against recoverability.

The same concern applies to steganography and concealed information. Hidden information may be useful under certain circumstances, but hidden information that nobody knows how to locate can become lost information. Preservation requires discoverability by authorized people. Security is not equivalent to maximum concealment. If the legitimate custodian cannot distinguish the genuine archive from irrelevant material, the system has protected the information from everyone, including those it was designed to help. The architecture must therefore define a controlled path to discovery.

Cryptographic failure deserves particular attention because encryption is often treated as an absolute solution. Encryption can be extraordinarily effective when correctly implemented, but it introduces a dependency on keys. If the key is destroyed, forgotten, corrupted, or inaccessible, the ciphertext may become effectively useless. If the key is copied and exposed, confidentiality may be lost. If the encryption algorithm eventually becomes vulnerable, protection may weaken. The creator therefore needs to think about both key survival and cryptographic longevity. The objective is not simply to encrypt the archive but to ensure that authorized access remains possible in the future.

Key escrow and distributed key arrangements can address some of these problems, but they also create new trust relationships. If a third party holds a recovery key, that party becomes important to the system. If several people hold fragments, coordination becomes necessary. If a threshold is required and too many participants disappear, recovery may fail. Every recovery mechanism therefore has its own failure modes. The correct question is not whether recovery exists but whether the recovery design remains functional under realistic adverse conditions.

Another common mistake is assuming that cloud storage constitutes a backup. A cloud copy can be valuable, but synchronization is not necessarily backup. If a file is accidentally deleted and the deletion synchronizes across devices, multiple synchronized copies may disappear together. If ransomware encrypts an account and synchronized systems reproduce the encrypted files, redundancy can collapse. A backup should therefore have some degree of historical separation and protection from the primary environment. The principle of independent recovery matters more than simply having multiple copies.

Offline archives provide a useful counterbalance. A disconnected storage device can be insulated from certain online attacks. A physical archive can survive an Internet outage. Paper records can remain readable without specialized software, although they have their own vulnerabilities. But offline storage is not automatically permanent. Physical media can degrade. Storage environments can become unsuitable. Devices can be lost or stolen. A forgotten archive can become inaccessible. Offline preservation therefore solves some problems while creating others.

Geographic separation is another form of resilience. If all copies of an archive are stored in the same building, one fire, flood, theft, or other disaster can destroy them simultaneously. Separating copies can reduce correlated physical risk. Yet geography also introduces custodial and logistical complications. A remote archive may become inaccessible. A custodian may relocate. A jurisdiction may impose restrictions. The principle remains useful, but it must be incorporated into a broader architecture. Geographic diversity is one layer, not a complete solution.

Communication failure can be just as damaging as storage failure. The archive may survive while the notification mechanism fails. An email may bounce. A phone number may be disconnected. A messaging platform may experience an outage. A recipient may ignore an unfamiliar message because they suspect phishing. This means that the system should distinguish between evidence preservation and notification. They should not necessarily depend upon the same infrastructure. If one communication channel fails, another may still function.

Authentication problems can make legitimate messages look fraudulent. A recipient receiving an unexpected encrypted archive from an unfamiliar account may reasonably assume it is malicious. A creator can reduce this problem through prior communication, documented verification procedures, and independent authentication methods. The recipient needs a way to determine that the message is genuine without relying solely upon the message itself. This is especially important when the system activates after a long period during which the creator has not been communicating normally. Trust must be engineered into the process.

Phishing represents the inverse problem. Attackers may imitate legitimate communications to trick custodians into surrendering credentials. A recipient who knows that a dead man's switch exists may become a particularly attractive target because the archive could contain valuable or sensitive information. Security awareness therefore remains important even after the technical architecture is established. Recipients should know how legitimate instructions are authenticated. They should know which channels are expected. They should be cautious about unexpected requests for passwords or keys. The human recipient remains part of the security perimeter.

Testing is the best defense against many of these failures. A system should not be considered operational simply because it was configured successfully once. The creator should periodically verify that messages can still be sent, archives can still be opened, credentials work, recipients remain reachable, and backups remain intact. Test procedures should avoid exposing sensitive information unnecessarily. The objective is to verify function without creating new risks. Regular testing turns an assumed system into a demonstrated system.

Testing should also include failure simulations. What happens if the primary email account becomes inaccessible? What happens if the main recipient cannot be contacted? What happens if the encryption key is lost? What happens if the cloud provider is unavailable? What happens if the creator misses several scheduled confirmations? What happens if a custodian receives the notification but cannot open the archive? These questions can reveal weaknesses that ordinary operational testing misses. A system is often best understood by examining how it behaves when something goes wrong.

Documentation of the testing process can create an additional layer of confidence. A record can show when a backup was last verified, when recipient details were updated, and when access procedures were tested. This creates an operational history rather than relying upon memory. It also helps future custodians understand how the system was maintained. The record itself should be protected because it may reveal information about the architecture. Documentation is therefore another asset requiring appropriate security.

Maintenance should also include deliberate retirement. Some systems should not operate indefinitely. A creator may decide that an archive is no longer necessary. A recipient may become unsuitable. A technology may become insecure. A legal situation may change. The ability to deactivate or replace obsolete components is part of responsible design. A system that cannot be safely retired can become a liability. Continuity includes knowing when not to continue.

The possibility of changed intentions is particularly important. A person may create a dead man's switch during a period of intense fear and later decide that disclosure would be inappropriate. If the mechanism is completely automatic and irreversible, the creator may be unable to correct the decision. A system that provides controlled cancellation or review can accommodate changing circumstances. This is another reason why immediate irreversible publication should not necessarily be the default. Human intentions evolve.

The failure problem also reveals why a dead man's switch should never be treated as an act of technological faith. No application, blockchain, encrypted drive, cloud service, or automated agent can guarantee survival. Each technology has an operating environment. Each depends upon assumptions. Each has failure modes. The objective is not to find the one perfect technology but to construct an architecture in which failures are expected and contained. Reliability emerges from relationships between components rather than from the supposed perfection of one component.

The strongest architecture therefore resembles a series of concentric safeguards. Evidence exists in more than one location. Access does not depend upon one credential. Notification does not depend upon one communication channel. Responsibility does not depend upon one person. Activation does not depend upon one ambiguous signal. Technology does not operate without appropriate human oversight. Each layer reduces the consequences of another layer failing. This is the essence of resilience.

There is also an important distinction between preventing failure and detecting failure. Prevention attempts to stop something from going wrong. Detection identifies when something has gone wrong. Recovery attempts to restore function afterward. A dead man's switch needs all three. Encryption can help prevent unauthorized access. Monitoring can reveal that a service has stopped operating. Independent backups can permit recovery. No single measure replaces the others. A resilient system assumes that prevention will eventually fail and prepares for detection and recovery.

The ultimate lesson is that the most dangerous failure may be the one nobody knows about. A broken mechanism that announces its failure can be repaired. A broken mechanism that silently appears functional can create false confidence. A creator may believe that their evidence is protected when the account has already expired, the backup has become corrupted, or the recipient can no longer be reached. Silent failure is therefore particularly important to detect. Systems designed for high-consequence situations should favor verifiability over assumption.

The dead man's switch is ultimately a promise made to the future. It says that information important enough to preserve should not depend entirely upon the physical survival of one person. But that promise can be broken by surprisingly ordinary things: a forgotten password, a dead battery, an obsolete application, a corrupted file, an unavailable recipient, or a mistaken interpretation of silence. These are not peripheral technical details. They are the central engineering problem. A system that survives only under ideal conditions is not a safety system at all.

The mature approach is therefore to design for failure from the beginning. Assume the password will be forgotten. Assume a service will eventually change. Assume one recipient will become unavailable. Assume one copy will become corrupted. Assume one communication channel will fail. Assume that a human being will misunderstand an instruction. Then ask whether the remaining architecture can still preserve the essential information and route it toward an appropriate decision-maker. If the answer is yes, the system has resilience. If the answer is no, the system has merely postponed its failure.

A dead man's switch does not become trustworthy because it never fails. It becomes trustworthy when its designer understands how it can fail and builds enough independent protection around those weaknesses that failure in one place does not become failure everywhere. That principle transforms the switch from a dramatic technological device into something more useful: a carefully engineered continuity system. The objective is not certainty, because certainty is impossible. The objective is to make the survival of important information substantially more likely than its disappearance, while making accidental disclosure substantially less likely than deliberate and justified release. In the end, resilience is not the absence of failure but the ability to survive it.

Resources

1. NIST Cybersecurity Framework 2.0[1] — framework for managing cybersecurity risk through governance, identification, protection, detection, response, and recovery.

2. NIST Special Publication 800-34 — Contingency Planning Guide for Federal Information Systems[2] — foundational guidance on contingency planning, system recovery, redundancy, and continuity.

1. https://www.nist.gov/cyberframework?utm_source=chatgpt.com

2. https://csrc.nist.gov/publications/detail/sp/800-34/rev-1/final?utm_source=chatgpt.com

3. NIST Special Publication 800-53 — Security and Privacy Controls[3] — extensive catalog of controls covering contingency planning, access control, authentication, system integrity, and resilience.

4. NIST Special Publication 800-57 — Recommendation for Key Management — authoritative guidance on cryptographic key protection, backup, recovery, compromise, and lifecycle management.

5. NIST Special Publication 800-63B — Authentication and Authenticator Management[4] — guidance on authentication, authenticators, recovery, and account-security considerations.

6. NIST Special Publication 800-61 — Computer Security Incident Handling Guide[5] — guidance concerning preparation, detection, response, and recovery from security incidents.

7. NIST Special Publication 800-160 — Systems Security Engineering — systems-engineering principles relevant to resilience, trustworthy architecture, risk management, and life-cycle security.

8. NIST Special Publication 800-160 Volume 2 — Developing Cyber-Resilient Systems — detailed treatment of cyber resilience, including anticipation, withstanding, recovery, and adaptation.

9. NIST Special Publication 800-184 — Guide for Cybersecurity Event Recovery[6] — guidance concerning recovery planning and restoring systems after disruptive cybersecurity events.

10. NIST Special Publication 800-209 — Security Guidelines for Storage Infrastructure — guidance concerning storage security, availability, integrity, access, and resilience.

11. NIST Special Publication 800-88 — Guidelines for Media Sanitization[7] — guidance relevant to the secure lifecycle and disposal of digital storage media.

12. NIST Special Publication 800-30 — Guide for Conducting Risk Assessments[8] — methodology for identifying threats, vulnerabilities, likelihood, and consequences.

13. OWASP — Threat Modeling[9] — methodology for understanding assets, threats, attack surfaces, and mitigations.

14. OWASP — Authentication Cheat Sheet[10] — practical guidance concerning authentication, account security, and common authentication weaknesses.

15. OWASP — Multifactor Authentication Cheat Sheet[11] — guidance on multifactor authentication and associated implementation considerations.

---

3. https://csrc.nist.gov/publications/detail/sp/800-53/rev-5/final?utm_source=chatgpt.com

4. https://pages.nist.gov/800-63-4/sp800-63b.html?utm_source=chatgpt.com

5. https://csrc.nist.gov/publications/detail/sp/800-61/rev-2/final?utm_source=chatgpt.com

6. https://csrc.nist.gov/publications/detail/sp/800-184/final?utm_source=chatgpt.com

7. https://csrc.nist.gov/publications/detail/sp/800-88/rev-1/final?utm_source=chatgpt.com

8. https://csrc.nist.gov/publications/detail/sp/800-30/rev-1/final?utm_source=chatgpt.com

9. https://owasp.org/www-community/Threat_Modeling?utm_source=chatgpt.com

10. https://cheatsheetseries.owasp.org/cheatsheets/Authentication_Cheat_Sheet.html?utm_source=chatgpt.com

11. https://cheatsheetseries.owasp.org/cheatsheets/Multifactor_Authentication_Cheat_Sheet.html?utm_source=chatgpt.com

16. Electronic Frontier Foundation — Surveillance Self-Defense[12] — practical resources on threat modeling, account security, encryption, authentication, and protecting sensitive information.

17. CISA — Cybersecurity Best Practices[13] — U.S. government guidance on account protection, resilience, incident preparation, and cybersecurity practices.

18. CISA — Secure by Design[14] — principles emphasizing that security, resilience, and failure considerations should be incorporated into system design.

19. ISO 22301 — Security and Resilience: Business Continuity Management Systems[15] — international standard concerning organizational continuity, disruption planning, and recovery.

20. ISO/IEC 27001 — Information Security Management Systems[16] — international framework for managing information-security risks and maintaining appropriate controls.

21. ISO/IEC 27002 — Information Security Controls[17] — guidance concerning access management, cryptography, operational security, backup, and resilience controls.

22. National Archives — Digital Preservation — resources concerning preservation, authenticity, accessibility, and long-term digital information management.

23. Library of Congress — Digital Preservation[18] — resources concerning digital preservation, storage, file formats, metadata, and long-term accessibility.

24. Digital Preservation Coalition — Digital Preservation Handbook[19] — professional guidance on preservation planning, storage, integrity, technological obsolescence, and continuity.

25. Internet Engineering Task Force — RFC 4949: Internet Security Glossary[20] — standardized terminology for security concepts including authentication, availability, integrity, threats, and vulnerabilities.

26. Internet Engineering Task Force — RFC 8446: TLS 1.3[21] — technical standard relevant to secure communications and protection against network-level interception.

27. NIST — Cryptographic Standards and Guidelines[22] — current cryptographic standards and guidance relevant to long-term protection and algorithm selection.

---

12. https://ssd.eff.org/?utm_source=chatgpt.com

13. https://www.cisa.gov/topics/cybersecurity-best-practices?utm_source=chatgpt.com

14. https://www.cisa.gov/securebydesign?utm_source=chatgpt.com

15. https://www.iso.org/standard/75106.html?utm_source=chatgpt.com

16. https://www.iso.org/isoiec-27001-information-security.html?utm_source=chatgpt.com

17. https://www.iso.org/standard/75652.html?utm_source=chatgpt.com

18. https://www.loc.gov/preservation/digital/?utm_source=chatgpt.com

19. https://www.dpconline.org/handbook?utm_source=chatgpt.com

20. https://www.rfc-editor.org/rfc/rfc4949?utm_source=chatgpt.com

21. https://www.rfc-editor.org/rfc/rfc8446?utm_source=chatgpt.com

22. https://csrc.nist.gov/projects/cryptographic-standards-and-guidelines?utm_source=chatgpt.com

28. National Institute of Standards and Technology — Secure Software Development Framework[23] — practices for reducing software vulnerabilities throughout the development lifecycle.

29. NIST — Cybersecurity Supply Chain Risk Management[24] — guidance concerning dependencies on external technologies, suppliers, and service providers.

30. Berkeley Protocol on Digital Open Source Investigations — methodological guidance for preserving, authenticating, documenting, and assessing digital information as evidence.

---

23. https://csrc.nist.gov/Projects/ssdf?utm_source=chatgpt.com

24. https://csrc.nist.gov/Projects/cyber-supply-chain-risk-management?utm_source=chatgpt.com

When Disclosure Becomes a Crime

There is a dangerous assumption hiding inside the idea of a dead man's switch: if information is important enough to preserve, then releasing it must automatically be justified. That assumption is understandable, particularly when the information concerns corruption, abuse, criminal conduct, institutional misconduct, or threats to the public. But importance and legality are not the same thing. A person may possess information of enormous public significance and still violate the law by obtaining it improperly, transmitting it to an unauthorized recipient, publishing protected personal information, revealing classified material, or disclosing confidential commercial information. The legal system may also distinguish sharply between reporting wrongdoing through a protected channel and making the same material available to the entire world. A responsible dead man's switch therefore has to confront the uncomfortable possibility that the truth can matter profoundly while the manner of disclosure remains legally consequential.

The first distinction is between information and disclosure. Simply possessing a document does not necessarily create the same legal consequences as publishing it. Giving information to a lawyer may be treated differently from giving it to a journalist. Providing evidence to a competent investigative authority may be treated differently from posting it anonymously on the Internet. Sending a classified document to an unauthorized person may create a different offense from reporting the existence of the classified program without revealing the protected document itself. These distinctions are highly dependent upon jurisdiction and circumstance. A system designed for serious information protection must therefore identify the intended pathway rather than treating "release" as a single event.

Classification is among the clearest examples. Governments classify certain information because they believe unauthorized disclosure could damage national security or other protected interests. Classification systems differ between countries, and the legal consequences of mishandling classified information vary accordingly. In the United States, for example, the federal classification framework distinguishes among Confidential, Secret, and Top Secret levels, while separate statutes and regulations govern particular categories of protected information. The existence of a classification marking is therefore significant, but it does not by itself answer every legal question surrounding the material. Classification must be considered alongside the circumstances in which the information was obtained, possessed, transmitted, and disclosed.

A particularly important distinction is between classified information and information that is merely embarrassing or politically damaging. A government may classify information for legitimate national-security reasons, but classification should not be casually treated as synonymous with proof of wrongdoing. Conversely, the fact that a document is classified does not necessarily mean that every disclosure involving it is automatically justified or automatically criminal in every conceivable circumstance. Different legal systems establish different rules. Some protections concern the information itself, some concern the person's employment or access authorization, and some concern the method of disclosure. A serious analysis must therefore avoid both extremes: treating classification as proof of corruption and treating classification as proof that disclosure can never be legitimate.

The United States provides an especially complicated example because its legal framework does not contain a single comprehensive "official secrets act" covering all classified information in the manner found in some other countries. Instead, various statutes can apply to particular categories of information and conduct, while executive orders and regulations govern classification and handling. The Espionage Act, for example, contains provisions concerning national-defense information, while other statutes address specific protected categories. The result is a legal environment in which the precise nature of the information and the conduct involved can matter enormously.

Anyone contemplating disclosure of national-security information therefore needs qualified legal advice rather than assumptions derived from popular culture.

National-security law also illustrates why a dead man's switch can create an unintended legal problem. A creator might believe that an automated system merely preserves information until an emergency occurs. But if the system automatically transmits protected material to unauthorized recipients, the creator may have created a mechanism for deliberate disclosure rather than merely a backup. Automation does not necessarily remove responsibility for the underlying act. A computer executing instructions does not make the consequences disappear. The legal system can still examine who created the mechanism, what they intended, what information was involved, and who ultimately received it.

Whistleblower law introduces another important distinction. Whistleblower protections exist in many jurisdictions to protect certain people who report wrongdoing through designated channels. These protections can address retaliation, dismissal, discrimination, or other adverse employment actions. They may apply differently depending upon whether the report concerns public-sector misconduct, private-sector misconduct, securities violations, fraud, health and safety, environmental violations, or other regulated subjects. Protection may also depend upon whether the person followed particular reporting procedures. A whistleblower protection law should therefore never be interpreted as a universal license to disclose anything to anyone.

In the United States, the Whistleblower Protection Act and related statutes provide important protections for certain federal employees and other categories of workers, while specialized laws protect particular types of reporting. The False Claims Act, securities laws, and various sector-specific statutes can create additional reporting mechanisms or protections. The legal landscape is fragmented because different forms of wrongdoing are governed by different statutory regimes. A person may therefore have strong protection for one kind of report and little or no protection for another. The existence of a whistleblower system does not eliminate the need to understand which system actually applies.

The difference between protected reporting and unrestricted publication is particularly important. A whistleblower may be entitled to report misconduct to an inspector general, regulator, law-enforcement agency, designated congressional body, or other authorized recipient. That does not necessarily mean the person can legally publish the underlying records on a public website. The legal system may protect the act of reporting while imposing restrictions on unauthorized dissemination. This distinction should be built into the conceptual design of a dead man's switch. The safest destination for sensitive information may be an institution capable of evaluating it rather than the entire public.

Trade secrets create a different problem because they concern privately held information rather than government secrets. Under U.S. law, the federal Defend Trade Secrets Act provides a civil cause of action for misappropriation of trade secrets under specified conditions. State laws also play an important role. Trade-secret protection generally concerns information that derives economic value from not being generally known and that is subject to reasonable efforts to maintain secrecy. The mere fact that information is confidential inside a company does not automatically make every disclosure a criminal offense. But unauthorized acquisition, use, or disclosure can create serious legal consequences.

The law also recognizes an important public-policy tension involving whistleblowing and trade secrets. U.S. federal law contains an immunity provision protecting certain disclosures of trade-secret information when made confidentially to government officials or attorneys for the purpose of reporting or investigating suspected violations of law, as well as certain disclosures in legal proceedings under specified conditions. This is a good illustration of the principle that the legal system may distinguish between responsible reporting and unrestricted publication. The same information can therefore present very different legal issues depending upon who receives it, why it is disclosed, and how the disclosure occurs.

Privacy law introduces another layer. Evidence may contain names, addresses, medical information, financial records, photographs, private correspondence, employment records, or intimate personal details concerning people who have nothing to do with the underlying wrongdoing. A creator who wants to expose corruption may unintentionally expose innocent individuals as well. The legal and ethical consequences can be significant. Privacy is not merely an obstacle placed in the way of truth. It is a recognition that people other than the alleged wrongdoer can be harmed by indiscriminate disclosure. Responsible disclosure therefore requires distinguishing evidence relevant to the allegation from unrelated personal information.

Data-protection regimes can be especially complicated because they may regulate the collection, processing, storage, transfer, and disclosure of personal information. The European Union's General Data Protection Regulation, for example, establishes a comprehensive framework for processing personal data and includes specific provisions concerning freedom of expression and information. Other jurisdictions have their own privacy statutes and exemptions. A dead man's switch operating internationally may therefore encounter multiple overlapping legal frameworks. Geographic distribution does not necessarily eliminate legal exposure. It can multiply the number of legal systems that must be considered.

Defamation creates another difficult boundary. A creator may possess information that appears to prove misconduct, but publishing an accusation as fact can create legal exposure if the underlying claim is false or insufficiently supported. Defamation law varies significantly between jurisdictions, particularly concerning public figures, standards of fault, defenses, and available remedies. In some systems, truth is a fundamental defense, but proving truth can itself require substantial evidence. Opinions, factual assertions, implications, and allegations can also be treated differently depending upon the jurisdiction. A dead man's switch should therefore preserve evidence, not merely conclusions.

This is one reason evidentiary discipline matters so much. A statement saying that someone committed a crime is not equivalent to a document showing that a particular transaction occurred. A photograph is not necessarily proof of the circumstances surrounding the photograph. A recording may be authentic while its interpretation remains disputed. An anonymous allegation is not equivalent to corroborated testimony. The stronger the potential legal consequences, the more important it becomes to preserve original material and its context. The purpose of a dead man's switch should be to preserve the ability to investigate, not to substitute the creator's conclusions for investigation.

Copyright and intellectual property law can also become relevant. Documents, photographs, recordings, software, technical drawings, and publications may be protected by copyright or other intellectual-property rights. A person may possess a copy without owning the copyright. Publishing that material can therefore raise questions separate from whether the information itself is true. Copyright law also contains doctrines such as fair use in the United States, but fair use is highly contextual and is not a universal permission to republish entire archives. Other jurisdictions use different exceptions and limitations.

The distinction between information and expression is particularly useful here. Facts themselves may not receive copyright protection in the same way as original expressive works. But the document containing those facts may still be protected. A creator who possesses a corporate report, for example, may have evidence of important facts without automatically acquiring unrestricted rights to publish the report in full. Responsible disclosure may sometimes involve describing the relevant information, providing necessary excerpts, or supplying the material to an appropriate investigative party. The precise legal analysis depends upon the jurisdiction and circumstances.

Attorney-client privilege introduces another boundary. Lawyers may receive sensitive information under legal confidentiality obligations, but privilege generally protects certain communications between attorney and client rather than automatically transforming every document given to a lawyer into privileged material. A person cannot necessarily shield preexisting evidence from disclosure simply by handing it to an attorney. At the same time, a lawyer may provide an important channel for evaluating legal risks before information is released. The distinction between legal advice and evidentiary custody therefore matters. A lawyer can be a valuable intermediary without being a magic legal shield.

Journalistic source protection creates a related but distinct framework. Investigative journalists often have professional practices designed to protect sources and evaluate evidence. Some jurisdictions also recognize legal protections for journalistic sources, while others provide weaker or more conditional protections. Even where strong source protections exist, they may not provide absolute immunity from every legal demand. Journalists must also consider defamation, privacy, national-security restrictions, evidentiary standards, and editorial responsibility. Sending sensitive information to a journalist is therefore not equivalent to placing it outside the law.

This is one reason professional media can sometimes be a more appropriate recipient than anonymous public publication. An established investigative organization may have lawyers, editors, fact-checkers, security specialists, and procedures for corroborating claims. It may also understand the consequences of publishing sensitive material. None of this guarantees responsible reporting. Journalists can make mistakes, organizations can disagree about publication, and legal restrictions can vary. But professional review can provide an important layer between raw evidence and irreversible public dissemination.

The legal concept of prior restraint also deserves careful distinction from subsequent liability. In some legal systems, governments face significant restrictions on preventing publication before it occurs, while people may still face legal consequences after publication under certain laws. The United States has particularly strong constitutional protections for freedom of the press, but those protections coexist with laws concerning classified information, privacy, intellectual property, defamation, and other interests. The existence of a constitutional right to publish does not mean that every publication is immune from legal consequences. Constitutional protections must be understood within the broader legal framework.

The phrase "public interest" is equally susceptible to misunderstanding. Something can be interesting to the public without being genuinely in the public interest. The private life of an uninvolved individual may attract enormous attention without contributing meaningfully to accountability. Conversely, information about serious misconduct may have substantial public value even if it is embarrassing to powerful people. Professional journalists and courts often distinguish these concepts in different ways. A responsible dead man's switch should make the same conceptual distinction.

National-security information creates perhaps the sharpest tension between public interest and legal restriction. A document may reveal government wrongdoing while simultaneously containing information that could endanger intelligence sources, military capabilities, diplomatic relationships, or individuals. The solution is not always complete secrecy or complete publication. Redaction, controlled disclosure, secure review, and staged publication can sometimes preserve the accountability value while reducing unnecessary harm. The creator should therefore avoid assuming that the only choices are "hide everything" and "publish everything." There is often a much wider range of responsible disclosure options.

This is where proportionality becomes useful as a decision principle. The question is not merely whether information is important but whether the proposed disclosure is proportionate to the legitimate objective. Does the recipient need the entire archive? Are certain personal details irrelevant? Can a claim be independently verified? Can sensitive identities be protected? Is immediate publication necessary? Could an authorized investigative body examine the evidence first? These questions do not produce universal legal answers, but they encourage disciplined thinking. They also reduce the possibility that a dead man's switch becomes an instrument of indiscriminate exposure.

Evidence preservation itself can be legally significant. Maintaining original files, metadata, timestamps, correspondence, and contextual records can help investigators determine what happened. Altering or selectively editing material can undermine credibility. In some circumstances, destroying or concealing evidence can create additional legal problems. The safest general principle is therefore preservation rather than manipulation. The creator should preserve original material and clearly distinguish it from copies, annotations, interpretations, and summaries. A future investigator should be able to see what was originally received or created.

Chain of custody can become important when information may eventually be used in legal proceedings. Investigators need to understand where evidence came from, who possessed it, how it was stored, and whether it may have been altered. Digital evidence presents additional challenges because copying a file can change metadata or create uncertainty about provenance. Cryptographic hashes, forensic imaging, access logs, and documented handling procedures can help establish continuity. But even technical evidence requires contextual interpretation. A hash can demonstrate that two files match; it cannot explain why the file exists.

There is also a crucial distinction between lawful whistleblowing and theft. A person may discover wrongdoing while legitimately accessing information as part of their employment. Another person may break into a system to obtain evidence of alleged misconduct. The public importance of the information does not automatically legalize the method by which it was acquired. Computer misuse laws, trespass laws, theft statutes, confidentiality agreements, and other rules may apply. This is another reason why a dead man's switch should not be understood as a justification for obtaining information through unlawful means.

The same principle applies to hacking. Someone might argue that accessing a compromised system is justified because it contains evidence of corruption. But unauthorized access can create independent legal consequences and can also contaminate evidence. The fact that a person believes their objective is morally justified does not necessarily create legal authorization. Responsible investigative practices emphasize lawful acquisition wherever possible. A dead man's switch should preserve legitimately obtained information rather than encourage illegal collection.

Jurisdiction makes almost every aspect of this subject more complicated. Information can be stored in one country, controlled by a person in another, transmitted through infrastructure located elsewhere, and ultimately published to a global audience. Different countries may have different rules concerning privacy, national security, trade secrets, defamation, data transfer, and journalistic privilege. A decentralized network can further complicate the question of where an act legally occurred. The international nature of modern technology does not create a single international law of disclosure. Instead, it creates overlapping legal systems.

This is why the idea of "putting it on the blockchain" is not a legal solution. Recording a document's fingerprint on a distributed ledger may provide useful technical evidence of integrity or existence. It does not make the underlying disclosure lawful. Nor does distributing encrypted fragments across countries automatically immunize the creator or recipients from legal obligations. Technology can change the physical and technical architecture of information. It does not repeal national legislation. Legal responsibility remains a separate layer.

The existence of a dead man's switch can itself become relevant to intent. If someone deliberately establishes an automated mechanism to release protected information after their death, investigators may examine what they intended, what information they selected, and whom they intended to receive it. The precise legal significance will vary dramatically. Intent can matter in criminal law, civil litigation, employment disputes, and regulatory proceedings. A carefully documented purpose may help explain the creator's motives, but documentation does not guarantee legal protection. The system should therefore not be designed around the assumption that automation obscures responsibility.

There is also an ethical distinction between truth and harm. Some information may be accurate but unnecessary to disclose. A report about institutional corruption might contain the home addresses of employees who played no role in the misconduct. A scientific dataset might contain identifiable information about research participants. A financial archive might expose innocent customers. A military document might identify people whose safety depends upon confidentiality. Publishing everything because everything is available can cause harm that has nothing to do with accountability. Responsible disclosure requires separating relevant evidence from collateral information.

Redaction can therefore be a legitimate part of responsible disclosure. A recipient may determine that names, account numbers, medical information, contact details, or operational information should be removed before publication. Redaction must itself be done carefully because poorly redacted digital documents can sometimes retain hidden information. The broader principle is that disclosure should reveal what is necessary for the legitimate purpose while minimizing unnecessary exposure. A dead man's switch should ideally preserve the complete archive while allowing professional recipients to determine what portion should become public. Preservation and publication do not have to be identical.

A particularly important safeguard is staged disclosure. Instead of releasing the entire archive immediately, the system can first notify a designated professional recipient that the archive exists. The recipient can then verify the material, assess legal restrictions, contact relevant parties, and determine whether publication is appropriate. Additional disclosure can occur after that review. This approach does not eliminate risk, but it creates opportunities for correction. It also recognizes that evidence often becomes more useful when contextualized.

There are circumstances, however, in which delay may itself be harmful. If information concerns an immediate threat to public safety, waiting indefinitely for perfect verification may allow harm to continue. The challenge is to balance urgency against accuracy. Emergency reporting channels may exist precisely because ordinary investigative timelines are too slow. A dead man's switch intended for high-risk circumstances should therefore distinguish between ordinary disclosure and emergency notification. Again, this is primarily a question of judgment rather than technology.

The creator also needs to distinguish between a legal prohibition and a legal risk. Some disclosures may clearly violate a statute. Others may fall within uncertain areas where litigation is possible but the legal outcome is difficult to predict. Still others may be lawful but ethically questionable. A sophisticated risk assessment should not collapse these categories. "Illegal," "potentially actionable," "legally uncertain," and "ethically problematic" are not interchangeable descriptions. Precision matters because the appropriate response differs in each case.

The role of legal counsel becomes particularly important at this stage. A lawyer familiar with the relevant jurisdiction can help identify applicable statutes, privileges, reporting channels, contractual obligations, and potential defenses. Legal advice can also help distinguish evidence that should be preserved from material that should not be disseminated. The lawyer may recommend disclosure to a regulator, inspector general, court, journalist, or other authorized recipient rather than direct publication. A dead man's switch should therefore be capable of routing information to professional review rather than assuming public release is the ultimate objective.

This leads to a broader principle: the purpose of a dead man's switch should be preservation of agency, not automatic publication. The creator wants the truth to remain capable of reaching the appropriate people even when the creator is no longer available. That does not necessarily mean deciding in advance that every future circumstance should produce the same public disclosure. Circumstances change. Laws change. Individuals named in the evidence may change. New corroborating information may emerge. A flexible system can preserve the evidence while allowing qualified decision-makers to determine the appropriate form of disclosure.

The law also reminds us that responsibility cannot be outsourced completely. A person cannot simply say that a computer published the information, a blockchain executed the contract, or a service provider transmitted the files. The underlying architecture was created by people. Decisions about recipients, conditions, information, and timing were made by people. The technology may complicate the chain of events, but it does not necessarily erase the human decisions that produced it. Accountability remains connected to intention and conduct.

At the same time, the possibility of legal consequences should not become an excuse for suppressing legitimate wrongdoing. Whistleblower protections, investigative journalism, regulatory reporting, public-record laws, constitutional protections, and other legal mechanisms exist partly because societies recognize that institutions can abuse power. The answer is not to assume that secrecy is always legitimate. Nor is it to assume that every secret deserves immediate publication. The mature position is to examine the legal basis for secrecy, the evidence of wrongdoing, the available protected reporting channels, and the likely consequences of disclosure.

The dead man's switch therefore sits at an uncomfortable but productive intersection of technology, law, ethics, and public accountability. Its technical architecture determines whether information can survive. Its evidentiary architecture determines whether that information can be evaluated. Its legal architecture determines who may lawfully receive or disclose it. Its ethical architecture determines whether the resulting action respects innocent people while addressing legitimate wrongdoing. Neglect any one of these dimensions and the entire system becomes weaker.

The ultimate lesson is that truth does not exist outside consequences. A person can possess genuine evidence and still cause injustice through careless disclosure. A government can invoke secrecy and still conceal genuine wrongdoing. A corporation can claim confidentiality and still face legitimate whistleblowing. A journalist can defend publication and still have an obligation to protect innocent people. A dead man's switch must navigate these tensions rather than pretending they do not exist.

When disclosure becomes a crime, the central question is therefore not simply whether the information is true. It is how the information was obtained, what legal protections apply, who receives it, what is disclosed, why it is disclosed, and what consequences reasonably follow. The strongest system preserves the original evidence, protects it against unauthorized access, and creates a pathway toward competent human review. It does not assume that secrecy is always wrong or that exposure is always right. It preserves the possibility of accountability while respecting the reality that law and responsibility remain part of the story.

A dead man's switch should ultimately make one promise above all others: the disappearance of the person should not automatically mean the disappearance of the evidence. What happens after that point requires judgment. Sometimes the appropriate response may be a lawyer. Sometimes it may be an investigative journalist. Sometimes it may be a regulator, inspector general, court, or law-enforcement authority. Sometimes the material may need to remain confidential because publication would create disproportionate harm. The technology can preserve the pathway, but it cannot responsibly decide every destination.

The difference between preserving truth and recklessly exposing information is therefore the difference between a safety system and a weapon. A responsible dead man's switch does not exist to make disclosure inevitable. It exists to make legitimate disclosure possible when ordinary channels fail. Its ultimate measure is not how dramatically it can reveal secrets, but how carefully it can preserve evidence until someone capable of evaluating its truth, legality, significance, and consequences can take responsibility for what happens next.

Resources

1. U.S. Executive Order 13526 — Classified National Security Information[1] — establishes the U.S. executive-branch classification framework and categories of classified national-security information.

2. Information Security Oversight Office — National Archives[2] — official U.S. government resources concerning classification, declassification, and national-security information management.

3. 18 U.S.C. § 793 — Gathering, Transmitting or Losing Defense Information[3] — federal statutory provisions concerning certain national-defense information.

4. 18 U.S.C. § 798 — Disclosure of Classified Communications Intelligence[4] — federal statute addressing particular disclosures concerning classified communications intelligence.

5. U.S. Department of Justice — Justice Manual: Classified Information Procedures Act — Department of Justice guidance concerning litigation involving classified information.

6. Classified Information Procedures Act — 18 U.S.C. Appendix 3 — statutory framework governing the use of classified information in federal criminal proceedings.

7. U.S. Office of Special Counsel — Whistleblower Disclosures — official guidance concerning protected disclosures by covered federal employees and applicants.

8. Whistleblower Protection Act — U.S. Office of Special Counsel — official resources concerning prohibited personnel practices and whistleblower protections.

---

1. https://www.archives.gov/isoo/policy-documents/cnsi-eo.html?utm_source=chatgpt.com

2. https://www.archives.gov/isoo?utm_source=chatgpt.com

3. https://www.law.cornell.edu/uscode/text/18/793?utm_source=chatgpt.com

4. https://www.law.cornell.edu/uscode/text/18/798?utm_source=chatgpt.com

9. U.S. Securities and Exchange Commission — Whistleblower Program[5] — official information concerning securities-law whistleblower reporting and protections.

10. U.S. Commodity Futures Trading Commission — Whistleblower Program — official information concerning reporting and whistleblower protections under commodities law.

11. 18 U.S.C. § 1833 — Protection from Liability for Confidential Disclosure of Trade Secrets[6] — statutory whistleblower immunity concerning certain confidential disclosures of trade secrets.

12. 18 U.S.C. § 1836 — Federal Civil Cause of Action for Trade Secret Misappropriation[7] — federal civil remedy concerning trade-secret misappropriation.

13. U.S. Copyright Office — Copyright Law[8] — official resources concerning copyright protection and limitations.

14. U.S. Copyright Office — Fair Use[9] — official explanation of the fair-use doctrine and its contextual nature.

15. U.S. Supreme Court — New York Times Co. v. United States[10] — landmark litigation concerning publication of classified material and the First Amendment, commonly known as the Pentagon Papers case.

16. Reporters Committee for Freedom of the Press — Reporter's Privilege Compendium — comparative resources concerning journalist-source protections and reporter's privilege in the United States.

17. Electronic Frontier Foundation — Legal Guide[11] — resources concerning online speech, privacy, intellectual property, and legal issues affecting publication.

18. European Union — General Data Protection Regulation[12] — comprehensive European data-protection framework, including provisions concerning personal data and freedom of expression.

19. European Commission — Data Protection Rules[13] — official European Commission resources explaining the GDPR and data-protection framework.

20. UNESCO — Journalism, "Fake News" and Disinformation Handbook — guidance concerning verification, evidence assessment, misinformation, and responsible journalism.

21. Berkeley Protocol on Digital Open Source Investigations — methodological framework for collecting, preserving, verifying, and analyzing digital evidence.

22. National Institute of Standards and Technology — Digital Identity Guidelines[14] — guidance relevant to authentication and establishing confidence in digital identities.

---

5. https://www.sec.gov/whistleblower?utm_source=chatgpt.com

6. https://www.law.cornell.edu/uscode/text/18/1833?utm_source=chatgpt.com

7. https://www.law.cornell.edu/uscode/text/18/1836?utm_source=chatgpt.com

8. https://www.copyright.gov/title17/?utm_source=chatgpt.com

9. https://www.copyright.gov/fair-use/?utm_source=chatgpt.com

10. https://www.supremecourt.gov/?utm_source=chatgpt.com

11. https://www.eff.org/issues/bloggers/legal?utm_source=chatgpt.com

12. https://eur-lex.europa.eu/eli/reg/2016/679/oj?utm_source=chatgpt.com

13. https://commission.europa.eu/law/law-topic/data-protection/data-protection-eu_en?utm_source=chatgpt.com

14. https://pages.nist.gov/800-63-4/?utm_source=chatgpt.com

23. NIST Special Publication 800-57 — Recommendation for Key Management — guidance concerning cryptographic keys, access, protection, recovery, and lifecycle management.

24. NIST Special Publication 800-88 — Guidelines for Media Sanitization[15] — guidance concerning digital storage media and secure handling across the information lifecycle.

25. National Archives — Digital Preservation — authoritative resources concerning long-term preservation, authenticity, accessibility, and management of digital records.

26. Library of Congress — Digital Preservation[16] — resources concerning preservation of digital information, formats, metadata, and long-term accessibility.

27. ISO/IEC 27001 — Information Security Management Systems[17] — international framework for information-security risk management and organizational controls.

28. ISO 22301 — Security and Resilience: Business Continuity Management Systems[18] — international standard concerning continuity, disruption planning, and recovery.

29. CISA — Cybersecurity Best Practices[19] — U.S. government guidance concerning account security, resilience, recovery, and cybersecurity risk management.

30. U.S. Department of Justice — Justice Manual — official reference for federal criminal-law and prosecution policies relevant to understanding the legal environment surrounding sensitive disclosures.

---

15. https://csrc.nist.gov/publications/detail/sp/800-88/rev-1/final?utm_source=chatgpt.com

16. https://www.loc.gov/preservation/digital/?utm_source=chatgpt.com

17. https://www.iso.org/isoiec-27001-information-security.html?utm_source=chatgpt.com

18. https://www.iso.org/standard/75106.html?utm_source=chatgpt.com

19. https://www.cisa.gov/topics/cybersecurity-best-practices?utm_source=chatgpt.com

The Ethics of Revealing Dangerous Truths

Truth has an extraordinary moral reputation because societies depend upon accurate information to make intelligent decisions, hold institutions accountable, and correct wrongdoing. Yet truth alone does not answer every ethical question surrounding disclosure. A fact can be true and still be dangerous to reveal in a particular form, at a particular time, or to a particular audience. A photograph can accurately identify someone who should never have been exposed. A document can genuinely prove misconduct while containing information that places an uninvolved person in danger. A scientific discovery can be authentic while its premature publication creates consequences that nobody has adequately considered. The ethics of a dead man's switch therefore begins with an uncomfortable proposition: knowing something is true does not automatically establish that everyone has a moral right to receive it.

The problem becomes particularly acute because disclosure is often irreversible. Once information has been placed on the Internet, copied, downloaded, indexed, mirrored, translated, and redistributed, the original publisher may have almost no practical ability to retrieve it. A person can apologize, delete a webpage, withdraw a statement, or request removal, but copies may survive indefinitely. This creates an asymmetry between disclosure and nondisclosure. Choosing not to release information today may leave open the possibility of releasing it tomorrow after further verification. Releasing it today may permanently eliminate the possibility of reconsidering the decision. Ethical decision-making therefore has to account not only for what disclosure might accomplish but also for what it might make impossible.

This reversibility problem is one of the strongest arguments for staged disclosure. A dead man's switch does not necessarily have to move directly from private storage to worldwide publication. It can preserve information while directing it first toward people capable of evaluating its significance. A lawyer, investigative journalist, regulator, inspector general, court, or qualified investigator may be able to determine whether publication is warranted. Such review cannot eliminate every mistake, but it introduces opportunities for verification and harm reduction. The principle is similar to other high-consequence systems in which irreversible actions require greater scrutiny than reversible ones.

The first ethical question should therefore be necessity. Why does this information need to be released at all? The answer should be more substantial than curiosity, revenge, embarrassment, political advantage, personal vindication, or the desire to punish an opponent. If the information demonstrates serious wrongdoing, exposes an ongoing danger, protects victims, or contributes significantly to public accountability, the moral case for disclosure becomes stronger. If the principal purpose is retaliation, the ethical case becomes considerably weaker. A dead man's switch created during an emotionally charged conflict may preserve a legitimate concern while also preserving the creator's anger. Future recipients need to distinguish those things.

Public interest is another important concept, but it must be used carefully. Information can attract enormous public attention without serving the public interest in any meaningful sense. A celebrity's private medical information may generate intense curiosity while contributing nothing to accountability. By contrast, evidence that a public institution has systematically concealed serious wrongdoing may have substantial public value even if the information is embarrassing to powerful individuals. The ethical question is therefore not simply whether people would want to know. It is whether society has a legitimate reason to know.

The distinction matters because disclosure affects people who may have had no role in the underlying events. An archive concerning corruption might contain the names and contact details of employees who merely followed ordinary procedures. A database might include customers or patients who had nothing to do with the alleged misconduct. Photographs may identify relatives, witnesses, or bystanders. Personal correspondence may reveal intimate information about people who never consented to publication. Ethical disclosure requires separating the information necessary to establish wrongdoing from information that merely happens to be contained within the evidence.

This is the principle of collateral harm. Every disclosure should be examined for foreseeable consequences beyond its intended target. Who could be identified? Who could lose employment? Who could become the subject of harassment? Could a witness be threatened? Could a vulnerable person be exposed? Could an investigation be compromised? Could an innocent individual become associated with allegations simply because their name appears in a document? These questions do not automatically prohibit disclosure. They determine whether the disclosure needs modification.

Redaction can therefore be an ethical act rather than merely a legal precaution. Removing irrelevant personal information can preserve the accountability value of evidence while reducing unnecessary harm. A journalist might publish a document demonstrating institutional misconduct while withholding private addresses and unrelated personal details. An investigator might receive the complete archive while the public receives a carefully edited version. A regulator might need access to information that should never be published publicly. The ethical goal is not maximum exposure. It is appropriate exposure.

The problem becomes harder when personal information itself is relevant. Sometimes the identity of an individual is central to understanding what happened. In other cases, revealing the identity may expose someone to retaliation without adding meaningful evidentiary value. There is no universal rule that names should always be hidden or always be published. The relevant question is whether identification materially contributes to the legitimate purpose of disclosure and whether the resulting risks are proportionate. This requires judgment rather than a mechanical formula.

Evidence quality presents another ethical difficulty. People who create dead man's switches may sincerely believe their information is accurate. Sincerity, however, is not the same as reliability. Memories can be mistaken. Documents can be misunderstood. Photographs can be misidentified. Audio recordings can lack context. Statistical patterns can be interpreted incorrectly. A collection of individually plausible pieces of evidence can also create a misleading narrative when assembled selectively.

This is why corroboration matters. Important allegations become more credible when independent sources converge on the same conclusion. An original document may be supported by metadata, correspondence, testimony, financial records, photographs, or other independent evidence. A witness statement may become more persuasive when contemporaneous records support it. Corroboration does not guarantee truth, but it reduces dependence upon a single interpretation. The ethical obligation increases as the potential harm of publication increases.

Uncertainty should also be communicated honestly. A responsible disclosure does not present a disputed allegation as an established fact merely because the creator believed it. Evidence can be labeled according to its status: documented, independently corroborated, disputed, unverified, or speculative. Such distinctions protect the audience from false certainty. They also preserve the possibility that future evidence may change the interpretation. A dead man's switch should preserve uncertainty when uncertainty genuinely exists.

The temptation to simplify is particularly strong when the information concerns dramatic wrongdoing. A complex investigation may involve contradictory testimony, incomplete records, institutional failures, and ambiguous motives. A short narrative can transform that complexity into a simple story of heroes and villains. Such narratives are powerful because they are easy to understand. They are also dangerous when the evidence does not support the certainty implied by the story. Ethical disclosure requires resisting the psychological attraction of simple explanations when reality is complicated.

Investigations can be damaged by premature disclosure. Law-enforcement investigations may depend upon witnesses who have not yet been interviewed, suspects who have not yet been confronted, or evidence that has not yet been secured. Publicizing sensitive details can allow suspects to destroy evidence, coordinate accounts, intimidate witnesses, flee, or alter behavior. In some circumstances, publication can therefore reduce the likelihood that wrongdoing will ever be proven. The ethical irony is profound: an attempt to expose wrongdoing can inadvertently make accountability more difficult.

Journalists confront this problem regularly. Responsible investigative reporting may involve delaying publication until sources have been corroborated, legal issues reviewed, and affected individuals given an opportunity to respond. This does not mean allowing powerful institutions to veto reporting. It means recognizing that publication can change the conditions under which an investigation takes place. The timing of disclosure can therefore be as important as the content. A truth revealed at the wrong moment can produce a different outcome from the same truth revealed after the relevant evidence has been secured.

National-security information presents an especially difficult example. A disclosure might expose government misconduct while also revealing intelligence sources, military capabilities, operational methods, or identities of people whose safety depends upon secrecy. The ethical question cannot be reduced to whether the government says the information is classified. Classification can be legitimate, overused, disputed, or politically controversial. The ethical assessment must consider the actual information, the public interest, the likelihood of harm, and the availability of safer alternatives. Sometimes the strongest disclosure is not the complete document but carefully selected evidence demonstrating the underlying misconduct.

The same principle applies to scientific information. Scientists have an ethical obligation to communicate important discoveries, but scientific knowledge can have consequences beyond the laboratory. Research involving dangerous pathogens, sensitive technologies, or potentially dual-use capabilities can create difficult publication questions. The existence of scientific value does not necessarily settle the question of unrestricted dissemination. At the same time, excessive secrecy can prevent legitimate scientific scrutiny and slow beneficial research. Ethical scientific communication therefore requires balancing openness with responsible risk assessment.

Corporate information creates similar tensions. A whistleblower might possess internal documents showing serious financial misconduct, environmental violations, unsafe practices, or deceptive conduct. The public interest in exposing such behavior may be substantial. Yet the same files might contain trade secrets unrelated to the wrongdoing, customer information, employee records, or proprietary technology. Publishing the entire archive could harm people who were never responsible for the misconduct. The ethical approach is to identify what is necessary to establish the allegation and protect what is not.

The possibility of retaliation must also be considered. Disclosure can protect some people while exposing others. A whistleblower may want the truth known, but witnesses, family members, colleagues, or local investigators may face consequences. A dead man's switch can unintentionally reveal relationships that the creator had deliberately kept confidential. The ethical responsibility therefore extends beyond the creator. A person creating a disclosure system should consider whether the information contains hidden dependencies that become dangerous when exposed. Protection of truth cannot be separated entirely from protection of people.

This creates a tension between the creator's autonomy and the rights of others. A person may have a moral claim to tell their own story. They may not have an equivalent moral claim to reveal every secret belonging to someone else. Personal correspondence, medical information, intimate photographs, confidential testimony, and private family matters can involve multiple people's interests simultaneously. A dead man's switch can transfer control of information but cannot transfer ownership of every moral interest contained within that information. Future custodians therefore need to distinguish personal testimony from information concerning third parties.

The creator's motives deserve examination as well. Someone can simultaneously be a genuine whistleblower and a deeply angry person. The existence of personal grievance does not invalidate evidence. Conversely, the existence of compelling evidence does not make every motive noble. Human motivations are rarely pure. A person might expose genuine corruption while also seeking revenge against an individual involved. Ethical analysis should therefore focus primarily on the evidence and foreseeable consequences rather than attempting to determine whether the creator was morally perfect.

The possibility of manipulation is another concern. A dead man's switch can create enormous psychological pressure because recipients may believe that failure to publish means allowing wrongdoing to remain hidden. That pressure can discourage careful verification. A creator might explicitly instruct recipients to publish everything immediately and accuse anyone who hesitates of participating in a cover-up. Such framing can transform an information-preservation system into a moral coercion mechanism. A responsible architecture should preserve evidence while allowing recipients to exercise independent judgment.

Independence is therefore ethically valuable. The person receiving the archive should not automatically become an obedient executor of the creator's final wishes. They should have the freedom to determine whether the evidence is authentic, whether circumstances have changed, and whether publication remains justified. This is especially important if the creator is no longer alive and cannot answer questions about context. The dead man's switch should preserve the creator's information, not necessarily eliminate the recipient's conscience. Responsible custody requires independent judgment.

There is also an ethical distinction between exposure and punishment. A whistleblower may want evidence released because they believe wrongdoing has occurred. They may also want the people responsible to suffer consequences. Those objectives should not automatically be combined. Publication can initiate public scrutiny, but determining guilt is ordinarily the responsibility of appropriate legal or institutional processes. A dead man's switch should not become a substitute for a court. Preserving evidence is fundamentally different from deciding the punishment of those accused.

The risk of vigilantism becomes particularly serious in the age of instantaneous communication. Social media can transform an allegation into a global accusation within minutes. Once a person's identity becomes associated with a serious allegation, later corrections may receive only a fraction of the original attention. Even a completely innocent person can suffer permanent reputational damage. This is another reason that high-impact allegations require unusually careful verification. The speed of digital communication does not reduce the ethical obligation to be accurate.

Artificial intelligence introduces additional complications because automated systems can now summarize, classify, translate, compare, and distribute enormous volumes of information. An AI system might identify patterns across thousands of documents or automatically prepare material for publication. These capabilities can increase efficiency. They can also amplify mistakes at unprecedented speed. An incorrect classification or misleading summary generated automatically could propagate across thousands of documents before a human notices. Automation should therefore assist responsible review rather than replace it where the consequences are irreversible.

The same concern applies to automated triggering. A system might determine that a condition has been satisfied and release an archive without understanding the circumstances surrounding the event. It may not know that the creator was traveling, hospitalized, under coercion, or temporarily unable to communicate. It cannot necessarily distinguish genuine death from a technical failure. It certainly cannot understand the moral significance of revealing a witness's identity. Automation can execute conditions. It cannot reliably supply human ethical judgment unless carefully designed within a broader process.

Coercion deserves particular attention. What if the creator establishes a dead man's switch and later changes their mind because someone threatens them? What if they are forced to provide credentials? What if they are imprisoned? What if they are suffering under extreme psychological pressure? What if someone else gains control of the mechanism? These circumstances complicate the assumption that silence or action represents free choice. A responsible system should recognize that human behavior under coercion can be ambiguous. The meaning of a trigger cannot always be inferred from a single signal.

There is also the problem of changing circumstances. Evidence that was dangerous to release five years ago may become less sensitive later. Conversely, information that seemed relatively harmless when stored may become dangerous after political, technological, or geopolitical conditions change. People may move. Institutions may collapse. Investigations may conclude. Individuals may become public figures. New evidence may overturn old interpretations. A dead man's switch should therefore avoid assuming that the ethical value of disclosure remains permanently fixed.

This is one reason archival systems should preserve context and chronology. A recipient needs to know when evidence was created, when it was collected, what was known at the time, and what happened afterward. Without chronology, historical evidence can easily be misinterpreted. A document created before an important event may be mistakenly treated as a response to it. A statement made under one set of circumstances may be interpreted under another. Context does not merely improve historical accuracy. It can change the ethical meaning of disclosure.

The principle of proportionality provides another useful framework. The greater the potential harm caused by disclosure, the stronger the evidence and public-interest justification should generally be. A minor allegation should not justify exposing hundreds of people's private information. A serious and immediate threat may justify stronger measures when evidence is compelling. The relationship between benefit and harm should be considered explicitly. Proportionality does not produce a mathematical answer, but it forces decision-makers to confront consequences rather than focusing solely on principle.

A related concept is the minimum necessary disclosure. If ten pages are required to establish the relevant facts, there may be no ethical reason to publish ten thousand pages containing unrelated personal information. If one person's identity is necessary to establish accountability, that does not automatically justify revealing the identities of everyone mentioned in the archive. If a technical report proves a dangerous institutional failure, publishing unrelated engineering details may create unnecessary risk. The ethical objective is therefore often precision rather than volume.

The strongest ethical systems separate preservation from publication. Preservation seeks to prevent information from disappearing. Publication determines what should eventually become public. These are different functions and should not necessarily occur simultaneously. A dead man's switch can preserve the complete evidentiary record while directing recipients toward an evaluation process. This separation creates room for verification, legal review, redaction, contextualization, and ethical judgment.

The distinction is particularly important because future recipients may possess information that the creator did not have. An investigator may discover that an allegation was false. A journalist may find corroborating evidence that strengthens it. A court may issue an order affecting disclosure. A regulator may already be investigating the matter. A person identified in the archive may have been exonerated. The creator cannot predict all future developments. A responsible system therefore preserves the evidence while allowing the future to remain capable of changing the decision.

The ethical purpose of redundancy also becomes clearer here. Redundancy is not merely about preventing technological failure. It can prevent premature or inappropriate disclosure by allowing multiple independent custodians to examine the evidence. If one custodian acts recklessly, another may provide a corrective perspective. If one archive becomes corrupted, another may preserve the original. If one recipient becomes unavailable, another can continue the process. Independence creates resilience not only against technical failure but also against human judgment failure.

None of this means that disclosure should be endlessly delayed. There are circumstances in which immediate action may be ethically necessary. An imminent threat to life, evidence of ongoing violence, or a rapidly developing danger may justify urgent notification. Waiting for perfect certainty can itself have moral consequences. The ethical challenge is therefore to distinguish reasonable caution from paralysis. A system designed for emergencies should include pathways for urgent escalation rather than forcing every circumstance through the same slow procedure.

The deepest ethical question is perhaps this: who gets to decide what the truth costs? The creator may believe that public exposure is worth any consequence. The affected individuals may strongly disagree. Journalists may prioritize public accountability. Lawyers may prioritize legal exposure. Investigators may prioritize preserving a case. Family members may prioritize safety. Regulators may prioritize institutional remedies. There is no neutral position from which every interest can be perfectly reconciled. Responsible disclosure therefore requires acknowledging competing interests rather than pretending that one moral principle automatically resolves everything.

This is why the language surrounding disclosure matters. Calling someone a criminal before the evidence has been adjudicated can transform an allegation into a perceived fact. Describing disputed material as "proof" can exaggerate its evidentiary status. Claiming that anyone who questions the material is part of a conspiracy can discourage legitimate scrutiny. Ethical disclosure uses precise language because language itself can create harm. The credibility of a serious archive depends partly upon the discipline with which its custodians describe what it contains.

The creator can help by separating evidence from interpretation. Original documents should be preserved alongside explanations of what the creator believes they demonstrate, but the distinction should remain visible. A future investigator should be able to examine the material without being forced to accept the creator's interpretation. This approach actually strengthens the archive because it permits independent analysis. Evidence that survives scrutiny is more powerful than evidence protected from scrutiny. The objective should be to make investigation possible, not to make disagreement impossible.

Ultimately, the ethics of a dead man's switch is the ethics of power over information. Information can protect people, expose institutions, destroy reputations, trigger investigations, change elections, destabilize organizations, and alter lives. The person who creates the switch may intend to use that power defensively, but the consequences can extend far beyond their original intention. This is why preservation must be accompanied by responsibility. The fact that a person can release information does not establish that they should.

A mature dead man's switch therefore embodies restraint as well as determination. It preserves evidence because truth can disappear when witnesses die, records are destroyed, institutions close ranks, or individuals become unable to speak. But it also preserves the possibility of review because evidence can be incomplete, circumstances can change, and innocent people can be harmed. It treats disclosure as a decision rather than an inevitable mechanical event. It recognizes that the ethical value of information depends partly upon how, when, and to whom it is revealed. Most importantly, it refuses to confuse courage with recklessness.

The ultimate responsibility is to preserve the truth without manufacturing certainty, expose wrongdoing without unnecessarily exposing innocent people, protect evidence without protecting falsehood, and create accountability without turning information into an instrument of revenge. These objectives will sometimes conflict. There will be cases in which no available option is completely safe or morally clean. The purpose of a responsible system is not to eliminate those dilemmas. It is to ensure that when the moment comes, the evidence survives long enough for someone capable of confronting those dilemmas to make an informed decision.

The dead man's switch is therefore best understood not as a command from the dead but as a responsibility handed to the living. The creator can preserve the information, explain its significance, and establish safeguards. The future custodian must then determine what the evidence actually means and what society needs to know. That final responsibility cannot be automated completely. Truth may demand courage, but responsible truth also demands judgment. The most powerful disclosure is not necessarily the largest disclosure; it is the disclosure that reveals what needs to be known while causing no greater harm than the circumstances require.

Resources

1. UNESCO — Journalism, "Fake News" and Disinformation — guidance on verification, accuracy, source evaluation, misinformation, and responsible journalism.

2. Berkeley Protocol on Digital Open Source Investigations — methodological guidance for collecting, preserving, verifying, analyzing, and presenting digital evidence.

3. Society of Professional Journalists — Code of Ethics[1] — professional principles concerning truth, minimizing harm, independence, and accountability in journalism.

4. Reuters Handbook of Journalism — professional guidance concerning verification, accuracy, sourcing, fairness, and publication decisions.

5. Associated Press — News Values and Principles[2] — editorial principles concerning accuracy, fairness, source evaluation, and minimizing harm.

1. https://www.spj.org/ethicscode.asp?utm_source=chatgpt.com

6. Committee to Protect Journalists — Safety Resources[3] — resources addressing threats to journalists and sources, including digital and physical security considerations.

7. Reporters Without Borders — Journalism Trust Initiative[4] — standards emphasizing transparency, accountability, editorial independence, and reliability in journalism.

8. International Federation of Journalists — Global Charter of Ethics for Journalists[5] — international ethical principles concerning truth, verification, privacy, source protection, and harm.

9. UNESCO — World Trends in Freedom of Expression and Media Development[6] — research and resources concerning media freedom, information integrity, safety, and public-interest journalism.

10. European Union — General Data Protection Regulation[7] — legal framework concerning personal-data processing and protections relevant to publication and disclosure.

11. European Commission — Data Protection and Privacy[8] — official explanation of European data-protection principles and rights.

12. U.S. Department of Health and Human Services — HIPAA Privacy Rule[9] — official resources concerning protected health information and privacy obligations in covered contexts.

13. U.S. Department of Justice — Justice Manual — official reference for federal criminal-law principles and prosecutorial considerations relevant to sensitive information.

14. NIST Special Publication 800-30 — Guide for Conducting Risk Assessments[10] — framework for identifying threats, vulnerabilities, likelihood, and consequences.

15. NIST Special Publication 800-160 Volume 2 — Developing Cyber-Resilient Systems — principles of anticipating, withstanding, recovering from, and adapting to disruptive events.

16. NIST Cybersecurity Framework 2.0[11] — framework for managing cybersecurity risk and building resilient information systems.

17. Electronic Frontier Foundation — Surveillance Self-Defense[12] — practical resources concerning threat modeling, privacy, secure communications, and protecting sensitive information.

---

2. https://www.ap.org/about/news-values-and-principles/?utm_source=chatgpt.com
3. https://cpj.org/safety-kit/?utm_source=chatgpt.com
4. https://rsf.org/en/journalism-trust-initiative?utm_source=chatgpt.com
5. https://www.ifj.org/who/rules-and-policy/global-charter-of-ethics-for-journalists?utm_source=chatgpt.com
6. https://www.unesco.org/en/world-media-trends?utm_source=chatgpt.com
7. https://eur-lex.europa.eu/eli/reg/2016/679/oj?utm_source=chatgpt.com
8. https://commission.europa.eu/law/law-topic/data-protection/data-protection-eu_en?utm_source=chatgpt.com
9. https://www.hhs.gov/hipaa/for-professionals/privacy/index.html?utm_source=chatgpt.com
10. https://csrc.nist.gov/publications/detail/sp/800-30/rev-1/final?utm_source=chatgpt.com
11. https://www.nist.gov/cyberframework?utm_source=chatgpt.com
12. https://ssd.eff.org/?utm_source=chatgpt.com

18. Electronic Frontier Foundation — Free Speech and Privacy — resources concerning the relationship between publication, privacy, speech, and digital rights.

19. National Archives — Digital Preservation — resources concerning authenticity, preservation, accessibility, and long-term management of digital evidence.

20. Library of Congress — Digital Preservation[13] — authoritative resources on preserving digital information, metadata, file formats, and authenticity.

21. National Academies — Responsible Conduct of Research[14] — resources concerning research integrity, responsible scientific conduct, and evidentiary reliability.

22. National Academies — Dual Use Research of Concern[15] — institutional resources relevant to the ethical tension between scientific openness and risks associated with potentially harmful applications of research.

23. World Health Organization — Guidance on Ethics and Governance of Artificial Intelligence for Health[16] — framework illustrating broader principles of human oversight, transparency, accountability, and risk management in consequential automated systems.

24. OECD AI Principles[17] — internationally recognized principles concerning trustworthy AI, human oversight, transparency, robustness, and accountability.

25. UNESCO Recommendation on the Ethics of Artificial Intelligence[18] — international framework addressing human rights, transparency, accountability, safety, and ethical governance of AI.

26. The Menlo Report — Ethical Principles Guiding Information and Communication Technology Research — framework applying principles of respect for persons, beneficence, justice, and respect for law to information and communications technology research.

27. U.S. Department of Justice — Evaluation of Corporate Compliance Programs[19] — framework containing useful principles concerning internal reporting, investigations, documentation, and organizational responses to misconduct.

28. International Organization for Standardization — ISO 31000 Risk Management[20] — international risk-management principles relevant to identifying, assessing, and responding to foreseeable consequences.

29. United Nations — Universal Declaration of Human Rights[21] — foundational international human-rights framework relevant to dignity, privacy, expression, and access to information.

---

13. https://www.loc.gov/preservation/digital/?utm_source=chatgpt.com

14. https://www.nationalacademies.org/our-work/responsible-science-ensuring-the-integrity-of-the-research-process?utm_source=chatgpt.com

15. https://www.nationalacademies.org/?utm_source=chatgpt.com

16. https://www.who.int/publications/i/item/9789240029200?utm_source=chatgpt.com

17. https://oecd.ai/en/ai-principles?utm_source=chatgpt.com

18. https://www.unesco.org/en/artificial-intelligence/recommendation-ethics?utm_source=chatgpt.com

19. https://www.justice.gov/criminal/criminal-fraud/page/file/937501/dl?utm_source=chatgpt.com

20. https://www.iso.org/iso-31000-risk-management.html?utm_source=chatgpt.com

21. https://www.un.org/en/about-us/universal-declaration-of-human-rights?utm_source=chatgpt.com

30. United Nations — International Covenant on Civil and Political Rights[22] — international framework addressing freedom of expression, privacy, and related rights that can come into tension during sensitive disclosure.

22. https://www.ohchr.org/en/instruments-mechanisms/instruments/international-covenant-civil-and-political-rights?utm_source=chatgpt.com

The Last Message: Dead Man's Switches and the Future of Truth

The original dead man's switch was never designed to reveal a secret. It was designed to keep a machine operating, stop a mechanism, or initiate a predetermined action when the person controlling it could no longer do so. The modern idea has transformed that simple mechanical principle into something much more profound: a way of ensuring that information can survive the disappearance of the person who possesses it. That transformation reflects a changing world in which information can be more valuable than physical objects and where a single archive can contain evidence capable of affecting governments, corporations, institutions, scientific communities, and individuals. The modern dead man's switch is therefore not merely a device but an architecture of continuity. It asks whether a person's knowledge can remain available after the person themselves is no longer available to explain it.

That question has always contained an element of fear. People create contingencies because they recognize that life is uncertain and that information can disappear through death, disappearance, imprisonment, coercion, incapacitation, accident, technological failure, or deliberate destruction. History provides countless examples of records being lost, witnesses becoming unavailable, archives being destroyed, and institutions denying events that others remembered differently. Yet history also demonstrates that preserving information does not automatically preserve truth. A document can survive while its context disappears. A photograph can survive while its provenance becomes uncertain. A testimony can survive while nobody can determine whether it was accurate. The ultimate challenge is therefore not simply keeping information alive but keeping enough context, evidence, provenance, and independent verification alive with it.

This distinction has shaped everything we have examined in this book. The dead man's switch begins with the fear that silence might follow disappearance. It develops into a psychological strategy for people who believe that possessing certain information creates personal danger. It becomes a technical problem when the creator must determine what should happen if communication stops. It becomes an evidentiary problem when sensitive material must be preserved without alteration. It becomes a legal problem when the information concerns classified material, trade secrets, privacy, intellectual property, or protected communications. And finally, it becomes an ethical problem when the truth itself can cause harm to people who had nothing to do with the wrongdoing being exposed.

The historical record provides an important warning against exaggeration. There have been documented cases in which whistleblowers, journalists, investigators, activists, witnesses, and dissidents have faced intimidation, retaliation, imprisonment, professional destruction, or violence. There have also been allegations of suspicious deaths and political assassinations that remain disputed or unresolved. These categories must never be casually merged. An unexplained death is not automatically an assassination, and a person's claim that they were threatened is not automatically evidence that a conspiracy existed. A responsible dead man's switch must begin where responsible historical investigation begins: with the distinction between what is documented, what is corroborated, what is alleged, and what remains unknown.

That distinction is more important than ever because modern technology can amplify uncertainty as quickly as it amplifies truth. A claim can move around the world before a journalist has verified its source. A manipulated image can acquire millions of views before anyone establishes that it is false. A fragment of an authentic document can be stripped from its original context and transformed into a misleading narrative. Artificial intelligence can now generate convincing text, images, audio, and video that may be difficult for ordinary viewers to distinguish from genuine material. The survival of information therefore no longer guarantees the survival of reliable information. In the future, provenance may become as important as preservation itself.

This creates a paradox at the heart of the dead man's switch. Technology makes it easier than ever to ensure that a file survives. At the same time, technology makes it increasingly difficult to establish what that file actually represents. A digital archive can be copied perfectly thousands of times, but those copies can preserve a mistake just as faithfully as they preserve a fact. Encryption can prevent unauthorized access without establishing whether the underlying information is true. Blockchain technology can create durable records of transactions or cryptographic fingerprints without independently verifying the truth of the material being recorded. Artificial intelligence can identify patterns across enormous datasets without necessarily understanding whether the underlying sources are authentic.

The future therefore belongs not simply to information preservation but to evidence preservation. Evidence requires context. It requires a chain of provenance that explains where material came from and how it was handled. It requires chronology so that later investigators can reconstruct events in their proper sequence. It requires independent corroboration where possible. It requires preservation of original files rather than relying solely upon screenshots, transcripts, summaries, or edited copies. It requires documentation of what the creator believed and what the evidence itself demonstrates. The difference between an archive and an evidentiary archive is the difference between storing information and preserving the possibility of investigation.

This is why the evidence vault developed earlier in the book is so important. Documents, photographs, recordings, correspondence, financial records, scientific data, and testimony should not exist as isolated objects. Their meaning depends upon relationships. A photograph may become powerful evidence when its original file, metadata, location, date, and accompanying correspondence are preserved. A financial record becomes more meaningful when it can be compared with invoices, bank statements, contracts, and testimony. A recording becomes more reliable when its origin and continuity can be established. Evidence gains strength through context.

The same principle applies to human testimony. People are not databases, and memory is not a perfect recording mechanism. A person may remember an event sincerely and still remember parts of it incorrectly. Trauma, stress, time, suggestion, fear, and ordinary human limitations can affect recollection. That does not mean testimony is worthless. It means testimony should be treated as one form of evidence whose reliability can be strengthened or weakened by independent corroboration. A dead man's switch should preserve testimony without pretending that testimony is automatically equivalent to proof.

The psychological dimension of the system is equally important. Someone who believes they possess dangerous information may live with fear, hypervigilance, isolation, distrust, and constant uncertainty. Creating a contingency mechanism can provide a sense of control because it transforms an unpredictable future into a series of planned possibilities. The person no longer has to believe that everything depends upon their physical survival. Yet the psychological benefit can become dangerous if the system reinforces paranoia or convinces the creator that every setback is evidence of persecution. A responsible framework must therefore separate genuine risk assessment from fear-driven interpretation.

Trust remains the central human vulnerability. No technical system can eliminate the need for people to make decisions. Someone has to maintain the archive, preserve credentials, verify recipients, assess evidence, interpret circumstances, or decide whether publication is justified. Family members may be deeply loyal but emotionally overwhelmed. Friends may be trustworthy but technically inexperienced. Lawyers may understand legal exposure but have professional obligations that restrict what they can do. Journalists may possess the investigative resources to evaluate the material but may decide that publication is not justified. There is no universally perfect custodian.

The strongest systems therefore distribute responsibility. One person should not necessarily control every copy, password, decision, and trigger. Multiple independent custodians can provide resilience against individual failure. Geographical separation can protect against localized disasters. Different forms of storage can protect against technological failure. Multiple authentication methods can reduce the consequences of a lost credential. Independent review can reduce the possibility that one person's interpretation becomes the only interpretation. Redundancy, in other words, is not merely a technical principle. It is a principle of human judgment.

The transition from physical to digital systems has expanded these possibilities enormously. A physical archive can survive without electricity and may be difficult to alter remotely, but it can be destroyed, stolen, lost, or physically inaccessible. Digital archives can be duplicated, encrypted, synchronized, and transmitted across continents, but they depend upon hardware, software, credentials, networks, service providers, and evolving technical standards. Cloud storage provides convenience and geographic redundancy while introducing account-security, provider-dependence, and access-control risks. Offline storage reduces some online threats while creating its own problems of degradation, loss, and forgotten access credentials.

The lesson is not that one medium is superior. The lesson is that every medium fails differently. A resilient information-preservation strategy therefore uses different forms of redundancy rather than assuming that one technology can provide absolute security. A copy stored on a laptop can be lost with the laptop. A cloud account can become inaccessible. A physical drive can fail. A password can be forgotten. An encryption key can disappear. A trusted person can die or become unavailable. The architecture must assume failure rather than treating failure as an exceptional event.

The same logic applies to activation. A dead man's switch can be manual, automatic, conditional, scheduled, or hybrid. Each approach creates different risks. Manual activation depends upon a person making the decision. Automatic activation depends upon technology correctly interpreting the absence of a signal. Conditional activation depends upon the reliability of the conditions being evaluated. Hybrid systems can combine strengths but also introduce complexity. The perfect trigger does not exist because the future contains circumstances that cannot be predicted completely.

This is why false positives can be as dangerous as false negatives. A false positive releases information when no release should have occurred. A false negative fails to release information when release was intended. Both represent failures of the system. A creator focused exclusively on preventing silence may design an overly aggressive mechanism that publishes material after a temporary technical failure. A creator focused exclusively on preventing accidental disclosure may create so many safeguards that the system becomes useless when a genuine emergency occurs. Reliability requires balancing both possibilities.

The password problem reveals an especially human vulnerability. Information can be perfectly encrypted and still effectively lost if nobody possesses the necessary credentials. Security and accessibility are opposing requirements that must be balanced carefully. If nobody can access the archive, the system has failed its purpose. If everyone can access it, the archive may not be secure. Digital inheritance therefore becomes a critical component of information preservation. The future custodian needs a legitimate and reliable pathway to obtain access without requiring the original creator to be present.

Encryption itself remains one of the most important technologies in this environment. Properly implemented cryptography can protect confidentiality and help establish integrity. It can prevent unauthorized people from casually reading sensitive material even if they obtain the storage device. But encryption does not establish truth. It does not prove that the encrypted document is genuine. It does not guarantee that the person holding the key is trustworthy. It does not protect against a compromised endpoint, malicious insider, social engineering, or poor operational security. Encryption is a powerful layer, not a complete information-preservation system.

Distributed technologies introduce another possible layer. Blockchain systems can create tamper-evident records and allow information about transactions or cryptographic commitments to exist across distributed networks. Smart contracts can execute predefined conditions within their technical environment. These characteristics can reduce dependence upon certain centralized intermediaries. But decentralization is frequently exaggerated. A decentralized ledger does not make a person anonymous by default, does not guarantee the truth of information entered into it, and does not eliminate legal jurisdiction. Technology can distribute trust without eliminating the need for trust.

Artificial intelligence may become the most significant new development in this field. An AI system could eventually help classify enormous archives, identify duplicated documents, compare testimony against records, detect anomalies, construct timelines, identify relationships among entities, and flag material requiring human review. Such capabilities could transform the investigation of large information dumps. A future dead man's switch might therefore contain not merely an archive but an intelligent system capable of explaining the relationships within that archive. Yet the dangers are equally profound. AI systems can hallucinate, misclassify evidence, amplify biased assumptions, and generate plausible but unsupported conclusions.

Human oversight therefore becomes more important rather than less important as AI capabilities increase. An AI system should not be allowed to transform uncertainty into certainty merely because its output sounds authoritative. Machine-generated summaries should be traceable to underlying documents. Claims should be independently verifiable. Important conclusions should remain open to human examination. Automated classification should be treated as assistance rather than unquestionable judgment. The future of evidence preservation may therefore involve a partnership between machine-scale analysis and human-scale responsibility.

AI may also change the meaning of authenticity itself. If synthetic audio can imitate a person's voice and synthetic video can create convincing images of events that never occurred, future investigators will need stronger methods of provenance. Cryptographic signatures, secure capture systems, trusted timestamps, hardware-backed identity, forensic analysis, and independent corroboration may become increasingly important. The question will no longer be merely "Does this recording exist?" but "Can we establish how this recording came into existence?" That shift could fundamentally change investigative journalism, courts, intelligence analysis, scientific research, and historical scholarship.

The future may therefore produce a new kind of dead man's switch: not simply a mechanism that releases information but an evidence continuity system. Such a system could preserve original files, maintain cryptographic integrity checks, document provenance, store contextual records, distribute encrypted copies, maintain independent custodians, and create carefully defined review procedures. It might use automated monitoring to detect system failures without automatically publishing everything. It might notify designated recipients rather than releasing material directly to the public. It might preserve a complete archive while allowing different recipients to receive different levels of access.

This distinction between notification and publication may become one of the most important developments in the field. A system does not necessarily need to say everything to everyone. It may first need to say one thing to one person: the archive exists, the creator is unavailable, and the evidence requires review. From there, the process can proceed according to legal and ethical considerations. Investigators may receive one portion. Lawyers may receive another. Journalists may receive material after verification. The public may ultimately receive only what can responsibly be published.

Such a system would also change the psychological meaning of the dead man's switch. It would no longer be primarily an expression of fear that says, "If something happens to me, everything comes out." Instead, it could become an expression of confidence that says, "If I cannot continue, the evidence will still have a pathway forward." That is a profound difference. The first model is built around retaliation and deterrence. The second is built around continuity and accountability. One threatens exposure. The other preserves the possibility of investigation.

This distinction matters because deterrence is one of the most misunderstood aspects of dead man's switches. The existence of a credible contingency can discourage someone from attempting to silence the creator if they believe the information will be released afterward. But deterrence only works when the threat is credible. An alleged switch that nobody knows about, cannot verify, or cannot activate may have little practical deterrent value. Conversely, an unnecessarily aggressive disclosure mechanism can create its own dangers. The most effective system may therefore be the one whose existence is credible without requiring reckless public exposure.

Whistleblowing will remain one of the most important applications. Institutions inevitably develop information asymmetries. Employees may know what executives do not know. Engineers may know what managers do not know. Investigators may discover misconduct that senior officials would prefer not to confront. The ability to preserve evidence outside the immediate institution can provide an important safeguard against information being suppressed internally. But whistleblowing works best when evidence can be evaluated independently. A dead man's switch should strengthen accountability rather than undermine the evidentiary standards necessary to establish it.

Journalism will also remain central because professional investigative organizations can provide something technology alone cannot: editorial judgment. Journalists can ask whether a claim is corroborated, whether publication is in the public interest, whether innocent people will be harmed, whether the accused has been given an opportunity to respond, and whether publication might compromise an investigation. They can consult lawyers and specialists. They can decide to publish, delay publication, redact material, or decline to publish. That independence can be frustrating to a creator who wants everything released immediately, but it is part of what makes responsible journalism possible.

The legal environment will continue to evolve as technology changes. Governments will confront new questions concerning encrypted archives, decentralized networks, artificial intelligence, cross-border data storage, digital evidence, and automated disclosure. Courts will have to consider how existing legal principles apply to technologies that did not exist when older statutes were written. Legislatures will create new rules while old rules continue to apply in unexpected ways. The result will not be a simple legal environment. Anyone creating a sophisticated dead man's switch in the future will need to consider not only technology but jurisdiction, applicable reporting protections, privacy, intellectual property, national security, and the laws governing the information itself.

Ethics may prove even more difficult than law. Law establishes boundaries, but morality often begins where legal rules end. A disclosure may be lawful and still cruel. It may be technically permissible and still irresponsible. It may expose a genuine wrong while unnecessarily destroying innocent lives. It may reveal important information while compromising an investigation that could have produced stronger accountability. Legal permission is therefore a floor rather than a complete ethical framework. Responsible disclosure requires asking not only "Can this be released?" but "Should it be released, in this form, at this time, to these people?"

That question brings us back to the concept of dangerous truth. Some truths are dangerous because powerful people want them hidden. Other truths are dangerous because their careless release can harm vulnerable people. Some truths require immediate exposure. Others require years of verification. Some truths should become public. Others may need to remain restricted to investigators or courts. The challenge is not to decide that truth is always dangerous or always liberating. The challenge is to understand what kind of truth we possess and what responsibilities accompany it.

The greatest mistake would be to imagine that technology can solve this problem for us. A blockchain cannot determine whether an allegation is morally justified. Encryption cannot determine whether a victim's privacy should be protected. Artificial intelligence cannot automatically determine whether a government secret is legitimate. An automated timer cannot understand the difference between temporary silence and death. A distributed network cannot decide whether publication will compromise an investigation. Technology can preserve, transmit, authenticate, and execute instructions. The final responsibility remains human.

This is why the dead man's switch is ultimately a philosophical idea disguised as a technical one. It asks what should happen to knowledge when its owner disappears. It asks whether a person's responsibility to the truth can continue beyond their physical existence. It asks whether information can be separated from the person who discovered it. It asks whether evidence can survive long enough to be judged by people who were not present when the events occurred. And it asks whether society can build systems in which truth does not depend entirely upon the survival of a single witness.

The answer is cautiously hopeful. Information can survive. Evidence can survive. Testimony can survive. Archives can survive. Cryptographic records can survive. Digital copies can survive across generations and continents. But survival alone is not enough. The information must remain accessible without becoming uncontrolled. It must remain authentic without becoming unquestionable. It must retain context without becoming overwhelmed by irrelevant material. It must reach people capable of evaluating it. And when disclosure occurs, it must be governed by law, evidence, ethics, and a recognition that innocent people can be harmed by truths they did not create.

The most resilient dead man's switch is therefore not necessarily the most technologically sophisticated one. It is the one that anticipates failure at every level. It anticipates that hardware will fail, accounts will disappear, passwords will be forgotten, services will close, people will die, recipients will become unavailable, circumstances will change, evidence will be challenged, laws will evolve, and interpretations will conflict. It creates alternatives without creating chaos. It preserves evidence without forcing publication. It distributes responsibility without eliminating accountability. It accepts that no system can guarantee the future and builds resilience precisely because certainty is impossible.

There is another lesson hidden in the idea of redundancy. If the truth depends upon one person, it is vulnerable. If it depends upon one hard drive, it is vulnerable. If it depends upon one password, it is vulnerable. If it depends upon one journalist, one lawyer, one government, or one technology company, it is vulnerable. The strongest information architecture distributes not only copies but knowledge about how those copies should be interpreted and accessed. A resilient archive is therefore a network of evidence, people, procedures, and principles. Its strength comes from the relationships among those elements.

The same principle applies to historical truth. Civilizations remember because people preserve records. They also forget because records disappear, institutions collapse, archives are destroyed, witnesses die, and political narratives change. The modern digital age gives humanity an unprecedented ability to preserve enormous quantities of information. Yet abundance can itself become a problem. Future historians may have millions of documents but still struggle to determine which were authentic, which were manipulated, which were misunderstood, and which mattered. The challenge of the future may therefore be less about saving information than about preserving trustworthy pathways through it.

A dead man's switch can contribute to that future by creating continuity where disappearance would otherwise create silence. It can ensure that an archive exists somewhere. It can preserve a testimony that might otherwise be forgotten. It can provide investigators with documents that might otherwise disappear. It can create a mechanism by which a creator's evidence reaches someone capable of examining it. It can provide psychological reassurance to someone living under genuine threat. But it cannot decide the truth of what it preserves. That remains the responsibility of the living.

Perhaps this is the deepest meaning of the last message. It is not necessarily a dramatic confession, a secret dossier, a final accusation, or a package of documents released at midnight after a mysterious disappearance. It may simply be a carefully preserved record saying, in effect, "I was here. I saw something. I recorded what I could. I preserved the evidence. Now you must decide what it means." That message carries a different kind of power because it does not demand belief. It demands investigation. It does not ask the future to accept one person's interpretation. It asks the future to examine what remains.

And that may be the most responsible legacy anyone can leave. Not certainty, but evidence. Not an accusation that cannot be questioned, but a record that can be investigated. Not revenge disguised as disclosure, but accountability supported by documentation. Not a technological promise that everything will automatically become public, but a resilient pathway ensuring that important information does not disappear simply because one person does. The purpose of the dead man's switch is therefore not to guarantee that the creator will be believed. It is to guarantee that the creator's evidence has a chance to be heard.

The future will almost certainly make this question more complicated. Artificial intelligence will make evidence easier to analyze and easier to fabricate. Decentralized systems will make information harder for any single institution to control while creating new questions about governance and responsibility. Encryption will continue to protect sensitive archives while governments and adversaries search for new ways to penetrate them. Whistleblowers will continue to face difficult choices about whether to remain silent, report internally, approach regulators, contact journalists, or disclose publicly. Technology will continue to evolve, but the underlying human problem will remain remarkably familiar.

Someone will still know something that others do not know. Someone will still fear what might happen if they speak. Someone will still wonder whether the institution they work for can be trusted. Someone will still consider what happens if they disappear tomorrow. Someone will still ask whether their family should know, whether a journalist should know, whether a lawyer should know, and whether the public should know. And someone will still need to decide whether preserving the truth is worth the risk of releasing it.

The dead man's switch exists in that space between silence and disclosure. It is neither inherently heroic nor inherently dangerous. It is a tool whose consequences depend upon the information it contains, the people who control it, the systems that preserve it, the triggers that activate it, and the judgment applied when those triggers are reached. Used responsibly, it can preserve evidence when ordinary channels fail. Used carelessly, it can amplify misinformation, expose innocent people, compromise investigations, or create legal and ethical consequences that cannot be undone.

The central lesson of this book is therefore not that everyone should create a dead man's switch. It is that anyone who chooses to preserve dangerous information must understand the responsibility that comes with doing so. Security without accessibility creates a locked archive. Accessibility without security creates uncontrolled exposure. Evidence without context creates confusion. Context without evidence creates narrative. Technology without judgment creates automation without wisdom. And truth without responsibility can become another form of harm.

A genuine dead man's switch should ultimately be measured by what happens when the person who created it is no longer there to explain it. Does the archive still exist? Can its authenticity be examined? Can legitimate recipients access it? Can innocent people be protected? Can investigators distinguish evidence from speculation? Can lawyers assess legal exposure? Can journalists evaluate public interest? Can the system survive technological failure? Can its custodians resist the temptation to turn uncertainty into certainty? Can the truth move forward without becoming a weapon?

If the answer to those questions is yes, then something extraordinary has been achieved. A person's disappearance has not necessarily produced silence. Their knowledge has been given a pathway beyond their lifetime. Their evidence has been separated from their physical survival without being separated from responsibility. The future has been given something that the creator could no longer personally provide: the opportunity to investigate.

That is the real promise of the dead man's switch. It is not immortality, because the person is still gone. It is not certainty, because evidence can still be challenged. It is not justice, because justice requires institutions, procedures, and human judgment. It is something more modest and, in some circumstances, more important: continuity. It is the preservation of a possibility that might otherwise disappear with the person who carried the information.

When a person disappears, the truth they carried with them does not have to disappear as well. But for that to happen responsibly, the truth must be preserved with its evidence, its provenance, its context, its uncertainty, and its safeguards. It must be protected from destruction without being released recklessly. It must be accessible to those capable of examining it without becoming available to everyone indiscriminately. It must survive not merely as data but as a credible record of something that happened, something someone discovered, or something someone believed important enough to preserve.

The final message, then, is not necessarily the message that appears on a screen when the switch activates. It is the message contained within the architecture itself: that knowledge matters enough to preserve, evidence matters enough to protect, and truth matters enough to give it a future. A dead man's switch cannot guarantee that the world will believe what it contains. It can ensure only that the world has the opportunity to examine it. And sometimes, when everything else has failed, that opportunity is the difference between a truth that dies with its witness and a truth that survives long enough to be discovered.

Resources

1. National Archives — Digital Preservation — resources concerning long-term preservation, authenticity, accessibility, and management of digital records.

2. Library of Congress — Digital Preservation[1] — authoritative resources concerning preservation of digital information, formats, metadata, and long-term accessibility.

3. NIST Cybersecurity Framework 2.0[2] — framework for managing cybersecurity risk, resilience, and organizational information-security practices.

4. NIST Special Publication 800-57 — Recommendation for Key Management — guidance concerning cryptographic keys, access, protection, recovery, and lifecycle management.

5. NIST Special Publication 800-61 — Computer Security Incident Handling Guide[3] — framework concerning preparation, detection, response, and recovery from information-security incidents.

6. NIST Special Publication 800-160 Volume 2 — Developing Cyber-Resilient Systems — principles for anticipating, withstanding, recovering from, and adapting to disruptive events.

7. Berkeley Protocol on Digital Open Source Investigations — methodological guidance for collecting, preserving, verifying, and analyzing digital evidence.

8. United Nations Office on Drugs and Crime — Electronic Evidence — resources concerning electronic evidence and its role in criminal investigations.

9. ISO/IEC 27001 — Information Security Management Systems[4] — international information-security management framework.

10. ISO 22301 — Business Continuity Management Systems[5] — international framework for continuity and resilience planning.

11. Electronic Frontier Foundation — Surveillance Self-Defense[6] — practical resources concerning threat modeling, privacy, secure communications, and protection of sensitive information.

12. Electronic Frontier Foundation — Encryption — resources explaining the role of encryption in protecting communications and information.

13. OECD AI Principles[7] — internationally recognized principles concerning trustworthy AI, human oversight, transparency, robustness, and accountability.

14. UNESCO Recommendation on the Ethics of Artificial Intelligence[8] — international framework addressing transparency, accountability, human rights, safety, and ethical governance of AI.

15. NIST Artificial Intelligence Risk Management Framework[9] — framework for managing risks associated with artificial-intelligence systems.

---

1. https://www.loc.gov/preservation/digital/?utm_source=chatgpt.com
2. https://www.nist.gov/cyberframework?utm_source=chatgpt.com
3. https://csrc.nist.gov/publications/detail/sp/800-61/rev-2/final?utm_source=chatgpt.com
4. https://www.iso.org/isoiec-27001-information-security.html?utm_source=chatgpt.com
5. https://www.iso.org/standard/75106.html?utm_source=chatgpt.com
6. https://ssd.eff.org/?utm_source=chatgpt.com
7. https://oecd.ai/en/ai-principles?utm_source=chatgpt.com
8. https://www.unesco.org/en/artificial-intelligence/recommendation-ethics?utm_source=chatgpt.com

16. NIST AI 600-1 — Generative Artificial Intelligence Profile — guidance concerning risks associated with generative AI, including misinformation and synthetic content.

17. C2PA — Coalition for Content Provenance and Authenticity[10] — technical standards initiative focused on establishing provenance and authenticity information for digital content.

18. W3C — Verifiable Credentials Data Model[11] — technical framework for representing digitally verifiable claims and credentials.

19. NIST Digital Identity Guidelines[12] — guidance concerning digital identity, authentication, and establishing confidence in digital identities.

20. UNESCO — Journalism, "Fake News" and Disinformation — guidance concerning verification, misinformation, source evaluation, and responsible journalism.

21. Society of Professional Journalists — Code of Ethics[13] — professional principles concerning accuracy, minimizing harm, independence, and accountability.

22. Reuters Handbook of Journalism — professional guidance concerning verification, sourcing, fairness, and responsible publication.

23. Committee to Protect Journalists — Safety Kit[14] — resources concerning the physical and digital safety of journalists and sources.

24. U.S. Office of Special Counsel — Whistleblower Disclosures — official guidance concerning protected whistleblower disclosures involving covered federal personnel.

25. U.S. Securities and Exchange Commission — Whistleblower Program[15] — official resources concerning securities-law whistleblower reporting and protections.

26. U.S. Department of Justice — Justice Manual — official reference concerning federal criminal law and prosecution policies relevant to sensitive disclosures.

27. U.S. Executive Order 13526 — Classified National Security Information[16] — U.S. framework concerning classification and handling of national-security information.

28. European Union — General Data Protection Regulation[17] — legal framework concerning personal-data protection and processing.

9. https://www.nist.gov/itl/ai-risk-management-framework?utm_source=chatgpt.com

10. https://c2pa.org/?utm_source=chatgpt.com

11. https://www.w3.org/TR/vc-data-model/?utm_source=chatgpt.com

12. https://pages.nist.gov/800-63-4/?utm_source=chatgpt.com

13. https://www.spj.org/ethicscode.asp?utm_source=chatgpt.com

14. https://cpj.org/safety-kit/?utm_source=chatgpt.com

15. https://www.sec.gov/whistleblower?utm_source=chatgpt.com

16. https://www.archives.gov/isoo/policy-documents/cnsi-eo.html?utm_source=chatgpt.com

17. https://eur-lex.europa.eu/eli/reg/2016/679/oj?utm_source=chatgpt.com

29. United Nations — Universal Declaration of Human Rights[18] — foundational international framework concerning dignity, privacy, expression, and fundamental rights.

30. International Covenant on Civil and Political Rights — United Nations Human Rights Office[19] — international framework addressing freedom of expression, privacy, and related rights relevant to information disclosure.

---

18. https://www.un.org/en/about-us/universal-declaration-of-human-rights?utm_source=chatgpt.com

19. https://www.ohchr.org/en/instruments-mechanisms/instruments/international-covenant-civil-and-political-rights?utm_source=chatgpt.com

Epilogue — When the Keeper of the Truth Is Gone

Every generation creates new ways to preserve what it fears losing, and every generation discovers that preservation is more complicated than simply making a copy. Ancient civilizations carved laws into stone because memory could fail. Governments created archives because institutions needed records that outlived individual officials. Scientists preserved observations because discoveries could disappear with the death of their authors. Journalists maintained source documents because allegations without evidence could vanish into rumor. In the digital age, humanity has acquired an extraordinary capacity to preserve information almost indefinitely, yet the fundamental problem remains surprisingly old. What happens when the person who knows something important is suddenly no longer there to explain it?

The dead man's switch emerged from this basic human problem and gradually became something larger than its original mechanical meaning. At its simplest, it represents a contingency against absence, a mechanism designed to produce a predetermined consequence when a person can no longer perform an expected action. Applied to information, the concept becomes a form of continuity planning in which knowledge does not depend entirely upon the physical survival of its creator. That idea can be reassuring to someone carrying sensitive information, but it can also be dangerous if misunderstood. A system that automatically releases information cannot distinguish by itself between truth and falsehood, justice and revenge, legitimate secrecy and illegitimate concealment, or genuine death and temporary silence. The mechanism can preserve a message, but only human beings can determine what that message means.

That distinction is perhaps the most important lesson of this book. We have examined whistleblowers who confronted powerful institutions, witnesses who found themselves exposed to retaliation, journalists who protected sources, investigators who accumulated sensitive evidence, and ordinary people who suddenly found themselves possessing information they believed could matter enormously. Some faced documented intimidation or retaliation, while other stories remain allegations whose facts are disputed. History contains genuine conspiracies, genuine assassinations, genuine cover-ups, genuine institutional abuses, and genuine miscarriages of justice, but it also contains mistaken interpretations, unreliable memories, fabricated evidence, coincidences presented as patterns, and accusations that could never be substantiated. The responsible preservation of truth therefore requires the courage to protect information without automatically believing everything that information claims.

That may seem like a contradiction, but it is not. Protecting evidence does not mean endorsing it. Preserving a testimony does not mean declaring the testimony true. Maintaining an archive does not mean guaranteeing the conclusions that future investigators will draw from it. In fact, the strongest preservation systems are those that allow evidence to be challenged. They preserve original material, chronology, provenance, metadata, surrounding correspondence, and other contextual information precisely because future investigators need the ability to reconstruct what happened. A record becomes more valuable when it can withstand scrutiny rather than when it is protected from scrutiny. The objective is not to create an untouchable narrative but to create a durable evidentiary record.

This principle becomes especially important as technology advances. The future will make information easier to copy, transmit, encrypt, distribute, analyze, and automate. It will also make information easier to manipulate. Artificial intelligence can already produce synthetic text, images, audio, and video, and increasingly sophisticated systems will make the distinction between authentic and fabricated material more difficult for ordinary observers. A future archive may contain thousands of files that appear convincing while only a portion of them represent genuine historical evidence. Provenance, authentication, independent corroboration, and reliable chains of custody will therefore become increasingly important.

The dead man's switch of the future may consequently look very different from the systems imagined by earlier generations. It may not simply send an email after a missed check-in. It may maintain encrypted repositories across multiple locations, preserve cryptographic records of important files, notify designated custodians, monitor system integrity, and use artificial intelligence to organize enormous collections of evidence. It may distinguish between an emergency notification and a public release. It may require several independent confirmations before sensitive material moves from one stage to another. It may even preserve evidence for decades before circumstances justify its review.

Yet technological sophistication will never eliminate the human problem. Someone must decide what deserves protection. Someone must determine who should have access. Someone must establish whether the information is authentic. Someone must evaluate the legal consequences of disclosure. Someone must consider whether innocent people could be harmed. Someone must decide whether publication serves the public interest. And someone must accept responsibility when the consequences cannot be reversed. The more powerful the technology becomes, the more important these human decisions may become.

This is why trust has remained such a persistent theme throughout our exploration. Every system eventually reaches a point at which trust becomes unavoidable. You may distribute the files, encrypt the archive, separate the passwords, use multiple custodians, and employ sophisticated authentication, but eventually someone must interpret the situation. A lawyer must decide what can lawfully be disclosed. A journalist must decide what can responsibly be published. An investigator must decide what deserves further examination. A family member may have to make a decision under extraordinary emotional pressure. A technical custodian may have to determine whether an automated trigger has genuinely occurred. There is no architecture without people.

The most resilient system is therefore not necessarily the one with the most technology. It is the one that understands its weaknesses. It recognizes that computers fail, accounts become inaccessible, services disappear, storage media deteriorate, passwords are forgotten, organizations change, custodians become unavailable, laws evolve, and assumptions turn out to be wrong. It builds redundancy because failure is normal. It separates critical functions because concentration creates vulnerability. It preserves multiple forms of evidence because any individual source can be incomplete. And it leaves enough context behind that people who were never present at the beginning can understand what they are looking at.

There is a profound philosophical idea hidden inside that architecture. The creator of a dead man's switch is attempting to communicate with people who may never have known them. The recipient may be a future journalist, investigator, lawyer, historian, regulator, scientist, or ordinary citizen. The creator cannot answer questions when that moment arrives. They cannot explain an ambiguous sentence, identify an unfamiliar person in a photograph, clarify why a particular document mattered, or correct a misunderstanding. The archive must therefore speak for them, but it must also contain enough information to allow others to speak back through investigation. Preservation becomes a conversation between the past and the future.

That conversation is one of the foundations of civilization. Much of what humanity knows about previous generations exists because someone preserved a record. We know about wars because people wrote about them. We understand scientific discoveries because researchers recorded observations. We reconstruct financial scandals because transactions left documentary trails. We investigate abuses because victims, witnesses, investigators, and institutions preserved evidence. We remember political crimes because records survived attempts to erase them. The survival of evidence does not guarantee justice, but without surviving evidence justice becomes much harder to pursue.

The same principle applies to individual lives. A person does not need to possess a government secret or uncover a global conspiracy for preservation to matter. Someone might document workplace corruption. Someone might preserve evidence of financial fraud. Someone might record an environmental violation. Someone might discover that an institution is concealing abuse. Someone might simply need to ensure that important personal records survive an unexpected death. The scale of the information does not determine whether preservation is meaningful. Sometimes the most important archive in existence is the one that allows a single family, investigation, or community to understand what actually happened.

But there is another side to this responsibility that cannot be ignored. Not every secret deserves to be revealed. Privacy matters. Confidentiality matters. Legitimate national-security interests exist. Scientific research can involve sensitive information. Journalists have ethical obligations to protect vulnerable sources. Lawyers have professional duties concerning confidential communications. Businesses have legitimate proprietary information. Families contain private matters that do not automatically become public simply because someone created an archive. The existence of a dead man's switch does not override these responsibilities.

This is where responsible disclosure differs from indiscriminate disclosure. The purpose is not to create a mechanism that publishes everything merely because its creator is absent. The purpose is to create a pathway through which important information can reach people capable of evaluating it. Sometimes the correct destination will be a journalist. Sometimes it will be a lawyer. Sometimes it will be a regulator, investigator, court, scientific institution, or other legitimate authority. Sometimes the responsible decision may be to withhold material because the evidence is insufficient or the foreseeable harm is disproportionate. A mature dead man's switch therefore contains judgment within its architecture rather than attempting to eliminate judgment altogether.

The temptation to automate everything will grow as artificial intelligence becomes more capable. Automation appears attractive because human beings are unpredictable, emotional, forgetful, and vulnerable to pressure. A machine seems more dependable because it can execute instructions without fear. Yet machines inherit the assumptions of the people who design them. An automated system can faithfully execute a flawed instruction. It can interpret a technical failure as silence. It can release an authentic document without understanding that the document contains an innocent person's private information. It can summarize contradictory evidence into an apparently coherent story that is nevertheless wrong. Automation can remove certain human errors while introducing new categories of error.

The wisest approach is therefore not to choose between humans and machines but to understand what each is capable of doing. Machines excel at repetition, organization, comparison, searching, pattern detection, and large-scale processing. Humans remain essential for contextual judgment, moral reasoning, interpretation, accountability, and decisions involving competing values. The future dead man's switch will probably combine both. Artificial intelligence may help determine what is in an archive, while human investigators determine what it means. Automated systems may preserve the evidence, while independent professionals determine what should happen next. Technology can create continuity without being granted ultimate authority.

The idea of decentralization introduces another important possibility. For centuries, control over information was often concentrated in institutions capable of deciding what records survived and what records disappeared.

Digital networks can distribute copies across jurisdictions and organizations, making complete suppression more difficult. But decentralization should never be confused with freedom from responsibility. A distributed network can preserve false information just as effectively as true information. A decentralized database can record something permanently without proving that the recorded claim was accurate. Distribution protects against certain forms of centralized failure, but it does not replace verification.

The same caution applies to the concept of anonymity. People sometimes imagine that sophisticated technology can make the creator, recipient, or archive completely invisible. In reality, digital systems leave complicated traces, identities can be inferred from behavior, accounts can be compromised, metadata can reveal relationships, and legal authorities may have powers that ordinary users do not anticipate. Security is always contextual. A method that protects against casual access may be inadequate against a determined adversary. A system that works today may become vulnerable tomorrow. No responsible preservation strategy should promise absolute secrecy.

Perhaps the greatest protection is therefore not secrecy alone but resilience. If one copy disappears, another survives. If one custodian becomes unavailable, another can act. If one interpretation is challenged, the underlying evidence remains available for independent review. If one technology becomes obsolete, another pathway exists. If one jurisdiction becomes inaccessible, another may still contain legitimate copies. Resilience changes the objective from creating an impenetrable system to creating a system that can continue functioning after individual components fail. That is a much more realistic goal.

The psychological significance of this resilience should not be underestimated. Someone living with sensitive information may experience fear, isolation, hypervigilance, and a constant awareness of vulnerability. The existence of a carefully designed contingency can reduce some of that psychological burden because the individual knows that their information does not depend entirely upon their physical survival. But there is a danger in allowing the system to become an obsession. Constantly anticipating assassination, disappearance, or betrayal can distort judgment and damage relationships. A contingency mechanism should provide resilience, not become a machine for manufacturing fear.

The mature approach is to begin with evidence and risk rather than imagination. What information actually exists? How reliable is it? What is its potential significance? What realistic threats exist? What legitimate protections already exist? What would happen if the information were lost? What would happen if it were released prematurely? Who could evaluate it? Who could be harmed? These questions are less dramatic than stories of secret assassins and hidden organizations, but they are much more useful. Responsible preparation depends upon distinguishing plausible risk from speculative fear.

That principle also provides a way of understanding the darker cases examined in this book. History contains genuine examples of people being threatened or killed because of political beliefs, journalism, whistleblowing, activism, investigations, or conflicts with powerful interests. It also contains cases where suspicious circumstances generated theories that later proved unsupported or remained unresolved. A responsible investigation does not need to choose between believing everything and believing nothing. It can preserve the evidence while acknowledging uncertainty. Sometimes the most intellectually honest conclusion is that the available record does not allow us to know.

That humility is essential because the dead man's switch itself can create a dangerous illusion of certainty. When a message appears automatically after someone's disappearance, recipients may instinctively assume that the disappearance validates the message. It does not. The person's death, disappearance, or silence may establish that the trigger condition occurred, but it does not establish the truth of every claim contained in the archive. The evidence still requires examination. A final message is not a final verdict. It is the beginning of an investigation.

And perhaps that is where the idea of justice enters most meaningfully. Justice does not require that every accusation be believed. It requires that credible evidence have an opportunity to be examined. It requires that powerful institutions cannot simply erase inconvenient records. It requires that victims and witnesses have pathways through which evidence can reach independent authorities. It requires that accusations be investigated rather than automatically accepted or dismissed. A properly designed information-preservation system can contribute to that process by ensuring that evidence survives long enough to be considered.

The legacy of a dead man's switch therefore should not be measured by how spectacularly it activates. A dramatic release may attract attention, but attention is not the same as truth. A quiet archive that allows investigators to reconstruct a complicated event may ultimately be far more valuable. A collection of original documents preserved for decades may matter more than a viral accusation. A carefully authenticated recording may matter more than a thousand anonymous claims. The most important outcome is not that information becomes famous. It is that information becomes available for responsible examination.

There is something deeply human about wanting one's knowledge to survive. Every writer who leaves a manuscript, every scientist who records an experiment, every journalist who saves source material, every historian who preserves documents, and every ordinary person who keeps a family archive is participating in the same ancient act. We create records because we know that memory fades and people disappear. We write because we will not always be present to speak. We preserve because the future will ask questions that we cannot yet imagine. The dead man's switch is an unusually dramatic expression of that universal impulse.

Its darker side is equally human. Fear of being silenced has existed throughout history. People who believe they have discovered something important may fear that powerful interests will attempt to suppress it. Sometimes those fears are justified. Sometimes they are not. The responsibility is to create systems that remain useful in either circumstance. Evidence should survive whether the perceived threat is real, exaggerated, or misunderstood. The archive should remain open to investigation rather than being designed solely to confirm the creator's interpretation.

This is ultimately why the title of this book refers to a switch rather than a weapon. The central concept is not destruction. It is transition. The switch represents the moment when responsibility passes from one person to another. The creator can no longer maintain the archive, answer questions, or control circumstances. The system transfers the possibility of action to those who remain. What they do with that responsibility determines whether the creator's final act becomes a contribution to truth or simply another source of confusion.

The best legacy is therefore not a final accusation. It is a carefully constructed opportunity for the truth to be examined. It is an archive that survives. It is evidence that retains its provenance. It is a message that acknowledges uncertainty where uncertainty exists. It is a system that protects innocent people while allowing legitimate wrongdoing to be investigated. It is a structure that anticipates technical failure, human error, legal complications, and ethical consequences. Above all, it is an act of trust placed not blindly in one person but carefully distributed across people, evidence, technology, and time.

Eventually every keeper of information becomes a former keeper. That is the unavoidable condition of human life. We cannot guarantee that we will be present when the consequences of our discoveries unfold. We cannot know who will need the information we preserve or what circumstances will surround its eventual examination. We can only determine whether we leave behind confusion or clarity, speculation or evidence, inaccessible secrets or responsibly preserved records. The difference may be invisible when the archive is created. Years later, it may become everything.

The future will decide what becomes of the information we leave behind. It may confirm it, reject it, reinterpret it, or discover that it was more complicated than anyone understood. That is not a failure of preservation. It is the purpose of preservation. Evidence belongs to the future precisely because the future has the right to examine it with knowledge and perspectives that the present does not possess. A responsible archive does not dictate what future generations must believe. It gives them enough reliable material to make their own judgment.

So the final question is not whether the dead man's switch can guarantee that the truth will come out. No mechanism can make such a guarantee. The deeper question is whether we can build systems that give truth a chance to survive when the person who carried it cannot. The answer is yes, but only if we understand that preservation is inseparable from responsibility. Evidence must survive with context. Security must exist alongside legitimate access. Automation must remain subject to judgment. Disclosure must remain subject to law and ethics. And every claim, however powerful, must remain open to verification.

When the keeper of the truth is gone, the truth does not automatically become clearer. It becomes more dependent upon the quality of what was left behind. If there is nothing but an accusation, the future receives a story. If there is carefully preserved evidence, the future receives a question that can be investigated. If there is evidence accompanied by provenance, chronology, corroboration, and context, the future receives something much more valuable: a genuine opportunity to discover what happened.

That is the enduring meaning of the dead man's switch. It is not a promise that secrets will explode into the world after someone dies. It is not a guarantee that powerful institutions will be exposed. It is not a technological shortcut around law, evidence, or ethical responsibility. It is the recognition that important knowledge should not necessarily vanish simply because its keeper does. At its best, it is a bridge between a person who knows and a future that may need to know. And when that bridge is built carefully, the final message is no longer about death at all, but about the possibility that something worth remembering can survive.

About the Author

Andrew Parry is a researcher and nonfiction writer whose work explores some of the most compelling mysteries of our time, including UAPs, extraterrestrial contact, hidden history, ancient civilizations, suppressed knowledge, consciousness, advanced technology, and the possibility of humanity entering a new era of disclosure. His books are written for readers who are curious, open-minded, and willing to look beyond the limits of official explanations while still wanting information presented in a clear, thoughtful, and well-researched way.

Andrew has long been fascinated by reports of unidentified aerial phenomena, extraterrestrial encounters, government secrecy, whistleblower testimony, ancient texts, and the recurring claim that humanity is not alone. In recent years, this fascination has deepened as public discussion around UAPs has moved from the margins into government hearings, military reports, mainstream media coverage, and international debate. His writing examines this shift with the belief that the world may be approaching a major turning point, with disclosure predicted by many researchers, experiencers, insiders, and contact traditions to accelerate in 2026, followed by the possibility of open contact in 2027.

His work brings together a wide range of available information from across the internet, including historical records, declassified documents, witness accounts, public testimony, scientific speculation, spiritual traditions, investigative research, and alternative perspectives. While many of the subjects he explores remain controversial or unresolved, Andrew's approach is to gather, compare, and present the available evidence so readers can examine the patterns for themselves. His books do not ask readers to accept every claim blindly; instead, they invite them to consider the possibility that history, human origins, consciousness, and our place in the universe may be far larger than conventional narratives allow.

Writing in an accessible and immersive style, Andrew aims to bridge the gap between mystery and research, speculation and documentation, ancient wisdom and modern revelation. His recent books reflect a continuing search for truth at the edges of accepted knowledge, where UAP disclosure, extraterrestrial life, hidden scriptures, lost technologies, and humanity's spiritual evolution may all be connected to a much greater story now beginning to unfold.

PLANET EARTH
PUBLISHING
IDEAS | STORIES | WORLDS

About the Publisher

Welcome to Planet Earth Publishing

Planet Earth Publishing was created for readers who believe that the greatest stories, mysteries, discoveries, and possibilities are still waiting to be explored. At a time when humanity is asking larger questions about our origins, our future, the nature of consciousness, the mysteries of the universe, and our place within a much greater cosmic reality, books remain one of the most powerful ways to investigate those questions. Planet Earth Publishing brings together thought-provoking nonfiction, investigative works, speculative ideas, extraordinary human experiences, science, alternative history, unexplained phenomena, and imaginative science fiction under one distinctive publishing identity. Our purpose is not simply to sell books, but to create a destination for curious readers who enjoy looking beyond conventional boundaries and considering possibilities that may challenge established assumptions. Whether you are fascinated by UFOs and UAPs, extraterrestrial life, ancient mysteries, consciousness, time travel, hidden history, emerging science, unexplained events, or the imagined worlds of science fiction, Planet Earth Publishing is a place where curiosity is encouraged.

The name Planet Earth Publishing reflects the perspective behind the business itself. We live on one extraordinary planet surrounded by a universe of almost unimaginable scale, and every generation inherits both the knowledge and the mysteries of those who came before it. Humanity has explored continents, oceans, atoms, genomes, distant galaxies, and the deepest questions of philosophy, yet we remain surrounded by unanswered questions about who we are and what may exist beyond the limits of our present understanding. Planet Earth Publishing exists at that frontier between what humanity already knows and what we are still attempting to discover. Our books explore established knowledge where appropriate, examine controversial claims carefully, investigate unusual testimony and historical records, and follow questions wherever the available evidence may lead. Some subjects may ultimately find conventional explanations, while others may remain genuinely unresolved, but every mystery deserves to be approached with curiosity, context, and an open mind.

A central part of Planet Earth Publishing will be the books of author and researcher Andrew Parry, whose growing body of nonfiction examines some of the most fascinating questions of our age. These works explore UFO and UAP encounters, government secrecy and disclosure, extraterrestrial-contact claims, consciousness, ancient civilizations, stargates, time travel, unexplained phenomena, future technologies, human potential, and the possibility that our understanding of reality is still incomplete. Rather than treating these subjects as isolated curiosities, the books examine their history, witnesses, documents, scientific possibilities, competing explanations, and wider implications. Readers are invited to investigate extraordinary claims without being told what they must believe, allowing evidence, testimony, history, science, and reasoned speculation to exist together within the same conversation.

www.ingramcontent.com/pod-product-compliance
Lightning Source LLC
LaVergne TN
LVHW060446061126
851857LV00016B/1738